Niccolò di Bernardo dei Machiavelli

SELECTIONS

THE PRINCE

❋

DESCRIPTION OF THE METHODS ADOPTED BY THE DUKE VALENTINO WHEN MURDERING VITELLOZZO VITELLI, OLIVEROTTO DA FERMO, THE SIGNOR PAGOLO, AND THE DUKE DI GRAVINA ORSINI

❋

THE LIFE OF CASTRUCCIO CASTRACANI OF LUCCA SENT TO HIS FRIENDS ZANOBI BUONDELMONTI AND LUIGI ALAMANNI

❋

DISCOURSES ON THE FIRST DECADE OF TITUS LIVIUS

From the editor

Niccolò Machiavelli (1469-1527), an Italian political philosopher, is remarkable for his self-contradictions. In his writings he appears sometimes as a cynical pragmatist, sometimes – as an ardent Republican. Perception of Machiavelli is also quite contradictory – sometimes entirely derogatory and scornful, sometimes – admiring and appreciative. Who was he, this peer of Leonardo da Vinci? A smart and cruel manipulator or a passionate libertarian? And if both are true, does not it shed a strange light on the heritage of High Renaissance? Our readers can now judge Machiavelli on the basis of his work.

THE PRINCE

DEDICATION

To the Magnificent Lorenzo Di Piero De' Medici:

Those who strive to obtain the good graces of a prince are accustomed to come before him with such things as they hold most precious, or in which they see him take most delight; whence one often sees horses, arms, cloth of gold, precious stones, and similar ornaments presented to princes, worthy of their greatness.

Desiring therefore to present myself to your Magnificence with some testimony of my devotion towards you, I have not found among my possessions anything which I hold more dear than, or value so much as, the knowledge of the actions of great men, acquired by long experience in contemporary affairs, and a continual study of antiquity; which, having reflected upon it with great and prolonged diligence, I now send, digested into a little volume, to your Magnificence.

And although I may consider this work unworthy of your countenance, nevertheless I trust much to your benignity that it may be acceptable, seeing that it is not possible for me to make a better gift than to offer you the opportunity of understanding in the shortest time all that I have learnt in so many years, and with so many troubles and dangers; which work I have not embellished with swelling or magnificent words, nor stuffed with rounded periods, nor with any extrinsic allurements or adornments whatever, with which so many are accustomed to embellish their works; for I have wished either that no honour should be given it, or else that the truth of the matter and the weightiness of the theme shall make it acceptable.

Nor do I hold with those who regard it as a presumption if a man of low and humble condition dare to discuss and settle the concerns of princes; because, just as those who draw landscapes place themselves below in the plain to contemplate the nature of the mountains and of lofty places, and in order to contemplate the plains place themselves upon high mountains, even so to understand the nature of the people it needs to be a prince, and to understand that of princes it needs to be of the people.

Take then, your Magnificence, this little gift in the spirit in which I send it; wherein, if it be diligently read and considered by you, you will learn my extreme desire that you should attain that greatness which fortune and your other attributes promise. And if your Magnificence from the summit of your greatness will sometimes turn your eyes to these lower regions, you will see how unmeritedly I suffer a great and continued malignity of fortune.

CHAPTER I

HOW MANY KINDS OF PRINCIPALITIES THERE ARE, AND BY WHAT MEANS THEY ARE ACQUIRED

All states, all powers, that have held and hold rule over men have been and are either republics or principalities.

Principalities are either hereditary, in which the family has been long established; or they are new.

The new are either entirely new, as was Milan to Francesco Sforza, or they are, as it were, members annexed to the hereditary state of the prince who has acquired them, as was the kingdom of Naples to that of the King of Spain.

Such dominions thus acquired are either accustomed to live under a prince, or to live in freedom; and are acquired either by the arms of the prince himself, or of others, or else by fortune or by ability.

CHAPTER II

CONCERNING HEREDITARY PRINCIPALITIES

I will leave out all discussion on republics, inasmuch as in another place I have written of them at length, and will address myself only to principalities. In doing so I will keep to the order indicated above, and discuss how such principalities are to be ruled and preserved.

I say at once there are fewer difficulties in holding hereditary states, and those long accustomed to the family of their prince, than new ones; for it is sufficient only not to transgress the customs of his ancestors, and to deal prudently with circumstances as they arise, for a prince of average powers to maintain himself in his state, unless he be deprived of it by some extraordinary and excessive force; and if he should be so deprived of it, whenever anything sinister happens to the usurper, he will regain it.

We have in Italy, for example, the Duke of Ferrara, who could not have withstood the attacks of the Venetians in '84, nor those of Pope Julius in '10, unless he had been long established in his dominions. For the hereditary prince has less cause and less necessity to offend; hence it happens that he will be more loved; and unless extraordinary vices cause him to be hated, it is reasonable to expect that his subjects will be naturally well disposed towards him; and in the antiquity and duration of his rule the memories and motives that make for change are lost, for one change always leaves the toothing for another.

CHAPTER III

CONCERNING MIXED PRINCIPALITIES

But the difficulties occur in a new principality. And firstly, if it be not entirely new, but is, as it were, a member of a state which, taken collectively, may be called composite, the changes arise chiefly from an inherent difficulty which there is in all new principalities; for men change their rulers willingly, hoping to better themselves, and this hope induces them to take up arms against him who rules: wherein they are deceived, because they afterwards find by experience they have gone from bad to worse. This follows also on another natural and common necessity, which always causes a new prince to burden those who have submitted to him with his soldiery and with infinite other hardships which he must put upon his new acquisition.

In this way you have enemies in all those whom you have injured in seizing that principality, and you are not able to keep those friends who put you there because of your not being able to satisfy them in the way they expected, and you cannot take strong measures against them, feeling bound to them. For, although one may be very strong in armed forces, yet in entering a province one has always need of the goodwill of the natives.

For these reasons Louis the Twelfth, King of France, quickly occupied Milan, and as quickly lost it; and to turn him out the first time it only needed Lodovico's own forces; because those who had opened the gates to him, finding themselves deceived in their hopes of future benefit, would not endure the ill-treatment of the new prince. It is very true that, after acquiring rebellious provinces a second time, they are not so lightly lost afterwards, because the prince, with little reluctance, takes the opportunity of the rebellion to punish the delinquents, to clear out the suspects, and to strengthen himself in the weakest places.

Thus to cause France to lose Milan the first time it was enough for the Duke Lodovico[1] to raise insurrections on the borders; but to cause him to lose it a second time it was necessary to bring the whole world against him, and that his armies should be defeated and driven out of Italy; which followed from the causes above mentioned.

Nevertheless Milan was taken from France both the first and the second time. The general reasons for the first have been discussed; it remains to name those for the second, and to see what resources he had, and what any one in his situation would have had for maintaining himself more securely in his acquisition than did the King of France.

Now I say that those dominions which, when acquired, are added to an ancient state by him who acquires them, are either of the same country and language, or they are not. When they are, it is easier to hold them, especially when they have not been accustomed to self-government; and to hold them securely it is enough to have destroyed the family of the prince who was ruling them; because the two peoples, preserving in other things the old conditions, and not being unlike in customs, will live quietly together, as one has seen in Brittany, Burgundy, Gascony, and Normandy, which have been bound to France for so long a time: and, although there may be some difference in language, nevertheless the customs are alike, and the people will easily be able to get on amongst themselves. He who has annexed them, if he wishes to hold them, has only to bear in mind two considerations: the one, that the family of their former lord is extinguished; the other, that neither their laws nor their taxes are altered, so that in a very short time they will become entirely one body with the old principality.

But when states are acquired in a country differing in language, customs, or laws, there are difficulties, and good fortune and great energy are needed to hold them, and one of the greatest and most real helps would be that he who has acquired them

---

[1] Duke Lodovico was Lodovico Moro, a son of Francesco Sforza, who married Beatrice d'Este. He ruled over Milan from 1494 to 1500, and died in 1510.

should go and reside there. This would make his position more secure and durable, as it has made that of the Turk in Greece, who, notwithstanding all the other measures taken by him for holding that state, if he had not settled there, would not have been able to keep it. Because, if one is on the spot, disorders are seen as they spring up, and one can quickly remedy them; but if one is not at hand, they are heard of only when they are great, and then one can no longer remedy them. Besides this, the country is not pillaged by your officials; the subjects are satisfied by prompt recourse to the prince; thus, wishing to be good, they have more cause to love him, and wishing to be otherwise, to fear him. He who would attack that state from the outside must have the utmost caution; as long as the prince resides there it can only be wrested from him with the greatest difficulty.

The other and better course is to send colonies to one or two places, which may be as keys to that state, for it is necessary either to do this or else to keep there a great number of cavalry and infantry. A prince does not spend much on colonies, for with little or no expense he can send them out and keep them there, and he offends a minority only of the citizens from whom he takes lands and houses to give them to the new inhabitants; and those whom he offends, remaining poor and scattered, are never able to injure him; whilst the rest being uninjured are easily kept quiet, and at the same time are anxious not to err for fear it should happen to them as it has to those who have been despoiled. In conclusion, I say that these colonies are not costly, they are more faithful, they injure less, and the injured, as has been said, being poor and scattered, cannot hurt. Upon this, one has to remark that men ought either to be well treated or crushed, because they can avenge themselves of lighter injuries, of more serious ones they cannot; therefore the injury that is to be done to a man ought to be of such a kind that one does not stand in fear of revenge.

But in maintaining armed men there in place of colonies one spends much more, having to consume on the garrison all the income from the state, so that the acquisition turns into a loss, and many more are exasperated, because the whole state is injured; through the shifting of the garrison up and down all become acquainted with hardship, and all become hostile, and they are enemies who, whilst beaten on their own ground, are yet able to do hurt. For every reason, therefore, such guards are as useless as a colony is useful.

Again, the prince who holds a country differing in the above respects ought to make himself the head and defender of his less powerful neighbours, and to weaken the more powerful amongst them, taking care that no foreigner as powerful as himself shall, by any accident, get a footing there; for it will always happen that such a one will be introduced by those who are discontented, either through excess of ambition or through fear, as one has seen already. The Romans were brought into Greece by the Aetolians; and in every other country where they obtained a footing they were brought in by the inhabitants. And the usual course of affairs is that, as soon as a powerful foreigner enters a country, all the subject states are drawn to him, moved by the hatred which they feel against the ruling power. So that in respect to those subject states he has not to take any trouble to gain them over to himself, for the whole of them quickly rally to the state which he has acquired there. He has only to take care that they do not get hold of too much power and too much authority, and then with his own forces, and with their goodwill, he can easily keep down the more powerful of them, so as to remain entirely master in the country. And he who does not properly manage this business will soon lose what he has acquired, and whilst he does hold it he will have endless difficulties and troubles.

The Romans, in the countries which they annexed, observed closely these measures; they sent colonies and maintained friendly relations with the minor powers, without increasing their strength; they kept down the greater, and did not allow any strong foreign powers to gain authority. Greece appears to me sufficient for an example. The Achaeans and Aetolians were kept friendly by them, the kingdom of Macedonia was humbled,

Antiochus was driven out; yet the merits of the Achaeans and Aetolians never secured for them permission to increase their power, nor did the persuasions of Philip ever induce the Romans to be his friends without first humbling him, nor did the influence of Antiochus make them agree that he should retain any lordship over the country. Because the Romans did in these instances what all prudent princes ought to do, who have to regard not only present troubles, but also future ones, for which they must prepare with every energy, because, when foreseen, it is easy to remedy them; but if you wait until they approach, the medicine is no longer in time because the malady has become incurable; for it happens in this, as the physicians say it happens in hectic fever, that in the beginning of the malady it is easy to cure but difficult to detect, but in the course of time, not having been either detected or treated in the beginning, it becomes easy to detect but difficult to cure. This it happens in affairs of state, for when the evils that arise have been foreseen (which it is only given to a wise man to see), they can be quickly redressed, but when, through not having been foreseen, they have been permitted to grow in a way that every one can see them, there is no longer a remedy. Therefore, the Romans, foreseeing troubles, dealt with them at once, and, even to avoid a war, would not let them come to a head, for they knew that war is not to be avoided, but is only to be put off to the advantage of others; moreover they wished to fight with Philip and Antiochus in Greece so as not to have to do it in Italy; they could have avoided both, but this they did not wish; nor did that ever please them which is for ever in the mouths of the wise ones of our time: — Let us enjoy the benefits of the time — but rather the benefits of their own valour and prudence, for time drives everything before it, and is able to bring with it good as well as evil, and evil as well as good.

But let us turn to France and inquire whether she has done any of the things mentioned. I will speak of Louis[2] (and not

---

[2] Louis XII, King of France, "The Father of the People," born 1462, died 1515.

of Charles)³ as the one whose conduct is the better to be observed, he having held possession of Italy for the longest period; and you will see that he has done the opposite to those things which ought to be done to retain a state composed of divers elements.

King Louis was brought into Italy by the ambition of the Venetians, who desired to obtain half the state of Lombardy by his intervention. I will not blame the course taken by the king, because, wishing to get a foothold in Italy, and having no friends there — seeing rather that every door was shut to him owing to the conduct of Charles — he was forced to accept those friendships which he could get, and he would have succeeded very quickly in his design if in other matters he had not made some mistakes. The king, however, having acquired Lombardy, regained at once the authority which Charles had lost: Genoa yielded; the Florentines became his friends; the Marquess of Mantua, the Duke of Ferrara, the Bentivogli, my lady of Forli, the Lords of Faenza, of Pesaro, of Rimini, of Camerino, of Piombino, the Lucchese, the Pisans, the Sienese — everybody made advances to him to become his friend. Then could the Venetians realize the rashness of the course taken by them, which, in order that they might secure two towns in Lombardy, had made the king master of two-thirds of Italy.

Let any one now consider with what little difficulty the king could have maintained his position in Italy had he observed the rules above laid down, and kept all his friends secure and protected; for although they were numerous they were both weak and timid, some afraid of the Church, some of the Venetians, and thus they would always have been forced to stand in with him, and by their means he could easily have made himself secure against those who remained powerful. But he was no sooner in Milan than he did the contrary by assisting Pope Alexander to occupy the Romagna. It never occurred to him that by this action he was weakening himself, depriving himself of friends and of

---

³ Charles VIII, King of France, born 1470, died 1498.

those who had thrown themselves into his lap, whilst he aggrandized the Church by adding much temporal power to the spiritual, thus giving it greater authority. And having committed this prime error, he was obliged to follow it up, so much so that, to put an end to the ambition of Alexander, and to prevent his becoming the master of Tuscany, he was himself forced to come into Italy.

And as if it were not enough to have aggrandized the Church, and deprived himself of friends, he, wishing to have the kingdom of Naples, divides it with the King of Spain, and where he was the prime arbiter in Italy he takes an associate, so that the ambitious of that country and the malcontents of his own should have somewhere to shelter; and whereas he could have left in the kingdom his own pensioner as king, he drove him out, to put one there who was able to drive him, Louis, out in turn.

The wish to acquire is in truth very natural and common, and men always do so when they can, and for this they will be praised not blamed; but when they cannot do so, yet wish to do so by any means, then there is folly and blame. Therefore, if France could have attacked Naples with her own forces she ought to have done so; if she could not, then she ought not to have divided it. And if the partition which she made with the Venetians in Lombardy was justified by the excuse that by it she got a foothold in Italy, this other partition merited blame, for it had not the excuse of that necessity.

Therefore Louis made these five errors: he destroyed the minor powers, he increased the strength of one of the greater powers in Italy, he brought in a foreign power, he did not settle in the country, he did not send colonies. Which errors, had he lived, were not enough to injure him had he not made a sixth by taking away their dominions from the Venetians; because, had he not aggrandized the Church, nor brought Spain into Italy, it would have been very reasonable and necessary to humble them; but having first taken these steps, he ought never to have consented to their ruin, for they, being powerful, would always have kept off others from designs on Lombardy, to which the Venetians would never have consented except to become masters themselves there; also because the others would not wish to take Lombardy from France in order to give it to the Venetians, and to run counter to both they would not have had the courage.

And if any one should say: "King Louis yielded the Romagna to Alexander and the kingdom to Spain to avoid war," I answer for the reasons given above that a blunder ought never to be perpetrated to avoid war, because it is not to be avoided, but is only deferred to your disadvantage. And if another should allege the pledge which the king had given to the Pope that he would assist him in the enterprise, in exchange for the dissolution of his marriage[4] and for the cap to Rouen,[5] to that I reply what I shall write later on concerning the faith of princes, and how it ought to be kept.

Thus King Louis lost Lombardy by not having followed any of the conditions observed by those who have taken possession of countries and wished to retain them. Nor is there any miracle in this, but much that is reasonable and quite natural. And on these matters I spoke at Nantes with Rouen, when Valentino, as Cesare Borgia, the son of Pope Alexander, was usually called, occupied the Romagna, and on Cardinal Rouen observing to me that the Italians did not understand war, I replied to him that the French did not understand statecraft, meaning that otherwise they would not have allowed the Church to reach such greatness. And in fact is has been seen that the greatness of the Church and of Spain in Italy has been caused by France, and her ruin may be attributed to them. From this a general rule is drawn which never or rarely fails: that he who is the cause of another becoming powerful is ruined; because that predominancy has been brought about either by astuteness or else by force, and both are distrusted by him who has been raised to power.

---

[4] Louis XII divorced his wife, Jeanne, daughter of Louis XI, and married in 1499 Anne of Brittany, widow of Charles VIII, in order to retain the Duchy of Brittany for the crown.

[5] The Archbishop of Rouen. He was Georges d'Amboise, created a cardinal by Alexander VI. Born 1460, died 1510.

CHAPTER IV

WHY THE KINGDOM OF DARIUS, CONQUERED BY ALEXANDER, DID NOT REBEL AGAINST THE SUCCESSORS OF ALEXANDER AT HIS DEATH

Considering the difficulties which men have had to hold to a newly acquired state, some might wonder how, seeing that Alexander the Great became the master of Asia in a few years, and died whilst it was scarcely settled (whence it might appear reasonable that the whole empire would have rebelled), nevertheless his successors maintained themselves, and had to meet no other difficulty than that which arose among themselves from their own ambitions.

I answer that the principalities of which one has record are found to be governed in two different ways; either by a prince, with a body of servants, who assist him to govern the kingdom as ministers by his favour and permission; or by a prince and barons, who hold that dignity by antiquity of blood and not by the grace of the prince. Such barons have states and their own subjects, who recognize them as lords and hold them in natural affection. Those states that are governed by a prince and his servants hold their prince in more consideration, because in all the country there is no one who is recognized as superior to him, and if they yield obedience to another they do it as to a minister and official, and they do not bear him any particular affection.

The examples of these two governments in our time are the Turk and the King of France. The entire monarchy of the Turk is governed by one lord, the others are his servants; and, dividing his kingdom into sanjaks, he sends there different administrators, and shifts and changes them as he chooses. But the

King of France is placed in the midst of an ancient body of lords, acknowledged by their own subjects, and beloved by them; they have their own prerogatives, nor can the king take these away except at his peril. Therefore, he who considers both of these states will recognize great difficulties in seizing the state of the Turk, but, once it is conquered, great ease in holding it. The causes of the difficulties in seizing the kingdom of the Turk are that the usurper cannot be called in by the princes of the kingdom, nor can he hope to be assisted in his designs by the revolt of those whom the lord has around him. This arises from the reasons given above; for his ministers, being all slaves and bondmen, can only be corrupted with great difficulty, and one can expect little advantage from them when they have been corrupted, as they cannot carry the people with them, for the reasons assigned. Hence, he who attacks the Turk must bear in mind that he will find him united, and he will have to rely more on his own strength than on the revolt of others; but, if once the Turk has been conquered, and routed in the field in such a way that he cannot replace his armies, there is nothing to fear but the family of this prince, and, this being exterminated, there remains no one to fear, the others having no credit with the people; and as the conqueror did not rely on them before his victory, so he ought not to fear them after it.

The contrary happens in kingdoms governed like that of France, because one can easily enter there by gaining over some baron of the kingdom, for one always finds malcontents and such as desire a change. Such men, for the reasons given, can open the way into the state and render the victory easy; but if you wish to hold it afterwards, you meet with infinite difficulties, both from those who have assisted you and from those you have crushed. Nor is it enough for you to have exterminated the family of the prince, because the lords that remain make themselves the heads of fresh movements against you, and as you are unable either to satisfy or exterminate them, that state is lost whenever time brings the opportunity.

Now if you will consider what was the nature of the government of Darius, you will find it similar to the kingdom of the Turk, and therefore it was only necessary for Alexander, first to overthrow him in the field, and then to take the country from him. After which victory, Darius being killed, the state remained secure to Alexander, for the above reasons. And if his successors had been united they would have enjoyed it securely and at their ease, for there were no tumults raised in the kingdom except those they provoked themselves.

But it is impossible to hold with such tranquillity states constituted like that of France. Hence arose those frequent rebellions against the Romans in Spain, France, and Greece, owing to the many principalities there were in these states, of which, as long as the memory of them endured, the Romans always held an insecure possession; but with the power and long continuance of the empire the memory of them passed away, and the Romans then became secure possessors. And when fighting afterwards amongst themselves, each one was able to attach to himself his own parts of the country, according to the authority he had assumed there; and the family of the former lord being exterminated, none other than the Romans were acknowledged.

When these things are remembered no one will marvel at the ease with which Alexander held the Empire of Asia, or at the difficulties which others have had to keep an acquisition, such as Pyrrhus and many more; this is not occasioned by the little or abundance of ability in the conqueror, but by the want of uniformity in the subject state.

CHAPTER V

CONCERNING THE WAY TO GOVERN CITIES OR PRINCIPALITIES WHICH LIVED UNDER THEIR OWN LAWS BEFORE THEY WERE ANNEXED

Whenever those states which have been acquired as stated have been accustomed to live under their own laws and in freedom, there are three courses for those who wish to hold them: the first is to ruin them, the next is to reside there in person, the third is to permit them to live under their own laws, drawing a tribute, and establishing within it an oligarchy which will keep it friendly to you. Because such a government, being created by the prince, knows that it cannot stand without his friendship and interest, and does it utmost to support him; and therefore he who would keep a city accustomed to freedom will hold it more easily by the means of its own citizens than in any other way.

There are, for example, the Spartans and the Romans. The Spartans held Athens and Thebes, establishing there an oligarchy, nevertheless they lost them. The Romans, in order to hold Capua, Carthage, and Numantia, dismantled them, and did not lose them. They wished to hold Greece as the Spartans held it, making it free and permitting its laws, and did not succeed. So to hold it they were compelled to dismantle many cities in the country, for in truth there is no safe way to retain them otherwise than by ruining them. And he who becomes master of a city accustomed to freedom and does not destroy it, may expect to be destroyed by it, for in rebellion it has always the watchword of liberty and its ancient privileges as a rallying point, which neither time nor benefits will ever cause it to forget. And whatever you may do or provide against, they never forget that name or their privileges unless they are disunited or dispersed, but at every chance they immediately rally to them, as Pisa after the hundred years she had been held in bondage by the Florentines.

But when cities or countries are accustomed to live under a prince, and his family is exterminated, they, being on the one hand accustomed to obey and on the other hand not having the old prince, cannot agree in making one from amongst themselves, and they do not know how to govern themselves. For this reason they are very slow to take up arms, and a prince can gain them to himself and secure them much more easily. But in republics there is more vitality, greater hatred, and more desire for vengeance, which will never permit them to allow the memory of their former liberty to rest; so that the safest way is to destroy them or to reside there.

CHAPTER VI

CONCERNING NEW PRINCIPALITIES WHICH ARE ACQUIRED BY ONE'S OWN ARMS AND ABILITY

Let no one be surprised if, in speaking of entirely new principalities as I shall do, I adduce the highest examples both of prince and of state; because men, walking almost always in paths beaten by others, and following by imitation their deeds, are yet unable to keep entirely to the ways of others or attain to the power of those they imitate. A wise man ought always to follow the paths beaten by great men, and to imitate those who have been supreme, so that if his ability does not equal theirs, at least it will savour of it. Let him act like the clever archers who, designing to hit the mark which yet appears too far distant, and knowing the limits to which the strength of their bow attains, take aim much higher than the mark, not to reach by their strength or arrow to so great a height, but to be able with the aid of so high an aim to hit the mark they wish to reach.

I say, therefore, that in entirely new principalities, where there is a new prince, more or less difficulty is found in keeping them, accordingly as there is more or less ability in him who has acquired the state. Now, as the fact of becoming a prince from a private station presupposes either ability or fortune, it is clear that one or other of these things will mitigate in some degree many difficulties. Nevertheless, he who has relied least on fortune is established the strongest. Further, it facilitates matters when the prince, having no other state, is compelled to reside there in person.

But to come to those who, by their own ability and not through fortune, have risen to be princes, I say that Moses, Cyrus,

Romulus, Theseus, and such like are the most excellent examples. And although one may not discuss Moses, he having been a mere executor of the will of God, yet he ought to be admired, if only for that favour which made him worthy to speak with God. But in considering Cyrus and others who have acquired or founded kingdoms, all will be found admirable; and if their particular deeds and conduct shall be considered, they will not be found inferior to those of Moses, although he had so great a preceptor. And in examining their actions and lives one cannot see that they owed anything to fortune beyond opportunity, which brought them the material to mould into the form which seemed best to them. Without that opportunity their powers of mind would have been extinguished, and without those powers the opportunity would have come in vain.

    It was necessary, therefore, to Moses that he should find the people of Israel in Egypt enslaved and oppressed by the Egyptians, in order that they should be disposed to follow him so as to be delivered out of bondage. It was necessary that Romulus should not remain in Alba, and that he should be abandoned at his birth, in order that he should become King of Rome and founder of the fatherland. It was necessary that Cyrus should find the Persians discontented with the government of the Medes, and the Medes soft and effeminate through their long peace. Theseus could not have shown his ability had he not found the Athenians dispersed. These opportunities, therefore, made those men fortunate, and their high ability enabled them to recognize the opportunity whereby their country was ennobled and made famous.

    Those who by valorous ways become princes, like these men, acquire a principality with difficulty, but they keep it with ease. The difficulties they have in acquiring it rise in part from the new rules and methods which they are forced to introduce to establish their government and its security. And it ought to be remembered that there is nothing more difficult to take in hand, more perilous to conduct, or more uncertain in its success, then to take the lead in the introduction of a new order of things. Because the innovator has for enemies all those who have done well under the old conditions, and lukewarm defenders in those who may do well under the new. This coolness arises partly from fear of the opponents, who have the laws on their side, and partly from the incredulity of men, who do not readily believe in new things until they have had a long experience of them. Thus it happens that whenever those who are hostile have the opportunity to attack they do it like partisans, whilst the others defend lukewarmly, in such wise that the prince is endangered along with them.

It is necessary, therefore, if we desire to discuss this matter thoroughly, to inquire whether these innovators can rely on themselves or have to depend on others: that is to say, whether, to consummate their enterprise, have they to use prayers or can they use force? In the first instance they always succeed badly, and never compass anything; but when they can rely on themselves and use force, then they are rarely endangered. Hence it is that all armed prophets have conquered, and the unarmed ones have been destroyed. Besides the reasons mentioned, the nature of the people is variable, and whilst it is easy to persuade them, it is difficult to fix them in that persuasion. And thus it is necessary to take such measures that, when they believe no longer, it may be possible to make them believe by force.

If Moses, Cyrus, Theseus, and Romulus had been unarmed they could not have enforced their constitutions for long — as happened in our time to Fra Girolamo Savonarola, who was ruined with his new order of things immediately the multitude believed in him no longer, and he had no means of keeping steadfast those who believed or of making the unbelievers to believe. Therefore such as these have great difficulties in consummating their enterprise, for all their dangers are in the ascent, yet with ability they will overcome them; but when these are overcome, and those who envied them their success are exterminated, they will begin to be respected, and they will continue afterwards powerful, secure, honoured, and happy.

To these great examples I wish to add a lesser one; still it bears some resemblance to them, and I wish it to suffice me for all of a like kind: it is Hiero the Syracusan.[6] This man rose from a private station to be Prince of Syracuse, nor did he, either, owe anything to fortune but opportunity; for the Syracusans, being oppressed, chose him for their captain, afterwards he was rewarded by being made their prince. He was of so great ability, even as a private citizen, that one who writes of him says he wanted nothing but a kingdom to be a king. This man abolished the old soldiery, organized the new, gave up old alliances, made new ones; and as he had his own soldiers and allies, on such foundations he was able to build any edifice: thus, whilst he had endured much trouble in acquiring, he had but little in keeping.

---

[6] Hiero II, born about 307 B.C., died 216 B.C.

CHAPTER VII

CONCERNING NEW PRINCIPALITIES WHICH ARE ACQUIRED EITHER BY THE ARMS OF OTHERS OR BY GOOD FORTUNE

Those who solely by good fortune become princes from being private citizens have little trouble in rising, but much in keeping atop; they have not any difficulties on the way up, because they fly, but they have many when they reach the summit. Such are those to whom some state is given either for money or by the favour of him who bestows it; as happened to many in Greece, in the cities of Ionia and of the Hellespont, where princes were made by Darius, in order that they might hold the cities both for his security and his glory; as also were those emperors who, by the corruption of the soldiers, from being citizens came to empire. Such stand simply elevated upon the goodwill and the fortune of him who has elevated them — two most inconstant and unstable things. Neither have they the knowledge requisite for the position; because, unless they are men of great worth and ability, it is not reasonable to expect that they should know how to command, having always lived in a private condition; besides, they cannot hold it because they have not forces which they can keep friendly and faithful.

States that rise unexpectedly, then, like all other things in nature which are born and grow rapidly, cannot leave their foundations and correspondencies fixed in such a way that the first storm will not overthrow them; unless, as is said, those who unexpectedly become princes are men of so much ability that they know they have to be prepared at once to hold that which fortune has thrown into their laps, and that those foundations, which others have laid BEFORE they became princes, they must lay AFTERWARDS.

Concerning these two methods of rising to be a prince by ability or fortune, I wish to adduce two examples within our own recollection, and these are Francesco Sforza[7] and Cesare Borgia. Francesco, by proper means and with great ability, from being a private person rose to be Duke of Milan, and that which he had acquired with a thousand anxieties he kept with little trouble. On the other hand, Cesare Borgia, called by the people Duke Valentino, acquired his state during the ascendancy of his father, and on its decline he lost it, notwithstanding that he had taken every measure and done all that ought to be done by a wise and able man to fix firmly his roots in the states which the arms and fortunes of others had bestowed on him.

Because, as is stated above, he who has not first laid his foundations may be able with great ability to lay them afterwards, but they will be laid with trouble to the architect and danger to the building. If, therefore, all the steps taken by the duke be considered, it will be seen that he laid solid foundations for his future power, and I do not consider it superfluous to discuss them, because I do not know what better precepts to give a new prince than the example of his actions; and if his dispositions were of no avail, that was not his fault, but the extraordinary and extreme malignity of fortune.

Alexander the Sixth, in wishing to aggrandize the duke, his son, had many immediate and prospective difficulties. Firstly, he did not see his way to make him master of any state that was

---

[7] Francesco Sforza, born 1401, died 1466. He married Bianca Maria Visconti, a natural daughter of Filippo Visconti, the Duke of Milan, on whose death he procured his own elevation to the duchy. Machiavelli was the accredited agent of the Florentine Republic to Cesare Borgia (1478-1507) during the transactions which led up to the assassinations of the Orsini and Vitelli at Sinigalia, and along with his letters to his chiefs in Florence he has left an account, written ten years before "The Prince," of the proceedings of the duke in his "Descritione del modo tenuto dal duca Valentino nello ammazzare Vitellozzo Vitelli," etc., a translation of which is appended to the present work.

not a state of the Church; and if he was willing to rob the Church he knew that the Duke of Milan and the Venetians would not consent, because Faenza and Rimini were already under the protection of the Venetians. Besides this, he saw the arms of Italy, especially those by which he might have been assisted, in hands that would fear the aggrandizement of the Pope, namely, the Orsini and the Colonnesi and their following. It behoved him, therefore, to upset this state of affairs and embroil the powers, so as to make himself securely master of part of their states. This was easy for him to do, because he found the Venetians, moved by other reasons, inclined to bring back the French into Italy; he would not only not oppose this, but he would render it more easy by dissolving the former marriage of King Louis. Therefore the king came into Italy with the assistance of the Venetians and the consent of Alexander. He was no sooner in Milan than the Pope had soldiers from him for the attempt on the Romagna, which yielded to him on the reputation of the king. The duke, therefore, having acquired the Romagna and beaten the Colonnesi, while wishing to hold that and to advance further, was hindered by two things: the one, his forces did not appear loyal to him, the other, the goodwill of France: that is to say, he feared that the forces of the Orsini, which he was using, would not stand to him, that not only might they hinder him from winning more, but might themselves seize what he had won, and that the king might also do the same. Of the Orsini he had a warning when, after taking Faenza and attacking Bologna, he saw them go very unwillingly to that attack. And as to the king, he learned his mind when he himself, after taking the Duchy of Urbino, attacked Tuscany, and the king made him desist from that undertaking; hence the duke decided to depend no more upon the arms and the luck of others.

    For the first thing he weakened the Orsini and Colonnesi parties in Rome, by gaining to himself all their adherents who were gentlemen, making them his gentlemen, giving them good pay, and, according to their rank, honouring them with office and command in such a way that in a few months all attachment to the factions was destroyed and turned entirely to the duke. After this he awaited an opportunity to crush the Orsini, having scattered the adherents of the Colonna house. This came to him soon and he used it well; for the Orsini, perceiving at length that the aggrandizement of the duke and the Church was ruin to them, called a meeting of the Magione in Perugia. From this sprung the rebellion at Urbino and the tumults in the Romagna, with endless dangers to the duke, all of which he overcame with the help of the French. Having restored his authority, not to leave it at risk by trusting either to the French or other outside forces, he had recourse to his wiles, and he knew so well how to conceal his mind that, by the mediation of Signor Pagolo — whom the duke did not fail to secure with all kinds of attention, giving him money, apparel, and horses — the Orsini were reconciled, so that their simplicity brought them into his power at Sinigalia. Having exterminated the leaders, and turned their partisans into his friends, the duke laid sufficiently good foundations to his power, having all the Romagna and the Duchy of Urbino; and the people now beginning to appreciate their prosperity, he gained them all over to himself. And as this point is worthy of notice, and to be imitated by others, I am not willing to leave it out.

    When the duke occupied the Romagna he found it under the rule of weak masters, who rather plundered their subjects than ruled them, and gave them more cause for disunion than for union, so that the country was full of robbery, quarrels, and every kind of violence; and so, wishing to bring back peace and obedience to authority, he considered it necessary to give it a good governor. Thereupon he promoted Messer Ramiro d'Orco, a swift and cruel man, to whom he gave the fullest power. This man in a short time restored peace and unity with the greatest success. Afterwards the duke considered that it was not advisable to confer such excessive authority, for he had no doubt but that he would become odious, so he set up a court of judgment in the country, under a most excellent president, wherein all cities had their advocates. And because he knew that the past severity had caused some hatred against himself, so, to clear himself in the minds of the people, and gain them entirely to himself, he desired to show that, if any cruelty had been practised, it had not originated with him, but in the natural sternness of the minister. Under this pretence he took Ramiro, and one morning caused him to be executed and left on the piazza at Cesena with the block and a bloody knife at his side. The barbarity of this spectacle caused the people to be at once satisfied and dismayed.

But let us return whence we started. I say that the duke, finding himself now sufficiently powerful and partly secured from immediate dangers by having armed himself in his own way, and having in a great measure crushed those forces in his vicinity that could injure him if he wished to proceed with his conquest, had next to consider France, for he knew that the king, who too late was aware of his mistake, would not support him. And from this time he began to seek new alliances and to temporize with France in the expedition which she was making towards the kingdom of Naples against the Spaniards who were besieging Gaeta. It was his intention to secure himself against them, and this he would have quickly accomplished had Alexander lived.

Such was his line of action as to present affairs. But as to the future he had to fear, in the first place, that a new successor to the Church might not be friendly to him and might seek to take from him that which Alexander had given him, so he decided to act in four ways. Firstly, by exterminating the families of those lords whom he had despoiled, so as to take away that pretext from the Pope. Secondly, by winning to himself all the gentlemen of Rome, so as to be able to curb the Pope with their aid, as has been observed. Thirdly, by converting the college more to himself. Fourthly, by acquiring so much power before the Pope should die that he could by his own measures resist the first shock. Of these four things, at the death of Alexander, he had accomplished three. For he had killed as many of the dispossessed lords as he could lay hands on, and few had escaped; he had won over the Roman gentlemen, and he had the most numerous party in the college. And as to any fresh acquisition, he intended to become master of Tuscany, for he already possessed Perugia and Piombino, and Pisa was under his protection. And as he had no longer to study France (for the French were already driven out of the kingdom of Naples by the Spaniards, and in this way both were compelled to buy his goodwill), he pounced down upon Pisa. After this, Lucca and Siena yielded at once, partly through hatred and partly through fear of the Florentines; and the Florentines would have had no remedy had he continued to prosper, as he was prospering the year that Alexander died, for he had acquired so much power and reputation that he would have stood by himself, and no longer have depended on the luck and the forces of others, but solely on his own power and ability.

But Alexander died five years after he had first drawn the sword. He left the duke with the state of Romagna alone consolidated, with the rest in the air, between two most powerful hostile armies, and sick unto death. Yet there were in the duke such boldness and ability, and he knew so well how men are to be won or lost, and so firm were the foundations which in so short a time he had laid, that if he had not had those armies on his back, or if he had been in good health, he would have overcome all difficulties. And it is seen that his foundations were good, for the Romagna awaited him for more than a month. In Rome, although but half alive, he remained secure; and whilst the Baglioni, the Vitelli, and the Orsini might come to Rome, they could not effect anything against him. If he could not have made Pope him whom he wished, at least the one whom he did not wish would not have been elected. But if he had been in sound health at the death of Alexander,[8] everything would have been different to him. On the day that Julius the Second[9] was elected, he told me that he had thought of everything that might occur at the death of his father, and had provided a remedy for all, except that he had never anticipated that, when the death did happen, he himself would be on the point to die.

When all the actions of the duke are recalled, I do not know how to blame him, but rather it appears to be, as I have

---

[8] Alexander VI died of fever, 18th August 1503.
[9] Julius II was Giuliano della Rovere, Cardinal of San Pietro ad Vincula, born 1443, died 1513.

said, that I ought to offer him for imitation to all those who, by the fortune or the arms of others, are raised to government. Because he, having a lofty spirit and far-reaching aims, could not have regulated his conduct otherwise, and only the shortness of the life of Alexander and his own sickness frustrated his designs. Therefore, he who considers it necessary to secure himself in his new principality, to win friends, to overcome either by force or fraud, to make himself beloved and feared by the people, to be followed and revered by the soldiers, to exterminate those who have power or reason to hurt him, to change the old order of things for new, to be severe and gracious, magnanimous and liberal, to destroy a disloyal soldiery and to create new, to maintain friendship with kings and princes in such a way that they must help him with zeal and offend with caution, cannot find a more lively example than the actions of this man.

Only can he be blamed for the election of Julius the Second, in whom he made a bad choice, because, as is said, not being able to elect a Pope to his own mind, he could have hindered any other from being elected Pope; and he ought never to have consented to the election of any cardinal whom he had injured or who had cause to fear him if they became pontiffs. For men injure either from fear or hatred. Those whom he had injured, amongst others, were San Pietro ad Vincula, Colonna, San Giorgio, and Ascanio.[10] The rest, in becoming Pope, had to fear him, Rouen and the Spaniards excepted; the latter from their relationship and obligations, the former from his influence, the kingdom of France having relations with him. Therefore, above everything, the duke ought to have created a Spaniard Pope, and, failing him, he ought to have consented to Rouen and not San Pietro ad Vincula. He who believes that new benefits will cause great personages to forget old injuries is deceived. Therefore, the duke erred in his choice, and it was the cause of his ultimate ruin.

---

[10] San Giorgio is Raffaello Riario. Ascanio is Ascanio Sforza.

CHAPTER VIII

CONCERNING THOSE WHO HAVE OBTAINED A PRINCIPALITY BY WICKEDNESS

Although a prince may rise from a private station in two ways, neither of which can be entirely attributed to fortune or genius, yet it is manifest to me that I must not be silent on them, although one could be more copiously treated when I discuss republics. These methods are when, either by some wicked or nefarious ways, one ascends to the principality, or when by the favour of his fellow-citizens a private person becomes the prince of his country. And speaking of the first method, it will be illustrated by two examples — one ancient, the other modern — and without entering further into the subject, I consider these two examples will suffice those who may be compelled to follow them.

Agathocles, the Sicilian,[11] became King of Syracuse not only from a private but from a low and abject position. This man, the son of a potter, through all the changes in his fortunes always led an infamous life. Nevertheless, he accompanied his infamies with so much ability of mind and body that, having devoted himself to the military profession, he rose through its ranks to be Praetor of Syracuse. Being established in that position, and having deliberately resolved to make himself prince and to seize by violence, without obligation to others, that which had been conceded to him by assent, he came to an understanding for this purpose with Amilcar, the Carthaginian, who, with his army, was fighting in Sicily. One morning he assembled the people and the

---

[11] Agathocles the Sicilian, born 361 B.C., died 289 B.C.

senate of Syracuse, as if he had to discuss with them things relating to the Republic, and at a given signal the soldiers killed all the senators and the richest of the people; these dead, he seized and held the princedom of that city without any civil commotion. And although he was twice routed by the Carthaginians, and ultimately besieged, yet not only was he able to defend his city, but leaving part of his men for its defence, with the others he attacked Africa, and in a short time raised the siege of Syracuse. The Carthaginians, reduced to extreme necessity, were compelled to come to terms with Agathocles, and, leaving Sicily to him, had to be content with the possession of Africa.

Therefore, he who considers the actions and the genius of this man will see nothing, or little, which can be attributed to fortune, inasmuch as he attained pre-eminence, as is shown above, not by the favour of any one, but step by step in the military profession, which steps were gained with a thousand troubles and perils, and were afterwards boldly held by him with many hazardous dangers. Yet it cannot be called talent to slay fellow-citizens, to deceive friends, to be without faith, without mercy, without religion; such methods may gain empire, but not glory. Still, if the courage of Agathocles in entering into and extricating himself from dangers be considered, together with his greatness of mind in enduring and overcoming hardships, it cannot be seen why he should be esteemed less than the most notable captain. Nevertheless, his barbarous cruelty and inhumanity with infinite wickedness do not permit him to be celebrated among the most excellent men. What he achieved cannot be attributed either to fortune or genius.

In our times, during the rule of Alexander the Sixth, Oliverotto da Fermo, having been left an orphan many years before, was brought up by his maternal uncle, Giovanni Fogliani, and in the early days of his youth sent to fight under Pagolo Vitelli, that, being trained under his discipline, he might attain some high position in the military profession. After Pagolo died, he fought under his brother Vitellozzo, and in a very short time, being endowed with wit and a vigorous body and mind, he became the first man in his profession. But it appearing a paltry thing to serve under others, he resolved, with the aid of some citizens of Fermo, to whom the slavery of their country was dearer than its liberty, and with the help of the Vitelleschi, to seize Fermo. So he wrote to Giovanni Fogliani that, having been away from home for many years, he wished to visit him and his city, and in some measure to look upon his patrimony; and although he had not laboured to acquire anything except honour, yet, in order that the citizens should see he had not spent his time in vain, he desired to come honourably, so would be accompanied by one hundred horsemen, his friends and retainers; and he entreated Giovanni to arrange that he should be received honourably by the Fermians, all of which would be not only to his honour, but also to that of Giovanni himself, who had brought him up.

Giovanni, therefore, did not fail in any attentions due to his nephew, and he caused him to be honourably received by the Fermians, and he lodged him in his own house, where, having passed some days, and having arranged what was necessary for his wicked designs, Oliverotto gave a solemn banquet to which he invited Giovanni Fogliani and the chiefs of Fermo. When the viands and all the other entertainments that are usual in such banquets were finished, Oliverotto artfully began certain grave discourses, speaking of the greatness of Pope Alexander and his son Cesare, and of their enterprises, to which discourse Giovanni and others answered; but he rose at once, saying that such matters ought to be discussed in a more private place, and he betook himself to a chamber, whither Giovanni and the rest of the citizens went in after him. No sooner were they seated than soldiers issued from secret places and slaughtered Giovanni and the rest. After these murders Oliverotto, mounted on horseback, rode up and down the town and besieged the chief magistrate in the palace, so that in fear the people were forced to obey him, and to form a government, of which he made himself the prince. He killed all the malcontents who were able to injure him, and strengthened himself with new civil and military ordinances, in such a way that, in the year during which he held the principality, not only was he secure in the city of Fermo, but he had become formidable to all his neighbours. And his destruction would have been as difficult as that of Agathocles if he had not allowed himself to be overreached by Cesare Borgia, who took him with the Orsini and Vitelli at Sinigalia, as was stated above. Thus one year after he had committed this parricide, he was strangled, together with Vitellozzo, whom he had made his leader in valour and wickedness.

Some may wonder how it can happen that Agathocles, and his like, after infinite treacheries and cruelties, should live for long secure in his country, and defend himself from external enemies, and never be conspired against by his own citizens; seeing that many others, by means of cruelty, have never been able even in peaceful times to hold the state, still less in the doubtful times of war. I believe that this follows from severities being badly or properly used. Those may be called properly used, if of evil it is possible to speak well, that are applied at one blow and are necessary to one's security, and that are not persisted in afterwards unless they can be turned to the advantage of the subjects. The badly employed are those which, notwithstanding they may be few in the commencement, multiply with time rather than decrease. Those who practise the first system are able, by aid of God or man, to mitigate in some degree their rule, as Agathocles did. It is impossible for those who follow the other to maintain themselves.

Hence it is to be remarked that, in seizing a state, the usurper ought to examine closely into all those injuries which it is necessary for him to inflict, and to do them all at one stroke so as not to have to repeat them daily; and thus by not unsettling men he will be able to reassure them, and win them to himself by benefits. He who does otherwise, either from timidity or evil advice, is always compelled to keep the knife in his hand; neither can he rely on his subjects, nor can they attach themselves to him, owing to their continued and repeated wrongs. For injuries ought to be done all at one time, so that, being tasted less, they offend less; benefits ought to be given little by little, so that the flavour of them may last longer.

And above all things, a prince ought to live amongst his people in such a way that no unexpected circumstances, whether of good or evil, shall make him change; because if the necessity for this comes in troubled times, you are too late for harsh measures; and mild ones will not help you, for they will be considered as forced from you, and no one will be under any obligation to you for them.

CHAPTER IX

CONCERNING A CIVIL PRINCIPALITY

But coming to the other point — where a leading citizen becomes the prince of his country, not by wickedness or any intolerable violence, but by the favour of his fellow citizens — this may be called a civil principality: nor is genius or fortune altogether necessary to attain to it, but rather a happy shrewdness. I say then that such a principality is obtained either by the favour of the people or by the favour of the nobles. Because in all cities these two distinct parties are found, and from this it arises that the people do not wish to be ruled nor oppressed by the nobles, and the nobles wish to rule and oppress the people; and from these two opposite desires there arises in cities one of three results, either a principality, self-government, or anarchy.

A principality is created either by the people or by the nobles, accordingly as one or other of them has the opportunity; for the nobles, seeing they cannot withstand the people, begin to cry up the reputation of one of themselves, and they make him a prince, so that under his shadow they can give vent to their ambitions. The people, finding they cannot resist the nobles, also cry up the reputation of one of themselves, and make him a prince so as to be defended by his authority. He who obtains sovereignty by the assistance of the nobles maintains himself with more difficulty than he who comes to it by the aid of the people, because the former finds himself with many around him who consider themselves his equals, and because of this he can neither rule nor manage them to his liking. But he who reaches sovereignty by popular favour finds himself alone, and has none around him, or few, who are not prepared to obey him.

Besides this, one cannot by fair dealing, and without injury to others, satisfy the nobles, but you can satisfy the people, for their object is more righteous than that of the nobles, the latter wishing to oppress, while the former only desire not to be oppressed. It is to be added also that a prince can never secure himself against a hostile people, because of their being too many, whilst from the nobles he can secure himself, as they are few in number. The worst that a prince may expect from a hostile people is to be abandoned by them; but from hostile nobles he has not only to fear abandonment, but also that they will rise against him; for they, being in these affairs more far-seeing and astute, always come forward in time to save themselves, and to obtain favours from him whom they expect to prevail. Further, the prince is compelled to live always with the same people, but he can do well without the same nobles, being able to make and unmake them daily, and to give or take away authority when it pleases him.

Therefore, to make this point clearer, I say that the nobles ought to be looked at mainly in two ways: that is to say, they either shape their course in such a way as binds them entirely to your fortune, or they do not. Those who so bind themselves, and are not rapacious, ought to be honoured and loved; those who do not bind themselves may be dealt with in two ways; they may fail to do this through pusillanimity and a natural want of courage, in which case you ought to make use of them, especially of those who are of good counsel; and thus, whilst in prosperity you honour them, in adversity you do not have to fear them. But when for their own ambitious ends they shun binding themselves, it is a token that they are giving more thought to themselves than to you, and a prince ought to guard against such, and to fear them as if they were open enemies, because in adversity they always help to ruin him.

Therefore, one who becomes a prince through the favour of the people ought to keep them friendly, and this he can easily do seeing they only ask not to be oppressed by him. But one who, in opposition to the people, becomes a prince by the favour of the nobles, ought, above everything, to seek to win the people over to himself, and this he may easily do if he takes them under his protection. Because men, when they receive good from him of whom they were expecting evil, are bound more closely to their benefactor; thus the people quickly become more devoted to him than if he had been raised to the principality by their favours; and the prince can win their affections in many ways, but as these vary according to the circumstances one cannot give fixed rules, so I omit them; but, I repeat, it is necessary for a prince to have the people friendly, otherwise he has no security in adversity.

Nabis,[12] Prince of the Spartans, sustained the attack of all Greece, and of a victorious Roman army, and against them he defended his country and his government; and for the overcoming of this peril it was only necessary for him to make himself secure against a few, but this would not have been sufficient had the people been hostile. And do not let any one impugn this statement with the trite proverb that "He who builds on the people, builds on the mud," for this is true when a private citizen makes a foundation there, and persuades himself that the people will free him when he is oppressed by his enemies or by the magistrates; wherein he would find himself very often deceived, as happened to the Gracchi in Rome and to Messer Giorgio Scali[13] in Florence. But granted a prince who has established himself as above, who can command, and is a man of courage, undismayed in adversity, who does not fail in other qualifications, and who, by his resolution and energy, keeps the whole people encouraged — such a one will never find himself deceived in them, and it will be shown that he has laid his foundations well.

These principalities are liable to danger when they are passing from the civil to the absolute order of government, for such princes either rule personally or through magistrates. In the latter case their government is weaker and more insecure, because it rests entirely on the goodwill of those citizens who are raised to

---

[12] Nabis, tyrant of Sparta, conquered by the Romans under Flamininus in 195 B.C.; killed 192 B.C.

[13] Messer Giorgio Scali. This event is to be found in Machiavelli's "Florentine History," Book III.

the magistracy, and who, especially in troubled times, can destroy the government with great ease, either by intrigue or open defiance; and the prince has not the chance amid tumults to exercise absolute authority, because the citizens and subjects, accustomed to receive orders from magistrates, are not of a mind to obey him amid these confusions, and there will always be in doubtful times a scarcity of men whom he can trust. For such a prince cannot rely upon what he observes in quiet times, when citizens have need of the state, because then every one agrees with him; they all promise, and when death is far distant they all wish to die for him; but in troubled times, when the state has need of its citizens, then he finds but few. And so much the more is this experiment dangerous, inasmuch as it can only be tried once. Therefore a wise prince ought to adopt such a course that his citizens will always in every sort and kind of circumstance have need of the state and of him, and then he will always find them faithful.

CHAPTER X

CONCERNING THE WAY IN WHICH THE STRENGTH OF ALL PRINCIPALITIES OUGHT TO BE MEASURED

It is necessary to consider another point in examining the character of these principalities: that is, whether a prince has such power that, in case of need, he can support himself with his own resources, or whether he has always need of the assistance of others. And to make this quite clear I say that I consider those who are able to support themselves by their own resources who can, either by abundance of men or money, raise a sufficient army to join battle against any one who comes to attack them; and I consider those always to have need of others who cannot show themselves against the enemy in the field, but are forced to defend themselves by sheltering behind walls. The first case has been discussed, but we will speak of it again should it recur. In the second case one can say nothing except to encourage such princes to provision and fortify their towns, and not on any account to defend the country. And whoever shall fortify his town well, and shall have managed the other concerns of his subjects in the way stated above, and to be often repeated, will never be attacked without great caution, for men are always adverse to enterprises where difficulties can be seen, and it will be seen not to be an easy thing to attack one who has his town well fortified, and is not hated by his people.

The cities of Germany are absolutely free, they own but little country around them, and they yield obedience to the emperor when it suits them, nor do they fear this or any other power they may have near them, because they are fortified in such a way that every one thinks the taking of them by assault would be tedious and difficult, seeing they have proper ditches and walls, they have sufficient artillery, and they always keep in public depots enough for one year's eating, drinking, and firing. And beyond this, to keep the people quiet and without loss to the state, they always have the means of giving work to the community in those labours that are the life and strength of the city, and on the pursuit of which the people are supported; they also hold military exercises in repute, and moreover have many ordinances to uphold them.

Therefore, a prince who has a strong city, and had not made himself odious, will not be attacked, or if any one should attack he will only be driven off with disgrace; again, because that the affairs of this world are so changeable, it is almost impossible to keep an army a whole year in the field without being interfered with. And whoever should reply: If the people have property outside the city, and see it burnt, they will not remain patient, and the long siege and self-interest will make them forget their prince; to this I answer that a powerful and courageous prince will overcome all such difficulties by giving at one time hope to his subjects that the evil will not be for long, at another time fear of the cruelty of the enemy, then preserving himself adroitly from those subjects who seem to him to be too bold.

Further, the enemy would naturally on his arrival at once burn and ruin the country at the time when the spirits of the people are still hot and ready for the defence; and, therefore, so much the less ought the prince to hesitate; because after a time, when spirits have cooled, the damage is already done, the ills are incurred, and there is no longer any remedy; and therefore they are so much the more ready to unite with their prince, he appearing to be under obligations to them now that their houses have been burnt and their possessions ruined in his defence. For it is the nature of men to be bound by the benefits they confer as much as by those they receive. Therefore, if everything is well considered, it will not be difficult for a wise prince to keep the minds of his citizens steadfast from first to last, when he does not fail to support and defend them.

CHAPTER XI

CONCERNING ECCLESIASTICAL PRINCIPALITIES

It only remains now to speak of ecclesiastical principalities, touching which all difficulties are prior to getting possession, because they are acquired either by capacity or good fortune, and they can be held without either; for they are sustained by the ancient ordinances of religion, which are so all-powerful, and of such a character that the principalities may be held no matter how their princes behave and live. These princes alone have states and do not defend them; and they have subjects and do not rule them; and the states, although unguarded, are not taken from them, and the subjects, although not ruled, do not care, and they have neither the desire nor the ability to alienate themselves. Such principalities only are secure and happy. But being upheld by powers, to which the human mind cannot reach, I shall speak no more of them, because, being exalted and maintained by God, it would be the act of a presumptuous and rash man to discuss them.

Nevertheless, if any one should ask of me how comes it that the Church has attained such greatness in temporal power, seeing that from Alexander backwards the Italian potentates (not only those who have been called potentates, but every baron and lord, though the smallest) have valued the temporal power very slightly — yet now a king of France trembles before it, and it has been able to drive him from Italy, and to ruin the Venetians — although this may be very manifest, it does not appear to me superfluous to recall it in some measure to memory.

Before Charles, King of France, passed into Italy,[14] this country was under the dominion of the Pope, the Venetians, the King of Naples, the Duke of Milan, and the Florentines. These potentates had two principal anxieties: the one, that no foreigner should enter Italy under arms; the other, that none of themselves should seize more territory. Those about whom there was the most anxiety were the Pope and the Venetians. To restrain the Venetians the union of all the others was necessary, as it was for the defence of Ferrara; and to keep down the Pope they made use of the barons of Rome, who, being divided into two factions, Orsini and Colonnesi, had always a pretext for disorder, and, standing with arms in their hands under the eyes of the Pontiff, kept the pontificate weak and powerless. And although there might arise sometimes a courageous pope, such as Sixtus, yet neither fortune nor wisdom could rid him of these annoyances. And the short life of a pope is also a cause of weakness; for in the ten years, which is the average life of a pope, he can with difficulty lower one of the factions; and if, so to speak, one people should almost destroy the Colonnesi, another would arise hostile to the Orsini, who would support their opponents, and yet would not have time to ruin the Orsini. This was the reason why the temporal powers of the pope were little esteemed in Italy.

Alexander the Sixth arose afterwards, who of all the pontiffs that have ever been showed how a pope with both money and arms was able to prevail; and through the instrumentality of the Duke Valentino, and by reason of the entry of the French, he brought about all those things which I have discussed above in the actions of the duke. And although his intention was not to aggrandize the Church, but the duke, nevertheless, what he did contributed to the greatness of the Church, which, after his death and the ruin of the duke, became the heir to all his labours.

Pope Julius came afterwards and found the Church strong, possessing all the Romagna, the barons of Rome reduced to impotence, and, through the chastisements of Alexander, the

---

[14] Charles VIII invaded Italy in 1494.

factions wiped out; he also found the way open to accumulate money in a manner such as had never been practised before Alexander's time. Such things Julius not only followed, but improved upon, and he intended to gain Bologna, to ruin the Venetians, and to drive the French out of Italy. All of these enterprises prospered with him, and so much the more to his credit, inasmuch as he did everything to strengthen the Church and not any private person. He kept also the Orsini and Colonnesi factions within the bounds in which he found them; and although there was among them some mind to make disturbance, nevertheless he held two things firm: the one, the greatness of the Church, with which he terrified them; and the other, not allowing them to have their own cardinals, who caused the disorders among them. For whenever these factions have their cardinals they do not remain quiet for long, because cardinals foster the factions in Rome and out of it, and the barons are compelled to support them, and thus from the ambitions of prelates arise disorders and tumults among the barons. For these reasons his Holiness Pope Leo[15] found the pontificate most powerful, and it is to be hoped that, if others made it great in arms, he will make it still greater and more venerated by his goodness and infinite other virtues.

---

[15] Pope Leo X was the Cardinal de' Medici.

CHAPTER XII

HOW MANY KINDS OF SOLDIERY THERE ARE, AND CONCERNING MERCENARIES

Having discoursed particularly on the characteristics of such principalities as in the beginning I proposed to discuss, and having considered in some degree the causes of their being good or bad, and having shown the methods by which many have sought to acquire them and to hold them, it now remains for me to discuss generally the means of offence and defence which belong to each of them.

We have seen above how necessary it is for a prince to have his foundations well laid, otherwise it follows of necessity he will go to ruin. The chief foundations of all states, new as well as old or composite, are good laws and good arms; and as there cannot be good laws where the state is not well armed, it follows that where they are well armed they have good laws. I shall leave the laws out of the discussion and shall speak of the arms.

I say, therefore, that the arms with which a prince defends his state are either his own, or they are mercenaries, auxiliaries, or mixed. Mercenaries and auxiliaries are useless and dangerous; and if one holds his state based on these arms, he will stand neither firm nor safe; for they are disunited, ambitious, and without discipline, unfaithful, valiant before friends, cowardly before enemies; they have neither the fear of God nor fidelity to men, and destruction is deferred only so long as the attack is; for in peace one is robbed by them, and in war by the enemy. The fact is, they have no other attraction or reason for keeping the field than a trifle of stipend, which is not sufficient to make them willing to die for you. They are ready enough to be your soldiers whilst you do not make war, but if war comes they take themselves off or run from the foe; which I should have little trouble to prove, for the ruin of Italy has been caused by nothing else than by resting all her hopes for many years on mercenaries, and although they formerly made some display and appeared valiant amongst themselves, yet when the foreigners came they showed what they were. Thus it was that Charles, King of France, was allowed to seize Italy with chalk in hand;[16] and he who told us that our sins were the cause of it told the truth, but they were not the sins he imagined, but those which I have related. And as they were the sins of princes, it is the princes who have also suffered the penalty.

I wish to demonstrate further the infelicity of these arms. The mercenary captains are either capable men or they are not; if they are, you cannot trust them, because they always aspire to their own greatness, either by oppressing you, who are their master, or others contrary to your intentions; but if the captain is not skilful, you are ruined in the usual way.

And if it be urged that whoever is armed will act in the same way, whether mercenary or not, I reply that when arms have to be resorted to, either by a prince or a republic, then the prince ought to go in person and perform the duty of a captain; the republic has to send its citizens, and when one is sent who does not turn out satisfactorily, it ought to recall him, and when one is worthy, to hold him by the laws so that he does not leave the command. And experience has shown princes and republics, single-handed, making the greatest progress, and mercenaries doing nothing except damage; and it is more difficult to bring a

---

[16] "With chalk in hand," "col gesso." This is one of the *bons mots* of Alexander VI, and refers to the ease with which Charles VIII seized Italy, implying that it was only necessary for him to send his quartermasters to chalk up the billets for his soldiers to conquer the country. Cf. "The History of Henry VII," by Lord Bacon: "King Charles had conquered the realm of Naples, and lost it again, in a kind of a felicity of a dream. He passed the whole length of Italy without resistance: so that it was true what Pope Alexander was wont to say: That the Frenchmen came into Italy with chalk in their hands, to mark up their lodgings, rather than with swords to fight."

republic, armed with its own arms, under the sway of one of its citizens than it is to bring one armed with foreign arms. Rome and Sparta stood for many ages armed and free. The Switzers are completely armed and quite free.

Of ancient mercenaries, for example, there are the Carthaginians, who were oppressed by their mercenary soldiers after the first war with the Romans, although the Carthaginians had their own citizens for captains. After the death of Epaminondas, Philip of Macedon was made captain of their soldiers by the Thebans, and after victory he took away their liberty.

Duke Filippo being dead, the Milanese enlisted Francesco Sforza against the Venetians, and he, having overcome the enemy at Caravaggio,[17] allied himself with them to crush the Milanese, his masters. His father, Sforza, having been engaged by Queen Johanna[18] of Naples, left her unprotected, so that she was forced to throw herself into the arms of the King of Aragon, in order to save her kingdom. And if the Venetians and Florentines formerly extended their dominions by these arms, and yet their captains did not make themselves princes, but have defended them, I reply that the Florentines in this case have been favoured by chance, for of the able captains, of whom they might have stood in fear, some have not conquered, some have been opposed, and others have turned their ambitions elsewhere. One who did not conquer was Giovanni Acuto,[19] and since he did not conquer his fidelity cannot be proved; but every one will acknowledge that, had he conquered, the Florentines would have stood at his discretion. Sforza had the Bracceschi always against him, so they watched each other. Francesco turned his ambition to Lombardy; Braccio

---

[17] Battle of Caravaggio, 15th September 1448.
[18] Johanna II of Naples, the widow of Ladislao, King of Naples.
[19] Giovanni Acuto. An English knight whose name was Sir John Hawkwood. He fought in the English wars in France, and was knighted by Edward III; afterwards he collected a body of troops and went into Italy. These became the famous "White Company." He took part in many wars, and died in Florence in 1394. He was born about 1320 at Sible Hedingham, a village in Essex. He married Domnia, a daughter of Bernabo Visconti.

against the Church and the kingdom of Naples. But let us come to that which happened a short while ago. The Florentines appointed as their captain Pagolo Vitelli, a most prudent man, who from a private position had risen to the greatest renown. If this man had taken Pisa, nobody can deny that it would have been proper for the Florentines to keep in with him, for if he became the soldier of their enemies they had no means of resisting, and if they held to him they must obey him. The Venetians, if their achievements are considered, will be seen to have acted safely and gloriously so long as they sent to war their own men, when with armed gentlemen and plebians they did valiantly. This was before they turned to enterprises on land, but when they began to fight on land they forsook this virtue and followed the custom of Italy. And in the beginning of their expansion on land, through not having much territory, and because of their great reputation, they had not much to fear from their captains; but when they expanded, as under Carmignuola[20] they had a taste of this mistake; for, having found him a most valiant man (they beat the Duke of Milan under his leadership), and, on the other hand, knowing how lukewarm he was in the war, they feared they would no longer conquer under him, and for this reason they were not willing, nor were they able, to let him go; and so, not to lose again that which they had acquired, they were compelled, in order to secure themselves, to murder him. They had afterwards for their captains Bartolomeo da Bergamo, Roberto da San Severino, the count of Pitigliano,[21] and the like, under whom they had to dread loss and not gain, as happened afterwards at Vaila,[22] where in one battle they lost that which in eight hundred years they had acquired with so much trouble. Because from such arms conquests

---

[20] Carmignuola. Francesco Bussone, born at Carmagnola about 1390, executed at Venice, 5th May 1432.

[21] Bartolomeo Colleoni of Bergamo; died 1457. Roberto of San Severino; died fighting for Venice against Sigismund, Duke of Austria, in 1487. "Primo capitano in Italia." — Machiavelli. Count of Pitigliano; Nicolo Orsini, born 1442, died 1510.

[22] Battle of Vaila in 1509.

come but slowly, long delayed and inconsiderable, but the losses sudden and portentous.

And as with these examples I have reached Italy, which has been ruled for many years by mercenaries, I wish to discuss them more seriously, in order that, having seen their rise and progress, one may be better prepared to counteract them. You must understand that the empire has recently come to be repudiated in Italy, that the Pope has acquired more temporal power, and that Italy has been divided up into more states, for the reason that many of the great cities took up arms against their nobles, who, formerly favoured by the emperor, were oppressing them, whilst the Church was favouring them so as to gain authority in temporal power: in many others their citizens became princes. From this it came to pass that Italy fell partly into the hands of the Church and of republics, and, the Church consisting of priests and the republic of citizens unaccustomed to arms, both commenced to enlist foreigners.

The first who gave renown to this soldiery was Alberigo da Conio,[23] the Romagnian. From the school of this man sprang, among others, Braccio and Sforza, who in their time were the arbiters of Italy. After these came all the other captains who till now have directed the arms of Italy; and the end of all their valour has been, that she has been overrun by Charles, robbed by Louis, ravaged by Ferdinand, and insulted by the Switzers. The principle that has guided them has been, first, to lower the credit of infantry so that they might increase their own. They did this because, subsisting on their pay and without territory, they were unable to support many soldiers, and a few infantry did not give them any authority; so they were led to employ cavalry, with a moderate force of which they were maintained and honoured; and affairs were brought to such a pass that, in an army of twenty thousand soldiers, there were not to be found two thousand foot soldiers. They had, besides this, used every art to lessen fatigue

---

[23] Alberigo da Conio. Alberico da Barbiano, Count of Cunio in Romagna. He was the leader of the famous "Company of St George," composed entirely of Italian soldiers. He died in 1409.

and danger to themselves and their soldiers, not killing in the fray, but taking prisoners and liberating without ransom. They did not attack towns at night, nor did the garrisons of the towns attack encampments at night; they did not surround the camp either with stockade or ditch, nor did they campaign in the winter. All these things were permitted by their military rules, and devised by them to avoid, as I have said, both fatigue and dangers; thus they have brought Italy to slavery and contempt.

CHAPTER XIII

CONCERNING AUXILIARIES, MIXED SOLDIERY, AND ONE'S OWN

Auxiliaries, which are the other useless arm, are employed when a prince is called in with his forces to aid and defend, as was done by Pope Julius in the most recent times; for he, having, in the enterprise against Ferrara, had poor proof of his mercenaries, turned to auxiliaries, and stipulated with Ferdinand, King of Spain,[24] for his assistance with men and arms. These arms may be useful and good in themselves, but for him who calls them in they are always disadvantageous; for losing, one is undone, and winning, one is their captive.

And although ancient histories may be full of examples, I do not wish to leave this recent one of Pope Julius the Second, the peril of which cannot fail to be perceived; for he, wishing to get Ferrara, threw himself entirely into the hands of the foreigner. But his good fortune brought about a third event, so that he did not reap the fruit of his rash choice; because, having his auxiliaries routed at Ravenna, and the Switzers having risen and driven out the conquerors (against all expectation, both his and others), it so came to pass that he did not become prisoner to his enemies, they having fled, nor to his auxiliaries, he having conquered by other arms than theirs.

The Florentines, being entirely without arms, sent ten thousand Frenchmen to take Pisa, whereby they ran more danger than at any other time of their troubles.

---

[24] Ferdinand V (F. II of Aragon and Sicily, F. III of Naples), surnamed "The Catholic," born 1542, died 1516.

The Emperor of Constantinople,[25] to oppose his neighbours, sent ten thousand Turks into Greece, who, on the war being finished, were not willing to quit; this was the beginning of the servitude of Greece to the infidels.

Therefore, let him who has no desire to conquer make use of these arms, for they are much more hazardous than mercenaries, because with them the ruin is ready made; they are all united, all yield obedience to others; but with mercenaries, when they have conquered, more time and better opportunities are needed to injure you; they are not all of one community, they are found and paid by you, and a third party, which you have made their head, is not able all at once to assume enough authority to injure you. In conclusion, in mercenaries dastardy is most dangerous; in auxiliaries, valour. The wise prince, therefore, has always avoided these arms and turned to his own; and has been willing rather to lose with them than to conquer with the others, not deeming that a real victory which is gained with the arms of others.

I shall never hesitate to cite Cesare Borgia and his actions. This duke entered the Romagna with auxiliaries, taking there only French soldiers, and with them he captured Imola and Forli; but afterwards, such forces not appearing to him reliable, he turned to mercenaries, discerning less danger in them, and enlisted the Orsini and Vitelli; whom presently, on handling and finding them doubtful, unfaithful, and dangerous, he destroyed and turned to his own men. And the difference between one and the other of these forces can easily be seen when one considers the difference there was in the reputation of the duke, when he had the French, when he had the Orsini and Vitelli, and when he relied on his own soldiers, on whose fidelity he could always count and found it ever increasing; he was never esteemed more highly than when every one saw that he was complete master of his own forces.

I was not intending to go beyond Italian and recent examples, but I am unwilling to leave out Hiero, the Syracusan, he

---

[25] Joannes Cantacuzenus, born 1300, died 1383.

being one of those I have named above. This man, as I have said, made head of the army by the Syracusans, soon found out that a mercenary soldiery, constituted like our Italian condottieri, was of no use; and it appearing to him that he could neither keep them not let them go, he had them all cut to pieces, and afterwards made war with his own forces and not with aliens.

I wish also to recall to memory an instance from the Old Testament applicable to this subject. David offered himself to Saul to fight with Goliath, the Philistine champion, and, to give him courage, Saul armed him with his own weapons; which David rejected as soon as he had them on his back, saying he could make no use of them, and that he wished to meet the enemy with his sling and his knife. In conclusion, the arms of others either fall from your back, or they weigh you down, or they bind you fast.

Charles the Seventh,[26] the father of King Louis the Eleventh,[27] having by good fortune and valour liberated France from the English, recognized the necessity of being armed with forces of his own, and he established in his kingdom ordinances concerning men-at-arms and infantry. Afterwards his son, King Louis, abolished the infantry and began to enlist the Switzers, which mistake, followed by others, is, as is now seen, a source of peril to that kingdom; because, having raised the reputation of the Switzers, he has entirely diminished the value of his own arms, for he has destroyed the infantry altogether; and his men-at-arms he has subordinated to others, for, being as they are so accustomed to fight along with Switzers, it does not appear that they can now conquer without them. Hence it arises that the French cannot stand against the Switzers, and without the Switzers they do not come off well against others. The armies of the French have thus become mixed, partly mercenary and partly national, both of which arms together are much better than mercenaries alone or auxiliaries alone, but much inferior to one's own forces. And this example proves it, for the kingdom of France would be

---

[26] Charles VII of France, surnamed "The Victorious," born 1403, died 1461.
[27] Louis XI, son of the above, born 1423, died 1483.

unconquerable if the ordinance of Charles had been enlarged or maintained.

But the scanty wisdom of man, on entering into an affair which looks well at first, cannot discern the poison that is hidden in it, as I have said above of hectic fevers. Therefore, if he who rules a principality cannot recognize evils until they are upon him, he is not truly wise; and this insight is given to few. And if the first disaster to the Roman Empire should be examined, it will be found to have commenced only with the enlisting of the Goths; because from that time the vigour of the Roman Empire began to decline, and all that valour which had raised it passed away to others.

I conclude, therefore, that no principality is secure without having its own forces; on the contrary, it is entirely dependent on good fortune, not having the valour which in adversity would defend it. And it has always been the opinion and judgment of wise men that nothing can be so uncertain or unstable as fame or power not founded on its own strength. And one's own forces are those which are composed either of subjects, citizens, or dependents; all others are mercenaries or auxiliaries. And the way to make ready one's own forces will be easily found if the rules suggested by me shall be reflected upon, and if one will consider how Philip, the father of Alexander the Great, and many republics and princes have armed and organized themselves, to which rules I entirely commit myself.

CHAPTER XIV

THAT WHICH CONCERNS A PRINCE ON THE SUBJECT OF THE ART OF WAR

A prince ought to have no other aim or thought, nor select anything else for his study, than war and its rules and discipline; for this is the sole art that belongs to him who rules, and it is of such force that it not only upholds those who are born princes, but it often enables men to rise from a private station to that rank. And, on the contrary, it is seen that when princes have thought more of ease than of arms they have lost their states. And the first cause of your losing it is to neglect this art; and what enables you to acquire a state is to be master of the art. Francesco Sforza, through being martial, from a private person became Duke of Milan; and the sons, through avoiding the hardships and troubles of arms, from dukes became private persons. For among other evils which being unarmed brings you, it causes you to be despised, and this is one of those ignominies against which a prince ought to guard himself, as is shown later on. Because there is nothing proportionate between the armed and the unarmed; and it is not reasonable that he who is armed should yield obedience willingly to him who is unarmed, or that the unarmed man should be secure among armed servants. Because, there being in the one disdain and in the other suspicion, it is not possible for them to work well together. And therefore a prince who does not understand the art of war, over and above the other misfortunes already mentioned, cannot be respected by his soldiers, nor can he rely on them. He ought never, therefore, to have out of his thoughts this subject of war, and in peace he should addict himself more to its exercise than in war; this he can do in two ways, the one by action, the other by study.

As regards action, he ought above all things to keep his men well organized and drilled, to follow incessantly the chase, by which he accustoms his body to hardships, and learns something of the nature of localities, and gets to find out how the mountains rise, how the valleys open out, how the plains lie, and to understand the nature of rivers and marshes, and in all this to take the greatest care. Which knowledge is useful in two ways. Firstly, he learns to know his country, and is better able to undertake its defence; afterwards, by means of the knowledge and observation of that locality, he understands with ease any other which it may be necessary for him to study hereafter; because the hills, valleys, and plains, and rivers and marshes that are, for instance, in Tuscany, have a certain resemblance to those of other countries, so that with a knowledge of the aspect of one country one can easily arrive at a knowledge of others. And the prince that lacks this skill lacks the essential which it is desirable that a captain should possess, for it teaches him to surprise his enemy, to select quarters, to lead armies, to array the battle, to besiege towns to advantage.

Philopoemen,[28] Prince of the Achaeans, among other praises which writers have bestowed on him, is commended because in time of peace he never had anything in his mind but the rules of war; and when he was in the country with friends, he often stopped and reasoned with them: "If the enemy should be upon that hill, and we should find ourselves here with our army, with whom would be the advantage? How should one best advance to meet him, keeping the ranks? If we should wish to retreat, how ought we to pursue?" And he would set forth to them, as he went, all the chances that could befall an army; he would listen to their opinion and state his, confirming it with reasons, so that by these continual discussions there could never

---

[28] Philopoemen, "the last of the Greeks," born 252 B.C., died 183 B.C.

arise, in time of war, any unexpected circumstances that he could not deal with.

But to exercise the intellect the prince should read histories, and study there the actions of illustrious men, to see how they have borne themselves in war, to examine the causes of their victories and defeat, so as to avoid the latter and imitate the former; and above all do as an illustrious man did, who took as an exemplar one who had been praised and famous before him, and whose achievements and deeds he always kept in his mind, as it is said Alexander the Great imitated Achilles, Caesar Alexander, Scipio Cyrus. And whoever reads the life of Cyrus, written by Xenophon, will recognize afterwards in the life of Scipio how that imitation was his glory, and how in chastity, affability, humanity, and liberality Scipio conformed to those things which have been written of Cyrus by Xenophon. A wise prince ought to observe some such rules, and never in peaceful times stand idle, but increase his resources with industry in such a way that they may be available to him in adversity, so that if fortune chances it may find him prepared to resist her blows.

CHAPTER XV

CONCERNING THINGS FOR WHICH MEN, AND ESPECIALLY PRINCES, ARE PRAISED OR BLAMED

It remains now to see what ought to be the rules of conduct for a prince towards subject and friends. And as I know that many have written on this point, I expect I shall be considered presumptuous in mentioning it again, especially as in discussing it I shall depart from the methods of other people. But, it being my intention to write a thing which shall be useful to him who apprehends it, it appears to me more appropriate to follow up the real truth of the matter than the imagination of it; for many have pictured republics and principalities which in fact have never been known or seen, because how one lives is so far distant from how one ought to live, that he who neglects what is done for what ought to be done, sooner effects his ruin than his preservation; for a man who wishes to act entirely up to his professions of virtue soon meets with what destroys him among so much that is evil.

Hence it is necessary for a prince wishing to hold his own to know how to do wrong, and to make use of it or not according to necessity. Therefore, putting on one side imaginary things concerning a prince, and discussing those which are real, I say that all men when they are spoken of, and chiefly princes for being more highly placed, are remarkable for some of those qualities which bring them either blame or praise; and thus it is that one is reputed liberal, another miserly, using a Tuscan term (because an avaricious person in our language is still he who desires to possess by robbery, whilst we call one miserly who deprives himself too much of the use of his own); one is reputed generous, one rapacious; one cruel, one compassionate; one faithless, another faithful; one effeminate and cowardly, another bold and brave; one affable, another haughty; one lascivious, another chaste; one sincere, another cunning; one hard, another easy; one grave, another frivolous; one religious, another unbelieving, and the like. And I know that every one will confess that it would be most praiseworthy in a prince to exhibit all the above qualities that are considered good; but because they can neither be entirely possessed nor observed, for human conditions do not permit it, it is necessary for him to be sufficiently prudent that he may know how to avoid the reproach of those vices which would lose him his state; and also to keep himself, if it be possible, from those which would not lose him it; but this not being possible, he may with less hesitation abandon himself to them. And again, he need not make himself uneasy at incurring a reproach for those vices without which the state can only be saved with difficulty, for if everything is considered carefully, it will be found that something which looks like virtue, if followed, would be his ruin; whilst something else, which looks like vice, yet followed brings him security and prosperity.

CHAPTER XVI

CONCERNING LIBERALITY AND MEANNESS

Commencing then with the first of the above-named characteristics, I say that it would be well to be reputed liberal. Nevertheless, liberality exercised in a way that does not bring you the reputation for it, injures you; for if one exercises it honestly and as it should be exercised, it may not become known, and you will not avoid the reproach of its opposite. Therefore, any one wishing to maintain among men the name of liberal is obliged to avoid no attribute of magnificence; so that a prince thus inclined will consume in such acts all his property, and will be compelled in the end, if he wish to maintain the name of liberal, to unduly weigh down his people, and tax them, and do everything he can to get money. This will soon make him odious to his subjects, and becoming poor he will be little valued by any one; thus, with his liberality, having offended many and rewarded few, he is affected by the very first trouble and imperilled by whatever may be the first danger; recognizing this himself, and wishing to draw back from it, he runs at once into the reproach of being miserly.

Therefore, a prince, not being able to exercise this virtue of liberality in such a way that it is recognized, except to his cost, if he is wise he ought not to fear the reputation of being mean, for in time he will come to be more considered than if liberal, seeing that with his economy his revenues are enough, that he can defend himself against all attacks, and is able to engage in enterprises without burdening his people; thus it comes to pass that he exercises liberality towards all from whom he does not take, who are numberless, and meanness towards those to whom he does not give, who are few.

We have not seen great things done in our time except by those who have been considered mean; the rest have failed. Pope Julius the Second was assisted in reaching the papacy by a reputation for liberality, yet he did not strive afterwards to keep it up, when he made war on the King of France; and he made many wars without imposing any extraordinary tax on his subjects, for he supplied his additional expenses out of his long thriftiness. The present King of Spain would not have undertaken or conquered in so many enterprises if he had been reputed liberal. A prince, therefore, provided that he has not to rob his subjects, that he can defend himself, that he does not become poor and abject, that he is not forced to become rapacious, ought to hold of little account a reputation for being mean, for it is one of those vices which will enable him to govern.

And if any one should say: Caesar obtained empire by liberality, and many others have reached the highest positions by having been liberal, and by being considered so, I answer: Either you are a prince in fact, or in a way to become one. In the first case this liberality is dangerous, in the second it is very necessary to be considered liberal; and Caesar was one of those who wished to become pre-eminent in Rome; but if he had survived after becoming so, and had not moderated his expenses, he would have destroyed his government. And if any one should reply: Many have been princes, and have done great things with armies, who have been considered very liberal, I reply: Either a prince spends that which is his own or his subjects' or else that of others. In the first case he ought to be sparing, in the second he ought not to neglect any opportunity for liberality. And to the prince who goes forth with his army, supporting it by pillage, sack, and extortion, handling that which belongs to others, this liberality is necessary, otherwise he would not be followed by soldiers. And of that which is neither yours nor your subjects' you can be a ready giver, as were Cyrus, Caesar, and Alexander; because it does not take away your reputation if you squander that of others, but adds to it; it is only squandering your own that injures you.

And there is nothing wastes so rapidly as liberality, for even whilst you exercise it you lose the power to do so, and so become either poor or despised, or else, in avoiding poverty, rapacious and hated. And a prince should guard himself, above all things, against being despised and hated; and liberality leads you to both. Therefore it is wiser to have a reputation for meanness which brings reproach without hatred, than to be compelled through seeking a reputation for liberality to incur a name for rapacity which begets reproach with hatred.

CHAPTER XVII

CONCERNING CRUELTY AND CLEMENCY, AND WHETHER IT IS BETTER TO BE LOVED THAN FEARED

Coming now to the other qualities mentioned above, I say that every prince ought to desire to be considered clement and not cruel. Nevertheless he ought to take care not to misuse this clemency. Cesare Borgia was considered cruel; notwithstanding, his cruelty reconciled the Romagna, unified it, and restored it to peace and loyalty. And if this be rightly considered, he will be seen to have been much more merciful than the Florentine people, who, to avoid a reputation for cruelty, permitted Pistoia to be destroyed.[29] Therefore a prince, so long as he keeps his subjects united and loyal, ought not to mind the reproach of cruelty; because with a few examples he will be more merciful than those who, through too much mercy, allow disorders to arise, from which follow murders or robberies; for these are wont to injure the whole people, whilst those executions which originate with a prince offend the individual only.

And of all princes, it is impossible for the new prince to avoid the imputation of cruelty, owing to new states being full of dangers. Hence Virgil, through the mouth of Dido, excuses the inhumanity of her reign owing to its being new, saying:

"*Res dura, et regni novitas me talia cogunt*
Moliri, et late fines custode tueri."

Nevertheless he ought to be slow to believe and to act, nor should he himself show fear, but proceed in a temperate

---

[29] During the rioting between the Cancellieri and Panciatichi factions in 1502 and 1503.

manner with prudence and humanity, so that too much confidence may not make him incautious and too much distrust render him intolerable.

Upon this a question arises: whether it be better to be loved than feared or feared than loved? It may be answered that one should wish to be both, but, because it is difficult to unite them in one person, it is much safer to be feared than loved, when, of the two, either must be dispensed with. Because this is to be asserted in general of men, that they are ungrateful, fickle, false, cowardly, covetous, and as long as you succeed they are yours entirely; they will offer you their blood, property, life, and children, as is said above, when the need is far distant; but when it approaches they turn against you. And that prince who, relying entirely on their promises, has neglected other precautions, is ruined; because friendships that are obtained by payments, and not by greatness or nobility of mind, may indeed be earned, but they are not secured, and in time of need cannot be relied upon; and men have less scruple in offending one who is beloved than one who is feared, for love is preserved by the link of obligation which, owing to the baseness of men, is broken at every opportunity for their advantage; but fear preserves you by a dread of punishment which never fails.

Nevertheless a prince ought to inspire fear in such a way that, if he does not win love, he avoids hatred; because he can endure very well being feared whilst he is not hated, which will always be as long as he abstains from the property of his citizens and subjects and from their women. But when it is necessary for him to proceed against the life of someone, he must do it on proper justification and for manifest cause, but above all things he must keep his hands off the property of others, because men more quickly forget the death of their father than the loss of their patrimony. Besides, pretexts for taking away the property are never wanting; for he who has once begun to live by robbery will always find pretexts for seizing what belongs to others; but reasons for taking life, on the contrary, are more difficult to find and sooner lapse. But when a prince is with his army, and has under control a multitude of soldiers, then it is quite necessary for him to disregard the reputation of cruelty, for without it he would never hold his army united or disposed to its duties.

Among the wonderful deeds of Hannibal this one is enumerated: that having led an enormous army, composed of many various races of men, to fight in foreign lands, no dissensions arose either among them or against the prince, whether in his bad or in his good fortune. This arose from nothing else than his inhuman cruelty, which, with his boundless valour, made him revered and terrible in the sight of his soldiers, but without that cruelty, his other virtues were not sufficient to produce this effect. And short-sighted writers admire his deeds from one point of view and from another condemn the principal cause of them. That it is true his other virtues would not have been sufficient for him may be proved by the case of Scipio, that most excellent man, not only of his own times but within the memory of man, against whom, nevertheless, his army rebelled in Spain; this arose from nothing but his too great forbearance, which gave his soldiers more license than is consistent with military discipline. For this he was upbraided in the Senate by Fabius Maximus, and called the corrupter of the Roman soldiery. The Locrians were laid waste by a legate of Scipio, yet they were not avenged by him, nor was the insolence of the legate punished, owing entirely to his easy nature. Insomuch that someone in the Senate, wishing to excuse him, said there were many men who knew much better how not to err than to correct the errors of others. This disposition, if he had been continued in the command, would have destroyed in time the fame and glory of Scipio; but, he being under the control of the Senate, this injurious characteristic not only concealed itself, but contributed to his glory.

Returning to the question of being feared or loved, I come to the conclusion that, men loving according to their own will and fearing according to that of the prince, a wise prince should establish himself on that which is in his own control and not in that of others; he must endeavour only to avoid hatred, as is noted.

CHAPTER XVIII

CONCERNING THE WAY IN WHICH PRINCES SHOULD KEEP FAITH

Every one admits how praiseworthy it is in a prince to keep faith, and to live with integrity and not with craft. Nevertheless our experience has been that those princes who have done great things have held good faith of little account, and have known how to circumvent the intellect of men by craft, and in the end have overcome those who have relied on their word. You must know there are two ways of contesting, the one by the law, the other by force; the first method is proper to men, the second to beasts; but because the first is frequently not sufficient, it is necessary to have recourse to the second. Therefore it is necessary for a prince to understand how to avail himself of the beast and the man. This has been figuratively taught to princes by ancient writers, who describe how Achilles and many other princes of old were given to the Centaur Chiron to nurse, who brought them up in his discipline; which means solely that, as they had for a teacher one who was half beast and half man, so it is necessary for a prince to know how to make use of both natures, and that one without the other is not durable. A prince, therefore, being compelled knowingly to adopt the beast, ought to choose the fox and the lion; because the lion cannot defend himself against snares and the fox cannot defend himself against wolves. Therefore, it is necessary to be a fox to discover the snares and a lion to terrify the wolves. Those who rely simply on the lion do not understand what they are about. Therefore a wise lord cannot, nor ought he to, keep faith when such observance may be turned against him, and when the reasons that caused him to pledge it exist no longer. If men were entirely good this precept would not hold, but because they are bad, and will not keep faith with you, you too are not bound to observe it with them. Nor will there ever be wanting to a prince legitimate reasons to excuse this non-observance. Of this endless modern examples could be given, showing how many treaties and engagements have been made void and of no effect through the faithlessness of princes; and he who has known best how to employ the fox has succeeded best.

But it is necessary to know well how to disguise this characteristic, and to be a great pretender and dissembler; and men are so simple, and so subject to present necessities, that he who seeks to deceive will always find someone who will allow himself to be deceived. One recent example I cannot pass over in silence. Alexander the Sixth did nothing else but deceive men, nor ever thought of doing otherwise, and he always found victims; for there never was a man who had greater power in asserting, or who with greater oaths would affirm a thing, yet would observe it less; nevertheless his deceits always succeeded according to his wishes, because he well understood this side of mankind.

Therefore it is unnecessary for a prince to have all the good qualities I have enumerated, but it is very necessary to appear to have them. And I shall dare to say this also, that to have them and always to observe them is injurious, and that to appear to have them is useful; to appear merciful, faithful, humane, religious, upright, and to be so, but with a mind so framed that should you require not to be so, you may be able and know how to change to the opposite.

And you have to understand this, that a prince, especially a new one, cannot observe all those things for which men are esteemed, being often forced, in order to maintain the state, to act contrary to fidelity, friendship, humanity, and religion. Therefore it is necessary for him to have a mind ready to turn itself accordingly as the winds and variations of fortune force it, yet, as I have said above, not to diverge from the good if he can avoid doing so, but, if compelled, then to know how to set about it.

For this reason a prince ought to take care that he never lets anything slip from his lips that is not replete with the above-named five qualities, that he may appear to him who sees and hears him altogether merciful, faithful, humane, upright, and religious. There is nothing more necessary to appear to have than this last quality, inasmuch as men judge generally more by the eye than by the hand, because it belongs to everybody to see you, to few to come in touch with you. Every one sees what you appear to be, few really know what you are, and those few dare not oppose themselves to the opinion of the many, who have the majesty of the state to defend them; and in the actions of all men, and especially of princes, which it is not prudent to challenge, one judges by the result.

For that reason, let a prince have the credit of conquering and holding his state, the means will always be considered honest, and he will be praised by everybody; because the vulgar are always taken by what a thing seems to be and by what comes of it; and in the world there are only the vulgar, for the few find a place there only when the many have no ground to rest on.

One prince[30] of the present time, whom it is not well to name, never preaches anything else but peace and good faith, and to both he is most hostile, and either, if he had kept it, would have deprived him of reputation and kingdom many a time.

---

[30] Ferdinand of Aragon.

CHAPTER XIX

THAT ONE SHOULD AVOID BEING DESPISED AND HATED

Now, concerning the characteristics of which mention is made above, I have spoken of the more important ones, the others I wish to discuss briefly under this generality, that the prince must consider, as has been in part said before, how to avoid those things which will make him hated or contemptible; and as often as he shall have succeeded he will have fulfilled his part, and he need not fear any danger in other reproaches.

It makes him hated above all things, as I have said, to be rapacious, and to be a violator of the property and women of his subjects, from both of which he must abstain. And when neither their property nor their honor is touched, the majority of men live content, and he has only to contend with the ambition of a few, whom he can curb with ease in many ways.

It makes him contemptible to be considered fickle, frivolous, effeminate, mean-spirited, irresolute, from all of which a prince should guard himself as from a rock; and he should endeavour to show in his actions greatness, courage, gravity, and fortitude; and in his private dealings with his subjects let him show that his judgments are irrevocable, and maintain himself in such reputation that no one can hope either to deceive him or to get round him.

That prince is highly esteemed who conveys this impression of himself, and he who is highly esteemed is not easily conspired against; for, provided it is well known that he is an excellent man and revered by his people, he can only be attacked with difficulty. For this reason a prince ought to have two fears, one from within, on account of his subjects, the other from without, on account of external powers. From the latter he is defended by being well armed and having good allies, and if he is well armed he will have good friends, and affairs will always remain quiet within when they are quiet without, unless they should have been already disturbed by conspiracy; and even should affairs outside be disturbed, if he has carried out his preparations and has lived as I have said, as long as he does not despair, he will resist every attack, as I said Nabis the Spartan did.

But concerning his subjects, when affairs outside are disturbed he has only to fear that they will conspire secretly, from which a prince can easily secure himself by avoiding being hated and despised, and by keeping the people satisfied with him, which it is most necessary for him to accomplish, as I said above at length. And one of the most efficacious remedies that a prince can have against conspiracies is not to be hated and despised by the people, for he who conspires against a prince always expects to please them by his removal; but when the conspirator can only look forward to offending them, he will not have the courage to take such a course, for the difficulties that confront a conspirator are infinite. And as experience shows, many have been the conspiracies, but few have been successful; because he who conspires cannot act alone, nor can he take a companion except from those whom he believes to be malcontents, and as soon as you have opened your mind to a malcontent you have given him the material with which to content himself, for by denouncing you he can look for every advantage; so that, seeing the gain from this course to be assured, and seeing the other to be doubtful and full of dangers, he must be a very rare friend, or a thoroughly obstinate enemy of the prince, to keep faith with you.

And, to reduce the matter into a small compass, I say that, on the side of the conspirator, there is nothing but fear, jealousy, prospect of punishment to terrify him; but on the side of the prince there is the majesty of the principality, the laws, the protection of friends and the state to defend him; so that, adding to all these things the popular goodwill, it is impossible that any one should be so rash as to conspire. For whereas in general the conspirator has to fear before the execution of his plot, in this case he has also to fear the sequel to the crime; because on account of it he has the people for an enemy, and thus cannot hope for any escape.

Endless examples could be given on this subject, but I will be content with one, brought to pass within the memory of our fathers. Messer Annibale Bentivogli, who was prince in Bologna (grandfather of the present Annibale), having been murdered by the Canneschi, who had conspired against him, not one of his family survived but Messer Giovanni,[31] who was in childhood: immediately after his assassination the people rose and murdered all the Canneschi. This sprung from the popular goodwill which the house of Bentivogli enjoyed in those days in Bologna; which was so great that, although none remained there after the death of Annibale who was able to rule the state, the Bolognese, having information that there was one of the Bentivogli family in Florence, who up to that time had been considered the son of a blacksmith, sent to Florence for him and gave him the government of their city, and it was ruled by him until Messer Giovanni came in due course to the government.

For this reason I consider that a prince ought to reckon conspiracies of little account when his people hold him in esteem; but when it is hostile to him, and bears hatred towards him, he ought to fear everything and everybody. And well-ordered states and wise princes have taken every care not to drive the nobles to desperation, and to keep the people satisfied and contented, for this is one of the most important objects a prince can have.

Among the best ordered and governed kingdoms of our times is France, and in it are found many good institutions on which depend the liberty and security of the king; of these the

---

[31] Giovanni Bentivogli, born in Bologna 1438, died at Milan 1508. He ruled Bologna from 1462 to 1506. Machiavelli's strong condemnation of conspiracies may get its edge from his own very recent experience (February 1513), when he had been arrested and tortured for his alleged complicity in the Boscoli conspiracy.

first is the parliament and its authority, because he who founded the kingdom, knowing the ambition of the nobility and their boldness, considered that a bit to their mouths would be necessary to hold them in; and, on the other side, knowing the hatred of the people, founded in fear, against the nobles, he wished to protect them, yet he was not anxious for this to be the particular care of the king; therefore, to take away the reproach which he would be liable to from the nobles for favouring the people, and from the people for favouring the nobles, he set up an arbiter, who should be one who could beat down the great and favour the lesser without reproach to the king. Neither could you have a better or a more prudent arrangement, or a greater source of security to the king and kingdom. From this one can draw another important conclusion, that princes ought to leave affairs of reproach to the management of others, and keep those of grace in their own hands. And further, I consider that a prince ought to cherish the nobles, but not so as to make himself hated by the people.

It may appear, perhaps, to some who have examined the lives and deaths of the Roman emperors that many of them would be an example contrary to my opinion, seeing that some of them lived nobly and showed great qualities of soul, nevertheless they have lost their empire or have been killed by subjects who have conspired against them. Wishing, therefore, to answer these objections, I will recall the characters of some of the emperors, and will show that the causes of their ruin were not different to those alleged by me; at the same time I will only submit for consideration those things that are noteworthy to him who studies the affairs of those times.

It seems to me sufficient to take all those emperors who succeeded to the empire from Marcus the philosopher down to Maximinus; they were Marcus and his son Commodus, Pertinax, Julian, Severus and his son Antoninus Caracalla, Macrinus, Heliogabalus, Alexander, and Maximinus.

There is first to note that, whereas in other principalities the ambition of the nobles and the insolence of the people only have to be contended with, the Roman emperors had a third difficulty in having to put up with the cruelty and avarice of their soldiers, a matter so beset with difficulties that it was the ruin of many; for it was a hard thing to give satisfaction both to soldiers and people; because the people loved peace, and for this reason they loved the unaspiring prince, whilst the soldiers loved the warlike prince who was bold, cruel, and rapacious, which qualities they were quite willing he should exercise upon the people, so that they could get double pay and give vent to their own greed and cruelty. Hence it arose that those emperors were always overthrown who, either by birth or training, had no great authority, and most of them, especially those who came new to the principality, recognizing the difficulty of these two opposing humours, were inclined to give satisfaction to the soldiers, caring little about injuring the people. Which course was necessary, because, as princes cannot help being hated by someone, they ought, in the first place, to avoid being hated by every one, and when they cannot compass this, they ought to endeavour with the utmost diligence to avoid the hatred of the most powerful. Therefore, those emperors who through inexperience had need of special favour adhered more readily to the soldiers than to the people; a course which turned out advantageous to them or not, accordingly as the prince knew how to maintain authority over them.

From these causes it arose that Marcus, Pertinax, and Alexander, being all men of modest life, lovers of justice, enemies to cruelty, humane, and benignant, came to a sad end except Marcus; he alone lived and died honoured, because he had succeeded to the throne by hereditary title, and owed nothing either to the soldiers or the people; and afterwards, being possessed of many virtues which made him respected, he always kept both orders in their places whilst he lived, and was neither hated nor despised.

But Pertinax was created emperor against the wishes of the soldiers, who, being accustomed to live licentiously under Commodus, could not endure the honest life to which Pertinax wished to reduce them; thus, having given cause for hatred, to which hatred there was added contempt for his old age, he was overthrown at the very beginning of his administration. And here it should be noted that hatred is acquired as much by good works as by bad ones, therefore, as I said before, a prince wishing to keep his state is very often forced to do evil; for when that body is corrupt whom you think you have need of to maintain yourself — it may be either the people or the soldiers or the nobles — you have to submit to its humours and to gratify them, and then good works will do you harm.

But let us come to Alexander, who was a man of such great goodness, that among the other praises which are accorded him is this, that in the fourteen years he held the empire no one was ever put to death by him unjudged; nevertheless, being considered effeminate and a man who allowed himself to be governed by his mother, he became despised, the army conspired against him, and murdered him.

Turning now to the opposite characters of Commodus, Severus, Antoninus Caracalla, and Maximinus, you will find them all cruel and rapacious-men who, to satisfy their soldiers, did not hesitate to commit every kind of iniquity against the people; and all, except Severus, came to a bad end; but in Severus there was so much valour that, keeping the soldiers friendly, although the people were oppressed by him, he reigned successfully; for his valour made him so much admired in the sight of the soldiers and people that the latter were kept in a way astonished and awed and the former respectful and satisfied. And because the actions of this man, as a new prince, were great, I wish to show briefly that he knew well how to counterfeit the fox and the lion, which natures, as I said above, it is necessary for a prince to imitate.

Knowing the sloth of the Emperor Julian, he persuaded the army in Sclavonia, of which he was captain, that it would be right to go to Rome and avenge the death of Pertinax, who had been killed by the praetorian soldiers; and under this pretext, without appearing to aspire to the throne, he moved the army on Rome, and reached Italy before it was known that he had started.

On his arrival at Rome, the Senate, through fear, elected him emperor and killed Julian. After this there remained for Severus, who wished to make himself master of the whole empire, two difficulties; one in Asia, where Niger, head of the Asiatic army, had caused himself to be proclaimed emperor; the other in the west where Albinus was, who also aspired to the throne. And as he considered it dangerous to declare himself hostile to both, he decided to attack Niger and to deceive Albinus. To the latter he wrote that, being elected emperor by the Senate, he was willing to share that dignity with him and sent him the title of Caesar; and, moreover, that the Senate had made Albinus his colleague; which things were accepted by Albinus as true. But after Severus had conquered and killed Niger, and settled oriental affairs, he returned to Rome and complained to the Senate that Albinus, little recognizing the benefits that he had received from him, had by treachery sought to murder him, and for this ingratitude he was compelled to punish him. Afterwards he sought him out in France, and took from him his government and life. He who will, therefore, carefully examine the actions of this man will find him a most valiant lion and a most cunning fox; he will find him feared and respected by every one, and not hated by the army; and it need not be wondered at that he, a new man, was able to hold the empire so well, because his supreme renown always protected him from that hatred which the people might have conceived against him for his violence.

But his son Antoninus was a most eminent man, and had very excellent qualities, which made him admirable in the sight of the people and acceptable to the soldiers, for he was a warlike man, most enduring of fatigue, a despiser of all delicate food and other luxuries, which caused him to be beloved by the armies. Nevertheless, his ferocity and cruelties were so great and so unheard of that, after endless single murders, he killed a large number of the people of Rome and all those of Alexandria. He became hated by the whole world, and also feared by those he had around him, to such an extent that he was murdered in the midst of his army by a centurion. And here it must be noted that such-like deaths, which are deliberately inflicted with a resolved and desperate courage, cannot be avoided by princes, because any one who does not fear to die can inflict them; but a prince may fear them the less because they are very rare; he has only to be careful not to do any grave injury to those whom he employs or has around him in the service of the state. Antoninus had not taken this care, but had contumeliously killed a brother of that centurion, whom also he daily threatened, yet retained in his bodyguard; which, as it turned out, was a rash thing to do, and proved the emperor's ruin.

But let us come to Commodus, to whom it should have been very easy to hold the empire, for, being the son of Marcus, he had inherited it, and he had only to follow in the footsteps of his father to please his people and soldiers; but, being by nature cruel and brutal, he gave himself up to amusing the soldiers and corrupting them, so that he might indulge his rapacity upon the people; on the other hand, not maintaining his dignity, often descending to the theatre to compete with gladiators, and doing other vile things, little worthy of the imperial majesty, he fell into contempt with the soldiers, and being hated by one party and despised by the other, he was conspired against and was killed.

It remains to discuss the character of Maximinus. He was a very warlike man, and the armies, being disgusted with the effeminacy of Alexander, of whom I have already spoken, killed him and elected Maximinus to the throne. This he did not possess for long, for two things made him hated and despised; the one, his having kept sheep in Thrace, which brought him into contempt (it being well known to all, and considered a great indignity by every one), and the other, his having at the accession to his dominions deferred going to Rome and taking possession of the imperial seat; he had also gained a reputation for the utmost ferocity by having, through his prefects in Rome and elsewhere in the empire, practised many cruelties, so that the whole world was moved to anger at the meanness of his birth and to fear at his barbarity. First Africa rebelled, then the Senate with all the people of Rome, and all Italy conspired against him, to which may be added his own army; this latter, besieging Aquileia and meeting with difficulties in taking it, were disgusted with his cruelties, and fearing him less when they found so many against him, murdered him.

I do not wish to discuss Heliogabalus, Macrinus, or Julian, who, being thoroughly contemptible, were quickly wiped out; but I will bring this discourse to a conclusion by saying that princes in our times have this difficulty of giving inordinate satisfaction to their soldiers in a far less degree, because, notwithstanding one has to give them some indulgence, that is soon done; none of these princes have armies that are veterans in the governance and administration of provinces, as were the armies of the Roman Empire; and whereas it was then more necessary to give satisfaction to the soldiers than to the people, it is now more necessary to all princes, except the Turk and the Soldan, to satisfy the people rather the soldiers, because the people are the more powerful.

From the above I have excepted the Turk, who always keeps round him twelve thousand infantry and fifteen thousand cavalry on which depend the security and strength of the kingdom, and it is necessary that, putting aside every consideration for the people, he should keep them his friends. The kingdom of the Soldan is similar; being entirely in the hands of soldiers, it follows again that, without regard to the people, he must keep them his friends. But you must note that the state of the Soldan is unlike all other principalities, for the reason that it is like the Christian pontificate, which cannot be called either an hereditary or a newly formed principality; because the sons of the old prince are not the heirs, but he who is elected to that position by those who have authority, and the sons remain only noblemen. And this being an ancient custom, it cannot be called a new principality, because there are none of those difficulties in it that are met with in new ones; for although the prince is new, the constitution of the state is old, and it is framed so as to receive him as if he were its hereditary lord.

But returning to the subject of our discourse, I say that whoever will consider it will acknowledge that either hatred or contempt has been fatal to the above-named emperors, and it will be recognized also how it happened that, a number of them acting in one way and a number in another, only one in each way came to a happy end and the rest to unhappy ones. Because it would have been useless and dangerous for Pertinax and Alexander, being new princes, to imitate Marcus, who was heir to the principality; and likewise it would have been utterly destructive to Caracalla, Commodus, and Maximinus to have imitated Severus, they not having sufficient valour to enable them to tread in his footsteps. Therefore a prince, new to the principality, cannot imitate the actions of Marcus, nor, again, is it necessary to follow those of Severus, but he ought to take from Severus those parts which are necessary to found his state, and from Marcus those which are proper and glorious to keep a state that may already be stable and firm.

CHAPTER XX

ARE FORTRESSES, AND MANY OTHER THINGS TO WHICH PRINCES OFTEN RESORT, ADVANTAGEOUS OR HURTFUL?

1. Some princes, so as to hold securely the state, have disarmed their subjects; others have kept their subject towns distracted by factions; others have fostered enmities against themselves; others have laid themselves out to gain over those whom they distrusted in the beginning of their governments; some have built fortresses; some have overthrown and destroyed them. And although one cannot give a final judgment on all of these things unless one possesses the particulars of those states in which a decision has to be made, nevertheless I will speak as comprehensively as the matter of itself will admit.

2. There never was a new prince who has disarmed his subjects; rather when he has found them disarmed he has always armed them, because, by arming them, those arms become yours, those men who were distrusted become faithful, and those who were faithful are kept so, and your subjects become your adherents. And whereas all subjects cannot be armed, yet when those whom you do arm are benefited, the others can be handled more freely, and this difference in their treatment, which they quite understand, makes the former your dependents, and the latter, considering it to be necessary that those who have the most danger and service should have the most reward, excuse you. But when you disarm them, you at once offend them by showing that you distrust them, either for cowardice or for want of loyalty, and either of these opinions breeds hatred against you. And because you cannot remain unarmed, it follows that you turn to

mercenaries, which are of the character already shown; even if they should be good they would not be sufficient to defend you against powerful enemies and distrusted subjects. Therefore, as I have said, a new prince in a new principality has always distributed arms. Histories are full of examples. But when a prince acquires a new state, which he adds as a province to his old one, then it is necessary to disarm the men of that state, except those who have been his adherents in acquiring it; and these again, with time and opportunity, should be rendered soft and effeminate; and matters should be managed in such a way that all the armed men in the state shall be your own soldiers who in your old state were living near you.

3. Our forefathers, and those who were reckoned wise, were accustomed to say that it was necessary to hold Pistoia by factions and Pisa by fortresses; and with this idea they fostered quarrels in some of their tributary towns so as to keep possession of them the more easily. This may have been well enough in those times when Italy was in a way balanced, but I do not believe that it can be accepted as a precept for to-day, because I do not believe that factions can ever be of use; rather it is certain that when the enemy comes upon you in divided cities you are quickly lost, because the weakest party will always assist the outside forces and the other will not be able to resist. The Venetians, moved, as I believe, by the above reasons, fostered the Guelph and Ghibelline factions in their tributary cities; and although they never allowed them to come to bloodshed, yet they nursed these disputes amongst them, so that the citizens, distracted by their differences, should not unite against them. Which, as we saw, did not afterwards turn out as expected, because, after the rout at Vaila, one party at once took courage and seized the state. Such methods argue, therefore, weakness in the prince, because these factions will never be permitted in a vigorous principality; such methods for enabling one the more easily to manage subjects are only useful in times of peace, but if war comes this policy proves fallacious.

4. Without doubt princes become great when they overcome the difficulties and obstacles by which they are confronted, and therefore fortune, especially when she desires to make a new prince great, who has a greater necessity to earn renown than an hereditary one, causes enemies to arise and form designs against him, in order that he may have the opportunity of overcoming them, and by them to mount higher, as by a ladder which his enemies have raised. For this reason many consider that a wise prince, when he has the opportunity, ought with craft to foster some animosity against himself, so that, having crushed it, his renown may rise higher.

5. Princes, especially new ones, have found more fidelity and assistance in those men who in the beginning of their rule were distrusted than among those who in the beginning were trusted. Pandolfo Petrucci, Prince of Siena, ruled his state more by those who had been distrusted than by others. But on this question one cannot speak generally, for it varies so much with the individual; I will only say this, that those men who at the commencement of a princedom have been hostile, if they are of a description to need assistance to support themselves, can always be gained over with the greatest ease, and they will be tightly held to serve the prince with fidelity, inasmuch as they know it to be very necessary for them to cancel by deeds the bad impression which he had formed of them; and thus the prince always extracts more profit from them than from those who, serving him in too much security, may neglect his affairs. And since the matter demands it, I must not fail to warn a prince, who by means of secret favours has acquired a new state, that he must well consider the reasons which induced those to favour him who did so; and if it be not a natural affection towards him, but only discontent with their government, then he will only keep them friendly with great trouble and difficulty, for it will be impossible to satisfy them. And weighing well the reasons for this in those examples which can be taken from ancient and modern affairs, we shall find that it is easier for the prince to make friends of those men who were contented under the former government, and are therefore

his enemies, than of those who, being discontented with it, were favourable to him and encouraged him to seize it.

6. It has been a custom with princes, in order to hold their states more securely, to build fortresses that may serve as a bridle and bit to those who might design to work against them, and as a place of refuge from a first attack. I praise this system because it has been made use of formerly. Notwithstanding that, Messer Nicolo Vitelli in our times has been seen to demolish two fortresses in Citta di Castello so that he might keep that state; Guido Ubaldo, Duke of Urbino, on returning to his dominion, whence he had been driven by Cesare Borgia, razed to the foundations all the fortresses in that province, and considered that without them it would be more difficult to lose it; the Bentivogli returning to Bologna came to a similar decision. Fortresses, therefore, are useful or not according to circumstances; if they do you good in one way they injure you in another. And this question can be reasoned thus: the prince who has more to fear from the people than from foreigners ought to build fortresses, but he who has more to fear from foreigners than from the people ought to leave them alone. The castle of Milan, built by Francesco Sforza, has made, and will make, more trouble for the house of Sforza than any other disorder in the state. For this reason the best possible fortress is — not to be hated by the people, because, although you may hold the fortresses, yet they will not save you if the people hate you, for there will never be wanting foreigners to assist a people who have taken arms against you. It has not been seen in our times that such fortresses have been of use to any prince, unless to the Countess of Forli,[32] when the Count Girolamo, her consort, was killed; for by that means

---

[32] Catherine Sforza, a daughter of Galeazzo Sforza and Lucrezia Landriani, born 1463, died 1509. It was to the Countess of Forli that Machiavelli was sent as envoy on 1499. A letter from Fortunati to the countess announces the appointment: "I have been with the signori," wrote Fortunati, "to learn whom they would send and when. They tell me that Nicolo Machiavelli, a learned young Florentine noble, secretary to my Lords of the Ten, is to leave with me at once."

she was able to withstand the popular attack and wait for assistance from Milan, and thus recover her state; and the posture of affairs was such at that time that the foreigners could not assist the people. But fortresses were of little value to her afterwards when Cesare Borgia attacked her, and when the people, her enemy, were allied with foreigners. Therefore, it would have been safer for her, both then and before, not to have been hated by the people than to have had the fortresses. All these things considered then, I shall praise him who builds fortresses as well as him who does not, and I shall blame whoever, trusting in them, cares little about being hated by the people.

CHAPTER XXI

HOW A PRINCE SHOULD CONDUCT HIMSELF SO AS TO GAIN RENOWN

Nothing makes a prince so much esteemed as great enterprises and setting a fine example. We have in our time Ferdinand of Aragon, the present King of Spain. He can almost be called a new prince, because he has risen, by fame and glory, from being an insignificant king to be the foremost king in Christendom; and if you will consider his deeds you will find them all great and some of them extraordinary. In the beginning of his reign he attacked Granada, and this enterprise was the foundation of his dominions. He did this quietly at first and without any fear of hindrance, for he held the minds of the barons of Castile occupied in thinking of the war and not anticipating any innovations; thus they did not perceive that by these means he was acquiring power and authority over them. He was able with the money of the Church and of the people to sustain his armies, and by that long war to lay the foundation for the military skill which has since distinguished him. Further, always using religion as a plea, so as to undertake greater schemes, he devoted himself with pious cruelty to driving out and clearing his kingdom of the Moors; nor could there be a more admirable example, nor one more rare. Under this same cloak he assailed Africa, he came down on Italy, he has finally attacked France; and thus his achievements and designs have always been great, and have kept the minds of his people in suspense and admiration and occupied with the issue of them. And his actions have arisen in such a way, one out of the other, that men have never been given time to work steadily against him.

Again, it much assists a prince to set unusual examples in internal affairs, similar to those which are related of Messer Bernabo da Milano, who, when he had the opportunity, by any one in civil life doing some extraordinary thing, either good or bad, would take some method of rewarding or punishing him, which would be much spoken about. And a prince ought, above all things, always endeavour in every action to gain for himself the reputation of being a great and remarkable man.

A prince is also respected when he is either a true friend or a downright enemy, that is to say, when, without any reservation, he declares himself in favour of one party against the other; which course will always be more advantageous than standing neutral; because if two of your powerful neighbours come to blows, they are of such a character that, if one of them conquers, you have either to fear him or not. In either case it will always be more advantageous for you to declare yourself and to make war strenuously; because, in the first case, if you do not declare yourself, you will invariably fall a prey to the conqueror, to the pleasure and satisfaction of him who has been conquered, and you will have no reasons to offer, nor anything to protect or to shelter you. Because he who conquers does not want doubtful friends who will not aid him in the time of trial; and he who loses will not harbour you because you did not willingly, sword in hand, court his fate.

Antiochus went into Greece, being sent for by the Aetolians to drive out the Romans. He sent envoys to the Achaeans, who were friends of the Romans, exhorting them to remain neutral; and on the other hand the Romans urged them to take up arms. This question came to be discussed in the council of the Achaeans, where the legate of Antiochus urged them to stand neutral. To this the Roman legate answered: "As for that which has been said, that it is better and more advantageous for your state not to interfere in our war, nothing can be more erroneous; because by not interfering you will be left, without favour or consideration, the guerdon of the conqueror." Thus it will always happen that he who is not your friend will demand your neutrality, whilst he who is your friend will entreat you to declare yourself with arms. And irresolute princes, to avoid present dangers, generally follow the neutral path, and are generally ruined. But when a prince declares himself gallantly in favour of one side, if the party with whom he allies himself conquers, although the victor may be powerful and may have him at his mercy, yet he is indebted to him, and there is established a bond of amity; and men are never so shameless as to become a monument of ingratitude by oppressing you. Victories after all are never so complete that the victor must not show some regard, especially to justice. But if he with whom you ally yourself loses, you may be sheltered by him, and whilst he is able he may aid you, and you become companions on a fortune that may rise again.

In the second case, when those who fight are of such a character that you have no anxiety as to who may conquer, so much the more is it greater prudence to be allied, because you assist at the destruction of one by the aid of another who, if he had been wise, would have saved him; and conquering, as it is impossible that he should not do with your assistance, he remains at your discretion. And here it is to be noted that a prince ought to take care never to make an alliance with one more powerful than himself for the purposes of attacking others, unless necessity compels him, as is said above; because if he conquers you are at his discretion, and princes ought to avoid as much as possible being at the discretion of any one. The Venetians joined with France against the Duke of Milan, and this alliance, which caused their ruin, could have been avoided. But when it cannot be avoided, as happened to the Florentines when the Pope and Spain sent armies to attack Lombardy, then in such a case, for the above reasons, the prince ought to favour one of the parties.

Never let any Government imagine that it can choose perfectly safe courses; rather let it expect to have to take very doubtful ones, because it is found in ordinary affairs that one never seeks to avoid one trouble without running into another;

but prudence consists in knowing how to distinguish the character of troubles, and for choice to take the lesser evil.

A prince ought also to show himself a patron of ability, and to honour the proficient in every art. At the same time he should encourage his citizens to practise their callings peaceably, both in commerce and agriculture, and in every other following, so that the one should not be deterred from improving his possessions for fear lest they be taken away from him or another from opening up trade for fear of taxes; but the prince ought to offer rewards to whoever wishes to do these things and designs in any way to honour his city or state.

Further, he ought to entertain the people with festivals and spectacles at convenient seasons of the year; and as every city is divided into guilds or into societies, he ought to hold such bodies in esteem, and associate with them sometimes, and show himself an example of courtesy and liberality; nevertheless, always maintaining the majesty of his rank, for this he must never consent to abate in anything.

CHAPTER XXII

CONCERNING THE SECRETARIES OF PRINCES

The choice of servants is of no little importance to a prince, and they are good or not according to the discrimination of the prince. And the first opinion which one forms of a prince, and of his understanding, is by observing the men he has around him; and when they are capable and faithful he may always be considered wise, because he has known how to recognize the capable and to keep them faithful. But when they are otherwise one cannot form a good opinion of him, for the prime error which he made was in choosing them.

There were none who knew Messer Antonio da Venafro as the servant of Pandolfo Petrucci, Prince of Siena, who would not consider Pandolfo to be a very clever man in having Venafro for his servant. Because there are three classes of intellects: one which comprehends by itself; another which appreciates what others comprehended; and a third which neither comprehends by itself nor by the showing of others; the first is the most excellent, the second is good, the third is useless. Therefore, it follows necessarily that, if Pandolfo was not in the first rank, he was in the second, for whenever one has judgment to know good and bad when it is said and done, although he himself may not have the initiative, yet he can recognize the good and the bad in his servant, and the one he can praise and the other correct; thus the servant cannot hope to deceive him, and is kept honest.

But to enable a prince to form an opinion of his servant there is one test which never fails; when you see the servant thinking more of his own interests than of yours, and seeking inwardly his own profit in everything, such a man will never make a good servant, nor will you ever be able to trust him; because he who has the state of another in his hands ought never to think of himself, but always of his prince, and never pay any attention to matters in which the prince is not concerned.

On the other hand, to keep his servant honest the prince ought to study him, honouring him, enriching him, doing him kindnesses, sharing with him the honours and cares; and at the same time let him see that he cannot stand alone, so that many honours may not make him desire more, many riches make him wish for more, and that many cares may make him dread chances. When, therefore, servants, and princes towards servants, are thus disposed, they can trust each other, but when it is otherwise, the end will always be disastrous for either one or the other.

CHAPTER XXIII

HOW FLATTERERS SHOULD BE AVOIDED

I do not wish to leave out an important branch of this subject, for it is a danger from which princes are with difficulty preserved, unless they are very careful and discriminating. It is that of flatterers, of whom courts are full, because men are so self-complacent in their own affairs, and in a way so deceived in them, that they are preserved with difficulty from this pest, and if they wish to defend themselves they run the danger of falling into contempt. Because there is no other way of guarding oneself from flatterers except letting men understand that to tell you the truth does not offend you; but when every one may tell you the truth, respect for you abates.

Therefore a wise prince ought to hold a third course by choosing the wise men in his state, and giving to them only the liberty of speaking the truth to him, and then only of those things of which he inquires, and of none others; but he ought to question them upon everything, and listen to their opinions, and afterwards form his own conclusions. With these councillors, separately and collectively, he ought to carry himself in such a way that each of them should know that, the more freely he shall speak, the more he shall be preferred; outside of these, he should listen to no one, pursue the thing resolved on, and be steadfast in his resolutions. He who does otherwise is either overthrown by flatterers, or is so often changed by varying opinions that he falls into contempt.

I wish on this subject to adduce a modern example. Fra Luca, the man of affairs to Maximilian,[33] the present emperor, speaking of his majesty, said: He consulted with no one, yet never got his own way in anything. This arose because of his following a practice the opposite to the above; for the emperor is a secretive man — he does not communicate his designs to any one, nor does he receive opinions on them. But as in carrying them into effect they become revealed and known, they are at once obstructed by those men whom he has around him, and he, being pliant, is diverted from them. Hence it follows that those things he does one day he undoes the next, and no one ever understands what he wishes or intends to do, and no one can rely on his resolutions.

A prince, therefore, ought always to take counsel, but only when he wishes and not when others wish; he ought rather to discourage every one from offering advice unless he asks it; but, however, he ought to be a constant inquirer, and afterwards a patient listener concerning the things of which he inquired; also, on learning that any one, on any consideration, has not told him the truth, he should let his anger be felt.

And if there are some who think that a prince who conveys an impression of his wisdom is not so through his own ability, but through the good advisers that he has around him, beyond doubt they are deceived, because this is an axiom which never fails: that a prince who is not wise himself will never take good advice, unless by chance he has yielded his affairs entirely to one person who happens to be a very prudent man. In this case indeed he may be well governed, but it would not be for long, because such a governor would in a short time take away his state from him.

---

[33] Maximilian I, born in 1459, died 1519, Emperor of the Holy Roman Empire. He married, first, Mary, daughter of Charles the Bold; after her death, Bianca Sforza; and thus became involved in Italian politics.

But if a prince who is not inexperienced should take counsel from more than one he will never get united counsels, nor will he know how to unite them. Each of the counsellors will think of his own interests, and the prince will not know how to control them or to see through them. And they are not to found otherwise, because men will always prove untrue to you unless they are kept honest by constraint. Therefore it must be inferred that good counsels, whencesoever they come, are born of the wisdom of the prince, and not the wisdom of the prince from good counsels.

CHAPTER XXIV

WHY THE PRINCES OF ITALY HAVE LOST THEIR STATES

The previous suggestions, carefully observed, will enable a new prince to appear well established, and render him at once more secure and fixed in the state than if he had been long seated there. For the actions of a new prince are more narrowly observed than those of an hereditary one, and when they are seen to be able they gain more men and bind far tighter than ancient blood; because men are attracted more by the present than by the past, and when they find the present good they enjoy it and seek no further; they will also make the utmost defence of a prince if he fails them not in other things. Thus it will be a double glory for him to have established a new principality, and adorned and strengthened it with good laws, good arms, good allies, and with a good example; so will it be a double disgrace to him who, born a prince, shall lose his state by want of wisdom.

And if those seigniors are considered who have lost their states in Italy in our times, such as the King of Naples, the Duke of Milan, and others, there will be found in them, firstly, one common defect in regard to arms from the causes which have been discussed at length; in the next place, some one of them will be seen, either to have had the people hostile, or if he has had the people friendly, he has not known how to secure the nobles. In the absence of these defects states that have power enough to keep an army in the field cannot be lost.

Philip of Macedon, not the father of Alexander the Great, but he who was conquered by Titus Quintius, had not much territory compared to the greatness of the Romans and of

Greece who attacked him, yet being a warlike man who knew how to attract the people and secure the nobles, he sustained the war against his enemies for many years, and if in the end he lost the dominion of some cities, nevertheless he retained the kingdom.

Therefore, do not let our princes accuse fortune for the loss of their principalities after so many years' possession, but rather their own sloth, because in quiet times they never thought there could be a change (it is a common defect in man not to make any provision in the calm against the tempest), and when afterwards the bad times came they thought of flight and not of defending themselves, and they hoped that the people, disgusted with the insolence of the conquerors, would recall them. This course, when others fail, may be good, but it is very bad to have neglected all other expedients for that, since you would never wish to fall because you trusted to be able to find someone later on to restore you. This again either does not happen, or, if it does, it will not be for your security, because that deliverance is of no avail which does not depend upon yourself; those only are reliable, certain, and durable that depend on yourself and your valour.

CHAPTER XXV

WHAT FORTUNE CAN EFFECT IN HUMAN AFFAIRS AND HOW TO WITHSTAND HER

It is not unknown to me how many men have had, and still have, the opinion that the affairs of the world are in such wise governed by fortune and by God that men with their wisdom cannot direct them and that no one can even help them; and because of this they would have us believe that it is not necessary to labour much in affairs, but to let chance govern them. This opinion has been more credited in our times because of the great changes in affairs which have been seen, and may still be seen, every day, beyond all human conjecture. Sometimes pondering over this, I am in some degree inclined to their opinion. Nevertheless, not to extinguish our free will, I hold it to be true that Fortune is the arbiter of one-half of our actions, but that she still leaves us to direct the other half, or perhaps a little less.

I compare her to one of those raging rivers, which when in flood overflows the plains, sweeping away trees and buildings, bearing away the soil from place to place; everything flies before it, all yield to its violence, without being able in any way to withstand it; and yet, though its nature be such, it does not follow therefore that men, when the weather becomes fair, shall not make provision, both with defences and barriers, in such a manner that, rising again, the waters may pass away by canal, and their force be neither so unrestrained nor so dangerous. So it happens with fortune, who shows her power where valour has not prepared to resist her, and thither she turns her forces where she knows that barriers and defences have not been raised to constrain her.

And if you will consider Italy, which is the seat of these changes, and which has given to them their impulse, you will see it to be an open country without barriers and without any defence. For if it had been defended by proper valour, as are Germany, Spain, and France, either this invasion would not have made the great changes it has made or it would not have come at all. And this I consider enough to say concerning resistance to fortune in general.

But confining myself more to the particular, I say that a prince may be seen happy to-day and ruined to-morrow without having shown any change of disposition or character. This, I believe, arises firstly from causes that have already been discussed at length, namely, that the prince who relies entirely on fortune is lost when it changes. I believe also that he will be successful who directs his actions according to the spirit of the times, and that he whose actions do not accord with the times will not be successful. Because men are seen, in affairs that lead to the end which every man has before him, namely, glory and riches, to get there by various methods; one with caution, another with haste; one by force, another by skill; one by patience, another by its opposite; and each one succeeds in reaching the goal by a different method. One can also see of two cautious men the one attain his end, the other fail; and similarly, two men by different observances are equally successful, the one being cautious, the other impetuous; all this arises from nothing else than whether or not they conform in their methods to the spirit of the times. This follows from what I have said, that two men working differently bring about the same effect, and of two working similarly, one attains his object and the other does not.

Changes in estate also issue from this, for if, to one who governs himself with caution and patience, times and affairs converge in such a way that his administration is successful, his fortune is made; but if times and affairs change, he is ruined if he does not change his course of action. But a man is not often found sufficiently circumspect to know how to accommodate himself to the change, both because he cannot deviate from what nature inclines him to do, and also because, having always prospered by acting in one way, he cannot be persuaded that it is well to leave it; and, therefore, the cautious man, when it is time to turn adventurous, does not know how to do it, hence he is ruined; but had he changed his conduct with the times fortune would not have changed.

Pope Julius the Second went to work impetuously in all his affairs, and found the times and circumstances conform so well to that line of action that he always met with success. Consider his first enterprise against Bologna, Messer Giovanni Bentivogli being still alive. The Venetians were not agreeable to it, nor was the King of Spain, and he had the enterprise still under discussion with the King of France; nevertheless he personally entered upon the expedition with his accustomed boldness and energy, a move which made Spain and the Venetians stand irresolute and passive, the latter from fear, the former from desire to recover the kingdom of Naples; on the other hand, he drew after him the King of France, because that king, having observed the movement, and desiring to make the Pope his friend so as to humble the Venetians, found it impossible to refuse him. Therefore Julius with his impetuous action accomplished what no other pontiff with simple human wisdom could have done; for if he had waited in Rome until he could get away, with his plans arranged and everything fixed, as any other pontiff would have done, he would never have succeeded. Because the King of France would have made a thousand excuses, and the others would have raised a thousand fears.

I will leave his other actions alone, as they were all alike, and they all succeeded, for the shortness of his life did not let him experience the contrary; but if circumstances had arisen which required him to go cautiously, his ruin would have followed, because he would never have deviated from those ways to which nature inclined him.

I conclude, therefore that, fortune being changeful and mankind steadfast in their ways, so long as the two are in agreement men are successful, but unsuccessful when they fall out.

For my part I consider that it is better to be adventurous than cautious, because fortune is a woman, and if you wish to keep her under it is necessary to beat and ill-use her; and it is seen that she allows herself to be mastered by the adventurous rather than by those who go to work more coldly. She is, therefore, always, woman-like, a lover of young men, because they are less cautious, more violent, and with more audacity command her.

CHAPTER XXVI

AN EXHORTATION TO LIBERATE ITALY FROM THE BARBARIANS

Having carefully considered the subject of the above discourses, and wondering within myself whether the present times were propitious to a new prince, and whether there were elements that would give an opportunity to a wise and virtuous one to introduce a new order of things which would do honour to him and good to the people of this country, it appears to me that so many things concur to favour a new prince that I never knew a time more fit than the present.

And if, as I said, it was necessary that the people of Israel should be captive so as to make manifest the ability of Moses; that the Persians should be oppressed by the Medes so as to discover the greatness of the soul of Cyrus; and that the Athenians should be dispersed to illustrate the capabilities of Theseus: then at the present time, in order to discover the virtue of an Italian spirit, it was necessary that Italy should be reduced to the extremity that she is now in, that she should be more enslaved than the Hebrews, more oppressed than the Persians, more scattered than the Athenians; without head, without order, beaten, despoiled, torn, overrun; and to have endured every kind of desolation.

Although lately some spark may have been shown by one, which made us think he was ordained by God for our redemption, nevertheless it was afterwards seen, in the height of his career, that fortune rejected him; so that Italy, left as without life, waits for him who shall yet heal her wounds and put an end to the ravaging and plundering of Lombardy, to the swindling and taxing of the kingdom and of Tuscany, and cleanse those sores that for long have festered. It is seen how she entreats God to send someone who shall deliver her from these wrongs and barbarous insolencies. It is seen also that she is ready and willing to follow a banner if only someone will raise it.

Nor is there to be seen at present one in whom she can place more hope than in your illustrious house,[34] with its valour and fortune, favoured by God and by the Church of which it is now the chief, and which could be made the head of this redemption. This will not be difficult if you will recall to yourself the actions and lives of the men I have named. And although they were great and wonderful men, yet they were men, and each one of them had no more opportunity than the present offers, for their enterprises were neither more just nor easier than this, nor was God more their friend than He is yours.

With us there is great justice, because that war is just which is necessary, and arms are hallowed when there is no other hope but in them. Here there is the greatest willingness, and where the willingness is great the difficulties cannot be great if you will only follow those men to whom I have directed your attention. Further than this, how extraordinarily the ways of God have been manifested beyond example: the sea is divided, a cloud has led the way, the rock has poured forth water, it has rained manna, everything has contributed to your greatness; you ought to do the rest. God is not willing to do everything, and thus take away our free will and that share of glory which belongs to us.

And it is not to be wondered at if none of the above-named Italians have been able to accomplish all that is expected from your illustrious house; and if in so many revolutions in Italy, and in so many campaigns, it has always appeared as if military virtue were exhausted, this has happened because the old order of things was not good, and none of us have known how to find a new one. And nothing honours a man more than to establish new laws and new ordinances when he himself was newly risen. Such

---

[34] Giuliano de Medici. He had just been created a cardinal by Leo X. In 1523 Giuliano was elected Pope, and took the title of Clement VII.

things when they are well founded and dignified will make him revered and admired, and in Italy there are not wanting opportunities to bring such into use in every form.

Here there is great valour in the limbs whilst it fails in the head. Look attentively at the duels and the hand-to-hand combats, how superior the Italians are in strength, dexterity, and subtlety. But when it comes to armies they do not bear comparison, and this springs entirely from the insufficiency of the leaders, since those who are capable are not obedient, and each one seems to himself to know, there having never been any one so distinguished above the rest, either by valour or fortune, that others would yield to him. Hence it is that for so long a time, and during so much fighting in the past twenty years, whenever there has been an army wholly Italian, it has always given a poor account of itself; the first witness to this is Il Taro, afterwards Allesandria, Capua, Genoa, Vaila, Bologna, Mestri.[35]

If, therefore, your illustrious house wishes to follow these remarkable men who have redeemed their country, it is necessary before all things, as a true foundation for every enterprise, to be provided with your own forces, because there can be no more faithful, truer, or better soldiers. And although singly they are good, altogether they will be much better when they find themselves commanded by their prince, honoured by him, and maintained at his expense. Therefore it is necessary to be prepared with such arms, so that you can be defended against foreigners by Italian valour.

And although Swiss and Spanish infantry may be considered very formidable, nevertheless there is a defect in both, by reason of which a third order would not only be able to oppose them, but might be relied upon to overthrow them. For the Spaniards cannot resist cavalry, and the Switzers are afraid of infantry whenever they encounter them in close combat. Owing to this, as has been and may again be seen, the Spaniards are unable to resist French cavalry, and the Switzers are overthrown by

---

[35] The battles of Il Taro, 1495; Alessandria, 1499; Capua, 1501; Genoa, 1507; Vaila, 1509; Bologna, 1511; Mestri, 1513.

Spanish infantry. And although a complete proof of this latter cannot be shown, nevertheless there was some evidence of it at the battle of Ravenna, when the Spanish infantry were confronted by German battalions, who follow the same tactics as the Swiss; when the Spaniards, by agility of body and with the aid of their shields, got in under the pikes of the Germans and stood out of danger, able to attack, while the Germans stood helpless, and, if the cavalry had not dashed up, all would have been over with them. It is possible, therefore, knowing the defects of both these infantries, to invent a new one, which will resist cavalry and not be afraid of infantry; this need not create a new order of arms, but a variation upon the old. And these are the kind of improvements which confer reputation and power upon a new prince.

This opportunity, therefore, ought not to be allowed to pass for letting Italy at last see her liberator appear. Nor can one express the love with which he would be received in all those provinces which have suffered so much from these foreign scourings, with what thirst for revenge, with what stubborn faith, with what devotion, with what tears. What door would be closed to him? Who would refuse obedience to him? What envy would hinder him? What Italian would refuse him homage? To all of us this barbarous dominion stinks. Let, therefore, your illustrious house take up this charge with that courage and hope with which all just enterprises are undertaken, so that under its standard our native country may be ennobled, and under its auspices may be verified that saying of Petrarch:

> *Virtu contro al Furore*
> *Prendera l'arme, e fia il combatter corto:*
> *Che l'antico valore*
> *Negli italici cuor non e ancor morto.*
> *Virtue against fury shall advance the fight,*
> *And it i' th' combat soon shall put to flight:*
> *For the old Roman valour is not dead,*
> *Nor in th' Italians' brests extinguished.*

DESCRIPTION OF THE METHODS ADOPTED BY THE DUKE VALENTINO WHEN MURDERING VITELLOZZO VITELLI, OLIVEROTTO DA FERMO, THE SIGNOR PAGOLO, AND THE DUKE DI GRAVINA ORSINI

The Duke Valentino had returned from Lombardy, where he had been to clear himself with the King of France from the calumnies which had been raised against him by the Florentines concerning the rebellion of Arezzo and other towns in the Val di Chiana, and had arrived at Imola, whence he intended with his army to enter upon the campaign against Giovanni Bentivogli, the tyrant of Bologna: for he intended to bring that city under his domination, and to make it the head of his Romagnian duchy.

These matters coming to the knowledge of the Vitelli and Orsini and their following, it appeared to them that the duke would become too powerful, and it was feared that, having seized Bologna, he would seek to destroy them in order that he might become supreme in Italy. Upon this a meeting was called at Magione in the district of Perugia, to which came the cardinal, Pagolo, and the Duke di Gravina Orsini, Vitellozzo Vitelli, Oliverotto da Fermo, Gianpagolo Baglioni, the tyrant of Perugia, and Messer Antonio da Venafro, sent by Pandolfo Petrucci, the Prince of Siena. Here were discussed the power and courage of the duke and the necessity of curbing his ambitions, which might otherwise bring danger to the rest of being ruined. And they decided not to abandon the Bentivogli, but to strive to win over the Florentines; and they send their men to one place and another, promising to one party assistance and to another encouragement to unite with them against the common enemy. This meeting was at once reported throughout all Italy, and those who were discontented under the duke, among whom were the people of Urbino, took hope of effecting a revolution.

Thus it arose that, men's minds being thus unsettled, it was decided by certain men of Urbino to seize the fortress of San Leo, which was held for the duke, and which they captured by the following means. The castellan was fortifying the rock and causing timber to be taken there; so the conspirators watched, and when certain beams which were being carried to the rock were upon the bridge, so that it was prevented from being drawn up by those inside, they took the opportunity of leaping upon the bridge and thence into the fortress. Upon this capture being effected, the whole state rebelled and recalled the old duke, being encouraged in this, not so much by the capture of the fort, as by the Diet at Magione, from whom they expected to get assistance.

Those who heard of the rebellion at Urbino thought they would not lose the opportunity, and at once assembled their men so as to take any town, should any remain in the hands of the duke in that state; and they sent again to Florence to beg that republic to join with them in destroying the common firebrand, showing that the risk was lessened and that they ought not to wait for another opportunity.

But the Florentines, from hatred, for sundry reasons, of the Vitelli and Orsini, not only would not ally themselves, but sent Nicolo Machiavelli, their secretary, to offer shelter and assistance to the duke against his enemies. The duke was found full of fear at Imola, because, against everybody's expectation, his soldiers had at once gone over to the enemy and he found himself disarmed and war at his door. But recovering courage from the offers of the Florentines, he decided to temporize before fighting with the few soldiers that remained to him, and to negotiate for a reconciliation, and also to get assistance. This latter he obtained in two ways, by sending to the King of France for men and by enlisting men-at-arms and others whom he turned into cavalry of a sort: to all he gave money.

Notwithstanding this, his enemies drew near to him, and approached Fossombrone, where they encountered some men of the duke and, with the aid of the Orsini and Vitelli, routed them. When this happened, the duke resolved at once to see if he could not close the trouble with offers of reconciliation, and being a most perfect dissembler he did not fail in any practices to make the insurgents understand that he wished every man who had acquired anything to keep it, as it was enough for him to have the title of prince, whilst others might have the principality.

And the duke succeeded so well in this that they sent Signor Pagolo to him to negotiate for a reconciliation, and they brought their army to a standstill. But the duke did not stop his preparations, and took every care to provide himself with cavalry and infantry, and that such preparations might not be apparent to the others, he sent his troops in separate parties to every part of the Romagna. In the meanwhile there came also to him five hundred French lancers, and although he found himself sufficiently strong to take vengeance on his enemies in open war, he considered that it would be safer and more advantageous to outwit them, and for this reason he did not stop the work of reconciliation.

And that this might be effected the duke concluded a peace with them in which he confirmed their former covenants; he gave them four thousand ducats at once; he promised not to injure the Bentivogli; and he formed an alliance with Giovanni; and moreover he would not force them to come personally into his presence unless it pleased them to do so. On the other hand, they promised to restore to him the duchy of Urbino and other places seized by them, to serve him in all his expeditions, and not to make war against or ally themselves with any one without his permission.

This reconciliation being completed, Guido Ubaldo, the Duke of Urbino, again fled to Venice, having first destroyed all the fortresses in his state; because, trusting in the people, he did not wish that the fortresses, which he did not think he could defend, should be held by the enemy, since by these means a check would be kept upon his friends. But the Duke Valentino, having completed this convention, and dispersed his men throughout the Romagna, set out for Imola at the end of November together with his French men-at-arms: thence he went to Cesena, where he stayed some time to negotiate with the envoys of the Vitelli and Orsini, who had assembled with their men in the duchy of Urbino, as to the enterprise in which they should now take part; but nothing being concluded, Oliverotto da Fermo was sent to propose that if the duke wished to undertake an expedition against Tuscany they were ready; if he did not wish it, then they would besiege Sinigalia. To this the duke replied that he did not wish to enter into war with Tuscany, and thus become hostile to the Florentines, but that he was very willing to proceed against Sinigalia.

It happened that not long afterwards the town surrendered, but the fortress would not yield to them because the castellan would not give it up to any one but the duke in person; therefore they exhorted him to come there. This appeared a good opportunity to the duke, as, being invited by them, and not going of his own will, he would awaken no suspicions. And the more to reassure them, he allowed all the French men-at-arms who were with him in Lombardy to depart, except the hundred lancers under Mons. di Candales, his brother-in-law. He left Cesena about the middle of December, and went to Fano, and with the utmost cunning and cleverness he persuaded the Vitelli and Orsini to wait for him at Sinigalia, pointing out to them that any lack of compliance would cast a doubt upon the sincerity and permanency of the reconciliation, and that he was a man who wished to make use of the arms and councils of his friends. But Vitellozzo remained very stubborn, for the death of his brother warned him that he should not offend a prince and afterwards trust him; nevertheless, persuaded by Pagolo Orsini, whom the duke had corrupted with gifts and promises, he agreed to wait.

Upon this the duke, before his departure from Fano, which was to be on 30th December 1502, communicated his designs to eight of his most trusted followers, among whom were

Don Michele and the Monsignor d'Euna, who was afterwards cardinal; and he ordered that, as soon as Vitellozzo, Pagolo Orsini, the Duke di Gravina, and Oliverotto should arrive, his followers in pairs should take them one by one, entrusting certain men to certain pairs, who should entertain them until they reached Sinigalia; nor should they be permitted to leave until they came to the duke's quarters, where they should be seized.

The duke afterwards ordered all his horsemen and infantry, of which there were more than two thousand cavalry and ten thousand footmen, to assemble by daybreak at the Metauro, a river five miles distant from Fano, and await him there. He found himself, therefore, on the last day of December at the Metauro with his men, and having sent a cavalcade of about two hundred horsemen before him, he then moved forward the infantry, whom he accompanied with the rest of the men-at-arms.

Fano and Sinigalia are two cities of La Marca situate on the shore of the Adriatic Sea, fifteen miles distant from each other, so that he who goes towards Sinigalia has the mountains on his right hand, the bases of which are touched by the sea in some places. The city of Sinigalia is distant from the foot of the mountains a little more than a bow-shot and from the shore about a mile. On the side opposite to the city runs a little river which bathes that part of the walls looking towards Fano, facing the high road. Thus he who draws near to Sinigalia comes for a good space by road along the mountains, and reaches the river which passes by Sinigalia. If he turns to his left hand along the bank of it, and goes for the distance of a bow-shot, he arrives at a bridge which crosses the river; he is then almost abreast of the gate that leads into Sinigalia, not by a straight line, but transversely. Before this gate there stands a collection of houses with a square to which the bank of the river forms one side.

The Vitelli and Orsini having received orders to wait for the duke, and to honour him in person, sent away their men to several castles distant from Sinigalia about six miles, so that room could be made for the men of the duke; and they left in Sinigalia only Oliverotto and his band, which consisted of one thousand infantry and one hundred and fifty horsemen, who were quartered in the suburb mentioned above. Matters having been thus arranged, the Duke Valentino left for Sinigalia, and when the leaders of the cavalry reached the bridge they did not pass over, but having opened it, one portion wheeled towards the river and the other towards the country, and a way was left in the middle through which the infantry passed, without stopping, into the town.

Vitellozzo, Pagolo, and the Duke di Gravina on mules, accompanied by a few horsemen, went towards the duke; Vitellozo, unarmed and wearing a cape lined with green, appeared very dejected, as if conscious of his approaching death — a circumstance which, in view of the ability of the man and his former fortune, caused some amazement. And it is said that when he parted from his men before setting out for Sinigalia to meet the duke he acted as if it were his last parting from them. He recommended his house and its fortunes to his captains, and advised his nephews that it was not the fortune of their house, but the virtues of their fathers that should be kept in mind. These three, therefore, came before the duke and saluted him respectfully, and were received by him with goodwill; they were at once placed between those who were commissioned to look after them.

But the duke noticing that Oliverotto, who had remained with his band in Sinigalia, was missing — for Oliverotto was waiting in the square before his quarters near the river, keeping his men in order and drilling them — signalled with his eye to Don Michelle, to whom the care of Oliverotto had been committed, that he should take measures that Oliverotto should not escape. Therefore Don Michele rode off and joined Oliverotto, telling him that it was not right to keep his men out of their quarters, because these might be taken up by the men of the duke; and he advised him to send them at once to their quarters and to come himself to meet the duke. And Oliverotto, having taken this advice, came before the duke, who, when he saw him, called to him; and Oliverotto, having made his obeisance, joined the others.

So the whole party entered Sinigalia, dismounted at the duke's quarters, and went with him into a secret chamber, where the duke made them prisoners; he then mounted on horseback, and issued orders that the men of Oliverotto and the Orsini should be stripped of their arms. Those of Oliverotto, being at hand, were quickly settled, but those of the Orsini and Vitelli, being at a distance, and having a presentiment of the destruction of their masters, had time to prepare themselves, and bearing in mind the valour and discipline of the Orsinian and Vitellian houses, they stood together against the hostile forces of the country and saved themselves.

But the duke's soldiers, not being content with having pillaged the men of Oliverotto, began to sack Sinigalia, and if the duke had not repressed this outrage by killing some of them they would have completely sacked it. Night having come and the tumult being silenced, the duke prepared to kill Vitellozzo and Oliverotto; he led them into a room and caused them to be strangled. Neither of them used words in keeping with their past lives: Vitellozzo prayed that he might ask of the pope full pardon for his sins; Oliverotto cringed and laid the blame for all injuries against the duke on Vitellozzo. Pagolo and the Duke di Gravina Orsini were kept alive until the duke heard from Rome that the pope had taken the Cardinal Orsino, the Archbishop of Florence, and Messer Jacopo da Santa Croce. After which news, on 18th January 1502, in the castle of Pieve, they also were strangled in the same way.

THE LIFE OF CASTRUCCIO CASTRACANI OF LUCCA SENT TO HIS FRIENDS ZANOBI BUONDELMONTI AND LUIGI ALAMANNI

CASTRUCCIO CASTRACANI 1284-1328

It appears, dearest Zanobi and Luigi, a wonderful thing to those who have considered the matter, that all men, or the larger number of them, who have performed great deeds in the world, and excelled all others in their day, have had their birth and beginning in baseness and obscurity; or have been aggrieved by Fortune in some outrageous way. They have either been exposed to the mercy of wild beasts, or they have had so mean a parentage that in shame they have given themselves out to be sons of Jove or of some other deity. It would be wearisome to relate who these persons may have been because they are well known to everybody, and, as such tales would not be particularly edifying to those who read them, they are omitted. I believe that these lowly beginnings of great men occur because Fortune is desirous of showing to the world that such men owe much to her and little to wisdom, because she begins to show her hand when wisdom can really take no part in their career: thus all success must be attributed to her. Castruccio Castracani of Lucca was one of those men who did great deeds, if he is measured by the times in which he lived and the city in which he was born; but, like many others, he was neither fortunate nor distinguished in his birth, as the course of this history will show. It appeared to be desirable to recall his memory, because I have discerned in him such indications of valour and fortune as should make him a great exemplar to men. I think also that I ought to call your attention to his actions, because you of all men I know delight most in noble deeds.

    The family of Castracani was formerly numbered among the noble families of Lucca, but in the days of which I speak it had somewhat fallen in estate, as so often happens in this world. To this family was born a son Antonio, who became a priest of the order of San Michele of Lucca, and for this reason was honoured with the title of Messer Antonio. He had an only sister, who had been married to Buonaccorso Cenami, but Buonaccorso dying she became a widow, and not wishing to marry again went to live with her brother. Messer Antonio had a vineyard behind the house where he resided, and as it was bounded on all sides by gardens, any person could have access to it without difficulty. One morning, shortly after sunrise, Madonna Dianora, as the sister of Messer Antonio was called, had occasion to go into the vineyard as usual to gather herbs for seasoning the dinner, and hearing a slight rustling among the leaves of a vine she turned her eyes in that direction, and heard something resembling the cry of an infant. Whereupon she went towards it, and saw the hands and face of a baby who was lying enveloped in the leaves and who seemed to be crying for its mother. Partly wondering and partly fearing, yet full of compassion, she lifted it up and carried it to the house, where she washed it and clothed it with clean linen as is customary, and showed it to Messer Antonio when he returned home. When he heard what had happened and saw the child he was not less surprised or compassionate than his sister. They discussed between themselves what should be done, and seeing that he was priest and that she had no children, they finally determined to bring it up. They had a nurse for it, and it was reared and loved as if it were their own child. They baptized it, and gave it the name of Castruccio after their father. As the years passed Castruccio grew very handsome, and gave evidence of wit and discretion, and learnt with a quickness beyond his years those lessons which Messer Antonio imparted to him. Messer Antonio intended to make a priest of him, and in time would have inducted him into his canonry and other benefices, and all his instruction was given with this object; but Antonio discovered that the character of Castruccio was quite unfitted for the priesthood. As soon as Castruccio reached the age of fourteen he began to take less notice of the chiding of Messer Antonio and Madonna Dianora and no longer to fear them; he left off reading ecclesiastical books, and turned to playing with arms, delighting in nothing so much as in learning their uses, and in running, leaping, and wrestling with other boys. In all exercises he far excelled his companions in courage and bodily strength, and if at any time he did turn to books, only those pleased him which told of wars and the mighty deeds of men. Messer Antonio beheld all this with vexation and sorrow.

There lived in the city of Lucca a gentleman of the Guinigi family, named Messer Francesco, whose profession was arms and who in riches, bodily strength, and valour excelled all other men in Lucca. He had often fought under the command of the Visconti of Milan, and as a Ghibelline was the valued leader of that party in Lucca. This gentleman resided in Lucca and was accustomed to assemble with others most mornings and evenings under the balcony of the Podesta, which is at the top of the square of San Michele, the finest square in Lucca, and he had often seen Castruccio taking part with other children of the street in those games of which I have spoken. Noticing that Castruccio far excelled the other boys, and that he appeared to exercise a royal authority over them, and that they loved and obeyed him, Messer Francesco became greatly desirous of learning who he was. Being informed of the circumstances of the bringing up of Castruccio he felt a greater desire to have him near to him. Therefore he called him one day and asked him whether he would more willingly live in the house of a gentleman, where he would learn to ride horses and use arms, or in the house of a priest, where he would learn nothing but masses and the services of the Church. Messer Francesco could see that it pleased Castruccio greatly to hear horses and arms spoken of, even though he stood silent, blushing modestly; but being encouraged by Messer Francesco to speak, he answered that, if his master were agreeable, nothing would please him more than to give up his priestly studies and take up those of a soldier. This reply delighted Messer Francesco, and in a very short time he obtained the consent of Messer Antonio, who was driven to yield by his knowledge of the nature of the lad, and the fear that he would not be able to hold him much longer.

Thus Castruccio passed from the house of Messer Antonio the priest to the house of Messer Francesco Guinigi the soldier, and it was astonishing to find that in a very short time he manifested all that virtue and bearing which we are accustomed to associate with a true gentleman. In the first place he became an accomplished horseman, and could manage with ease the most fiery charger, and in all jousts and tournaments, although still a youth, he was observed beyond all others, and he excelled in all exercises of strength and dexterity. But what enhanced so much the charm of these accomplishments, was the delightful modesty which enabled him to avoid offence in either act or word to others, for he was deferential to the great men, modest with his equals, and courteous to his inferiors. These gifts made him beloved, not only by all the Guinigi family, but by all Lucca. When Castruccio had reached his eighteenth year, the Ghibellines were driven from Pavia by the Guelphs, and Messer Francesco was sent by the Visconti to assist the Ghibellines, and with him went Castruccio, in charge of his forces. Castruccio gave ample proof of his prudence and courage in this expedition, acquiring greater reputation than any other captain, and his name and fame were known, not only in Pavia, but throughout all Lombardy.

Castruccio, having returned to Lucca in far higher estimation that he left it, did not omit to use all the means in his power to gain as many friends as he could, neglecting none of those arts which are necessary for that purpose. About this time Messer Francesco died, leaving a son thirteen years of age named Pagolo, and having appointed Castruccio to be his son's tutor and administrator of his estate. Before he died Francesco called Castruccio to him, and prayed him to show Pagolo that goodwill which he (Francesco) had always shown to HIM, and to render to the son the gratitude which he had not been able to repay to the father. Upon the death of Francesco, Castruccio became the governor and tutor of Pagolo, which increased enormously his power and position, and created a certain amount of envy against him in Lucca in place of the former universal goodwill, for many men suspected him of harbouring tyrannical intentions. Among these the leading man was Giorgio degli Opizi, the head of the Guelph party. This man hoped after the death of Messer Francesco to become the chief man in Lucca, but it seemed to him that Castruccio, with the great abilities which he already showed, and holding the position of governor, deprived him of his opportunity; therefore he began to sow those seeds which should rob Castruccio of his eminence. Castruccio at first treated this with scorn, but afterwards he grew alarmed, thinking that Messer Giorgio might be able to bring him into disgrace with the deputy of King Ruberto of Naples and have him driven out of Lucca.

The Lord of Pisa at that time was Uguccione of the Faggiuola of Arezzo, who being in the first place elected their captain afterwards became their lord. There resided in Paris some exiled Ghibellines from Lucca, with whom Castruccio held communications with the object of effecting their restoration by the help of Uguccione. Castruccio also brought into his plans friends from Lucca who would not endure the authority of the Opizi. Having fixed upon a plan to be followed, Castruccio cautiously fortified the tower of the Onesti, filling it with supplies and munitions of war, in order that it might stand a siege for a few days in case of need. When the night came which had been agreed upon with Uguccione, who had occupied the plain between the mountains and Pisa with many men, the signal was given, and without being observed Uguccione approached the gate of San Piero and set fire to the portcullis. Castruccio raised a great uproar within the city, calling the people to arms and forcing open the gate from his side. Uguccione entered with his men, poured through the town, and killed Messer Giorgio with all his family and many of his friends and supporters. The governor was driven out, and the government reformed according to the wishes of Uguccione, to the detriment of the city, because it was found that more than one hundred families were exiled at that time. Of those who fled, part went to Florence and part to Pistoia, which city was the headquarters of the Guelph party, and for this reason it became most hostile to Uguccione and the Lucchese.

As it now appeared to the Florentines and others of the Guelph party that the Ghibellines absorbed too much power in Tuscany, they determined to restore the exiled Guelphs to Lucca. They assembled a large army in the Val di Nievole, and seized Montecatini; from thence they marched to Montecarlo, in order to secure the free passage into Lucca. Upon this Uguccione assembled his Pisan and Lucchese forces, and with a number of German cavalry which he drew out of Lombardy, he moved against the quarters of the Florentines, who upon the appearance of the enemy withdrew from Montecarlo, and posted themselves between Montecatini and Pescia. Uguccione now took up a position near to Montecarlo, and within about two miles of the enemy, and slight skirmishes between the horse of both parties were of daily occurrence. Owing to the illness of Uguccione, the Pisans and Lucchese delayed coming to battle with the enemy. Uguccione, finding himself growing worse, went to Montecarlo to be cured, and left the command of the army in the hands of Castruccio. This change brought about the ruin of the Guelphs, who, thinking that the hostile army having lost its captain had lost its head, grew over-confident. Castruccio observed this, and allowed some days to pass in order to encourage this belief; he also showed signs of fear, and did not allow any of the munitions of the camp to be used. On the other side, the Guelphs grew more insolent the more they saw these evidences of fear, and every day they drew out in the order of battle in front of the army of Castruccio. Presently, deeming that the enemy was sufficiently emboldened, and having mastered their tactics, he decided to join battle with them. First he spoke a few words of encouragement to his soldiers, and pointed out to them the certainty of victory if they would but obey his commands. Castruccio had noticed how the enemy had placed all his best troops in the centre of the line of battle, and his less reliable men on the wings of the army; whereupon he did exactly the opposite, putting his most valiant men on the flanks, while those on whom he could not so strongly rely he moved to the centre. Observing this order of battle, he drew out of his lines and quickly came in sight of the hostile army, who, as usual, had come in their insolence to defy him. He then commanded his centre squadrons to march slowly, whilst he moved rapidly forward those on the wings. Thus, when they came into contact with the enemy, only the wings of the two armies became engaged, whilst the center battalions remained out of action, for these two portions of the line of battle were separated from each other by a long interval and thus unable to reach each other. By this expedient the more valiant part of Castruccio's men were opposed to the weaker part of the enemy's troops, and the most efficient men of the enemy were disengaged; and thus the Florentines were unable to fight with those who were arrayed opposite to them, or to give any assistance to their own flanks. So, without much difficulty, Castruccio put the enemy to flight on both flanks, and the centre battalions took to flight when they found themselves exposed to attack, without having a chance of displaying their valour. The defeat was complete, and the loss in men very heavy, there being more than ten thousand men killed with many officers and knights of the Guelph party in Tuscany, and also many princes who had come to help them, among whom were Piero, the brother of King Ruberto, and Carlo, his nephew, and Filippo, the lord of Taranto. On the part of Castruccio the loss did not amount to more than three hundred men, among whom was Francesco, the son of Uguccione, who, being young and rash, was killed in the first onset.

  This victory so greatly increased the reputation of Castruccio that Uguccione conceived some jealousy and suspicion of him, because it appeared to Uguccione that this victory had given him no increase of power, but rather than diminished it. Being of this mind, he only waited for an opportunity to give effect to it. This occurred on the death of Pier Agnolo Micheli, a man of great repute and abilities in Lucca, the murderer of whom fled to the house of Castruccio for refuge. On the sergeants of the captain going to arrest the murderer, they were driven off by Castruccio, and the murderer escaped. This affair coming to the knowledge of Uguccione, who was than at Pisa, it appeared to him a proper opportunity to punish Castruccio. He therefore sent for his son Neri, who was the governor of Lucca, and commissioned him to take Castruccio prisoner at a banquet and put him to death. Castruccio, fearing no evil, went to the governor in a friendly way, was entertained at supper, and then thrown into prison. But Neri, fearing to put him to death lest the people should be incensed, kept him alive, in order to hear further from his father concerning his intentions. Ugucionne cursed the hesitation and cowardice of his son, and at once set out from Pisa to Lucca with four hundred horsemen to finish the business in his own way; but he had not yet reached the baths when the Pisans rebelled and put his deputy to death and created Count Gaddo della Gherardesca their lord. Before Uguccione reached Lucca he heard of the occurrences at Pisa, but it did not appear wise to him to turn back, lest the Lucchese with the example of Pisa before them should close their gates against him. But the Lucchese, having heard of what had happened at Pisa, availed themselves of this opportunity to demand the liberation of Castruccio, notwithstanding that Uguccione had arrived in their city. They first began to speak of it in private circles, afterwards openly in the squares and streets; then they raised a tumult, and with arms in their hands went to Uguccione and demanded that Castruccio should be set at liberty. Uguccione, fearing that worse might happen, released him from prison. Whereupon Castruccio gathered his friends around him, and with the help of the people attacked Uguccione; who, finding he had no resource but in flight, rode away with his friends to Lombardy, to the lords of Scale, where he died in poverty.

But Castruccio from being a prisoner became almost a prince in Lucca, and he carried himself so discreetly with his friends and the people that they appointed him captain of their army for one year. Having obtained this, and wishing to gain renown in war, he planned the recovery of the many towns which had rebelled after the departure of Uguccione, and with the help of the Pisans, with whom he had concluded a treaty, he marched to Serezzana. To capture this place he constructed a fort against it, which is called to-day Zerezzanello; in the course of two months Castruccio captured the town. With the reputation gained at that siege, he rapidly seized Massa, Carrara, and Lavenza, and in a short time had overrun the whole of Lunigiana. In order to close the pass which leads from Lombardy to Lunigiana, he besieged Pontremoli and wrested it from the hands of Messer Anastagio Palavicini, who was the lord of it. After this victory he returned to Lucca, and was welcomed by the whole people. And now Castruccio, deeming it imprudent any longer to defer making himself a prince, got himself created the lord of Lucca by the help of Pazzino del Poggio, Puccinello dal Portico, Francesco Boccansacchi, and Cecco Guinigi, all of whom he had corrupted; and he was afterwards solemnly and deliberately elected prince by the people. At this time Frederick of Bavaria, the King of the Romans, came into Italy to assume the Imperial crown, and Castruccio, in order that he might make friends with him, met him at the head of five hundred horsemen. Castruccio had left as his deputy in Lucca, Pagolo Guinigi, who was held in high estimation, because of the people's love for the memory of his father. Castruccio was received in great honour by Frederick, and many privileges were conferred upon him, and he was appointed the emperor's lieutenant in Tuscany. At this time the Pisans were in great fear of Gaddo della Gherardesca, whom they had driven out of Pisa, and they had recourse for assistance to Frederick. Frederick created Castruccio the lord of Pisa, and the Pisans, in dread of the Guelph party, and particularly of the Florentines, were constrained to accept him as their lord.

Frederick, having appointed a governor in Rome to watch his Italian affairs, returned to Germany. All the Tuscan and Lombardian Ghibellines, who followed the imperial lead, had recourse to Castruccio for help and counsel, and all promised him the governorship of his country, if enabled to recover it with his assistance. Among these exiles were Matteo Guidi, Nardo Scolari, Lapo Uberti, Gerozzo Nardi, and Piero Buonaccorsi, all exiled Florentines and Ghibellines. Castruccio had the secret intention of becoming the master of all Tuscany by the aid of these men and of his own forces; and in order to gain greater weight in affairs, he entered into a league with Messer Matteo Visconti, the Prince of Milan, and organized for him the forces of his city and the country districts. As Lucca had five gates, he divided his own country districts into five parts, which he supplied with arms, and enrolled the men under captains and ensigns, so that he could quickly bring into the field twenty thousand soldiers, without those whom he could summon to his assistance from Pisa. While he surrounded himself with these forces and allies, it happened at Messer Matteo Visconti was attacked by the Guelphs of Piacenza, who had driven out the Ghibellines with the assistance of a Florentine army and the King Ruberto. Messer Matteo called upon Castruccio to invade the Florentines in their own territories, so that, being attacked at home, they should be compelled to draw their army out of Lombardy in order to defend themselves. Castruccio invaded the Valdarno, and seized Fucecchio and San Miniato, inflicting immense damage upon the country. Whereupon the Florentines recalled their army, which had scarcely reached Tuscany, when Castruccio was forced by other necessities to return to Lucca.

There resided in the city of Lucca the Poggio family, who were so powerful that they could not only elevate Castruccio, but even advance him to the dignity of prince; and it appearing to them they had not received such rewards for their services as they deserved, they incited other families to rebel and to drive Castruccio out of Lucca. They found their opportunity one morning, and arming themselves, they set upon the lieutenant whom Castruccio had left to maintain order and killed him. They endeavoured to raise the people in revolt, but Stefano di Poggio, a peaceable old man who had taken no hand in the rebellion, intervened and compelled them by his authority to lay down their arms; and he offered to be their mediator with Castruccio to obtain from him what they desired. Therefore they laid down their arms with no greater intelligence than they had taken them up. Castruccio, having heard the news of what had happened at Lucca, at once put Pagolo Guinigi in command of the army, and with a troop of cavalry set out for home. Contrary to his expectations, he found the rebellion at an end, yet he posted his men in the most advantageous places throughout the city. As it appeared to Stefano that Castruccio ought to be very much obliged to him, he sought him out, and without saying anything on his own behalf, for he did not recognize any need for doing so, he begged Castruccio to pardon the other members of his family by reason of their youth, their former friendships, and the obligations which Castruccio was under to their house. To this Castruccio graciously responded, and begged Stefano to reassure himself, declaring that it gave him more pleasure to find the tumult at an end than it had ever caused him anxiety to hear of its inception. He encouraged Stefano to bring his family to him, saying that he thanked God for having given him the opportunity of showing his clemency and liberality. Upon the word of Stefano and Castruccio they surrendered, and with Stefano were immediately thrown into prison and put to death. Meanwhile the Florentines had recovered San Miniato, whereupon it seemed advisable to Castruccio to make peace, as it did not appear to him that he was sufficiently secure at Lucca to leave him. He approached the Florentines with the proposal of a truce, which they readily entertained, for they were weary of the war, and desirous of getting rid of the expenses of it. A treaty was concluded with them for two years, by which both parties agreed to keep the conquests they had made. Castruccio thus released from this trouble, turned his attention to affairs in Lucca, and in order that he should not again be subject to the perils from which he had just escaped, he, under various pretences and reasons, first wiped out all those who by their ambition might aspire to the principality; not sparing one of them, but depriving them of country and property, and those whom he had in his hands of life also, stating that he had found by experience that none of them were to be trusted. Then for his further security he raised a fortress in Lucca with the stones of the towers of those whom he had killed or hunted out of the state.

Whilst Castruccio made peace with the Florentines, and strengthened his position in Lucca, he neglected no opportunity, short of open war, of increasing his importance elsewhere. It appeared to him that if he could get possession of Pistoia, he would have one foot in Florence, which was his great desire. He, therefore, in various ways made friends with the mountaineers, and worked matters so in Pistoia that both parties confided their secrets to him. Pistoia was divided, as it always had been, into the Bianchi and Neri parties; the head of the Bianchi was Bastiano di Possente, and of the Neri, Jacopo da Gia. Each of these men held secret communications with Castruccio, and each desired to drive the other out of the city; and, after many threatenings, they came to blows. Jacopo fortified himself at the Florentine gate, Bastiano at that of the Lucchese side of the city; both trusted more in Castruccio than in the Florentines, because they believed that Castruccio was far more ready and willing to fight than the Florentines, and they both sent to him for assistance. He gave promises to both, saying to Bastiano that he would come in person, and to Jacopo that he would send his pupil, Pagolo Guinigi. At the appointed time he sent forward Pagolo by way of Pisa, and went himself direct to Pistoia; at midnight both of them met outside the city, and both were admitted as friends. Thus the two leaders entered, and at a signal given by Castruccio, one killed Jacopo da Gia, and the other Bastiano di Possente, and both took prisoners or killed the partisans of either faction. Without further opposition Pistoia passed into the hands of Castruccio, who, having forced the Signoria to leave the palace, compelled the people to yield obedience to him, making them many promises and remitting their old debts. The countryside flocked to the city to see the new prince, and all were filled with hope and quickly settled down, influenced in a great measure by his great valour.

About this time great disturbances arose in Rome, owing to the dearness of living which was caused by the absence of the pontiff at Avignon. The German governor, Enrico, was much blamed for what happened — murders and tumults following each other daily, without his being able to put an end to them. This caused Enrico much anxiety lest the Romans should call in Ruberto, the King of Naples, who would drive the Germans out of the city, and bring back the Pope. Having no nearer friend to whom he could apply for help than Castruccio, he sent to him, begging him not only to give him assistance, but also to come in person to Rome. Castruccio considered that he ought not to hesitate to render the emperor this service, because he believed that he himself would not be safe if at any time the emperor ceased to hold Rome. Leaving Pagolo Guinigi in command at Lucca, Castruccio set out for Rome with six hundred horsemen, where he was received by Enrico with the greatest distinction. In a short time the presence of Castruccio obtained such respect for the emperor that, without bloodshed or violence, good order was restored, chiefly by reason of Castruccio having sent by sea from the country round Pisa large quantities of corn, and thus removed the source of the trouble. When he had chastised some of the Roman leaders, and admonished others, voluntary obedience was rendered to Enrico. Castruccio received many honours, and was made a Roman senator. This dignity was assumed with the greatest pomp, Castruccio being clothed in a brocaded toga, which had the following words embroidered on its front: "I am what God wills." Whilst on the back was: "What God desires shall be."

During this time the Florentines, who were much enraged that Castruccio should have seized Pistoia during the truce, considered how they could tempt the city to rebel, to do which they thought would not be difficult in his absence. Among the exiled Pistoians in Florence were Baldo Cecchi and Jacopo Baldini, both men of leading and ready to face danger. These men kept up communications with their friends in Pistoia, and with the aid of the Florentines entered the city by night, and after driving out some of Castruccio's officials and partisans, and killing others, they restored the city to its freedom. The news of this greatly angered Castruccio, and taking leave of Enrico, he pressed on in great haste to Pistoia. When the Florentines heard of his return, knowing that he would lose no time, they decided to intercept him with their forces in the Val di Nievole, under the belief that by doing so they would cut off his road to Pistoia. Assembling a great army of the supporters of the Guelph cause, the Florentines entered the Pistoian territories. On the other hand, Castruccio reached Montecarlo with his army; and having heard where the Florentines' lay, he decided not to encounter it in the plains of Pistoia, nor to await it in the plains of Pescia, but, as far as he possibly could, to attack it boldly in the Pass of Serravalle. He believed that if he succeeded in this design, victory was assured, although he was informed that the Florentines had thirty thousand men, whilst he had only twelve thousand. Although he had every confidence in his own abilities and the valour of his troops, yet he hesitated to attack his enemy in the open lest he should be overwhelmed by numbers. Serravalle is a castle between Pescia and Pistoia, situated on a hill which blocks the Val di Nievole, not in the exact pass, but about a bowshot beyond; the pass itself is in places narrow and steep, whilst in general it ascends gently, but is still narrow, especially at the summit where the waters divide, so that twenty men side by side could hold it. The lord of Serravalle was Manfred, a German, who, before Castruccio became lord of Pistoia, had been allowed to remain in possession of the castle, it being common to the Lucchese and the Pistoians, and unclaimed by either — neither of them wishing to displace Manfred as long as he kept his promise of neutrality, and came under obligations to no one. For these reasons, and also because the castle was well fortified, he had always been able to maintain his position. It was here that Castruccio had determined to fall upon his enemy, for here his few men would have the advantage, and there was no fear lest, seeing the large masses of the hostile force before they became engaged, they should not stand. As soon as this trouble with

Florence arose, Castruccio saw the immense advantage which possession of this castle would give him, and having an intimate friendship with a resident in the castle, he managed matters so with him that four hundred of his men were to be admitted into the castle the night before the attack on the Florentines, and the castellan put to death.

Castruccio, having prepared everything, had now to encourage the Florentines to persist in their desire to carry the seat of war away from Pistoia into the Val di Nievole, therefore he did not move his army from Montecarlo. Thus the Florentines hurried on until they reached their encampment under Serravalle, intending to cross the hill on the following morning. In the meantime, Castruccio had seized the castle at night, had also moved his army from Montecarlo, and marching from thence at midnight in dead silence, had reached the foot of Serravalle: thus he and the Florentines commenced the ascent of the hill at the same time in the morning. Castruccio sent forward his infantry by the main road, and a troop of four hundred horsemen by a path on the left towards the castle. The Florentines sent forward four hundred cavalry ahead of their army which was following, never expecting to find Castruccio in possession of the hill, nor were they aware of his having seized the castle. Thus it happened that the Florentine horsemen mounting the hill were completely taken by surprise when they discovered the infantry of Castruccio, and so close were they upon it they had scarcely time to pull down their visors. It was a case of unready soldiers being attacked by ready, and they were assailed with such vigour that with difficulty they could hold their own, although some few of them got through. When the noise of the fighting reached the Florentine camp below, it was filled with confusion. The cavalry and infantry became inextricably mixed: the captains were unable to get their men either backward or forward, owing to the narrowness of the pass, and amid all this tumult no one knew what ought to be done or what could be done. In a short time the cavalry who were engaged with the enemy's infantry were scattered or killed without having made any effective defence because of their unfortunate position, although in sheer desperation they had offered a stout resistance. Retreat had been impossible, with the mountains on both flanks, whilst in front were their enemies, and in the rear their friends. When Castruccio saw that his men were unable to strike a decisive blow at the enemy and put them to flight, he sent one thousand infantrymen round by the castle, with orders to join the four hundred horsemen he had previously dispatched there, and commanded the whole force to fall upon the flank of the enemy. These orders they carried out with such fury that the Florentines could not sustain the attack, but gave way, and were soon in full retreat — conquered more by their unfortunate position than by the valour of their enemy. Those in the rear turned towards Pistoia, and spread through the plains, each man seeking only his own safety. The defeat was complete and very sanguinary. Many captains were taken prisoners, among whom were Bandini dei Rossi, Francesco Brunelleschi, and Giovanni della Tosa, all Florentine noblemen, with many Tuscans and Neapolitans who fought on the Florentine side, having been sent by King Ruberto to assist the Guelphs. Immediately the Pistoians heard of this defeat they drove out the friends of the Guelphs, and surrendered to Castruccio. He was not content with occupying Prato and all the castles on the plains on both sides of the Arno, but marched his army into the plain of Peretola, about two miles from Florence. Here he remained many days, dividing the spoils, and celebrating his victory with feasts and games, holding horse races, and foot races for men and women. He also struck medals in commemoration of the defeat of the Florentines. He endeavoured to corrupt some of the citizens of Florence, who were to open the city gates at night; but the conspiracy was discovered, and the participators in it taken and beheaded, among whom were Tommaso Lupacci and Lambertuccio Frescobaldi. This defeat caused the Florentines great anxiety, and despairing of preserving their liberty, they sent envoys to King Ruberto of Naples, offering him the dominion of their city; and he, knowing of what immense importance the maintenance of the Guelph cause was to him, accepted it. He agreed with the Florentines to receive from them a yearly tribute of two hundred thousand florins, and he send his son Carlo to Florence with four thousand horsemen.

Shortly after this the Florentines were relieved in some degree of the pressure of Castruccio's army, owing to his being compelled to leave his positions before Florence and march on Pisa, in order to suppress a conspiracy that had been raised against him by Benedetto Lanfranchi, one of the first men in Pisa, who could not endure that his fatherland should be under the dominion of the Lucchese. He had formed this conspiracy, intending to seize the citadel, kill the partisans of Castruccio, and drive out the garrison. As, however, in a conspiracy paucity of numbers is essential to secrecy, so for its execution a few are not sufficient, and in seeking more adherents to his conspiracy Lanfranchi encountered a person who revealed the design to Castruccio. This betrayal cannot be passed by without severe reproach to Bonifacio Cerchi and Giovanni Guidi, two Florentine exiles who were suffering their banishment in Pisa. Thereupon Castruccio seized Benedetto and put him to death, and beheaded many other noble citizens, and drove their families into exile. It now appeared to Castruccio that both Pisa and Pistoia were thoroughly disaffected; he employed much thought and energy upon securing his position there, and this gave the Florentines their opportunity to reorganize their army, and to await the coming of Carlo, the son of the King of Naples. When Carlo arrived they decided to lose no more time, and assembled a great army of more than thirty thousand infantry and ten thousand cavalry — having called to their aid every Guelph there was in Italy. They consulted whether they should attack Pistoia or Pisa first, and decided that it would be better to march on the latter — a course, owing to the recent conspiracy, more likely to succeed, and of more advantage to them, because they believed that the surrender of Pistoia would follow the acquisition of Pisa.

In the early part of May 1328, the Florentines put in motion this army and quickly occupied Lastra, Signa, Montelupo, and Empoli, passing from thence on to San Miniato. When

Castruccio heard of the enormous army which the Florentines were sending against him, he was in no degree alarmed, believing that the time had now arrived when Fortune would deliver the empire of Tuscany into his hands, for he had no reason to think that his enemy would make a better fight, or had better prospects of success, than at Pisa or Serravalle. He assembled twenty thousand foot soldiers and four thousand horsemen, and with this army went to Fucecchio, whilst he sent Pagolo Guinigi to Pisa with five thousand infantry. Fucecchio has a stronger position than any other town in the Pisan district, owing to its situation between the rivers Arno and Gusciana and its slight elevation above the surrounding plain. Moreover, the enemy could not hinder its being victualled unless they divided their forces, nor could they approach it either from the direction of Lucca or Pisa, nor could they get through to Pisa, or attack Castruccio's forces except at a disadvantage. In one case they would find themselves placed between his two armies, the one under his own command and the other under Pagolo, and in the other case they would have to cross the Arno to get to close quarters with the enemy, an undertaking of great hazard. In order to tempt the Florentines to take this latter course, Castruccio withdrew his men from the banks of the river and placed them under the walls of Fucecchio, leaving a wide expanse of land between them and the river.

The Florentines, having occupied San Miniato, held a council of war to decide whether they should attack Pisa or the army of Castruccio, and, having weighed the difficulties of both courses, they decided upon the latter. The river Arno was at that time low enough to be fordable, yet the water reached to the shoulders of the infantrymen and to the saddles of the horsemen. On the morning of 10 June 1328, the Florentines commenced the battle by ordering forward a number of cavalry and ten thousand infantry. Castruccio, whose plan of action was fixed, and who well knew what to do, at once attacked the Florentines with five thousand infantry and three thousand horsemen, not allowing them to issue from the river before he charged them; he also sent one thousand light infantry up the river bank, and the same number down the Arno. The infantry of the Florentines were so much impeded by their arms and the water that they were not able to mount the banks of the river, whilst the cavalry had made the passage of the river more difficult for the others, by reason of the few who had crossed having broken up the bed of the river, and this being deep with mud, many of the horses rolled over with their riders and many of them had stuck so fast that they could not move. When the Florentine captains saw the difficulties their men were meeting, they withdrew them and moved higher up the river, hoping to find the river bed less treacherous and the banks more adapted for landing. These men were met at the bank by the forces which Castruccio had already sent forward, who, being light armed with bucklers and javelins in their hands, let fly with tremendous shouts into the faces and bodies of the cavalry. The horses, alarmed by the noise and the wounds, would not move forward, and trampled each other in great confusion. The fight between the men of Castruccio and those of the enemy who succeeded in crossing was sharp and terrible; both sides fought with the utmost desperation and neither would yield. The soldiers of Castruccio fought to drive the others back into the river, whilst the Florentines strove to get a footing on land in order to make room for the others pressing forward, who if they could but get out of the water would be able to fight, and in this obstinate conflict they were urged on by their captains. Castruccio shouted to his men that these were the same enemies whom they had before conquered at Serravalle, whilst the Florentines reproached each other that the many should be overcome by the few. At length Castruccio, seeing how long the battle had lasted, and that both his men and the enemy were utterly exhausted, and that both sides had many killed and wounded, pushed forward another body of infantry to take up a position at the rear of those who were fighting; he then commanded these latter to open their ranks as if they intended to retreat, and one part of them to turn to the right and another to the left. This cleared a space of which the Florentines at once took advantage, and thus gained possession of a portion of the battlefield. But when these tired soldiers found themselves at close quarters with Castruccio's reserves they could not stand against them and at once fell back into the river. The cavalry of either side had not as yet gained any decisive advantage over the other, because Castruccio, knowing his inferiority in this arm, had commanded his leaders only to stand on the defensive against the attacks of their adversaries, as he hoped that when he had overcome the infantry he would be able to make short work of the cavalry. This fell out as he had hoped, for when he saw the Florentine army driven back across the river he ordered the remainder of his infantry to attack the cavalry of the enemy. This they did with lance and javelin, and, joined by their own cavalry, fell upon the enemy with the greatest fury and soon put him to flight. The Florentine captains, having seen the difficulty their cavalry had met with in crossing the river, had attempted to make their infantry cross lower down the river, in order to attack the flanks of Castruccio's army. But here, also, the banks were steep and already lined by the men of Castruccio, and this movement was quite useless. Thus the Florentines were so completely defeated at all points that scarcely a third of them escaped, and Castruccio was again covered with glory. Many captains were taken prisoners, and Carlo, the son of King Ruberto, with Michelagnolo Falconi and Taddeo degli Albizzi, the Florentine commissioners, fled to Empoli. If the spoils were great, the slaughter was infinitely greater, as might be expected in such a battle. Of the Florentines there fell twenty thousand two hundred and thirty-one men, whilst Castruccio lost one thousand five hundred and seventy men.

But Fortune growing envious of the glory of Castruccio took away his life just at the time when she should have preserved it, and thus ruined all those plans which for so long a time he had worked to carry into effect, and in the successful prosecution of which nothing but death could have stopped him. Castruccio was in the thick of the battle the whole of the day; and when the end of it came, although fatigued and overheated, he stood at the gate of Fucecchio to welcome his men on their return from victory and personally thank them. He was also on the watch for any attempt of the enemy to retrieve the fortunes of the day; he being of the opinion that it was the duty of a good general to be the first man in the saddle and the last out of it. Here Castruccio stood exposed to a wind which often rises at midday on the banks of the Arno, and which is often very unhealthy; from this he took a chill, of which he thought nothing, as he was accustomed to such troubles; but it was the cause of his death. On the following night he was attacked with high fever, which increased so rapidly that the doctors saw it must prove fatal. Castruccio, therefore, called Pagolo Guinigi to him, and addressed him as follows:

"If I could have believed that Fortune would have cut me off in the midst of the career which was leading to that glory which all my successes promised, I should have laboured less, and I should have left thee, if a smaller state, at least with fewer enemies and perils, because I should have been content with the governorships of Lucca and Pisa. I should neither have subjugated the Pistoians, nor outraged the Florentines with so many injuries. But I would have made both these peoples my friends, and I should have lived, if no longer, at least more peacefully, and have left you a state without a doubt smaller, but one more secure and established on a surer foundation. But Fortune, who insists upon having the arbitrament of human affairs, did not endow me with sufficient judgment to recognize this from the first, nor the time to surmount it. Thou hast heard, for many have told thee, and I have never concealed it, how I entered the house of thy father whilst yet a boy — a stranger to all those ambitions which every generous soul should feel — and how I was brought up by him, and loved as though I had been born of his blood; how under his governance I learned to be valiant and capable of availing myself of all that fortune, of which thou hast been witness. When thy good father came to die, he committed thee and all his possessions to my care, and I have brought thee up with that love, and increased thy estate with that care, which I was bound to show. And in order that thou shouldst not only possess the estate which thy father left, but also that which my fortune and abilities have gained, I have never married, so that the love of children should never deflect my mind from that gratitude which I owed to the children of thy father. Thus I leave thee a vast estate, of which I am well content, but I am deeply concerned, inasmuch as I leave it thee unsettled and insecure. Thou hast the city of Lucca on thy hands, which will never rest contented under they government. Thou hast also Pisa, where the men are of nature changeable and unreliable, who, although they may be sometimes held in subjection, yet they will ever disdain to serve under a Lucchese. Pistoia is also disloyal to thee, she being eaten up with factions and deeply incensed against thy family by reason of the wrongs recently inflicted upon them. Thou hast for neighbours the offended Florentines, injured by us in a thousand ways, but not utterly destroyed, who will hail the news of my death with more delight than they would the acquisition of all Tuscany. In the Emperor and in the princes of Milan thou canst place no reliance, for they are far distant, slow, and their help is very long in coming. Therefore, thou hast no hope in anything but in thine own abilities, and in the memory of my valour, and in the prestige which this latest victory has brought thee; which, as thou knowest how to use it with prudence, will assist thee to come to terms with the Florentines, who, as they are suffering under this great defeat, should be inclined to listen to thee. And whereas I have sought to make them my enemies, because I believed that war with them would conduce to my power and glory, thou hast every inducement to make friends of them, because their alliance will bring thee advantages and security. It is of the greatest important in this world that a man should know himself, and the measure of his own strength and means; and he who knows that he has not a genius for fighting must learn how to govern by the arts of peace. And it will be well for thee to rule they conduct by my counsel, and to learn in this way to enjoy what my life-work and dangers have gained; and in this thou wilt easily succeed when thou hast learnt to believe that what I have told thee is true. And thou wilt be doubly indebted to me, in that I have left thee this realm and have taught thee how to keep it."

After this there came to Castruccio those citizens of Pisa, Pistoia, and Lucca, who had been fighting at his side, and whilst recommending Pagolo to them, and making them swear obedience to him as his successor, he died. He left a happy memory to those who had known him, and no prince of those times was ever loved with such devotion as he was. His obsequies were celebrated with every sign of mourning, and he was buried in San Francesco at Lucca. Fortune was not so friendly to Pagolo Guinigi as she had been to Castruccio, for he had not the abilities. Not long after the death of Castruccio, Pagolo lost Pisa, and then Pistoia, and only with difficulty held on to Lucca. This latter city continued in the family of Guinigi until the time of the great-grandson of Pagolo.

From what has been related here it will be seen that Castruccio was a man of exceptional abilities, not only measured by men of his own time, but also by those of an earlier date. In stature he was above the ordinary height, and perfectly proportioned. He was of a gracious presence, and he welcomed men with such urbanity that those who spoke with him rarely left him displeased. His hair was inclined to be red, and he wore it cut short above the ears, and, whether it rained or snowed, he always went without a hat. He was delightful among friends, but terrible to his enemies; just to his subjects; ready to play false with the unfaithful, and willing to overcome by fraud those whom he desired to subdue, because he was wont to say that it was the victory that brought the glory, not the methods of achieving it. No one was bolder in facing danger, none more prudent in extricating himself. He was accustomed to say that men ought to attempt everything and fear nothing; that God is a lover of strong men, because one always sees that the weak are chastised by the strong. He was also wonderfully sharp or biting though courteous in his answers; and as he did not look for any indulgence in this way of speaking from others, so he was not angered with others did not show it to him. It has often happened that he has listened quietly when others have spoken sharply to him, as on the following occasions. He had caused a ducat to be given for a partridge, and was taken to task for doing so by a friend, to whom Castruccio had said: "You would not have given more than a penny." "That is true," answered the friend. Then said Castruccio to him: "A ducat is much less to me." Having about him a flatterer on whom he had spat to show that he scorned him, the flatterer said to him: "Fisherman are willing to let the waters of the sea saturate them in order that they make take a few little fishes, and I allow myself to be wetted by spittle that I may catch a whale"; and this was not only heard by Castruccio with patience but rewarded. When told by a priest that it was wicked for him to live so sumptuously, Castruccio said: "If that be a vice than you should not fare so splendidly at the feasts of our saints." Passing through a street he saw a young man as he came out of a house of ill fame blush at being seen by Castruccio, and said to him: "Thou shouldst not be ashamed when thou comest out, but when thou goest into such places." A friend gave him a very curiously tied knot to undo and was told: "Fool, do you think that I wish to untie a thing which gave so much trouble to fasten." Castruccio said to one who professed to be a philosopher: "You are like the dogs who always run after those who will give them the best to eat," and was answered: "We are rather like the doctors who go to the houses of those who have the greatest need of them." Going by water from Pisa to Leghorn, Castruccio was much disturbed by a dangerous storm that sprang up, and was reproached for cowardice by one of those with him, who said that he did not fear anything. Castruccio answered that he did not wonder at that, since every man valued his soul for what is was worth. Being asked by one what he ought to do to gain estimation, he said: "When thou goest to a banquet take care that thou dost not seat one piece of wood upon another." To a person who was boasting that he had read many things, Castruccio said: "He knows better than to boast of remembering many things." Someone bragged that he could drink much without becoming intoxicated. Castruccio replied: "An ox does the same." Castruccio was acquainted with a girl with whom he had intimate relations, and being blamed by a friend who told him that it was undignified for him to be taken in by a woman, he said: "She has not taken me in, I have taken her." Being also blamed for eating very dainty foods, he answered: "Thou dost not spend as much as I do?" and being told that it was true, he continued: "Then thou art more avaricious than I am gluttonous." Being invited by Taddeo Bernardi, a very rich and splendid citizen of Luca, to supper, he went to the house and was shown by Taddeo into a chamber hung with silk and paved with fine stones representing flowers and foliage of the most beautiful colouring. Castruccio gathered some saliva in his mouth and spat it out upon Taddeo, and seeing him much disturbed by this, said to him: "I knew not where to spit in order to offend thee less." Being asked how Caesar died he said: "God willing I will die as he did." Being one night in the house of one of his gentlemen where many ladies were assembled, he was reproved by one of his friends for dancing and amusing himself with them more than was usual in one of his station, so he said: "He who is considered wise by day will not be considered a fool at night." A person came to demand a favour of Castruccio, and thinking he was not listening to his plea threw himself on his knees to the ground, and being sharply reproved by Castruccio, said: "Thou art the reason of my acting thus for thou hast thy ears in thy feet," whereupon he obtained double the favour he had asked. Castruccio used to say that the way to hell was an easy one, seeing that it was in a downward direction and you travelled blindfolded. Being asked a favour by one who used many superfluous words, he said to him: "When you have another request to make, send someone else to make it." Having been wearied by a similar man with a long oration who wound up by saying: "Perhaps I have fatigued you by speaking so long," Castruccio said: "You have not, because I have not listened to a word you said." He used to say of one who had been a beautiful child and who afterwards became a fine man, that he was dangerous, because he first took the husbands from the wives and now he took the wives from their husbands. To an envious man who laughed, he said: "Do you laugh because you are successful or because another is unfortunate?" Whilst he was still in the charge of Messer Francesco Guinigi, one of his companions said to him: "What shall I give you if you will let me give you a blow on the nose?" Castruccio answered: "A helmet." Having put to death a citizen of Lucca who had been instrumental in raising him to power, and being told that he had done wrong to kill one of his old friends, he answered that people deceived themselves; he had only killed a new enemy. Castruccio praised greatly those men who intended to take a wife and then did not do so, saying that they were like men who said they would go to sea, and then refused when the time came. He said that it always struck him with surprise that whilst men in buying an earthen or glass vase would sound it first to learn if it were good, yet in choosing a wife they were content with only looking at her. He was once asked in what manner he would wish to be buried when he died, and answered: "With the face turned downwards, for I know when I am gone this country will be turned upside down." On being asked if it had ever occurred to him to become a friar in order to save his soul, he answered that it had not, because it appeared strange to him that Fra Lazerone should go to Paradise and Uguccione della Faggiuola to the Inferno. He was once asked when should a man eat to preserve his health, and replied: "If the man be rich let him eat when he is hungry; if he be poor, then when he can." Seeing on of his gentlemen make a member of his family lace him up, he said to him: "I pray God that you will let him feed you also." Seeing that someone had written upon his house in Latin the words: "May God preserve this house from the wicked," he said, "The owner must never go in." Passing through one of the streets he saw a small house with a very large door, and remarked: "That house will fly through the door." He was having a discussion with the ambassador of the King of Naples concerning the property of some banished nobles, when a dispute arose between them, and the ambassador asked him if he had no fear of the king. "Is this king of yours a bad man or a good one?" asked Castruccio, and was told that he was a good one, whereupon he said, "Why should you suggest that I should be afraid of a good man?"

I could recount many other stories of his sayings both witty and weighty, but I think that the above will be sufficient testimony to his high qualities. He lived forty-four years, and was in every way a prince. And as he was surrounded by many evidences of his good fortune, so he also desired to have near him some memorials of his bad fortune; therefore the manacles with which he was chained in prison are to be seen to this day fixed up in the tower of his residence, where they were placed by him to testify for ever to his days of adversity. As in his life he was inferior neither to Philip of Macedon, the father of Alexander, nor to Scipio of Rome, so he died in the same year of his age as they did, and he would doubtless have excelled both of them had Fortune decreed that he should be born, not in Lucca, but in Macedonia or Rome.

DISCOURSES ON THE FIRST DECADE OF TITUS LIVIUS

NICCOLO MACHIAVELLI TO ZANOBI BUONDELMONTI AND COSIMO RUCELLAI

HEALTH.

I send you a gift, which if it answers ill the obligations I owe you, is at any rate the greatest which Niccolo Machiavelli has it in his power to offer. For in it I have expressed whatever I have learned, or have observed for myself during a long experience and constant study of human affairs. And since neither you nor any other can expect more at my hands, you cannot complain if I have not given you more.

You may indeed lament the poverty of my wit, since what I have to say is but poorly said; and tax the weakness of my judgment, which on many points may have erred in its conclusions. But granting all this, I know not which of us is less beholden to the other: I to you, who have forced me to write what of myself I never should have written; or you to me, who have written what can give you no content.

Take this, however, in the spirit in which all that comes from a friend should be taken, in respect whereof we always look more to the intention of the giver than to the quality of the gift. And, believe me, that in one thing only I find satisfaction, namely, in knowing that while in many matters I may have made mistakes, at least I have not been mistaken in choosing you before all others as the persons to whom I dedicate these Discourses; both because I seem to myself, in doing so, to have shown a little gratitude for kindness received, and at the same time to have departed from the hackneyed custom which leads many authors to inscribe their works to some Prince, and blinded by hopes of favour or reward, to praise him as possessed of every virtue; whereas with more reason they might reproach him as contaminated with every shameful vice.

To avoid which error I have chosen, not those who are but those who from their infinite merits deserve to be Princes; not such persons as have it in their power to load me with honours, wealth, and preferment, but such as though they lack the power, have all the will to do so. For men, if they would judge justly, should esteem those who are, and not those whose means enable them to be generous; and in like manner those who know how to govern kingdoms, rather than those who possess the government without such knowledge. For Historians award higher praise to Hiero of Syracuse when in a private station than to Perseus the Macedonian when a King affirming that while the former lacked nothing that a Prince should have save the name, the latter had nothing of the King but the kingdom.

Make the most, therefore, of this good or this evil, as you may esteem it, which you have brought upon yourselves; and should you persist in the mistake of thinking my opinions worthy your attention, I shall not fail to proceed with the rest of the History in the manner promised in my Preface. *Farewell.*

BOOK I

PREFACE

Albeit the jealous temper of mankind, ever more disposed to censure than to praise the work of others, has constantly made the pursuit of new methods and systems no less perilous than the search after unknown lands and seas; nevertheless, prompted by that desire which nature has implanted in me, fearlessly to undertake whatsoever I think offers a common benefit to all, I enter on a path which, being hitherto untrodden by any, though it involve me in trouble and fatigue, may yet win me thanks from those who judge my efforts in a friendly spirit. And although my feeble discernment, my slender experience of current affairs, and imperfect knowledge of ancient events, render these efforts of mine defective and of no great utility, they may at least open the way to some other, who, with better parts and sounder reasoning and judgment, shall carry out my design; whereby, if I gain no credit, at all events I ought to incur no blame.

When I see antiquity held in such reverence, that to omit other instances, the mere fragment of some ancient statue is often bought at a great price, in order that the purchaser may keep it by him to adorn his house, or to have it copied by those who take delight in this art; and how these, again, strive with all their skill to imitate it in their various works; and when, on the other hand, I find those noble labours which history shows to have been wrought on behalf of the monarchies and republics of old times, by kings, captains, citizens, lawgivers, and others who have toiled for the good of their country, rather admired than followed, nay, so absolutely renounced by every one that not a trace of that antique worth is now left among us, I cannot but at once marvel and grieve; at this inconsistency; and all the more because I perceive that, in civil disputes between citizens, and in the bodily disorders into which men fall, recourse is always had to the decisions and remedies, pronounced or prescribed by the ancients.

For the civil law is no more than the opinions delivered by the ancient jurisconsults, which, being reduced to a system, teach the jurisconsults of our own times how to determine; while the healing art is simply the recorded experience of the old physicians, on which our modern physicians found their practice. And yet, in giving laws to a commonwealth, in maintaining States and governing kingdoms, in organizing armies and conducting wars, in dealing with subject nations, and in extending a State's dominions, we find no prince, no republic, no captain, and no citizen who resorts to the example of the ancients.

This I persuade myself is due, not so much to the feebleness to which the present methods of education have brought the world, or to the injury which a pervading apathy has wrought in many provinces and cities of Christendom, as to the want of a right intelligence of History, which renders men incapable in reading it to extract its true meaning or to relish its flavour. Whence it happens that by far the greater number of those who read History, take pleasure in following the variety of incidents which it presents, without a thought to imitate them; judging such imitation to be not only difficult but impossible; as though the heavens, the sun, the elements, and man himself were no longer the same as they formerly were as regards motion, order, and power.

Desiring to rescue men from this error, I have thought fit to note down with respect to all those books of Titus Livius which have escaped the malignity of Time, whatever seems to me essential to a right understanding of ancient and modern affairs; so that any who shall read these remarks of mine, may reap from them that profit for the sake of which a knowledge of History is to be sought. And although the task be arduous, still, with the help of those at whose instance I assumed the burthen, I hope to carry it forward so far, that another shall have no long way to go to bring it to its destination.

CHAPTER I

Of the Beginnings of Cities in general, and in particular of that of Rome.

No one who reads how the city of Rome had its beginning, who were its founders, and what its ordinances and laws, will marvel that so much excellence was maintained in it through many ages, or that it grew afterwards to be so great an Empire.

And, first, as touching its origin, I say, that all cities have been founded either by the people of the country in which they stand, or by strangers. Cities have their origins in the former of these two ways when the inhabitants of a country find that they cannot live securely if they live dispersed in many and small societies, each of them unable, whether from its situation or its slender numbers, to stand alone against the attacks of its enemies; on whose approach there is no time left to unite for defence without abandoning many strongholds, and thus becoming an easy prey to the invader. To escape which dangers, whether of their own motion or at the instance of some of greater authority among them, they restrict themselves to dwell together in certain places, which they think will be more convenient to live in and easier to defend.

Among many cities taking their origin in this way were Athens and Venice; the former of which, for reasons like those just now mentioned, was built by a scattered population under the direction of Theseus. To escape the wars which, on the decay of the Roman Empire daily renewed in Italy by the arrival of fresh hordes of Barbarians, numerous refugees, sheltering in certain little islands in a corner of the Adriatic Sea, gave beginning to

Venice; where, without any recognized leader to direct them, they agreed to live together under such laws as they thought best suited to maintain them. And by reason of the prolonged tranquility which their position secured, they being protected by the narrow sea and by the circumstance that the tribes who then harassed Italy had no ships wherewith to molest them, they were able from very small beginnings to attain to that greatness they now enjoy.

In the second case, namely of a city being founded by strangers, the settlers are either wholly independent, or they are controlled by others, as where colonies are sent forth either by a prince or by a republic, to relieve their countries of an excessive population, or to defend newly acquired territories which it is sought to secure at small cost. Of this sort many cities were settled by the Romans, and in all parts of their dominions. It may also happen that such cities are founded by a prince merely to add to his renown, without any intention on his part to dwell there, as Alexandria was built by Alexander the Great. Cities like these, not having had their beginning in freedom, seldom make such progress as to rank among the chief towns of kingdoms.

The city of Florence belongs to that class of towns which has not been independent from the first; for whether we ascribe its origin to the soldiers of Sylla, or, as some have conjectured, to the mountaineers of Fiesole (who, emboldened by the long peace which prevailed throughout the world during the reign of Octavianus, came down to occupy the plain on the banks of the Arno), in either case, it was founded under the auspices of Rome nor could, at first, make other progress than was permitted by the grace of the sovereign State.

The origin of cities may be said to be independent when a people, either by themselves or under some prince, are constrained by famine, pestilence, or war to leave their native land and seek a new habitation. Settlers of this sort either establish themselves in cities which they find ready to their hand in the countries of which they take possession, as did Moses; or they build new ones, as did AEneas. It is in this last case that the merits of a founder and the good fortune of the city founded are best seen; and this good fortune will be more or less remarkable according to the greater or less capacity of him who gives the city its beginning.

The capacity of a founder is known in two ways: by his choice of a site, or by the laws which he frames. And since men act either of necessity or from choice, and merit may seem greater where choice is more restricted, we have to consider whether it may not be well to choose a sterile district as the site of a new city, in order that the inhabitants, being constrained to industry, and less corrupted by ease, may live in closer union, finding less cause for division in the poverty of their land; as was the case in Ragusa, and in many other cities built in similar situations. Such a choice were certainly the wisest and the most advantageous, could men be content to enjoy what is their own without seeking to lord it over others. But since to be safe they must be strong, they are compelled avoid these barren districts, and to plant themselves in more fertile regions; where, the fruitfulness of the soil enabling them to increase and multiply, they may defend themselves against any who attack them, and overthrow any who would withstand their power.

And as for that languor which the situation might breed, care must be had that hardships which the site does not enforce, shall be enforced by the laws; and that the example of those wise nations be imitated, who, inhabiting most fruitful and delightful countries, and such as were likely to rear a listless and effeminate race, unfit for all manly exercises, in order to obviate the mischief wrought by the amenity and relaxing influence of the soil and climate, subjected all who were to serve as soldiers to the severest training; whence it came that better soldiers were raised in these countries than in others by nature rugged and barren. Such, of old, was the kingdom of the Egyptians, which, though of all lands the most bountiful, yet, by the severe training which its laws enforced, produced most valiant soldiers, who, had their names not been lost in antiquity, might be thought to deserve more praise than Alexander the Great and many besides, whose memory is still fresh in men's minds. And even in recent times, any one contemplating the kingdom of the Soldan, and the military order of the Mamelukes before they were destroyed by Selim the Grand Turk, must have seen how carefully they trained their soldiers in every kind of warlike exercise; showing thereby how much they dreaded that indolence to which their genial soil and climate might have disposed them, unless neutralized by strenuous laws. I say, then, that it is a prudent choice to found your city in a fertile region when the effects of that fertility are duly balanced by the restraint of the laws.

When Alexander the Great thought to add to his renown by founding a city, Dinocrates the architect came and showed him how he might build it on Mount Athos, which not only offered a strong position, but could be handled that the city built there might present a semblance of the human form, which would be a thing strange and striking, and worthy of so great a monarch. But on Alexander asking how the inhabitants were to live, Dinocrates answered that he had not thought of that. Whereupon, Alexander laughed, and leaving Mount Athos as it stood, built Alexandria; where, the fruitfulness of the soil, and the vicinity of the Nile and the sea, might attract many to take up their abode.

To him, therefore, who inquires into the origin of Rome, if he assign its beginning to AEneas, it will seem to be of those cities which were founded by strangers if to Romulus, then of those founded by the natives of the country. But in whichever class we place it, it will be seen to have had its beginning in freedom, and not in subjection to another State. It will be seen, too, as hereafter shall be noted, how strict was the discipline which the laws instituted by Romulus, Numa, and its other founders made compulsory upon it; so that neither its fertility, the proximity of the sea, the number of its victories, nor the extent of its dominion, could for many centuries corrupt it, but, on the contrary, maintained it replete with such virtues as were never matched in any other commonwealth.

And because the things done by Rome, and which Titus Livius has celebrated, were effected at home or abroad by public or by private wisdom, I shall begin by treating, and noting the consequences of those things done at home in accordance with the public voice, which seem most to merit attention; and to this object the whole of this first Book or first Part of my Discourses, shall be directed.

CHAPTER II

Of the various kinds of Government; and to which of them the Roman Commonwealth belonged.

I forego all discussion concerning those cities which at the outset have been dependent upon others, and shall speak only of those which from their earliest beginnings have stood entirely clear of all foreign control, being governed from the first as pleased themselves, whether as republics or as princedoms.

These as they have had different origins, so likewise have had different laws and institutions. For to some at their very first commencement, or not long after, laws have been given by a single legislator, and all at one time; like those given by Lycurgus to the Spartans; while to others they have been given at different times, as need rose or accident determined; as in the case of Rome. That republic, indeed, may be called happy, whose lot has been to have a founder so prudent as to provide for it laws under which it can continue to live securely, without need to amend them; as we find Sparta preserving hers for eight hundred years, without deterioration and without any dangerous disturbance. On the other hand, some measure of unhappiness attaches to the State which, not having yielded itself once for all into the hands of a single wise legislator, is obliged to recast its institutions for itself; and of such States, by far the most unhappy is that which is furthest removed from a sound system of government, by which I mean that its institutions lie wholly outside the path which might lead it to a true and perfect end. For it is scarcely possible that a State in this position can ever, by any chance, set itself to rights, whereas another whose institutions are imperfect, if it have made a good beginning and such as admits of its amendment, may in the course of events arrive at perfection. It is certain, however, that such States can never be reformed without great risk; for, as a rule, men will accept no new law altering the institutions of their State, unless the necessity for such a change be demonstrated; and since this necessity cannot arise without danger, the State may easily be overthrown before the new order of things is established. In proof whereof we may instance the republic of Florence, which was reformed in the year 1502, in consequence of the affair of Arezzo, but was ruined in 1512, in consequence of the affair of Prato.

Desiring, therefore, to discuss the nature of the government of Rome, and to ascertain the accidental circumstances which brought it to its perfection, I say, as has been said before by many who have written of Governments, that of these there are three forms, known by the names Monarchy, Aristocracy, and Democracy, and that those who give its institutions to a State have recourse to one or other of these three, according as it suits their purpose. Other, and, as many have thought, wiser teachers, will have it, that there are altogether six forms of government, three of them utterly bad, the other three good in themselves, but so readily corrupted that they too are apt to become hurtful. The good are the three above named; the bad, three others dependent upon these, and each so like that to which it is related, that it is easy to pass imperceptibly from the one to the other. For a Monarchy readily becomes a Tyranny, an Aristocracy an Oligarchy, while a Democracy tends to degenerate into Anarchy. So that if the founder of a State should establish any one of these three forms of Government, he establishes it for a short time only, since no precaution he may take can prevent it from sliding into its contrary, by reason of the close resemblance which, in this case, the virtue bears to the vice.

These diversities in the form of Government spring up among men by chance. For in the beginning of the world, its inhabitants, being few in number, for a time lived scattered after the fashion of beasts; but afterwards, as they increased and multiplied, gathered themselves into societies, and, the better to protect themselves, began to seek who among them was the strongest and of the highest courage, to whom, making him their head, they tendered obedience. Next arose the knowledge of such things as are honourable and good, as opposed to those which are bad and shameful. For observing that when a man wronged his benefactor, hatred was universally felt for the one and sympathy for the other, and that the ungrateful were blamed, while those who showed gratitude were honoured, and reflecting that the wrongs they saw done to others might be done to themselves, to escape these they resorted to making laws and fixing punishments against any who should transgress them; and in this way grew the recognition of Justice. Whence it came that afterwards, in choosing their rulers, men no longer looked about for the strongest, but for him who was the most prudent and the most just.

But, presently, when sovereignty grew to be hereditary and no longer elective, hereditary sovereigns began to degenerate from their ancestors, and, quitting worthy courses, took up the notion that princes had nothing to do but to surpass the rest of the world in sumptuous display and wantonness, and whatever else ministers to pleasure so that the prince coming to be hated, and therefore to feel fear, and passing from fear to infliction of injuries, a tyranny soon sprang up. Forthwith there began movements to overthrow the prince, and plots and conspiracies against him undertaken not by those who were weak, or afraid for themselves, but by such as being conspicuous for their birth, courage, wealth, and station, could not tolerate the shameful life of the tyrant. The multitude, following the lead of these powerful men, took up arms against the prince and, he being got rid of, obeyed these others as their liberators; who, on their part, holding in hatred the name of sole ruler, formed themselves into a government and at first, while the recollection of past tyranny was still fresh, observed the laws they themselves made, and postponing personal advantage to the common welfare, administered affairs both publicly and privately with the utmost diligence and zeal. But this government passing, afterwards, to their descendants who, never having been taught in the school of Adversity, knew nothing of the vicissitudes of Fortune, these not choosing to rest content with mere civil equality, but abandoning themselves to avarice, ambition, and lust, converted, without respect to civil rights what had been a government of the best into a government of the few; and so very soon met with the same fate as the tyrant.

For the multitude loathing its rulers, lent itself to any who ventured, in whatever way, to attack them; when some one man speedily arose who with the aid of the people overthrew them. But the recollection of the tyrant and of the wrongs suffered at his hands being still fresh in the minds of the people, who therefore felt no desire to restore the monarchy, they had recourse to a popular government, which they established on such a footing that neither king nor nobles had any place in it. And because all governments inspire respect at the first, this government also lasted for a while, but not for long, and seldom after the generation which brought it into existence had died out. For, suddenly, liberty passed into license, wherein neither private worth nor public authority was respected, but, every one living as he liked, a thousand wrongs were done daily. Whereupon, whether driven by necessity, or on the suggestion of some wiser man among them and to escape anarchy, the people reverted to a monarchy, from which, step by step, in the manner and for the causes already assigned, they came round once more to license. For this is the circle revolving within which all States are and have been governed; although in the same State the same forms of Government rarely repeat themselves, because hardly any State can have such vitality as to pass through such a cycle more than once, and still together. For it may be expected that in some sea of disaster, when a State must always be wanting prudent counsels and in strength, it will become subject to some neighbouring and better-governed State; though assuming this not to happen, it might well pass for an indefinite period from one of these forms of government to another.

I say, then, that all these six forms of government are pernicious — the three good kinds, from their brief duration the three bad, from their inherent badness. Wise legislators therefore, knowing these defects, and avoiding each of these forms in its simplicity, have made choice of a form which shares in the qualities of all the first three, and which they judge to be more stable and lasting than any of these separately. For where we have a monarchy, an aristocracy, and a democracy existing together in the same city, each of the three serves as a check upon the other.

Among those who have earned special praise by devising a constitution of this nature, was Lycurgus, who so framed the laws of Sparta as to assign their proper functions to kings, nobles, and commons; and in this way established a government, which, to his great glory and to the peace and tranquility of his country, lasted for more than eight hundred years. The contrary, however, happened in the case of Solon; who by the turn he gave to the institutions of Athens, created there a purely democratic government, of such brief duration, that I himself lived to witness the beginning of the despotism of Pisistratus. And although, forty years later, the heirs of Pisistratus were driven out, and Athens recovered her freedom, nevertheless because she reverted to the same form government as had been established by Solon, she could maintain it for only a hundred years more; for though to preserve it, many ordinances were passed for repressing the ambition of the great and the turbulence of the people, against which Solon had not provided, still, since neither the monarchic nor the aristocratic element was given a place in her constitution, Athens, as compared with Sparta, had but a short life.

But let us now turn to Rome, which city, although she had no Lycurgus to give her from the first such a constitution as would preserve her long in freedom, through a series of accidents, caused by the contests between the commons and the senate, obtained by chance what the foresight of her founders failed to provide. So that Fortune, if she bestowed not her first favours on Rome, bestowed her second; because, although the original institutions of this city were defective, still they lay not outside the true path which could bring them to perfection. For Romulus and the other kings made many and good laws, and such as were not incompatible with freedom; but because they sought to found a kingdom and not a commonwealth, when the city became free many things were found wanting which in the interest of liberty it was necessary to supply, since these kings had not supplied them.

And although the kings of Rome lost their sovereignty, in the manner and for the causes mentioned above, nevertheless those who drove them out, by at once creating two consuls to take their place, preserved in Rome the regal authority while banishing from it the regal throne, so that as both senate and consuls were included in that republic, it in fact possessed two of the elements above enumerated, to wit, the monarchic and the aristocratic.

It then only remained to assign its place to the popular element, and the Roman nobles growing insolent from causes which shall be noticed hereafter, the commons against them, when, not to lose the whole of their power, they were forced to concede a share to the people; while with the share which remained, the senate and consuls retained so much authority that they still held their own place in the republic. In this way the tribunes of the people came to be created, after whose creation the stability of the State was much augmented, since each the three forms of government had now its due influence allowed it. And such was the good fortune of Rome that although her government passed from the kings to the nobles, and from these to the people, by the steps and for the reasons noticed above, still the entire authority of the kingly element was not sacrificed to strengthen the authority of the nobles, nor were the nobles divested of their authority to bestow it on the commons; but three, blending together, made up a perfect State; which perfection, as shall be fully shown in the next two Chapters, was reached through the dissensions of the commons and the senate.

CHAPTER III

Of the Accidents which led in Rome to the creation of Tribunes of the People; whereby the Republic was made more perfect.

They who lay the foundations of a State and furnish it with laws must, as is shown by all who have treated of civil government, and by examples of which history is full, assume that 'all men are bad, and will always, when they have free field, give loose to their evil inclinations; and that if these for a while remain hidden, it is owing to some secret cause, which, from our having no contrary experience, we do not recognize at once, but which is afterwards revealed by Time, of whom we speak as the father of all truth.

In Rome, after the expulsion of the Tarquins, it seemed as though the closest union prevailed between the senate and the commons, and that the nobles, laying aside their natural arrogance, had learned so to sympathize with the people as to have become supportable by all, even of the humblest rank. This dissimulation remained undetected, and its causes concealed, while the Tarquins lived; for the nobles dreading the Tarquins, and fearing that the people, if they used them ill, might take part against them, treated them with kindness. But no sooner were the Tarquins got rid of, and the nobles thus relieved of their fears, when they began to spit forth against the commons all the venom which before they had kept in their breasts, offending and insulting them in every way they could; confirming what I have observed already, that men never behave well unless compelled, and that whenever they are free to act as they please, and are under no restraint everything falls at once into confusion and disorder. Wherefore it has been said that as poverty and hunger are needed to make men industrious, so laws are needed to make them good. When we do well without laws, laws are not needed; but when good customs are absent, laws are at once required.

On the extinction of the Tarquins, therefore, the dread of whom had kept the nobles in check, some new safeguard had to be contrived, which should effect the same result as had been effected by the Tarquins while they lived. Accordingly, after much uproar and confusion, and much danger of violence ensuing between the commons and the nobles, to insure the safety of the former, tribunes were created, and were invested with such station and authority as always afterwards enabled them to stand between the people and the senate, and to resist the insolence of the nobles.

CHAPTER IV

That the Dissensions between the Senate and Commons of Rome, made Rome free and powerful.

Touching those tumults which prevailed in Rome from the extinction of the Tarquins to the creation of the tribunes the discussion of which I have no wish to avoid, and as to certain other matters of a like nature, I desire to say something in opposition to the opinion of many who assert that Rome was a turbulent city, and had fallen into utter disorder, that had not her good fortune and military prowess made amends for other defects, she would have been inferior to every other republic.

I cannot indeed deny that the good fortune and the armies of Rome were the causes of her empire; yet it certainly seems to me that those holding this opinion fail to perceive, that in a State where there are good soldiers there must be good order, and, generally speaking, good fortune. And looking to the other circumstances of this city, I affirm that those who condemn these dissensions between the nobles and the commons, condemn what was the prime cause of Rome becoming free; and give more heed to the tumult and uproar wherewith these dissensions were attended, than to the good results which followed from them; not reflecting that while in every republic there are two conflicting factions, that of the people and that of the nobles, it is in this conflict that all laws favourable to freedom have their origin, as may readily be seen to have been the case in Rome. For from the time of the Tarquins to that of the Gracchi, a period of over three hundred years, the tumults in Rome seldom gave occasion to punishment by exile, and very seldom to bloodshed. So that we cannot truly declare those tumults to have been disastrous, or that republic to have been disorderly, which during all that time, on account of her internal broils, banished no more than eight or ten of her citizens, put very few to death, and rarely inflicted money penalties. Nor can we reasonably pronounce that city ill-governed wherein we find so many instances of virtue; for virtuous actions have their origin in right training, right training in wise laws, and wise laws in these very tumults which many would thoughtlessly condemn. For he who looks well to the results of these tumults will find that they did not lead to banishments, nor to violence hurtful to the common good, but to laws and ordinances beneficial to the public liberty. And should any object that the behaviour of the Romans was extravagant and outrageous; that for the assembled people to be heard shouting against the senate, the senate against the people; for the whole commons to be seen rushing wildly through the streets, closing their shops, and quitting the town, were things which might well affright him even who only reads of them; it may be answered, that the inhabitants of all cities, more especially of cities which seek to make use of the people in matters of importance, have their own ways of giving expression to their wishes; among which the city of Rome had the custom, that when its people sought to have a law passed they followed one or another of those courses mentioned above, or else refused to be enrolled as soldiers when, to pacify them, something of their demands had to be conceded. But the demands of a free people are hurtful to freedom, since they originate either in being oppressed, or in the fear that they are about to be so. When this fear is groundless, it finds its remedy in public meetings, wherein some worthy person may come forward and show the people by argument that they are deceiving themselves. For though they be ignorant, the people are not therefore, as Cicero says, incapable of being taught the truth, but are readily convinced when it is told them by one in whose honesty they can trust.

We should, therefore, be careful how we censure the government of Rome, and should reflect that all the great results effected by that republic, could not have come about without good cause. And if the popular tumults led the creation of the tribunes, they merit all praise; since these magistrates not only gave its due influence to the popular voice in the government, but also acted as the guardians of Roman freedom, as shall be clearly shown in the following Chapter.

CHAPTER V

Whether the Guardianship of public Freedom is safer in the hands of the Commons or of the Nobles; and whether those who seek to acquire Power or they who seek to maintain it are the greater cause of Commotions.

Of the provisions made by wise founders of republics, one of the most necessary is for the creation of a guardianship of liberty; for according as this is placed in good or bad hands, the freedom of the State will be more or less lasting. And because in every republic we find the two parties of nobles and commons, the question arises, to which of these two this guardianship can most safely be entrusted. Among the Lacedaemonians of old, as now with the Venetians, it was placed in the hands of the nobles, but with the Romans it was vested in the commons. We have, therefore, to determine which of these States made the wiser choice. If we look to reasons, something is to be said on both sides of the question; though were we to look to results, we should have to pronounce in favour of the nobles, inasmuch as the liberty of Sparta and Venice has had a longer life than that of Rome.

As touching reasons, it may be pleaded for the Roman method, that they are most fit to have charge of a thing, who least desire to pervert it to their own ends. And, doubtless, if we examine the aims which the nobles and the commons respectively set before them, we shall find in the former a great desire to dominate, in the latter merely a desire not to be dominated over, and hence a greater attachment to freedom, since they have less to gain than the others by destroying it. Wherefore, when the commons are put forward as the defenders of liberty, they may be expected to take better care of it, and, as they have no desire to tamper with it themselves, to be less apt to suffer others to do so.

On the other hand, he who defends the method followed by the Spartans and Venetians, may urge, that by confiding this guardianship to the nobles, two desirable ends are served: first, that from being allowed to retain in their own hands a weapon which makes them the stronger party in the State, the ambition of this class is more fully satisfied; and, second, that an authority is withdrawn from the unstable multitude which as used by them is likely to lead to endless disputes and tumults, and to drive the nobles into dangerous and desperate courses. In instance whereof might be cited the case of Rome itself, wherein the tribunes of the people being vested with this authority, not content to have one consul a plebeian, insisted on having both; and afterwards laid claim to the censorship, the praetorship and all the other magistracies in the city. Nor was this enough for them, but, carried away by the same factious spirit, they began after a time to pay court to such men as they thought able to attack the nobility, and so gave occasion to the rise of Marius and the overthrow of Rome.

Wherefore one who weighs both sides of the question well, might hesitate which party he should choose as the guardian of public liberty, being uncertain which class is more mischievous in a commonwealth, that which would acquire what it has not, or that which would keep the authority which it has already. But, on the whole, on a careful balance of arguments we may sum up thus: — Either we have to deal with a republic eager like Rome to extend its power, or with one content merely to maintain itself; in the former case it is necessary to do in all things as Rome did; in the latter, for the reasons and in the manner to be shown in the following Chapter, we may imitate Venice and Sparta.

But reverting to the question which class of citizens is more mischievous in a republic, those who seek to acquire or those who fear to lose what they have acquired already, I note that when Marcus Menenius and Marcus Fulvius, both of them men of plebeian birth, were made the one dictator, the other master of the knights, that they might inquire into certain plots against Rome contrived in Capua, they had at the same time authority given them by the people to investigate whether, in Rome itself, irregular and corrupt practices had been used to obtain the consulship and other honours of the city. The nobles suspecting that the powers thus conferred were to be turned against them, everywhere gave out that if honours had been sought by any by irregular and unworthy means, it was not by them, but by the plebeians, who, with neither birth nor merit to recommend them, had need to resort to corruption. And more particularly they accused the dictator himself. And so telling was the effect of these charges, that Menenius, after haranguing the people and complaining to them of the calumnies circulated against him, laid down his dictatorship, and submitted himself to whatever judgment might be passed upon him. When his cause came to be tried he was acquitted; but at the hearing it was much debated, whether he who would retain power or he who would acquire it, is the more dangerous citizen; the desires of both being likely to lead to the greatest disorders.

Nevertheless, I believe that, as a rule, disorders are more commonly occasioned by those seeking to preserve power, because in them the fear of loss breeds the same passions as are felt by those seeking to acquire; since men never think they hold what they have securely, unless when they are gaining something new from others. It is also to be said that their position enables them to operate changes with less effort and greater efficacy. Further, it may be added, that their corrupt and insolent behaviour inflames the minds of those who have nothing, with the desire to have; either for the sake of punishing their adversaries by despoiling them, or to obtain for themselves a share of those riches and honours which they see the others abuse.

CHAPTER VI

Whether it was possible in Rome to contrive such a Government as would have composed the Differences between the Commons and the Senate.

I have spoken above of the effects produced in Rome by the controversies between the commons and the senate. Now, as these lasted down to the time of the Gracchi, when they brought about the overthrow of freedom, some may think it matter for regret that Rome should not have achieved the great things she did, without being torn by such disputes. Wherefore, it seems to me worth while to consider whether the government of Rome could ever have been constituted in such a way as to prevent like controversies.

In making this inquiry we must first look to those republics which have enjoyed freedom for a great while, undisturbed by any violent contentions or tumults, and see what their government was, and whether it would have been possible to introduce it into Rome. Of such republics we have an example in ancient times in Sparta, in modern times in Venice, of both which States I have already made mention. Sparta created for herself a government consisting of a king and a limited senate. Venice has made no distinction in the titles of her rulers, all qualified to take part in her government being classed under the one designation of "Gentlemen," an arrangement due rather to chance than to the foresight of those who gave this State its constitution. For many persons, from causes already noticed, seeking shelter on these rocks on which Venice now stands, after they had so multiplied that if they were to continue to live together it became necessary for them to frame laws, established a form of government; and assembling often in their councils to consult for the interests of their city, when it seemed to them that their numbers were sufficient for political existence, they closed the entrance to civil rights against all who came afterwards to live there, not allowing them to take any part in the management of affairs. And when in course of time there came to be many citizens excluded from the government, to add to the importance of the governing body, they named these "Gentlemen" (*gentiluomini*), the others "Plebeians" (*popolani*). And this distinction could grow up and maintain itself without causing disturbance; for as at the time of its origin, whosoever then lived in Venice was made one of the governing body, none had reason to complain; while those who came to live there afterwards, finding the government in a completed form, had neither ground nor opportunity to object. No ground, because nothing was taken from them; and no opportunity, because those in authority kept them under control, and never employed them in affairs in which they could acquire importance. Besides which, they who came later to dwell in Venice were not so numerous as to destroy all proportion between the governors and the governed; the number of the "Gentlemen" being as great as, or greater than that of the "Plebeians." For these reasons, therefore, it was possible for Venice to make her constitution what it is, and to maintain it without divisions.

Sparta, again, being governed, as I have said, by a king and a limited senate, was able to maintain herself for the long period she did, because, from the country being thinly inhabited and further influx of population forbidden, and from the laws of Lycurgus (the observance whereof removed all ground of disturbance) being held in high esteem, the citizens were able to continue long in unity. For Lycurgus having by his laws established in Sparta great equality as to property, but less equality as to rank, there prevailed there an equal poverty; and the commons were less ambitious, because the offices of the State, which were held to their exclusion, were confined to a few; and because the nobles never by harsh treatment aroused in them any desire to usurp these offices. And this was due to the Spartan kings, who, being appointed to that dignity for life, and placed in the midst of this nobility, had no stronger support to their authority than in defending the people against injustice. Whence it resulted that as the people neither feared nor coveted the power which they did not possess, the conflicts which might have arisen between them and the nobles were escaped, together with the causes which would have led to them; and in this way they were able to live long united. But of this unity in Sparta there were two chief causes: one, the fewness of its inhabitants, which allowed of their being governed by a few; the other, that by denying foreigners admission into their country, the people had less occasion to become corrupted, and never so increased in numbers as to prove troublesome to their few rulers.

Weighing all which circumstances, we see that to have kept Rome in the same tranquility wherein these republics were kept, one of two courses must have been followed by her legislators; for either, like the Venetians, they must have refrained from employing the commons in war, or else, like the Spartans, they must have closed their country to foreigners. Whereas, in both particulars, they did the opposite, arming the commons and increasing their number, and thus affording endless occasions for disorder. And had the Roman commonwealth grown to be more tranquil, this inconvenience would have resulted, that it must at the same time have grown weaker, since the road would have been closed to that greatness to which it came, for in removing the causes of her tumults, Rome must have interfered with the causes of her growth.

And he who looks carefully into the matter will find, that in all human affairs, we cannot rid ourselves of one inconvenience without running into another. So that if you would have your people numerous and warlike, to the end that with their aid you may establish a great empire, you will have them of such a sort as you cannot afterwards control at your pleasure; while should you keep them few and unwarlike, to the end that you may govern them easily, you will be unable, should you extend your dominions, to preserve them, and will become so contemptible as to be the prey of any who attack you. For which reason in all our deliberations we ought to consider where we are likely to encounter least inconvenience, and accept that as the course to be preferred, since we shall never find any line of action entirely free from disadvantage.

Rome might, therefore, following the example of Sparta, have created a king for life and a senate of limited numbers, but desiring to become a great empire, she could not, like Sparta, have restricted the number of her citizens. So that to have created a king for life and a limited senate had been of little service to her.

Were any one, therefore, about to found a wholly new republic, he would have to consider whether he desired it to increase as Rome did in territory and dominion, or to continue within narrow limits. In the former case he would have to shape its constitution as nearly as possible on the pattern of the Roman, leaving room for dissensions and popular tumults, for without a great and warlike population no republic can ever increase, or increasing maintain itself. In the second case he might give his republic a constitution like that of Venice or Sparta; but since extension is the ruin of such republics, the legislator would have to provide in every possible way against the State which he had founded making any additions to its territories. For these, when superimposed upon a feeble republic, are sure to be fatal to it: as we see to have been the case with Sparta and Venice, the former of which, after subjugating nearly all Greece, on sustaining a trifling reverse, betrayed the insufficiency of her foundations, for when, after the revolt of Thebes under Pelopidas, other cities also rebelled, the Spartan kingdom was utterly overthrown. Venice in like manner, after gaining possession of a great portion of Italy (most of it not by her arms but by her wealth and subtlety), when her strength was put to the proof, lost all in one pitched battle.

I can well believe, then, that to found a republic which shall long endure, the best plan may be to give it internal institutions like those of Sparta or Venice; placing it in a naturally strong situation, and so fortifying it that none can expect to get the better of it easily, yet, at the same time, not making it so great as to be formidable to its neighbours; since by taking these precautions, it might long enjoy its independence. For there are two causes which lead to wars being made against a republic; one, your desire to be its master, the other the fear lest it should master you; both of which dangers the precaution indicated will go far to remove. For if, as we are to assume, this republic be well prepared for defence, and consequently difficult of attack, it will seldom or never happen that any one will form the design to attack it, and while it keeps within its own boundaries, and is seen from experience not to be influenced by ambition, no one will be led, out of fear for himself, to make war upon it, more particularly when its laws and constitution forbid its extension. And were it possible to maintain things in this equilibrium, I veritably believe that herein would be found the true form of political life, and the true tranquility of a republic. But all human affairs being in movement, and incapable of remaining as they are, they must either rise or fall; and to many conclusions to which we are not led by reason, we are brought by necessity. So that when we have given institutions to a State on the footing that it is to maintain itself without enlargement, should necessity require its enlargement, its foundations will be cut from below it, and its downfall quickly ensue. On the other hand, were a republic so favoured by Heaven as to lie under no necessity of making war, the result of this ease would be to make it effeminate and divided which two evils together, and each by itself, would insure its ruin. And since it is impossible, as I believe, to bring about an equilibrium, or to adhere strictly to the mean path, we must, in arranging our republic, consider what is the more honourable course for it to take, and so contrive that even if necessity compel its enlargement, it may be able to keep what it gains.

But returning to the point first raised, I believe it necessary for us to follow the method of the Romans and not that of the other republics, for I know of no middle way. We must, consequently, put up with those dissensions which arise between commons and senate, looking on them as evils which cannot be escaped if we would arrive at the greatness of Rome.

In connection with the arguments here used to prove that the authority of the tribunes was essential in Rome to the guardianship of freedom, we may naturally go on to show what advantages result to a republic from the power of impeachment; which, together with others, was conferred upon the tribunes; a subject to be noticed in the following Chapter.

CHAPTER VII

That to preserve Liberty in a State there must exist the Right to accuse.

To those set forward in a commonwealth as guardians of public freedom, no more useful or necessary authority can be given than the power to accuse, either before the people, or before some council or tribunal, those citizens who in any way have offended against the liberty of their country.

A law of this kind has two effects most beneficial to a State: *first,* that the citizens from fear of being accused, do not engage in attempts hurtful to the State, or doing so, are put down at once and without respect of persons: and *next,* that a vent is given for the escape of all those evil humours which, from whatever cause, gather in cities against particular citizens; for unless an outlet be duly provided for these by the laws, they flow into irregular channels and overwhelm the State. There is nothing, therefore, which contributes so much to the stability and permanence of a State, as to take care that the fermentation of these disturbing humours be supplied by operation of law with a recognized outlet. This might be shown by many examples, but by none so clearly as by that of Coriolanus related by Livius, where he tells us, that at a time when the Roman nobles were angry with the plebeians (thinking that the appointment of tribunes for their protection had made them too powerful), it happened that Rome was visited by a grievous famine, to meet which the senate sent to Sicily for corn. But Coriolanus, hating the commons, sought to persuade the senate that now was the time to punish them, and to deprive them of the authority which they had usurped to the prejudice of the nobles, by withholding the distribution of corn, and so suffering them to perish of hunger. Which advice of his coming to the ears of the people, kindled them to such fury against him, that they would have slain him as he left the Senate House, had not the tribunes cited him to appear and answer before them to a formal charge.

In respect of this incident I repeat what I have just now said, how useful and necessary it is for republics to provide by their laws a channel by which the displeasure of the multitude against a single citizen may find a vent. For when none such is regularly provided, recourse will be had to irregular channels, and these will assuredly lead to much worse results. For when a citizen is borne down by the operation or the ordinary laws, even though he be wronged, little or no disturbance is occasioned to the state: the injury he suffers not being wrought by private violence, nor by foreign force, which are the causes of the overthrow of free institutions, but by public authority and in accordance with public ordinances, which, having definite limits set them, are not likely to pass beyond these so as to endanger the commonwealth. For proof of which I am content to rest on this old example of Coriolanus, since all may see what a disaster it would have been for Rome had he been violently put to death by the people. For, as between citizen and citizen, a wrong would have been done affording ground for fear, fear would have sought defence, defence have led to faction, faction to divisions in the State, and these to its ruin. But the matter being taken up by those whose office it was to deal with it, all the evils which must have followed had it been left in private hands were escaped.

In Florence, on the other hand, and in our own days, we have seen what violent commotions follow when the people cannot show their displeasure against particular citizens in a form recognized by the laws, in the instance of Francesco Valori, at one time looked upon as the foremost citizen of our republic. But many thinking him ambitious, and likely from his high spirit and daring to overstep the limits of civil freedom, and there being no way to oppose him save by setting up an adverse faction, the result was, that, apprehending irregular attacks, he sought to gain partisans for his support; while his opponents, on their side, having no course open to them of which the laws approved, resorted to courses of which the laws did not approve, and, at last, to open violence. And as his influence had to be attacked by unlawful methods, these were attended by injury not to him only, but to many other noble citizens; whereas, could he have been met by constitutional restraints, his power might have been broken without injury to any save himself. I might also cite from our Florentine history the fall of Piero Soderini, which had no other cause than there not being in our republic any law under which powerful and ambitious citizens can be impeached. For to form a tribunal by which a powerful citizen is to be tried, eight judges only are not enough; the judges must be numerous, because a few will always do the will of a few. But had there been proper methods for obtaining redress, either the people would have impeached Piero if he was guilty, and thus have given vent to their displeasure without calling in the Spanish army; or if he was innocent, would not have ventured, through fear of being accused themselves, to have taken proceedings against him. So that in either case the bitter spirit which was the cause of all the disorder would have had an end. Wherefore, when we find one of the parties in a State calling in a foreign power, we may safely conclude that it is because the defective laws of that State provide no escape for those malignant humours which are natural to men; which can best be done by arranging for an impeachment before a sufficient number of judges, and by giving countenance to this procedure. This was so well contrived in Rome that in spite of the perpetual struggle maintained between the commons and the senate, neither the senate nor the commons, nor any single citizen, ever sought redress at the hands of a foreign power; for having a remedy at home, there was no need to seek one abroad.

Although the examples above cited be proof sufficient of what I affirm, I desire to adduce one other, recorded by Titus Livius in his history, where he relates that a sister of Aruns having been violated by a Lucumo of Clusium, the chief of the Etruscan towns, Aruns being unable, from the interest of her ravisher, to avenge her, betook himself to the Gauls who ruled in the province we now name Lombardy, and besought them to come with an armed force to Clusium; showing them how with advantage to themselves they might avenge his wrongs. Now, had Aruns seen that he could have had redress through the laws of his country, he never would have resorted to these Barbarians for help.

But as the right to accuse is beneficial in a republic, so calumny, on the other hand, is useless and hurtful, as in the following Chapter I shall proceed to show.

CHAPTER VIII

That Calumny is as hurtful in a Commonwealth as the power to accuse is useful.

Such were the services rendered to Rome by Furius Camillus in rescuing her from the oppression of the Gauls, that no Roman, however high his degree or station, held it derogatory to yield place to him, save only Manlius Capitolinus, who could not brook such glory and distinction being given to another. For he thought that in saving the Capitol, he had himself done as much as Camillus to preserve Rome, and that in respect of his other warlike achievements he was no whit behind him. So that, bursting with jealousy, and unable to remain at rest by reason of the other's renown, and seeing no way to sow discord among the Fathers, he set himself to spread abroad sinister reports among the commons; throwing out, among other charges, that the treasure collected to be given to the Gauls, but which, afterwards, was withheld, had been embezzled by certain citizens, and if recovered might be turned to public uses in relieving the people from taxes or from private debts. These assertions so prevailed with the commons that they began to hold meetings and to raise what tumults they liked throughout the city. But this displeasing the senate, and the matter appearing to them grave and dangerous, they appointed a dictator to inquire into it, and to restrain the attacks of Manlius. The dictator, forthwith, caused Manlius to be cited before him; and these two were thus brought face to face in the presence of the whole city, the dictator surrounded by the nobles, and Manlius by the commons. The latter, being desired to say with whom the treasure of which he had spoken was to be found, since the senate were as anxious to know this as the commons, made no direct reply, but answered evasively that it was needless to tell them what they already knew. Whereupon the dictator ordered him to prison.

In this passage we are taught how hateful a thing is calumny in all free States, as, indeed, in every society, and how we must neglect no means which may serve to check it. And there can be no more effectual means for checking calumny than by affording ample facilities for impeachment, which is as useful in a commonwealth as the other is pernicious. And between them there is this difference, that calumny needs neither witness, nor circumstantial proof to establish it, so that any man may be calumniated by any other; but not impeached; since impeachment demands that there be substantive charges made, and trustworthy evidence to support them. Again, it is before the magistrates, the people, or the courts of justice that men are impeached; but in the streets and market places that they are calumniated. Calumny, therefore, is most rife in that State wherein impeachment is least practised, and the laws least favour it. For which reasons the legislator should so shape the laws of his State that it shall be possible therein to impeach any of its citizens without fear or favour; and, after duly providing for this, should visit calumniators with the sharpest punishments. Those punished will have no cause to complain, since it was in their power to have impeached openly where they have secretly calumniated. Where this is not seen to, grave disorders will always ensue. For calumnies sting without disabling; and those who are stung being more moved by hatred of their detractors than by fear of the things they say against them, seek revenge.

This matter, as we have said, was well arranged for in Rome, but has always been badly regulated in our city of Florence. And as the Roman ordinances with regard to it were productive of much good, so the want of them in Florence has bred much mischief. For any one reading the history of our city may perceive, how many calumnies have at all times been aimed against those of its citizens who have taken a leading part in its affairs. Thus, of one it would be said that he had plundered the public treasury, of another, that he had failed in some enterprise because he had been bribed; of a third, that this or the other disaster had originated in his ambition. Hence hatred sprung up on every side, and hatred growing to division, these led to factions, and these again to ruin. But had there existed in Florence some procedure whereby citizens might have been impeached, and calumniators punished, numberless disorders which have taken there would have been prevented. For citizens who were impeached, whether condemned or acquitted, would have had no power to injure the State; and they would have been impeached far seldomer than they have been calumniated; for calumny, as I have said already, is an easier matter than impeachment.

Some, indeed, have made use of calumny as a means for raising themselves to power, and have found their advantage in traducing eminent citizens who withstood their designs; for by taking the part of the people, and confirming them in their ill-opinion of these great men, they made them their friends. Of this, though I could give many instances, I shall content myself with one. At the siege of Lucca the Florentine army was commanded by Messer Giovanni Guicciardini, as its commissary, through whose bad generalship or ill-fortune the town was not taken. But whatever the cause of this failure, Messer Giovanni had the blame; and the rumour ran that he had been bribed by the people of Lucca. Which calumny being fostered by his enemies, brought Messer Giovanni to very verge of despair; and though to clear himself he would willingly have given himself up to the Captain of Justice he found he could not, there being no provision in the laws of the republic which allowed of his doing so. Hence arose the bitterest hostility between the friends of Messer Giovanni, who were mostly of the old nobility (*grandi*), and those who sought to reform the government of Florence; and from this and the like causes, the affair grew to such dimensions as to bring about the downfall of our republic.

Manlius Capitolinus, then, was a calumniator, not an accuser; and in their treatment of him the Romans showed how calumniators should be dealt with; by which I mean, that they should be forced to become accusers; and if their accusation be proved true, should be rewarded, or at least not punished, but if proved false should be punished as Manlius was.

CHAPTER IX

That to give new Institutions to a Commonwealth, or to reconstruct old Institutions on an entirely new basis, must be the work of one Man.

It may perhaps be thought that I should not have got so far into the history of Rome, without some mention of those who gave that city its institutions, and saying something of these institutions themselves, so far as they relate to religion and war. As I have no wish to keep those who would know my views on these matters in suspense, I say at once, that to many it might seem of evil omen that the founder of a civil government like Romulus, should first have slain his brother, and afterwards have consented to the death of Titus Tatius the Sabine, whom he had chosen to be his colleague in the kingship; since his countrymen, if moved by ambition and lust of power to inflict like injuries on any who opposed their designs, might plead the example of their prince. This view would be a reasonable one were we to disregard the object which led Romulus to put those men to death. But we must take it as a rule to which there are very few if any exceptions, that no commonwealth or kingdom ever has salutary institutions given it from the first or has its institutions recast in an entirely new mould, unless by a single person. On the contrary, it must be from one man that it receives its institutions at first, and upon one man that all similar reconstruction must depend. For this reason the wise founder of a commonwealth who seeks to benefit not himself only, or the line of his descendants, but his State and country, must endeavour to acquire an absolute and undivided authority. And none who is wise will ever blame any action, however extraordinary and irregular, which serves to lay the foundation of a kingdom or to establish a republic. For although the act condemn the doer, the end may justify him; and when, as in the case of Romulus, the end is good, it will always excuse the means; since it is he who does violence with intent to injure, not he who does it with the design to secure tranquility, who merits blame. Such a person ought however to be so prudent and moderate as to avoid transmitting the absolute authority he acquires, as an inheritance to another; for as men are, by nature, more prone to evil than to good, a successor may turn to ambitious ends the power which his predecessor has used to promote worthy ends. Moreover, though it be one man that must give a State its institutions, once given they are not so likely to last long resting for support on the shoulders of one man only, as when entrusted to the care of many, and when it is the business of many to maintain them. For though the multitude be unfit to set a State in order, since they cannot, by reason of the divisions which prevail among them, agree wherein the true well-being of the State lies, yet when they have once been taught the truth, they never will consent to abandon it. And that Romulus, though he put his brother to death, is yet of those who are to be pardoned, since what he did was done for the common good and not from personal ambition, is shown by his at once creating a senate, with whom he took counsel, and in accordance with whose voice he determined. And whosoever shall well examine the authority which Romulus reserved to himself, will find that he reserved nothing beyond the command of the army when war was resolved on, and the right to assemble the senate. This is seen later, on Rome becoming free by the expulsion of the Tarquins, when the Romans altered none of their ancient institutions save in appointing two consuls for a year instead of a king for life; for this proves that all the original institutions of that city were more in conformity with a free and constitutional government, than with an absolute and despotic one.

In support of what has been said above, I might cite innumerable instances, as of Moses, Lycurgus, Solon, and other founders of kingdoms and commonwealths, who, from the full powers given them, were enabled to shape their laws to the public advantage; but passing over these examples, as of common notoriety, I take one, not indeed so famous, but which merits the attention of all who desire to frame wise laws. Agis, King of Sparta, desiring to bring back his countrymen to those limits within which the laws of Lycurgus had held them, because he thought that, from having somewhat deviated from them, his city had lost much of its ancient virtue and, consequently much of its strength and power, was, at the very outset of his attempts, slain by the Spartan Ephori, as one who sought to make himself a tyrant. But Cleomenes coming after him in the kingdom, and, on reading the notes and writings which he found of Agis wherein his designs and intentions were explained, being stirred by the same desire, perceived that he could not confer this benefit on his country unless he obtained sole power. For he saw that the ambition of others made it impossible for him to do what was useful for many against the will of a few. Wherefore, finding fit occasion, he caused the Ephori and all others likely to throw obstacles in his way, to be put to death; after which, he completely renewed the laws of Lycurgus. And the result of his measures would have been to give fresh life to Sparta, and to gain for himself a renown not inferior to that of Lycurgus, had it not been for the power of the Macedonians and the weakness of the other Greek States. For while engaged with these reforms, he was attacked by the Macedonians, and being by himself no match for them, and having none to whom he could turn for help, he was overpowered; and his plans, though wise and praiseworthy, were never brought to perfection.

    All which circumstances considered, I conclude that he who gives new institutions to a State must stand alone; and that for the deaths of Remus and Tatius, Romulus is to be excused rather than blamed.

CHAPTER X

That in proportion as the Founder of a Kingdom or Commonwealth merits Praise, he who founds a Tyranny deserves Blame.

Of all who are praised they are praised the most, who are the authors and founders of religions. After whom come the founders of kingdoms and commonwealths. Next to these, they have the greatest name who as commanders of armies have added to their own dominions or those of their country. After these, again, are ranked men of letters, who being of various shades of merit are celebrated each in his degree. To all others, whose number is infinite, is ascribed that measure of praise to which his profession or occupation entitles him. And, conversely, all who contribute to the overthrow of religion, or to the ruin of kingdoms and commonwealths, all who are foes to letters and to the arts which confer honour and benefit on the human race (among whom I reckon the impious, the cruel, the ignorant, the indolent, the base and the worthless), are held in infamy and detestation.

No one, whether he be wise or foolish, bad or good, if asked to choose between these two kinds of men, will ever be found to withhold praise from what deserves praise, or blame from what is to be blamed. And yet almost all, deceived by a false good and a false glory, allow themselves either ignorantly or wilfully to follow in the footsteps such as deserve blame rather than praise; and, have it in their power to establish, to their lasting renown, a commonwealth or kingdom, turn aside to create a tyranny without a thought how much they thereby lose in name, fame, security, tranquility, and peace of mind; and in name how much infamy, scorn, danger, and disquiet they are? But were they to read history, and turn to profit the lessons of the past, it seems impossible that those living in a republic as private citizens, should not prefer their native city, to play the part of Scipio rather of Caesar; or that those who by good fortune or merit have risen to be rulers, should not seek rather to resemble Agesilaus, Timoleon, and Dion, than to Nabis, Phalaris and Dionysius; since they would see how the latter are loaded with infamy, while the former have been extolled beyond bounds. They would see, too, how Timoleon and others like him, had as great authority in their country as Dionysius or Phalaris in theirs, while enjoying far greater security. Nor let any one finding Caesar celebrated by a crowd of writers, be misled by his glory; for those who praise him have been corrupted by good fortune, and overawed by the greatness of that empire which, being governed in his name, would not suffer any to speak their minds openly concerning him. But let him who desires to know how historians would have written of Caesar had they been free to declare their thoughts mark what they say of Catiline, than whom Caesar is more hateful, in proportion as he who does is more to be condemned than he who only desires to do evil. Let him see also what praises they lavish upon Brutus, because being unable, out of respect for his power, to reproach Caesar, they magnify his enemy. And if he who has become prince in any State will but reflect, how, after Rome was made an empire, far greater praise was earned those emperors who lived within the laws, and worthily, than by those who lived in the contrary way, he will see that Titus, Nerva, Trajan, Hadrian, Antoninus and Marcus had no need of praetorian cohorts, or of countless legions to guard them, but were defended by their own good lives, the good-will of their subjects, and the attachment of the senate. In like manner he will perceive in the case of Caligula, Nero, Vitellius, and ever so many more of those evil emperors, that all the armies of the east and of the west were of no avail to protect them from the enemies whom their bad and depraved lives raised up against them. And were the history of these emperors rightly studied, it would be a sufficient lesson to any prince how to distinguish the paths which lead to honour and safety from those which end in shame and insecurity. For of the twenty-six emperors from Caesar to Maximinus, sixteen came to a violent, ten only to a natural death; and though one or two of those who died by violence may have been good princes, as Galba or Pertinax, they met their fate in consequence of that corruption which their predecessors had left behind in the army. And if among those who died a natural death, there be found some bad emperors, like Severus, it is to be ascribed to their signal good fortune and to their great abilities, advantages seldom found united in the same man. From the study this history we may also learn how a good government is to be established; for while all the emperors who succeeded to the throne by birth, except Titus, were bad, all were good who succeeded by adoption; as in the case of the five from Nerva to Marcus. But so soon as the empire fell once more to the heirs by birth, its ruin recommenced.

Let a prince therefore look to that period which extends from Nerva to Marcus, and contrast it with that which went before and that which came after, and then let him say in which of them he would wish to have been born or to have reigned. For during these times in which good men governed, he will see the prince secure in the midst of happy subjects, and the whole world filled with peace and justice. He will find the senate maintaining its authority, the magistrates enjoying their honours, rich citizens their wealth, rank and merit held in respect, ease and content everywhere prevailing, rancour, licence corruption and ambition everywhere quenched, and that golden age restored in which every one might hold and support what opinions he pleased. He will see, in short, the world triumphing, the sovereign honoured and revered, the people animated with love, and rejoicing in their security. But should he turn to examine the times of the other emperors, he will find them wasted by battles, torn by seditions, cruel alike in war and peace; many princes perishing by the sword; many wars foreign and domestic; Italy overwhelmed with unheard-of disasters; her towns destroyed and plundered; Rome burned; the Capitol razed to the ground by Roman citizens; the ancient temples desolated; the ceremonies of religion corrupted; the cities rank with adultery; the seas covered with exiles and the islands polluted with blood. He will see outrage follow outrage; rank, riches, honours, and, above all, virtue imputed as mortal crimes; informers rewarded; slaves bribed to betray their masters, freedmen their patrons, and those who were without enemies brought to destruction by their friends; and then he will know the true nature of the debt which Rome, Italy, and the world owe to Caesar; and if he possess a spark of human feeling, will turn from the example of those evil times, and kindle with a consuming passion to imitate those which were good.

And in truth the prince who seeks for worldly glory should desire to be the ruler of a corrupt city; not that, like Caesar, he may destroy it, but that, like Romulus, he may restore it; since man cannot hope for, nor Heaven offer any better opportunity of fame. Were it indeed necessary in giving a constitution to a State to forfeit its sovereignty, the prince who, to retain his station, should withhold a constitution, might plead excuse; but for him who in giving a constitution can still retain his sovereignty, no excuse is to be made.

Let those therefore to whom Heaven has afforded this opportunity, remember that two courses lie open to them; one which will render them secure while they live and glorious when they die; another which exposes them to continual difficulties in life, and condemns them to eternal infamy after death.

CHAPTER XI

Of the Religion of the Romans.

Though Rome had Romulus for her first founder, and as a daughter owed him her being and nurture, nevertheless, when the institutions of Romulus were seen by Heaven to be insufficient for so great a State, the Roman senate were moved to choose Numa Pompilius as his successor, that he might look to all matters which Romulus had neglected. He finding the people fierce and turbulent, and desiring with the help of the peaceful arts to bring them to order and obedience, called in the aid of religion as essential to the maintenance of civil society, and gave it such a form, that for many ages God was nowhere so much feared as in that republic. The effect of this was to render easy any enterprise in which the senate or great men of Rome thought fit to engage. And whosoever pays heed to an infinity of actions performed, sometimes by the Roman people collectively, often by single citizens, will see, that esteeming the power of God beyond that of man, they dreaded far more to violate their oath than to transgress the laws; as is clearly shown by the examples of Scipio and of Manlius Torquatus. For after the defeat of the Romans by Hannibal at Cannae, many citizens meeting together, resolved, in their terror and dismay, to abandon Italy and seek refuge in Sicily. But Scipio, getting word of this, went among them, and menacing them with his naked sword, made them swear never to abandon their country. Again, when Lucius Manlius was accused by the tribune Marcus Pomponius, before the day fixed for trial, Titus Manlius, afterwards named Torquatus, son to Lucius, went to seek this Marcus, and threatening him with death if he did not withdraw the charge against his father, compelled him to swear compliance; and he, through fear, having sworn, kept his oath. In the first of these two instances, therefore, citizens whom love of their country and its laws could not have retained in Italy, were kept there by the oath forced upon them; and in the second, the tribune Marcus, to keep his oath, laid aside the hatred he bore the father, and overlooked the injury done him by the son, and his own dishonour. And this from no other cause than the religion which Numa had impressed upon this city.

And it will be plain to any one who carefully studies Roman History, how much religion helped in disciplining the army, in uniting the people, in keeping good men good, and putting bad men to shame; so that had it to be decided to which prince, Romulus or Numa, Rome owed the greater debt, I think the balance must turn in favour of Numa; for when religion is once established you may readily bring in arms; but where you have arms without religion it is not easy afterwards to bring in religion. We see, too, that while Romulus in order to create a senate, and to establish his other ordinances civil and military, needed no support from Divine authority, this was very necessary to Numa, who feigned to have intercourse with a Nymph by whose advice he was guided in counselling the people. And this, because desiring to introduce in Rome new and untried institutions, he feared that his own authority might not effect his end. Nor, indeed, has any attempt ever been made to introduce unusual laws among a people, without resorting to Divine authority, since without such sanction they never would have been accepted. For the wise recognize many things to be good which do not bear such reasons on the face of them as command their acceptance by others; wherefore, wise men who would obviate these difficulties, have recourse to Divine aid. Thus did Lycurgus, thus Solon, and thus have done many besides who have had the same end in view.

The Romans, accordingly, admiring the prudence and virtues of Numa, assented to all the measures which he recommended. This, however, is to be said, that the circumstance of these times being deeply tinctured with religious feeling, and of the men with whom he had to deal being rude and ignorant, gave Numa better facility to carry out his plans, as enabling him to mould his subjects readily to any new impression. And, doubtless, he who should seek at the present day to form a new commonwealth, would find the task easier among a race of simple mountaineers, than among the dwellers in cities where society is corrupt; as the sculptor can more easily carve a fair statue from a rough block, than from the block which has been badly shaped out by another. But taking all this into account, I maintain that the religion introduced by Numa was one of the chief causes of the prosperity of Rome, since it gave rise to good ordinances, which in turn brought with them good fortune, and with good fortune, happy issues to whatsoever was undertaken.

And as the observance of the ordinances of religion is the cause of the greatness of a State, so their neglect is the occasion of its decline; since a kingdom without the fear of God must either fall to pieces, or must be maintained by the fear of some prince who supplies that influence not supplied by religion. But since the lives of princes are short, the life of this prince, also, and with it his influence, must soon come to an end; whence it happens that a kingdom which rests wholly on the qualities of its prince, lasts for a brief time only; because these qualities, terminating with his life, are rarely renewed in his successor. For as Dante wisely says: —

"Seldom through the boughs doth human worth renew itself; for such the will of Him who gives it, that to Him we may ascribe it."

It follows, therefore, that the safety of a commonwealth or kingdom lies, not in its having a ruler who governs it prudently while he lives, but in having one who so orders things, that when he dies, the State may still maintain itself. And though it be easier to impose new institutions or a new faith on rude and simple men, it is not therefore impossible to persuade their adoption by men who are civilized, and who do not think themselves rude. The people of Florence do not esteem themselves rude or ignorant, and yet were persuaded by the Friar Girolamo Savonarola that he spoke with God. Whether in this he said truth or no, I take not on me to pronounce, since of so great a man we must speak with reverence; but this I do say, that very many believed him without having witnessed anything extraordinary to warrant their belief; his life, his doctrines, the matter whereof he treated, being sufficient to enlist their faith.

Let no man, therefore, lose heart from thinking that he cannot do what others have done before him; for, as I said in my Preface, men are born, and live, and die, always in accordance with the same rules.

CHAPTER XII

That it is of much moment to make account of Religion; and that Italy, through the Roman Church, being wanting therein, has been ruined.

Princes and commonwealths that would save themselves from growing corrupted, should before all things keep uncorrupted the rites and ceremonies of religion, and always hold them in reverence; since we can have no surer sign of the decay of a province than to see Divine worship held therein in contempt. This is easily understood when it is seen on what foundation that religion rests in which a man is born. For every religion has its root in certain fundamental ordinances peculiar to itself.

The religion of the Gentiles had its beginning in the responses of the oracles and in the prognostics of the augurs and soothsayers. All their other ceremonies and observances depended upon these; because men naturally believed that the God who could forecast their future weal or woe, could also bring them to pass. Wherefore the temples, the prayers, the sacrifices, and all the other rites of their worship, had their origin in this, that the oracles of Delos, of Dodona, and others celebrated in antiquity, held the world admiring and devout. But, afterwards, when these oracles began to shape their answers to suit the interests of powerful men, and their impostures to be seen through by the multitude, men grew incredulous and ready to overturn every sacred institution. For which reason, the rulers of kingdoms and commonwealths should maintain the foundations of the faith which they hold; since thus it will be easy for them to keep their country religious, and, consequently, virtuous and united. To which end they should countenance and further whatsoever tells in favour of religion, even should they think it untrue; and the wiser they are, and the better they are acquainted with natural causes, the more ought they to do so. It is from this course having been followed by the wise, that the miracles celebrated even in false religions, have come to be held in repute; for from whatever source they spring, discreet men will extol them, whose authority afterwards gives them currency everywhere.

These miracles were common enough in Rome, and among others this was believed, that when the Roman soldiers were sacking the city of Veii, certain of them entered the temple of Juno and spoke to the statue of the goddess, saying, "*Wilt thou come with us to Rome?*" when to some it seemed that she inclined her head in assent, and to others that they heard her answer, "*Yea.*" For these men being filled with religious awe (which Titus Livius shows us by the circumstance that, in entering the temple, they entered devoutly, reverently, and without tumult), persuaded themselves they heard that answer to their question, which, perhaps, they had formed beforehand in their minds. But their faith and belief were wholly approved of and confirmed by Camillus and by the other chief men of the city.

Had religion been maintained among the princes of Christendom on the footing on which it was established by its Founder, the Christian States and republics had been far more united and far more prosperous than they now are; nor can we have surer proof of its decay than in witnessing how those countries which are the nearest neighbours of the Roman Church, the head of our faith, have less devoutness than any others; so that any one who considers its earliest beginnings and observes how widely different is its present practice, might well believe its ruin or its chastisement to be close at hand.

But since some are of opinion that the welfare of Italy depends upon the Church of Rome, I desire to put forward certain arguments which occur to me against that view, and shall adduce two very strong ones, which, to my mind, admit of no answer. The first is, that, through the ill example of the Roman

Court, the country has lost all religious feeling and devoutness, a loss which draws after it infinite mischiefs and disorders; for as the presence of religion implies every excellence, so the contrary is involved in its absence. To the Church, therefore, and to the priests, we Italians owe this first debt, that through them we have become wicked and irreligious. And a still greater debt we owe them for what is the immediate cause of our ruin, namely, that by the Church our country is kept divided. For no country was ever united or prosperous which did not yield obedience to some one prince or commonwealth, as has been the case with France and Spain. And the Church is the sole cause why Italy stands on a different footing, and is subject to no one king or commonwealth. For though she holds here her seat, and exerts her temporal authority, she has never yet gained strength and courage to seize upon the entire country, or make herself supreme; yet never has been so weak that when in fear of losing her temporal dominion, she could not call in some foreign potentate to aid her against any Italian State by which she was overmatched. Of which we find many instances, both in early times, as when by the intervention of Charles the Great she drove the Lombards, who had made themselves masters of nearly the whole country, out of Italy; and also in recent times, as when, with the help of France, she first stripped the Venetians of their territories, and then, with the help of the Swiss, expelled the French.

The Church, therefore, never being powerful enough herself to take possession of the entire country, while, at the same time, preventing any one else from doing so, has made it impossible to bring Italy under one head; and has been the cause of her always living subject to many princes or rulers, by whom she has been brought to such division and weakness as to have become a prey, not to Barbarian kings only, but to any who have thought fit to attack her. For this, I say, we Italians have none to thank but the Church. And were any man powerful enough to transplant the Court of Rome, with all the authority it now wields over the rest of Italy, into the territories of the Swiss (the only people who at this day, both as regards religion and military discipline, live like the ancients,) he would have clear proof of the truth of what I affirm, and would find that the corrupt manners of that Court had, in a little while, wrought greater mischief in these territories than any other disaster which could ever befall them.

CHAPTER XIII

Of the use the Romans made of Religion in giving Institutions to their City, in carrying out their Enterprises, and in quelling Tumults.

Here it seems to me not out of place to cite instances of the Romans seeking assistance from religion in reforming their institutions and in carrying out their warlike designs. And although many such are related by Titus Livius, I content myself with mentioning the following only: The Romans having appointed tribunes with consular powers, all of them, save one, plebeians, it so chanced that in that very year they were visited by plague and famine, accompanied by many strange portents. Taking occasion from this, the nobles, at the next creation of tribunes, gave out that the gods were angry with Rome for lowering the majesty of her government, nor could be appeased but by the choice of tribunes being restored to a fair footing. Whereupon the people, smitten with religious awe, chose all the tribunes from the nobles. Again, at the siege of Veii, we find the Roman commanders making use of religion to keep the minds of their men well disposed towards that enterprise. For when, in the last year of the siege, the soldiers, disgusted with their protracted service, began to clamour to be led back to Rome, on the Alban lake suddenly rising to an uncommon height, it was found that the oracles at Delphi and elsewhere had foretold that Veii should fall that year in which the Alban lake overflowed. The hope of near victory thus excited in the minds of the soldiers, led them to put up with the weariness of the war, and to continue in arms; until, on Camillus being named dictator, Veii was taken after a ten years' siege. In these cases, therefore, we see religion, wisely used, assist in the reduction of this city, and in restoring the tribuneship to the nobles; neither of which ends could well have been effected without it.

One other example bearing on the same subject I must not omit. Constant disturbances were occasioned in Rome by the tribune Terentillus, who, for reasons to be noticed in their place, sought to pass a certain law. The nobles, in their efforts to baffle him, had recourse to religion, which they sought to turn to account in two ways. For first they caused the Sibylline books to be searched, and a feigned answer returned, that in that year the city ran great risk of losing its freedom through civil discord; which fraud, although exposed by the tribunes, nevertheless aroused such alarm in the minds of the commons that they slackened in their support of their leaders. Their other contrivance was as follows: A certain Appius Herdonius, at the head of a band of slaves and outlaws, to the lumber of four thousand, having seized the Capitol by night, an alarm was spread that were the Equians and Volscians, those perpetual enemies of the Roman name, then to attack the city, they might succeed in taking it. And when, in spite of this, the tribunes stubbornly persisted in their efforts to pass the law, declaring the act of Herdonius to be a device of the nobles and no real danger. Publius Rubetius, a citizen of weight and authority, came forth from the Senate House, and in words partly friendly and partly menacing, showed them the peril in which the city stood, and that their demands were unseasonable; and spoke to such effect that the commons bound themselves by oath to stand by the consul; in fulfilment of which engagement they aided the consul, Publius Valerius, to carry the Capitol by assault. But Valerius being slain in the attack, Titus Quintius was at once appointed in his place, who, to leave the people no breathing time, nor suffer their thoughts to revert to the Terentillian law, ordered them to quit Rome and march against the Volscians; declaring them bound to follow him by virtue of the oath they had sworn not to desert the consul. And though the tribunes withstood him, contending that the oath had been sworn to the dead consul and not to Quintius, yet the people under the influence of religious awe, chose rather to obey the consul than believe the tribunes. And Titus Livius commends their behaviour when he says: "*That neglect of the gods which now prevails, had not then made its way nor was it then the practice for every man to interpret his oath, or the laws, to suit his private ends.*" The tribunes accordingly, fearing to lose their entire ascendency, consented to obey the consul, and to refrain for a year from moving in the matter of the Terentillian law; while the consuls, on their part, undertook that for a year the commons should not be called forth to war. And thus, with the help of religion, the senate were able to overcome a difficulty which they never could have overcome without it.

CHAPTER XIV

That the Romans interpreted the Auspices to meet the occasion; and made a prudent show of observing the Rites of Religion even when forced to disregard them; and any who rashly slighted Religion they punished.

Auguries were not only, as we have shown above, a main foundation of the old religion of the Gentiles, but were also the cause of the prosperity of the Roman commonwealth. Accordingly, the Romans gave more heed to these than to any other of their observances; resorting to them in their consular comitia; in undertaking new enterprises; in calling out their armies; in going into battle; and, in short, in every business of importance, whether civil or military. Nor would they ever set forth on any warlike expedition, until they had satisfied their soldiers that the gods had promised them victory.

Among other means of declaring the auguries, they had in their armies a class of soothsayers, named by them *pullarii*, whom, when they desired to give battle, they would ask to take the auspices, which they did by observing the behaviour of fowls. If the fowls pecked, the engagement was begun with a favourable omen. If they refused, battle was declined. Nevertheless, when it was plain on the face of it that a certain course had to be taken, they take it at all hazards, even though the auspices were adverse; contriving, however, to manage matters so adroitly as not to appear to throw any slight on religion; as was done by the consul Papirius in the great battle he fought with the Samnites wherein that nation was finally broken and overthrown. For Papirius being encamped over against the Samnites, and perceiving that he fought, victory was certain, and consequently being eager to engage, desired the omens to be taken. The fowls refused to peck; but the chief soothsayer observing the eagerness of the soldiers to fight and the confidence felt both by them and by their captain, not to deprive the army of such an opportunity of glory, reported to the consul that the auspices were favourable. Whereupon Papirius began to array his army for battle. But some among the soothsayers having divulged to certain of the soldiers that the fowls had not pecked, this was told to Spurius Papirius, the nephew of the consul, who reporting it to his uncle, the latter straightway bade him mind his own business, for that so far as he himself and the army were concerned, the auspices were fair; and if the soothsayer had lied, the consequences were on his head. And that the event might accord with the prognostics, he commanded his officers to place the soothsayers in front of the battle. It so chanced that as they advanced against the enemy, the chief soothsayer was killed by a spear thrown by a Roman soldier; which, the consul hearing of, said, *"All goes well, and as the Gods would have it, for by the death of this liar the army is purged of blame and absolved from whatever displeasure these may have conceived against it."* And contriving, in this way to make his designs tally with the auspices, he joined battle, without the army knowing that the ordinances of religion had in any degree been disregarded.

But an opposite course was taken by Appius Pulcher, in Sicily, in the first Carthaginian war. For desiring to join battle, he bade the soothsayers take the auspices, and on their announcing that the fowls refused to feed, he answered, *"Let us see, then, whether they will drink,"* and, so saying, caused them to be thrown into the sea. After which he fought and was defeated. For this he was condemned at Rome, while Papirius was honoured; not so much because the one had gained while the other had lost a battle, as because in their treatment of the auspices the one had behaved discreetly, the other with rashness. And, in truth, the sole object of this system of taking the auspices was to insure the army joining battle with that confidence of success which constantly leads to victory; a device followed not by the Romans only, but by foreign nations as well; of which I shall give an example in the following Chapter.

CHAPTER XV

How the Samnites, as a last resource in their broken Fortunes, had recourse to Religion.

The Samnites, who before had met with many defeats at the hands of the Romans, were at last decisively routed by them in Etruria, where their armies were cut to pieces and their commanders slain. And because their allies also, such as the Etruscans, the Umbrians, and the Gauls, were likewise vanquished, they "*could now no longer*" as Livius tells us, "*either trust to their own strength or to foreign aid; yet, for all that, would not cease from hostilities, nor resign themselves to forfeit the liberty which they had unsuccessfully defended, preferring new defeats to an inglorious submission.*" They resolved, therefore, to make a final effort; and as they knew that victory was only to be secured by inspiring their soldiers with a stubborn courage, to which end nothing could help so much as religion, at the instance of their high priest, Ovius Paccius, they revived an ancient sacrificial rite performed by them in the manner following. After offering solemn sacrifice they caused all the captains of their armies, standing between the slain victims and the smoking altars, to swear never to abandon the war. They then summoned the common soldiers, one by one, and before the same altars, and surrounded by a ring of many centurions with drawn swords, first bound them by oath never to reveal what they might see or hear; and then, after imprecating the Divine wrath, and reciting the most terrible incantations, made them vow and swear to the gods, as they would not have a curse light on their race and offspring, to follow wherever their captains led, never to turn back from battle, and to put any they saw turn back to death.

Some who in their terror declined to swear, were forthwith slain by the centurions. The rest, warned by their cruel fate, complied. Assembling thereafter to the number of forty thousand, one-half of whom, to render their appearance of unusual splendour were clad in white, with plumes and crests over their helmets, they took up their ground in the neighbourhood of Aquilonia. But Papirius, being sent against them, bade his soldiers be of good cheer, telling them *"that feathers made no wounds, and that a Roman spear would pierce a painted shield,"* and to lessen the effect which the oath taken by the Samnites had upon the minds of the Romans, he said that such an oath must rather distract than strengthen those bound by it, since they had to fear, at once, their enemies, their comrades, and their Gods. In the battle which ensued, the Samnites were routed, any firmness lent them by religion or by the oath they had sworn, being balanced by the Roman valour, and the terror inspired by past defeats. Still we see that, in their own judgment, they had no other refuge to which to turn, nor other remedy for restoring their broken hopes; and this is strong testimony to the spirit which religion rightly used can arouse.

Some of the incidents which I have now been considering may be thought to relate rather to the foreign than to the domestic affairs of Rome, which last alone form the proper subject of this Book; nevertheless since the matter connects itself with one of the most important institutions of the Roman republic, I have thought it convenient to notice it here, so as not to divide the subject and be obliged to return to it hereafter.

CHAPTER XVI

That a People accustomed to live under a Prince, if by any accident it become free, can hardly preserve that Freedom.

Should a people accustomed to live under a prince by any accident become free, as did the Romans on the expulsion of the Tarquins, we know from numberless instances recorded in ancient history, how hard it will be for it to maintain that freedom. And this is no more than we might expect. For a people in such circumstances may be likened to the wild animal which, though destined by nature to roam at large in the woods, has been reared in the cage and in constant confinement and which, should it chance to be set free in the open country, being unused to find its own food, and unfamiliar with the coverts where it might lie concealed, falls a prey to the first who seeks to recapture it. Even thus it fares with the people which has been accustomed to be governed by others; since ignorant how to act by itself either for attack or defence, and neither knowing foreign princes nor being known of them, it is speedily brought back under the yoke, and often under a heavier yoke than that from which it has just freed its neck. These difficulties will be met with, even where the great body of the citizens has not become wholly corrupted; but where the corruption is complete, freedom, as shall presently be shown, is not merely fleeting but impossible. Wherefore my remarks are to be taken as applying to those States only wherein corruption has as yet made no great progress, and in which there is more that is sound than unsound.

To the difficulties above noticed, another has to be added, which is, that a State in becoming free makes for itself bitter enemies but not warm friends. All become its bitter enemies who, drawing their support from the wealth of the tyrant, flourished under his government. For these men, when the causes which made them powerful are withdrawn, can no longer live contented, but are one and all impelled to attempt the restoration of the tyranny in hopes of regaining their former importance. On the other hand, as I have said, the State which becomes free does not gain for itself warm friends. For a free government bestows its honours and rewards in accordance with certain fixed rules, and on considerations of merit, without which none is honoured or rewarded. But when a man obtains only those honours or rewards which he seems to himself to deserve, he will never admit that he is under any obligation to those who bestow them. Moreover the common benefits that all derive from a free government, which consist in the power to enjoy what is our own, openly and undisturbed, in having to feel no anxiety for the honour of wife or child, nor any fear for personal safety, are hardly recognized by men while they still possess them, since none will ever confess obligation to him who merely refrains from injury. For these reasons, I repeat, a State which has recently become free, is likely to have bitter enemies and no warm friends.

Now, to meet these difficulties and their attendant disorders, there is no more potent, effectual, wholesome, and necessary remedy than *to slay the sons of Brutus*. They, as the historian tells us, were along with other young Romans led to conspire against their country, simply because the unusual privileges which they had enjoyed under the kings, were withheld under the consuls; so that to them it seemed as though the freedom of the people implied their servitude. Any one, therefore, who undertakes to control a people, either as their prince or as the head of a commonwealth, and does not make sure work with all who are hostile to his new institutions, founds a government which cannot last long. Undoubtedly those princes are to be reckoned unhappy, who, to secure their position, are forced to advance by unusual and irregular paths, and with the people for their enemies. For while he who has to deal with a few adversaries only, can easily and without much or serious difficulty secure himself, he who has an entire people against him can never feel safe and the greater the severity he uses the weaker his authority becomes; so that his best course is to strive to make the people his friends.

But since these views may seem to conflict with what I have said above, treating there of a republic and here of a prince, that I may not have to return to the subject again, I will in this place discuss it briefly. Speaking, then of those princes who have become the tyrants of their country, I say that the prince who seeks to gain over an unfriendly people should first of all examine what it is the people really desire, and he will always find that they desire two things: first, to be revenged upon those who are the cause of their servitude; and second, to regain their freedom. The first of these desires the prince can gratify wholly, the second in part. As regards the former, we have an instance exactly in point. Clearchus, tyrant of Heraclea, being in exile, it so happened that on a feud arising between the commons and the nobles of that city, the latter, perceiving they were weaker than their adversaries, began to look with favour on Clearchus, and conspiring with him, in opposition to the popular voice recalled him to Heraclea and deprived the people of their freedom. Clearchus finding himself thus placed between the arrogance of the nobles, whom he could in no way either satisfy or correct, and the fury of the people, who could not put up with the loss of their freedom, resolved to rid himself at a stroke from the harassment of the nobles and recommend himself to the people. Wherefore, watching his opportunity, he caused all the nobles to be put to death, and thus, to the extreme delight of the people, satisfied one of those desires by which they are possessed, namely, the desire for vengeance.

As for the other desire of the people, namely, to recover their freedom, the prince, since he never can content them in this, should examine what the causes are which make them long to be free; and he will find a very few of them desiring freedom that they may obtain power, but all the rest, whose number is countless, only desiring it that they may live securely. For in all republics, whatever the form of their government, barely forty or fifty citizens have any place in the direction of affairs; who, from their number being so small, can easily be reckoned with, either by making away with them, or by allowing them such a share of honours as, looking to their position, may reasonably content them. All those others whose sole aim it is to live safely, are well contented where the prince enacts such laws and ordinances as provide for the general security, while they establish his own authority; and when he does this, and the people see that nothing induces him to violate these laws, they soon begin to live happily and without anxiety. Of this we have an example in the kingdom of France, which enjoys perfect security from this cause alone, that its kings are bound to compliance with an infinity of laws upon which the well-being of the whole people depends. And he who gave this State its constitution allowed its kings to do as they pleased as regards arms and money; but provided that as regards everything else they should not interfere save as the laws might direct. Those rulers, therefore, who omit to provide sufficiently for the safety of their government at the outset, must, like the Romans, do so on the first occasion which offers; and whoever lets the occasion slip, will repent too late of not having acted as he should. The Romans, however, being still uncorrupted at the time when they recovered their freedom, were able, after slaying the sons of Brutus and getting rid of the Tarquins, to maintain it with all those safeguards and remedies which we have elsewhere considered. But had they already become corrupted, no remedy could have been found, either in Rome or out of it, by which their freedom could have been secured; as I shall show in the following Chapter.

CHAPTER XVII

That a corrupt People obtaining Freedom can hardly preserve it.

I believe that if her kings had not been expelled, Rome must very soon have become a weak and inconsiderable State. For seeing to what a pitch of corruption these kings had come, we may conjecture that if two or three more like reigns had followed, and the taint spread from the head to the members, so soon as the latter became infected, cure would have been hopeless. But from the head being removed while the trunk was still sound, it was not difficult for the Romans to return to a free and constitutional government.

It may be assumed, however, as most certain, that a corrupted city living under a prince can never recover its freedom, even were the prince and all his line to be exterminated. For in such a city it must necessarily happen that one prince will be replaced by another, and that things will never settle down until a new lord be established; unless, indeed, the combined goodness and valour of some one citizen should maintain freedom, which, even then, will endure only for his lifetime; as happened twice in Syracuse, first under the rule of Dion, and again under that of Timoleon, whose virtues while they lived kept their city free, but on whose death it fell once more under a tyranny.

But the strongest example that can be given is that of Rome, which on the expulsion of the Tarquins was able at once to seize on liberty and to maintain it; yet, on the deaths of Caesar, Caligula, and Nero, and on the extinction of the Julian line, was not only unable to establish her freedom, but did not even venture a step in that direction. Results so opposite arising in one and the same city can only be accounted for by this, that in the time of the Tarquins the Roman people were not yet corrupted, but in these later times had become utterly corrupt. For on the first occasion, nothing more was needed to prepare and determine them to shake off their kings, than that they should be bound by oath to suffer no king ever again to reign in Rome; whereas, afterwards, the authority and austere virtue of Brutus, backed by all the legions of the East, could not rouse them to maintain their hold of that freedom, which he, following in the footsteps of the first Brutus, had won for them; and this because of the corruption wherewith the people had been infected by the Marian faction, whereof Caesar becoming head, was able so to blind the multitude that it saw not the yoke under which it was about to lay its neck.

Though this example of Rome be more complete than any other, I desire to instance likewise, to the same effect, certain peoples well known in our own days; and I maintain that no change, however grave or violent, could ever restore freedom to Naples or Milan, because in these States the entire body of the people has grown corrupted. And so we find that Milan, although desirous to return to a free form of government, on the death of Filippo Visconti, had neither the force nor the skill needed to preserve it.

Most fortunate, therefore, was it for Rome that her kings grew corrupt soon, so as to be driven out before the taint of their corruption had reached the vitals of the city. For it was because these were sound that the endless commotions which took place in Rome, so far from being hurtful, were, from their object being good, beneficial to the commonwealth. From which we may draw this inference, that where the body of the people is still sound, tumults and other like disorders do little hurt, but that where it has become corrupted, laws, however well devised, are of no advantage, unless imposed by some one whose paramount authority causes them to be observed until the community be once more restored to a sound and healthy condition.

Whether this has ever happened I know not, nor whether it ever can happen. For we see, as I have said a little way back, that a city which owing to its pervading corruption has once begun to decline, if it is to recover at all, must be saved not by the excellence of the people collectively, but of some one man then living among them, on whose death it at once relapses into its former plight; as happened with Thebes, in which the virtue of Epaminondas made it possible while he lived to preserve the form of a free Government, but which fell again on his death into its old disorders; the reason being that hardly any ruler lives so long as to have time to accustom to right methods a city which has long been accustomed to wrong. Wherefore, unless things be put on a sound footing by some one ruler who lives to a very advanced age, or by two virtuous rulers succeeding one another, the city upon their death at once falls back into ruin; or, if it be preserved, must be so by incurring great risks, and at the cost of much blood. For the corruption I speak of, is wholly incompatible with a free government, because it results from an inequality which pervades the State and can only be removed by employing unusual and very violent remedies, such as few are willing or know how to employ, as in another place I shall more fully explain.

CHAPTER XVIII

How a Free Government existing in a corrupt City may be preserved, or not existing may be created.

I think it neither out of place, nor inconsistent with what has been said above, to consider whether a free government existing in a corrupt city can be maintained, or, not existing, can be introduced. And on this head I say that it is very difficult to bring about either of these results, and next to impossible to lay down rules as to how it may be done; because the measures to be taken must vary with the degree of corruption which prevails.

Nevertheless, since it is well to reason things out, I will not pass this matter by, but will assume, in the first place, the case of a very corrupt city, and then take the case of one in which corruption has reached a still greater height; but where corruption is universal, no laws or institutions will ever have force to restrain it. Because as good customs stand in need of good laws for their support, so laws, that they may be respected, stand in need of good customs. Moreover, the laws and institutions established in a republic at its beginning, when men were good, are no longer suitable when they have become bad; but while the laws of a city are altered to suit its circumstances, its institutions rarely or never change; whence it results that the introduction of new laws is of no avail, because the institutions, remaining unchanged, corrupt them.

And to make this plainer, I say that in Rome it was first of all the institutions of the State, and next the laws as enforced by the magistrates, which kept the citizens under control. The institutions of the State consisted in the authority of the people, the senate, the tribunes, and the consuls; in the methods of choosing and appointing magistrates; and in the arrangements for passing laws. These institutions changed little, if at all, with circumstances. But the laws by which the people were controlled, as for instance the law relating to adultery, the sumptuary laws, the law as to canvassing at elections, and many others, were altered as the citizens grew more and more corrupted. Hence, the institutions of the State remaining the same although from the corruption of the people no longer suitable, amendments in the laws could not keep men good, though they might have proved very useful if at the time when they were made the institutions had likewise been reformed.

That its original institutions are no longer adapted to a city that has become corrupted, is plainly seen in two matters of great moment, I mean in the appointment of magistrates and in the passing of laws. For the Roman people conferred the consulship and other great offices of their State on none save those who sought them; which was a good institution at first, because then none sought these offices save those who thought themselves worthy of them, and to be rejected was held disgraceful; so that, to be deemed worthy, all were on their best behaviour. But in a corrupted city this institution grew to be most mischievous. For it was no longer those of greatest worth, but those who had most influence, who sought the magistracies; while all who were without influence, however deserving, refrained through fear. This untoward result was not reached all at once, but like other similar results, by gradual steps. For after subduing Africa and Asia, and reducing nearly the whole of Greece to submission, the Romans became perfectly assured of their freedom, and seemed to themselves no longer to have any enemy whom they had cause to fear. But this security and the weakness of their adversaries led them in conferring the consulship, no longer to look to merit, but only to favour, selecting for the office those who knew best how to pay court to them, not those who knew best how to vanquish their enemies. And afterwards, instead of selecting those who were best liked, they came to select those who had most influence; and in this way, from the imperfection of their institutions, good men came to be wholly excluded.

Again, as to making laws, any of the tribunes and certain others of the magistrates were entitled to submit laws to the people; but before these were passed it was open to every citizen to speak either for or against them. This was a good system so long as the citizens were good, since it is always well that every man should be able to propose what he thinks may be of use to his country, and that all should be allowed to express their views with regard to his proposal; so that the people, having heard all, may resolve on what is best. But when the people grew depraved, this became a very mischievous institution; for then it was only the powerful who proposed laws, and these not in the interest of public freedom but of their own authority; and because, through fear, none durst speak against the laws they proposed, the people were either deceived or forced into voting their own destruction.

In order, therefore, that Rome after she had become corrupted might still preserve her freedom, it was necessary that, as in the course of events she had made new laws, so likewise she should frame new institutions, since different institutions and ordinances are needed in a corrupt State from those which suit a State which is not corrupted; for where the matter is wholly dissimilar, the form cannot be similar.

But since old institutions must either be reformed all at once, as soon as they are seen to be no longer expedient, or else gradually, as the imperfection of each is recognized, I say that each of these two courses is all but impossible. For to effect a gradual reform requires a sagacious man who can discern mischief while it is still remote and in the germ. But it may well happen that no such person is found in a city; or that, if found, he is unable to persuade others of what he is himself persuaded. For men used to live in one way are loath to leave it for another, especially when they are not brought face to face with the evil against which they should guard, and only have it indicated to them by conjecture. And as for a sudden reform of institutions which are seen by all to be no longer good, I say that defects which are easily discerned are not easily corrected, because for their correction it is not enough to use ordinary means, these being in themselves insufficient; but recourse must be had to extraordinary means, such as violence and arms; and, as a preliminary, you must become prince of the city, and be able to deal with it at your pleasure. But since the restoration of a State to new political life presupposes a good man, and to become prince of a city by violence presupposes a bad man, it can, consequently, very seldom happen that, although the end be good, a good man will be found ready to become a prince by evil ways, or that a bad man having become a prince will be disposed to act virtuously, or think of turning to good account his ill-acquired authority.

From all these causes comes the difficulty, or rather the impossibility, which a corrupted city finds in maintaining an existing free government, or in establishing a new one. So that had we to establish or maintain a government in that city, it would be necessary to give it a monarchical, rather than a popular form, in order that men too arrogant to be restrained by the laws, might in some measure be kept in check by a power almost absolute; since to attempt to make them good otherwise would be a very cruel or a wholly futile endeavour. This, as I have said, was the method followed by Cleomenes; and if he, that he might stand alone, put to death the Ephori; and if Romulus, with a like object, put to death his brother and Titus Tatius the Sabine, and if both afterwards made good use of the authority they thus acquired, it is nevertheless to be remembered that it was because neither Cleomenes nor Romulus had to deal with so corrupt a people as that of which I am now speaking, that they were able to effect their ends and to give a fair colour to their acts.

CHAPTER XIX

After a strong Prince a weak Prince may maintain himself: but after one weak Prince no Kingdom can stand a second.

When we contemplate the excellent qualities of Romulus, Numa, and Tullus, the first three kings of Rome, and note the methods which they followed, we recognize the extreme good fortune of that city in having her first king fierce and warlike, her second peaceful and religious, and her third, like the first, of a high spirit and more disposed to war than to peace. For it was essential for Rome that almost at the outset of her career, a ruler should be found to lay the foundations of her civil life; but, after that had been done, it was necessary that her rulers should return to the virtues of Romulus, since otherwise the city must have grown feeble, and become a prey to her neighbours.

And here we may note that a prince who succeeds to another of superior valour, may reign on by virtue of his predecessor's merits, and reap the fruits of his labours; but if he live to a great age, or if he be followed by another who is wanting in the qualities of the first, that then the kingdom must necessarily dwindle. Conversely, when two consecutive princes are of rare excellence, we commonly find them achieving results which win for them enduring renown. David, for example, not only surpassed in learning and judgment, but was so valiant in arms that, after conquering and subduing all his neighbours, he left to his young son Solomon a tranquil State, which the latter, though unskilled in the arts of war, could maintain by the arts of peace, and thus happily enjoy the inheritance of his father's valour. But Solomon could not transmit this inheritance to his son Rehoboam, who neither resembling his grandfather in valour, nor his father in good fortune, with difficulty made good his right to a sixth part of the kingdom. In like manner Bajazet, sultan of the Turks, though a man of peace rather than of war, was able to enjoy the labours of Mahomet his father, who, like David, having subdued his neighbours, left his son a kingdom so safely established that it could easily be retained by him by peaceful arts. But had Selim, son to Bajazet, been like his father, and not like his grandfather, the Turkish monarchy must have been overthrown; as it is, he seems likely to outdo the fame of his grandsire.

I affirm it to be proved by these examples, that after a valiant prince a feeble prince may maintain himself; but that no kingdom can stand when two feeble princes follow in succession, unless, as in the case of France, it be supported by its ancient ordinances. By feeble princes, I mean such as are not valiant in war. And, to put the matter shortly, it may be said, that the great valour of Romulus left Numa a period of many years within which to govern Rome by peaceful arts; that after Numa came Tullus, who renewed by his courage the fame of Romulus; and that he in turn was succeeded by Ancus, a prince so gifted by nature that he could equally avail himself of the methods of peace or war; who setting himself at first to pursue the former, when he found that his neighbours judged him to be effeminate, and therefore held him in slight esteem, understood that to preserve Rome he must resort to arms and resemble Romulus rather than Numa. From whose example every ruler of a State may learn that a prince like Numa will hold or lose his power according as fortune and circumstances befriend him; but that the prince who resembles Romulus, and like him is fortified with foresight and arms, will hold his State whatever befall, unless deprived of it by some stubborn and irresistible force. For we may reckon with certainty that if Rome had not had for her third king one who knew how to restore her credit by deeds of valour, she could not, or at any rate not without great difficulty, have afterwards held her ground, nor could ever have achieved the great exploits she did.

And for these reasons Rome, while she lived under her kings, was in constant danger of destruction through a king who might be weak or bad.

CHAPTER XX

That the consecutive Reigns of two valiant Princes produce great results: and that well-ordered Commonwealths are assured of a Succession of valiant Rulers by whom their Power and Growth are rapidly extended.

When Rome had driven out her kings, she was freed from those dangers to which, as I have said, she was exposed by the possible succession of a weak or wicked prince. For the chief share in the government then devolved upon the consuls, who took their authority not by inheritance, nor yet by craft or by ambitious violence, but by the free suffrages of their fellow-citizens, and were always men of signal worth; by whose valour and good fortune Rome being constantly aided, was able to reach the height of her greatness in the same number of years as she had lived under her kings. And since we find that two successive reigns of valiant princes, as of Philip of Macedon and his son Alexander, suffice to conquer the world, this ought to be still easier for a commonwealth, which has it in its power to choose, not two excellent rulers only, but an endless number in succession. And in every well ordered commonwealth provision will be made for a succession of this sort.

CHAPTER XXI

That it is a great reproach to a Prince or to a Commonwealth to be without a national Army.

Those princes and republics of the present day who lack forces of their own, whether for attack or defence, should take shame to themselves, and should be convinced by the example of Tullus, that their deficiency does not arise from want of men fit for warlike enterprises, but from their own fault in not knowing how to make their subjects good soldiers. For after Rome had been at peace for forty years, Tullus, succeeding to the kingdom, found not a single Roman who had ever been in battle. Nevertheless when he made up his mind to enter on a war, it never occurred to him to have recourse to the Samnites, or the Etruscans, or to any other of the neighbouring nations accustomed to arms, but he resolved, like the prudent prince he was, to rely on his own countrymen. And such was his ability that, under his rule, the people very soon became admirable soldiers. For nothing is more true than that where a country, having men, lacks soldiers, it results from some fault in its ruler, and not from any defect in the situation or climate. Of this we have a very recent instance. Every one knows, how, only the other day, the King of England invaded the realm of France with an army raised wholly from among his own people, although from his country having been at peace for thirty years, he had neither men nor officers who had ever looked an enemy in the face. Nevertheless, he did not hesitate with such troops as he had, to attack a kingdom well provided with officers and excellent soldiers who had been constantly under arms in the Italian wars. And this was possible through the prudence of the English king and the wise ordinances of his kingdom, which never in time of peace relaxes its warlike discipline. So too, in old times, Pelopidas and Epaminondas the Thebans, after they had freed Thebes from her tyrants, and rescued her from thraldom to Sparta, finding themselves in a city used to servitude and surrounded by an effeminate people, scrupled not, so great was their courage, to furnish these with arms, and go forth with them to meet and to conquer the Spartan forces on the field. And he who relates this, observes, that these two captains very soon showed that warriors are not bred in Lacedaemon alone, but in every country where men are found, if only some one arise among them who knows how to direct them to arms; as we see Tullus knew how to direct the Romans. Nor could Virgil better express this opinion, or show by fitter words that he was convinced of its truth than, when he says: —

"To arms shall Tullus rouse His sluggish warriors."

CHAPTER XXII

What is to be noted in the combat of the three Roman Horatii and the three Alban Curiatii.

It was agreed between Tullus king of Rome, and Metius king of Alba, that the nation whose champions were victorious in combat should rule over the other. The three Alban Curiatii were slain; one of the Roman Horatii survived. Whereupon the Alban king with all his people became subject to the Romans. The surviving Horatius returning victorious to Rome, and meeting his sister, wife to one of the dead Curiatii, bewailing the death of her husband, slew her; and being tried for this crime, was, after much contention, liberated, rather on the entreaties of his father than for his own deserts.

Herein three points are to be noted. *First*, that we should never peril our whole fortunes on the success of only a part of our forces. *Second*, that in a well-governed State, merit should never be allowed to balance crime. And *third*, that those are never wise covenants which we cannot or should not expect to be observed. Now, for a State to be enslaved is so terrible a calamity that it ought never to have been supposed possible that either of these kings or nations would rest content under a slavery resulting from the defeat of three only of their number. And so it appeared to Metius; for although on the victory of the Roman champions, he at once confessed himself vanquished, and promised obedience; nevertheless, in the very first expedition which he and Tullus undertook jointly against the people of Veii, we find him seeking to circumvent the Roman, as though perceiving too late the rash part he had played.

This is enough to say of the third point which I noted as deserving attention. Of the other two I shall speak in the next two Chapters.

CHAPTER XXIII

That we should never hazard our whole Fortunes where we put not forth our entire Strength; for which reason to guard a Defile is often hurtful.

It was never judged a prudent course to peril your whole fortunes where you put not forth your whole strength; as may happen in more ways than one. One of these ways was that taken by Tullus and Metius, when each staked the existence of his country and the credit of his army on the valour and good fortune of three only of his soldiers, that being an utterly insignificant fraction of the force at his disposal. For neither of these kings reflected that all the labours of their predecessors in framing such institutions for their States, as might, with the aid of the citizens themselves, maintain them long in freedom, were rendered futile, when the power to ruin all was left in the hands of so small a number. No rasher step, therefore, could have been taken, than was taken by these kings.

A like risk is almost always incurred by those who, on the approach of an enemy, resolve to defend some place of strength, or to guard the defiles by which their country is entered. For unless room be found in this place of strength for almost all your army, the attempt to hold it will almost always prove hurtful. If you can find room, it will be right to defend your strong places; but if these be difficult of access, and you cannot there keep your entire force together, the effort to defend is mischievous. I come to this conclusion from observing the example of those who, although their territories be enclosed by mountains and precipices, have not, on being attacked by powerful enemies, attempted to fight on the mountains or in the defiles, but have advanced beyond them to meet their foes; or, if unwilling to advance, have awaited attack behind their mountains, on level and not on broken ground. The reason of which is, as I have above explained, that many men cannot be assembled in these strong places for their defence; partly because a large number of men cannot long subsist there, and partly because such places being narrow and confined, afford room for a few only; so that no enemy can there be withstood, who comes in force to the attack; which he can easily do, his design being to pass on and not to make a stay; whereas he who stands on the defensive cannot do so in force, because, from not knowing when the enemy may enter the confined and sterile tracts of which I speak, he may have to lodge himself there for a long time. But should you lose some pass which you had reckoned on holding, and on the defence of which your country and army have relied, there commonly follows such panic among your people and among the troops which remain to you, that you are vanquished without opportunity given for any display of valour, and lose everything without bringing all your resources into play.

Every one has heard with what difficulty Hannibal crossed the Alps which divide France from Lombardy, and afterwards those which separate Lombardy from Tuscany. Nevertheless the Romans awaited him, in the first instance on the banks of the Ticino, in the second on the plain of Arezzo, preferring to be defeated on ground which at least gave them a chance of victory, to leading their army into mountain fastnesses where it was likely to be destroyed by the mere difficulties of the ground. And any who read history with attention will find, that very few capable commanders have attempted to hold passes of this nature, as well for the reasons already given, as because to close them all were impossible. For mountains, like plains, are traversed not only by well-known and frequented roads, but also by many by-ways, which, though unknown to strangers, are familiar to the people of the country, under whose guidance you may always, and in spite of any opposition, be easily conducted to whatever point you please. Of this we have a recent instance in the events of the year 1515. For when Francis I. of France resolved on invading Italy in order to recover the province of Lombardy, those hostile to his attempt looked mainly to the Swiss, who it was hoped would stop him in passing through their mountains. But this hope was disappointed by the event. For leaving on one side two or three defiles which were guarded by the Swiss, the king advanced by another unknown pass, and was in Italy and upon his enemies before they knew. Whereupon they fled terror-stricken into Milan; while the whole population of Lombardy, finding themselves deceived in their expectation that the French would be detained in the mountains, went over to their side.

CHAPTER XXIV

That well-ordered States always provide Rewards and Punishments for their Citizens; and never set off Deserts against Misdeeds.

The valour of Horatius in vanquishing the Curiatii deserved the highest reward. But in slaying his sister he had been guilty of a heinous crime. And so displeasing to the Romans was an outrage of this nature, that although his services were so great and so recent, they brought him to trial for his life. To one looking at it carelessly, this might seem an instance of popular ingratitude, but he who considers the matter more closely, and examines with sounder judgment what the ordinances of a State should be, will rather blame the Roman people for acquitting Horatius than for putting him on his trial. And this because no well-ordered State ever strikes a balance between the services of its citizens and their misdeeds; but appointing rewards for good actions and punishment for bad, when it has rewarded a man for acting well, will afterwards, should he act ill, chastise him, without regard to his former deserts. When these ordinances are duly observed, a city will live long in freedom, but when they are neglected, it must soon come to ruin. For when a citizen has rendered some splendid service to his country, if to the distinction which his action in itself confers, were added an overweening confidence that any crime he might thenceforth commit would pass unpunished, he would soon become so arrogant that no civil bonds could restrain him.

Still, while we would have punishment terrible to wrongdoers, it is essential that good actions should be rewarded, as we see to have been the case in Rome. For even where a republic is poor, and has but little to give, it ought not to withhold that little; since a gift, however small, bestowed as a reward for services however great, will always be esteemed most honourable and precious by him who receives it. The story of Horatius Cocles and that of Mutius Scaevola are well known: how the one withstood the enemy on the bridge while it was being cut down, and the other thrust his hand into the fire in punishment of the mistake made when he sought the life of Porsenna the Etruscan king. To each of these two, in requital of their splendid deeds, two ploughgates only of the public land were given. Another famous story is that of Manlius Capitolinus, to whom, for having saved the Capitol from the besieging Gauls, a small measure of meal was given by each of those who were shut up with him during the siege. Which recompense, in proportion to the wealth of the citizens of Rome at that time, was thought ample; so that afterwards, when Manlius, moved by jealousy and malice, sought to arouse sedition in Rome, and to gain over the people to his cause, they without regard to his past services threw him headlong from that Capitol in saving which he had formerly gained so great a renown.

CHAPTER XXV

That he who would reform the Institutions of a free State, must retain at least the semblance of old Ways.

Whoever takes upon him to reform the government of a city, must, if his measures are to be well received and carried out with general approval, preserve at least the semblance of existing methods, so as not to appear to the people to have made any change in the old order of things; although, in truth, the new ordinances differ altogether from those which they replace. For when this is attended to, the mass of mankind accept what seems as what is; nay, are often touched more nearly by appearances than by realities.

This tendency being recognized by the Romans at the very outset of their civil freedom, when they appointed two consuls in place of a single king, they would not permit the consuls to have more than twelve lictors, in order that the old number of the king's attendants might not be exceeded. Again, there being solemnized every year in Rome a sacrificial rite which could only be performed by the king in person, that the people might not be led by the absence of the king to remark the want of any ancient observance, a priest was appointed for the due celebration of this rite, to whom was given the name of *Rex sacrificulus*, and who was placed under the orders of the chief priest. In this way the people were contented, and had no occasion from any defect in the solemnities to desire the return of their kings. Like precautions should be used by all who would put an end to the old government of a city and substitute new and free institutions. For since novelty disturbs men's minds, we should seek in the changes we make to preserve as far as possible what is ancient, so that if the new magistrates differ from the old in number, in authority, or in the duration of their office, they shall at least retain the old names.

This, I say, should be seen to by him who would establish a constitutional government, whether in the form of a commonwealth or of a kingdom. But he who would create an absolute government of the kind which political writers term a tyranny, must renew everything, as shall be explained in the following Chapter.

CHAPTER XXVI

A new Prince in a City or Province of which he has taken Possession, ought to make Everything new.

Whosoever becomes prince of a city or State, more especially if his position be so insecure that he cannot resort to constitutional government either in the form of a republic or a monarchy, will find that the best way to preserve his princedom is to renew the whole institutions of that State; that is to say, to create new magistracies with new names, confer new powers, and employ new men, and like David when he became king, exalt the humble and depress the great, *"filling the hungry with good things, and sending the rich empty away."* Moreover, he must pull down existing towns and rebuild them, removing their inhabitants from one place to another; and, in short, leave nothing in the country as he found it; so that there shall be neither rank, nor condition, nor honour, nor wealth which its possessor can refer to any but to him. And he must take example from Philip of Macedon, the father of Alexander, who by means such as these, from being a petty prince became monarch of all Greece; and of whom it was written that he shifted men from province to province as a shepherd moves his flocks from one pasture to another.

These indeed are most cruel expedients, contrary not merely to every Christian, but to every civilized rule of conduct, and such as every man should shun, choosing rather to lead a private life than to be a king on terms so hurtful to mankind. But he who will not keep to the fair path of virtue, must to maintain himself enter this path of evil. Men, however, not knowing how to be wholly good or wholly bad, choose for themselves certain middle ways, which of all others are the most pernicious, as shall be shown by an instance in the following Chapter.

CHAPTER XXVII

That Men seldom know how to be wholly good or wholly bad.

When in the year 1505, Pope Julius II. went to Bologna to expel from that city the family of the Bentivogli, who had been princes there for over a hundred years, it was also in his mind, as a part of the general design he had planned against all those lords who had usurped Church lands, to remove Giovanpagolo Baglioni, tyrant of Perugia. And coming to Perugia with this intention and resolve, of which all men knew, he would not wait to enter the town with a force sufficient for his protection, but entered it unattended by troops, although Giovanpagolo was there with a great company of soldiers whom he had assembled for his defence. And thus, urged on by that impetuosity which stamped all his actions, accompanied only by his body-guard, he committed himself into the hands of his enemy, whom he forthwith carried away with him, leaving a governor behind to hold the town for the Church. All prudent men who were with the Pope remarked on his temerity, and on the pusillanimity of Giovanpagolo; nor could they conjecture why the latter had not, to his eternal glory, availed himself of this opportunity for crushing his enemy, and at the same time enriching himself with plunder, the Pope being attended by the whole College of Cardinals with all their luxurious equipage. For it could not be supposed that he was withheld by any promptings of goodness or scruples of conscience; because in the breast of a profligate living in incest with his sister, and who to obtain the princedom had put his nephews and kinsmen to death, no virtuous impulse could prevail. So that the only inference to be drawn was, that men know not how to be splendidly wicked or wholly good, and shrink in consequence from such crimes as are stamped with an inherent greatness or disclose a nobility of nature. For which reason Giovanpagolo, who thought nothing of incurring the guilt of incest, or of murdering his kinsmen, could not, or more truly durst not, avail himself of a fair occasion to do a deed which all would have admired; which would have won for him a deathless fame as the first to teach the prelates how little those who live and reign as they do are to be esteemed; and which would have displayed a greatness far transcending any infamy or danger that could attach to it.

CHAPTER XXVIII

Whence it came that the Romans were less ungrateful to their Citizens than were the Athenians.

In the histories of all republics we meet with instances of some sort of ingratitude to their great citizens, but fewer in the history of Rome than of Athens, or indeed of any other republic. Searching for the cause of this, I am persuaded that, so far as regards Rome and Athens, it was due to the Romans having had less occasion than the Athenians to look upon their fellow-citizens with suspicion For, from the expulsion of her kings down to the times of Sylla and Marius, the liberty of Rome was never subverted by any one of her citizens; so that there never was in that city grave cause for distrusting any man, and in consequence making him the victim of inconsiderate injustice. The reverse was notoriously the case with Athens; for that city, having, at a time when she was most flourishing, been deprived of her freedom by Pisistratus under a false show of good-will, remembering, after she regained her liberty, her former bondage and all the wrongs she had endured, became the relentless chastiser, not of offences only on the part of her citizens, but even of the shadow of an offence. Hence the banishment and death of so many excellent men, and hence the law of ostracism, and all those other violent measures which from time to time during the history of that city were directed against her foremost citizens. For this is most true which is asserted by the writers on civil government, that a people which has recovered its freedom, bites more fiercely than one which has always preserved it.

And any who shall weigh well what has been said, will not condemn Athens in this matter, nor commend Rome, but refer all to the necessity arising out of the different conditions prevailing in the two States. For careful reflection will show that had Rome been deprived of her freedom as Athens was, she would not have been a whit more tender to her citizens. This we may reasonably infer from remarking what, after the expulsion of the kings, befell Collatinus and Publius Valerius; the former of whom, though he had taken part in the liberation of Rome, was sent into exile for no other reason than that he bore the name of Tarquin; while the sole ground of suspicion against the latter, and what almost led to his banishment, was his having built a house upon the Caelian hill. Seeing how harsh and suspicious Rome was in these two instances, we may surmise that she would have shown the same ingratitude as Athens, had she, like Athens, been wronged by her citizens at an early stage of her growth, and before she had attained to the fulness of her strength.

That I may not have to return to this question of ingratitude, I shall say all that remains to be said about it in my next Chapter.

CHAPTER XXIX

Whether a People or a Prince is the more ungrateful.

In connection with what has been said above, it seems proper to consider whether more notable instances of ingratitude are supplied by princes or peoples. And, to go to the root of the matter, I affirm that this vice of ingratitude has its source either in avarice or in suspicion. For a prince or people when they have sent forth a captain on some important enterprise, by succeeding in which he earns a great name, are bound in return to reward him; and if moved by avarice and covetousness they fail to do so, or if, instead of rewarding, they wrong and disgrace him, they commit an error which is not only without excuse, but brings with it undying infamy. And, in fact, we find many princes who have sinned in this way, for the cause given by Cornelius Tacitus when he says, that *"men are readier to pay back injuries than benefits, since to requite a benefit is felt to be a burthen, to return an injury a gain."*

When, however, reward is withheld, or, to speak more correctly, where offence is given, not from avarice but from suspicion, the prince or people may deserve some excuse; and we read of many instances of ingratitude proceeding from this cause. For the captain who by his valour has won new dominions for his prince, since while overcoming his enemies, he at the same time covers himself with glory and enriches his soldiers, must needs acquire such credit with his own followers, and with the enemy, and also with the subjects of his prince, as cannot be wholly agreeable to the master who sent him forth. And since men are by nature ambitious as well as jealous, and none loves to set a limit to his fortunes, the suspicion which at once lays hold of the prince when he sees his captain victorious, is sure to be inflamed by some arrogant act or word of the captain himself. So that the prince will be unable to think of anything but how to secure himself; and to this end will contrive how he may put his captain to death, or at any rate deprive him of the credit he has gained with the army and among the people; doing all he can to show that the victory was not won by his valour, but by good fortune, or by the cowardice of the enemy, or by the skill and prudence of those commanders who were with him at this or the other battle.

After Vespasian, who was then in Judaea, had been proclaimed emperor by his army, Antonius Primus, who commanded another army in Illyria, adopted his cause, and marching into Italy against Vitellius who had been proclaimed emperor in Rome, courageously defeated two armies under that prince, and occupied Rome; so that Mutianus, who was sent thither by Vespasian, found everything done to his hand, and all difficulties surmounted by the valour of Antonius. But all the reward which Antonius had for his pains, was, that Mutianus forthwith deprived him of his command of the army, and by degrees diminished his authority in Rome till none was left him. Thereupon Antonius went to join Vespasian, who was still in Asia; by whom he was so coldly received and so little considered, that in despair he put himself to death. And of cases like this, history is full. Every man living at the present hour knows with what zeal and courage Gonsalvo of Cordova, while conducting the war in Naples against the French, conquered and subdued that kingdom for his master Ferdinand of Aragon; and how his services were requited by Ferdinand coming from Aragon to Naples, and first of all depriving him of the command of the army, afterwards of the fortresses, and finally carrying him back with him to Spain, where soon after he died in disgrace.

This jealousy, then, is so natural to princes, that they cannot guard themselves against it, nor show gratitude to those who serving under their standard have gained great victories and made great conquests on their behalf. And if it be impossible for princes to free their minds from such suspicions, there is nothing strange or surprising that a people should be unable to do so. For as a city living under free institutions has two ends always before it, namely to acquire liberty and to preserve it, it must of necessity be led by its excessive passion for liberty to make mistakes in the pursuit of both these objects. Of the mistakes it commits in the effort to acquire liberty, I shall speak, hereafter, in the proper place. Of mistakes committed in the endeavour to preserve liberty are to be noted, the injuring those citizens who ought to be rewarded, and the suspecting those who should be trusted. Now, although in a State which has grown corrupt these errors occasion great evils, and commonly lead to a tyranny, as happened in Rome when Caesar took by force what ingratitude had denied him, they are nevertheless the cause of much good in the republic which has not been corrupted, since they prolong the duration of its free institutions, and make men, through fear of punishment, better and less ambitious. Of all peoples possessed of great power, the Romans, for the reasons I have given, have undoubtedly been the least ungrateful, since we have no other instance of their ingratitude to cite, save that of Scipio. For both Coriolanus and Camillus were banished on account of the wrongs which they inflicted on the commons; and though the former was not forgiven because he constantly retained ill will against the people, the latter was not only recalled, but for the rest of his life honoured as a prince. But the ingratitude shown towards Scipio arose from the suspicion wherewith the citizens came to regard him, which they had not felt in the case of the others, and which was occasioned by the greatness of the enemy whom he had overthrown, the fame he had won by prevailing in so dangerous and protracted a war, the suddenness of his victories, and, finally, the favour which his youth, together with his prudence and his other memorable qualities had gained for him. These qualities were, in truth, so remarkable that the very magistrates, not to speak of others, stood in awe of his authority, a circumstance displeasing to prudent citizens, as before unheard of in Rome. In short, his whole bearing and character were so much out of the common, that even the elder Cato, so celebrated for his austere virtue, was the first to declare against him, saying that no city could be deemed free which contained a citizen who was feared by the magistrates. And since, in this instance, the Romans followed the opinion of Cato, they merit that excuse which, as I have said already, should be extended to the prince or people who are ungrateful through suspicion.

In conclusion it is to be said that while this vice of ingratitude has its origin either in avarice or in suspicion, commonwealths are rarely led into it by avarice, and far seldomer than princes by suspicion, having, as shall presently be shown, far less reason than princes for suspecting.

CHAPTER XXX

How Princes and Commonwealths may avoid the vice of Ingratitude; and how a Captain or Citizen may escape being undone by it.

That he may not be tormented by suspicion, nor show ungrateful, a prince should go himself on his wars as the Roman emperors did at first, as the Turk does now, and, in short, as all valiant princes have done and do. For when it is the prince himself who conquers, the glory and the gain are all his own; but when he is absent, since the glory is another's, it will seem to the prince that he profits nothing by the gain, unless that glory be quenched which he knew not how to win for himself; and when he thus becomes ungrateful and unjust, doubtless his loss is greater than his gain. To the prince, therefore, who, either through indolence or from want of foresight, sends forth a captain to conduct his wars while he himself remains inactive at home, I have no advice to offer which he does not already know. But I would counsel the captain whom he sends, since I am sure that he can never escape the attacks of ingratitude, to follow one or other of two courses, and either quit his command at once after a victory, and place himself in the hands of his prince, while carefully abstaining from every vainglorious or ambitious act, so that the prince, being relieved from all suspicion, may be disposed to reward, or at any rate not to injure him; or else, should he think it inexpedient for him to act in this way, to take boldly the contrary course, and fearlessly to follow out all such measures as he thinks will secure for himself, and not for his prince, whatever he has gained; conciliating the good-will of his soldiers and fellow-citizens, forming new friendships with neighbouring potentates, placing his own adherents in fortified towns, corrupting the chief officers of his army and getting rid of those whom he fails to corrupt, and by all similar means endeavouring to punish his master for the ingratitude which he looks for at his hands. These are the only two courses open; but since, as I said before, men know not how to be wholly good or wholly bad, it will never happen that after a victory a captain will quit his army and conduct himself modestly, nor yet that he will venture to use those hardy methods which have in them some strain of greatness; and so, remaining undecided, he will be crushed while he still wavers and doubts.

A commonwealth desiring to avoid the vice of ingratitude is, as compared with a prince, at this disadvantage, that while a prince can go himself on his expeditions, the commonwealth must send some one of its citizens. As a remedy, I would recommend that course being adopted which was followed by the Roman republic in order to be less ungrateful than others, having its origin in the nature of the Roman government. For the whole city, nobles and commons alike, taking part in her wars, there were always found in Rome at every stage of her history, so many valiant and successful soldiers, that by reason of their number, and from one acting as a check upon another, the nation had never ground to be jealous of any one man among them; while they, on their part, lived uprightly, and were careful to betray no sign of ambition, nor give the people the least cause to distrust them as ambitious; so that he obtained most glory from his dictatorship who was first to lay it down. Which conduct, as it excited no suspicion, could occasion no ingratitude.

We see, then, that the commonwealth which would have no cause to be ungrateful, must act as Rome did; and that the citizen who would escape ingratitude, must observe those precautions which were observed by Roman citizens.

CHAPTER XXXI

That the Roman Captains were never punished with extreme severity for Misconduct; and where loss resulted to the Republic merely through their Ignorance or Want of Judgment, were not punished at all.

The Romans were not only, as has been said above, less ungrateful than other republics, but were also more lenient and more considerate than others in punishing the captains of their armies. For if these erred of set purpose, they chastised them with gentleness; while if they erred through ignorance, so far from punishing, they even honoured and rewarded them. And this conduct was well considered. For as they judged it of the utmost moment, that those in command of their armies should, in all they had to do, have their minds undisturbed and free from external anxieties, they would not add further difficulty and danger to a task in itself both dangerous and difficult, lest none should ever be found to act with valour. For supposing them to be sending forth an army against Philip of Macedon in Greece or against Hannibal in Italy, or against any other enemy at whose hands they had already sustained reverses, the captain in command of that expedition would be weighted with all the grave and important cares which attend such enterprises. But if to all these cares, had been added the example of Roman generals crucified or otherwise put to death for having lost battles, it would have been impossible for a commander surrounded by so many causes for anxiety to have acted with vigour and decision. For which reason, and because they thought that to such persons the mere ignominy of defeat was in itself punishment enough, they would not dishearten their generals by inflicting on them any heavier penalty.

Of errors committed not through ignorance, the following is an instance. Sergius and Virginius were engaged in the siege of Veii, each being in command of a division of the army, and while Sergius was set to guard against the approach of the Etruscans, it fell to Virginius to watch the town. But Sergius being attacked by the Faliscans and other tribes, chose rather to be defeated and routed than ask aid from Virginius, who, on his part, awaiting the humiliation of his rival, was willing to see his country dishonoured and an army destroyed, sooner than go unasked to his relief. This was notable misconduct, and likely, unless both offenders were punished, to bring discredit on the Roman name. But whereas another republic would have punished these men with death, the Romans were content to inflict only a money fine: not because the offence did not in itself deserve severe handling, but because they were unwilling, for the reasons already given, to depart in this instance from their ancient practice.

Of errors committed through ignorance we have no better example than in the case of Varro, through whose rashness the Romans were defeated by Hannibal at Cannae, where the republic well-nigh lost its liberty. But because he had acted through ignorance and with no evil design, they not only refrained from punishing him, but even treated him with distinction; the whole senate going forth to meet him on his return to Rome, and as they could not thank him for having fought, thanking him for having come back, and for not having despaired of the fortunes his country.

Again, when Papirius Cursor would have had Fabius put to death, because, contrary to his orders, he had fought with the Samnites, among the reasons pleaded by the father of Fabius against the persistency of the dictator, he urged that never on the occasion of the defeat of any of their captains had the Romans done what Papirius desired them to do on the occasion of a victory.

CHAPTER XXXII

That a Prince or Commonwealth should not delay conferring Benefits until they are themselves in difficulties.

The Romans found it for their advantage to be generous to the commons at a season of danger, when Porsenna came to attack Rome and restore the Tarquins. For the senate, apprehending that the people might choose rather to take back their kings than to support a war, secured their adherence by relieving them of the duty on salt and of all their other burthens; saying that *"the poor did enough for the common welfare in rearing their offspring."* In return for which indulgence the commons were content to undergo war, siege, and famine. Let no one however, relying on this example, delay conciliating the people till danger has actually come; or, if he do, let him not hope to have the same good fortune as the Romans. For the mass of the people will consider that they have to thank not him, but his enemies, and that there is ground to fear that when the danger has passed away, he will take back what he gave under compulsion, and, therefore, that to him they lie under no obligation. And the reason why the course followed by the Romans succeeded, was that the State was still new and unsettled. Besides which, the people knew that laws had already been passed in their favour, as, for instance, the law allowing an appeal to the tribunes, and could therefore persuade themselves that the benefits granted them proceeded from the good-will entertained towards them by the senate, and were not due merely to the approach of an enemy. Moreover, the memory of their kings, by whom they had in many ways been wronged and ill-treated, was still fresh in their minds. But since like conditions seldom recur, it can only rarely happen that like remedies are useful. Wherefore, all, whether princes or republics, who hold the reins of government, ought to think beforehand of the adverse times which may await them, and of what help they may then stand in need; and ought so to live with their people as they would think right were they suffering under any calamity. And, whosoever, whether prince or republic, but prince more especially, behaves otherwise, and believes that after the event and when danger is upon him he will be able to win men over by benefits, deceives himself, and will not merely fail to maintain his place, but will even precipitate his downfall.

CHAPTER XXXIII

When a Mischief has grown up in, or against a State, it is safer to temporize with than to meet it with Violence.

As Rome grew in fame, power, and dominion, her neighbours, who at first had taken no heed to the injury which this new republic might do them, began too late to see their mistake, and desiring to remedy what should have been remedied before, combined against her to the number of forty nations. Whereupon the Romans, resorting to a method usual with them in seasons of peril, appointed a dictator; that is, gave power to one man to decide without advice, and carry out his resolves without appeal. Which expedient, as it then enabled them to overcome the dangers by which they were threatened, so always afterwards proved most serviceable, when, at any time during the growth of their power, difficulties arose to embarrass their republic.

In connection with this league against Rome we have first to note, that when a mischief which springs up either in or against a republic, and whether occasioned by internal or external causes, has grown to such proportions that it begins to fill the whole community with alarm, it is a far safer course to temporize with it than to attempt to quell it by violence. For commonly those who make this attempt only add fuel to the flame, and hasten the impending ruin. Such disorders arise in a republic more often from internal causes than external, either through some citizen being suffered to acquire undue influence, or from the corruption of some institution of that republic, which had once been the life and sinew of its freedom; and from this corruption being allowed to gain such head that the attempt to check it is more dangerous than to let it be. And it is all the harder to recognize these disorders in their beginning, because it seems natural to men to look with favour on the beginnings of things. Favour of this sort, more than by anything else, is attracted by those actions which seem to have in them a quality of greatness, or which are performed by the young. For when in a republic some young man is seen to come forward endowed with rare excellence, the eyes of all the citizens are at once turned upon him, and all, without distinction, concur to do him honour; so that if he have one spark of ambition, the advantages which he has from nature, together with those he takes from this favourable disposition of men's minds, raise him to such a pitch of power, that when the citizens at last see their mistake it is almost impossible for them to correct it; and when they do what they can to oppose his influence the only result is to extend it. Of this I might cite numerous examples, but shall content myself with one relating to our own city.

Cosimo de' Medici, to whom the house of the Medici in Florence owes the origin of its fortunes, acquired so great a name from the favour wherewith his own prudence and the blindness of others invested him, that coming to be held in awe by the government, his fellow-citizens deemed it dangerous to offend him, but still more dangerous to let him alone. Nicolo da Uzzano, his cotemporary, who was accounted well versed in all civil affairs, but who had made a first mistake in not discerning the dangers which might grow from the rising influence of Cosimo, would never while he lived, permit a second mistake to be made in attempting to crush him; judging that such an attempt would be the ruin of the State, as in truth it proved after his death. For some who survived him, disregarding his counsels, combined against Cosimo and banished him from Florence. And so it came about that the partisans of Cosimo, angry at the wrong done him, soon afterwards recalled him and made him prince of the republic, a dignity he never would have reached but for this open opposition. The very same thing happened in Rome in the case of Caesar. For his services having gained him the good-will of Pompey and other citizens, their favour was presently turned to fear, as Cicero testifies where he says that "it was late that Pompey began to fear Caesar." This fear led men to think of remedies, and the remedies to which they resorted accelerated the destruction of the republic.

I say, then, that since it is difficult to recognize these disorders in their beginning, because of the false impressions which things produce at the first, it is a wiser course when they become known, to temporize with them than to oppose them; for when you temporize, either they die out of themselves, or at any rate the injury they do is deferred. And the prince who would suppress such disorders or oppose himself to their force and onset, must always be on his guard, lest he help where he would hinder, retard when he would advance, and drown the plant he thinks to water. He must therefore study well the symptoms of the disease; and, if he believe himself equal to the cure, grapple with it fearlessly; if not, he must let it be, and not attempt to treat it in any way. For, otherwise, it will fare with him as it fared with those neighbours of Rome, for whom it would have been safer, after that city had grown to be so great, to have sought to soothe and restrain her by peaceful arts, than to provoke her by open war to contrive new means of attack and new methods of defence. For this league had no other effect than to make the Romans more united and resolute than before, and to bethink themselves of new expedients whereby their power was still more rapidly advanced; among which was the creation of a dictator; for this innovation not only enabled them to surmount the dangers which then threatened them, but was afterwards the means of escaping infinite calamities into which, without it, the republic must have fallen.

CHAPTER XXXIV

That the authority of the Dictator did good and not harm to the Roman Republic: and that it is not those Powers which are given by the free suffrages of the People, but those which ambitious Citizens usurp for themselves, that are pernicious to a State.

Those citizens who first devised a dictatorship for Rome have been blamed by certain writers, as though this had been the cause of the tyranny afterwards established there. For these authors allege that the first tyrant of Rome governed it with the title of Dictator, and that, but for the existence of the office, Caesar could never have cloaked his usurpation under a constitutional name. He who first took up this opinion had not well considered the matter, and his conclusion has been accepted without good ground. For it was not the name nor office of Dictator which brought Rome to servitude, but the influence which certain of her citizens were able to assume from the prolongation of their term of power; so that even had the name of Dictator been wanting in Rome, some other had been found to serve their ends, since power may readily give titles, but not titles power. We find, accordingly, that while the dictatorship was conferred in conformity with public ordinances, and not through personal influence, it was constantly beneficial to the city. For it is the magistracies created and the powers usurped in unconstitutional ways that hurt a republic, not those which conform to ordinary rule; so that in Rome, through the whole period of her history, we never find a dictator who acted otherwise than well for the republic. For which there were the plainest reasons. In the first place, to enable a citizen to work harm and to acquire undue authority, many circumstances must be present which never can be present in a State which is not corrupted. For such a citizen must be exceedingly rich, and must have many retainers and partisans, whom he cannot have where the laws are strictly observed, and who, if he had them, would occasion so much alarm, that the free suffrage of the people would seldom be in his favour. In the second place, the dictator was not created for life, but for a fixed term, and only to meet the emergency for which he was appointed. Power was indeed given him to determine by himself what measures the exigency demanded; to do what he had to do without consultation; and to punish without appeal. But he had no authority to do anything to the prejudice of the State, as it would have been to deprive the senate or the people of their privileges, to subvert the ancient institutions of the city, or introduce new. So that taking into account the brief time for which his office lasted, its limited authority, and the circumstance that the Roman people were still uncorrupted, it was impossible for him to overstep the just limits of his power so as to injure the city; and in fact we find that he was always useful to it.

And, in truth, among the institutions of Rome, this of the dictatorship deserves our special admiration, and to be linked with the chief causes of her greatness; for without some such safeguard a city can hardly pass unharmed through extraordinary dangers. Because as the ordinary institutions of a commonwealth work but slowly, no council and no magistrate having authority to act in everything alone, but in most matters one standing in need of the other, and time being required to reconcile their differences, the remedies which they provide are most dangerous when they have to be applied in cases which do not brook delay. For which reason, every republic ought to have some resource of this nature provided by its constitution; as we find that the Republic of Venice, one of the best of those now existing, has in cases of urgent danger reserved authority to a few of her citizens, if agreed among themselves, to determine without further consultation what course is to be followed. When a republic is not provided with some safeguard such as this, either it must be ruined by observing constitutional forms, or else, to save it, these must be broken through. But in a republic nothing should be left to be effected by irregular methods, because, although for the time the irregularity may be useful, the example will nevertheless be pernicious, as giving rise to a practice of violating the laws for good ends, under colour of which they may afterwards be violated for ends which are not good. For which reason, that can never become a perfect republic wherein every contingency has not been foreseen and provided for by the laws, and the method of dealing with it defined. To sum up, therefore, I say that those republics which cannot in sudden emergencies resort either to a dictator or to some similar authority, will, when the danger is serious, always be undone.

We may note, moreover, how prudently the Romans, in introducing this new office, contrived the conditions under which it was to be exercised. For perceiving that the appointment of a dictator involved something of humiliation for the consuls, who, from being the heads of the State, were reduced to render obedience like every one else, and anticipating that this might give offence, they determined that the power to appoint should rest with the consuls, thinking that when the occasion came when Rome should have need of this regal authority, they would have the consuls acting willingly and feeling the less aggrieved from the appointment being in their own hands. For those wounds or other injuries which a man inflicts upon himself by choice, and of his own free will, pain him far less than those inflicted by another. Nevertheless, in the later days of the republic the Romans were wont to entrust this power to a consul instead of to a dictator, using the formula, *Videat CONSUL ne quid respublica detrimenti capiat.*

But to return to the matter in hand, I say briefly, that when the neighbours of Rome sought to crush her, they led her to take measures not merely for her readier defence, but such as enabled her to attack them with a stronger force, with better skill, and with an undivided command.

CHAPTER XXXV

Why the Creation of the Decemvirate in Rome, although brought about by the free and open Suffrage of the Citizens, was hurtful to the Liberties of that Republic

The fact of those ten citizens who were chosen by the Roman people to make laws for Rome, in time becoming her tyrants and depriving her of her freedom, may seem contrary to what I have said above, namely that it is the authority which is violently usurped, and not that conferred by the free suffrages of the people which is injurious to a republic. Here, however, we have to take into account both the mode in which, and the term for which authority is given. Where authority is unrestricted and is conferred for a long term, meaning by that for a year or more, it is always attended with danger, and its results will be good or bad according as the men are good or bad to whom it is committed. Now when we compare the authority of the Ten with that possessed by the dictator, we see that the power placed in the hands of the former was out of all proportion greater than that entrusted to the latter. For when a dictator was appointed there still remained the tribunes, the consuls, and the senate, all of them invested with authority of which the dictator could not deprive them. For even if he could have taken his consulship from one man, or his status as a senator from another, he could not abolish the senatorial rank nor pass new laws. So that the senate, the consuls, and the tribunes continuing to exist with undiminished authority were a check upon him and kept him in the right road. But on the creation of the Ten, the opposite of all this took place. For on their appointment, consuls and tribunes were swept away, and express powers were given to the new magistrates to make laws and do whatever else they thought fit, with the entire authority of the whole Roman people. So that finding themselves alone without consuls or tribunes to control them, and with no appeal against them to the people, and thus there being none to keep a watch upon them, and further being stimulated by the ambition of Appius, in the second year of their office they began to wax insolent.

  Let it be noted, therefore, that when it is said that authority given by the public vote is never hurtful to any commonwealth, it is assumed that the people will never be led to confer that authority without due limitations, or for other than a reasonable term. Should they, however either from being deceived or otherwise blinded, be induced to bestow authority imprudently, as the Romans bestowed it on the Ten, it will always fare with them as with the Romans. And this may readily be understood on reflecting what causes operated to keep the dictator good, what to make the Ten bad, and by observing how those republics which have been accounted well governed, have acted when conferring authority for an extended period, as the Spartans on their kings and the Venetians on their doges; for it will be seen that in both these instances the authority was controlled by checks which made it impossible for it to be abused. But where an uncontrolled authority is given, no security is afforded by the circumstance that the body of the people is not corrupted; for in the briefest possible time absolute authority will make a people corrupt, and obtain for itself friends and partisans. Nor will it be any hindrance to him in whom such authority is vested, that he is poor and without connections, for wealth and every other advantage will quickly follow, as shall be shown more fully when we discuss the appointment of the Ten.

CHAPTER XXXVI

That Citizens who have held the higher Offices of a Commonwealth should not disdain the lower.

Under the consuls M. Fabius and Cn. Manlius, the Romans had a memorable victory in a battle fought with the Veientines and the Etruscans, in which Q. Fabius, brother of the consul, who had himself been consul the year before, was slain. This event may lead us to remark how well the methods followed by the city of Rome were suited to increase her power, and how great a mistake is made by other republics in departing from them. For, eager as the Romans were in the pursuit of glory, they never esteemed it a dishonour to obey one whom before they had commanded, or to find themselves serving in the ranks of an army which once they had led. This usage, however, is opposed to the ideas, the rules, and the practice which prevail at the present day, as, for instance, in Venice, where the notion still obtains that a citizen who has filled a great office should be ashamed to accept a less; and where the State itself permits him to decline it. This course, assuming it to lend lustre to individual citizens, is plainly to the disadvantage of the community, which has reason to hope more from, and to trust more to, the citizen who descends from a high office to fill a lower, than him who rises from a low office to fill a high one; for in the latter no confidence can reasonably be placed, unless he be seen to have others about him of such credit and worth that it may be hoped their wise counsels and influence will correct his inexperience. But had the usage which prevails in Venice and in other modern commonwealths and kingdoms, prevailed in Rome whereby he who had once been consul was never afterwards to go with the army except as consul, numberless results must have followed detrimental to the free institutions of that city; as well from the mistakes which the inexperience of new men would have occasioned, as because from their ambition having a freer course, and from their having none near them in whose presence they might fear to do amiss, they would have grown less scrupulous; and in this way the public service must have suffered grave harm.

CHAPTER XXXVII

Of the Mischief bred in Rome by the Agrarian Law: and how it is a great source of disorder in a Commonwealth to pass a Law opposed to ancient Usage and with stringent retrospective Effect.

It has been said by ancient writers that to be pinched by adversity or pampered by prosperity is the common lot of men, and that in whichever way they are acted upon the result is the same. For when no longer urged to war on one another by necessity, they are urged by ambition, which has such dominion in their hearts that it never leaves them to whatsoever heights they climb. For nature has so ordered it that while they desire everything, it is impossible for them to have everything, and thus their desires being always in excess of their capacity to gratify them, they remain constantly dissatisfied and discontented. And hence the vicissitudes in human affairs. For some seeking to enlarge their possessions, and some to keep what they have got, wars and enmities ensue, from which result the ruin of one country and the growth of another.

I am led to these reflections from observing that the commons of Rome were not content to secure themselves against the nobles by the creation of tribunes, a measure to which they were driven by necessity, but after effecting this, forthwith entered upon an ambitious contest with the nobles, seeking to share with them what all men most esteem, namely, their honours and their wealth. Hence was bred that disorder from which sprang the feuds relating to the Agrarian Laws, and which led in the end to the downfall of the Roman republic. And although it should be the object of every well-governed commonwealth to make the State rich and keep individual citizens poor it must be allowed that in the matter of this law the city of Rome was to blame; whether for having passed it at first in such a shape as to require it to be continually recast; or for having postponed it so long that its retrospective effect was the occasion of tumult; or else, because, although rightly framed at first, it had come in its operation to be perverted. But in whatever way it happened, so it was, that this law was never spoken of in Rome without the whole city being convulsed.

The law itself embraced two principal provisions. By one it was enacted that no citizen should possess more than a fixed number of acres of land; by the other that all lands taken from the enemy should be distributed among the whole people. A twofold blow was thus aimed at the nobles; since all who possessed more land than the law allowed, as most of the nobles did, fell to be deprived of it; while by dividing the lands of the enemy among the whole people, the road to wealth was closed. These two grounds of offence being given to a powerful class, to whom it appeared that by resisting the law they did a service to the State, the whole city, as I have said, was thrown into an uproar on the mere mention of its name. The nobles indeed sought to temporize, and to prevail by patience and address; sometimes calling out the army, sometimes opposing another tribune to the one who was promoting the law, and sometimes coming to a compromise by sending a colony into the lands which were to be divided; as was done in the case of the territory of Antium, whither, on a dispute concerning the law having arisen, settlers were sent from Rome, and the land made over to them. In speaking of which colony Titus Livius makes the notable remark, that hardly any one in Rome could be got to take part in it, so much readier were the commons to indulge in covetous schemes at home, than to realize them by leaving it.

The ill humour engendered by this contest continued to prevail until the Romans began to carry their arms into the remoter parts of Italy and to countries beyond its shores; after which it seemed for a time to slumber — and this, because the lands held by the enemies of Rome, out of sight of her citizens and too remote to be conveniently cultivated, came to be less desired. Whereupon the Romans grew less eager to punish their enemies by dividing their lands, and were content, when they deprived any city of its territory, to send colonists to occupy it. For causes such as these, the measure remained in abeyance down to the time of the Gracchi; but being by them revived, finally overthrew the liberty of Rome. For as it found the power of its adversaries doubled, such a flame of hatred was kindled between commons and senate, that, regardless of all civil restraints, they resorted to arms and bloodshed. And as the public magistrates were powerless to provide a remedy, each of the two factions having no longer any hopes from them, resolved to do what it could for itself, and to set up a chief for its own protection. On reaching this stage of tumult and disorder, the commons lent their influence to Marius, making him four times consul; whose authority, lasting thus long, and with very brief intervals, became so firmly rooted that he was able to make himself consul other three times. Against this scourge, the nobles, lacking other defence, set themselves to favour Sylla, and placing him at the head of their faction, entered on the civil wars; wherein, after much blood had been spilt, and after many changes of fortune, they got the better of their adversaries. But afterwards, in the time of Caesar and Pompey, the distemper broke out afresh; for Caesar heading the Marian party, and Pompey, that of Sylla, and war ensuing, the victory remained with Caesar, who was the first tyrant in Rome; after whose time that city was never again free. Such, therefore, was the beginning and such the end of the Agrarian Law.

But since it has elsewhere been said that the struggle between the commons and senate of Rome preserved her liberties, as giving rise to laws favourable to freedom, it might seem that the consequences of the Agrarian Law are opposed to that view. I am not, however, led to alter my opinion on this account; for I maintain that the ambition of the great is so pernicious that unless controlled and counteracted in a variety of ways, it will always reduce a city to speedy ruin. So that if the controversy over the Agrarian Laws took three hundred years to bring Rome to slavery, she would in all likelihood have been brought to slavery in a far shorter time, had not the commons, by means of this law, and by other demands, constantly restrained the ambition of the nobles.

We may also learn from this contest how much more men value wealth than honours; for in the matter of honours, the Roman nobles always gave way to the commons without any extraordinary resistance; but when it came to be a question of property, so stubborn were they in its defence, that the commons to effect their ends had to resort to those irregular methods which have been described above. Of which irregularities the prime movers were the Gracchi, whose motives are more to be commended than their measures; since to pass a law with stringent retrospective effect, in order to remove an abuse of long standing in a republic, is an unwise step, and one which, as I have already shown at length, can have no other result than to accelerate the mischief to which the abuse leads; whereas, if you temporize, either the abuse develops more slowly, or else, in course of time, and before it comes to a head, dies out of itself.

CHAPTER XXXVIII

That weak Republics are irresolute and undecided; and that the course they may take depends more on Necessity than Choice.

A terrible pestilence breaking out in Rome seemed to the Equians and Volscians to offer a fit opportunity for crushing her. The two nations, therefore, assembling a great army, attacked the Latins and Hernicians and laid waste their country. Whereupon the Latins and Hernicians were forced to make their case known to the Romans, and to ask to be defended by them. The Romans, who were sorely afflicted by the pestilence, answered that they must look to their own defence, and with their own forces, since Rome was in no position to succour them.

Here we recognize the prudence and magnanimity of the Roman senate, and how at all times, and in all changes of fortune, they assumed the responsibility of determining the course their country should take; and were not ashamed, when necessary, to decide on a course contrary to that which was usual with them, or which they had decided to follow on some other occasion. I say this because on other occasions this same senate had forbidden these nations to defend themselves; and a less prudent assembly might have thought it lowered their credit to withdraw that prohibition. But the Roman senate always took a sound view of things, and always accepted the least hurtful course as the best. So that, although it was distasteful to them not to be able to defend their subjects, and equally distasteful — both for the reasons given, and for others which may be understood — that their subjects should take up arms in their absence, nevertheless knowing that these must have recourse to arms in any case, since the enemy was upon them, they took an honourable course in deciding that what had to be done should be done with their leave, lest men driven to disobey by necessity should come afterwards to disobey from choice. And although this may seem the course which every republic ought reasonably to follow, nevertheless weak and badly-advised republics cannot make up their minds to follow it, not knowing how to do themselves honour in like extremities.

After Duke Valentino had taken Faenza and forced Bologna to yield to his terms, desiring to return to Rome through Tuscany, he sent one of his people to Florence to ask leave for himself and his army to pass. A council was held in Florence to consider how this request should be dealt with, but no one was favourable to the leave asked for being granted. Wherein the Roman method was not followed. For as the Duke had a very strong force with him, while the Florentines were so bare of troops that they could not have prevented his passage, it would have been far more for their credit that he should seem to pass with their consent, than that he should pass in spite of them; because, while discredit had to be incurred either way, they would have incurred less by acceding to his demand.

But of all courses the worst for a weak State is to be irresolute; for then whatever it does will seem to be done under compulsion, so that if by chance it should do anything well, this will be set down to necessity and not to prudence. Of this I shall cite two other instances happening in our own times, and in our own country. In the year 1500, King Louis of France, after recovering Milan, being desirous to restore Pisa to the Florentines, so as to obtain payment from them of the fifty thousand ducats which they had promised him on the restitution being completed, sent troops to Pisa under M. Beaumont, in whom, though a Frenchman, the Florentines put much trust. Beaumont accordingly took up his position with his forces between Cascina and Pisa, to be in readiness to attack the town. After he had been there for some days making arrangements for the assault, envoys came to him from Pisa offering to surrender their city to the French if a promise were given in the king's name, not to hand it over to the Florentines until four months had run. This condition was absolutely rejected by the Florentines, and the siege being proceeded with, they were forced to retire with disgrace. Now the proposal of the Pisans was rejected by the Florentines for no other reason than that they distrusted the good faith of the King, into whose hands their weakness obliged them to commit themselves, and did not reflect how much more it was for their interest that, by obtaining entrance into Pisa, he should have it in his power to restore the town to them, or, failing to restore it, should at once disclose his designs, than that remaining outside he should put them off with promises for which they had to pay. It would therefore have been a far better course for the Florentines to have agreed to Beaumont taking possession on whatever terms.

This was seen afterwards by experience in the year 1502, when, on the revolt of Arezzo, M. Imbalt was sent by the King of France with French troops to assist the Florentines. For when he got near Arezzo, and began to negotiate with the Aretines, who, like the Pisans, were willing to surrender their town on terms, the acceptance of these terms was strongly disapproved in Florence; which Imbalt learning, and thinking that the Florentines were acting with little sense, he took the entire settlement of conditions into his own hands, and, without consulting the Florentine commissioners, concluded an arrangement to his own satisfaction, in execution of which he entered Arezzo with his army. And he let the Florentines know that he thought them fools and ignorant of the ways of the world; since if they desired to have Arezzo, they could signify their wishes to the King, who would be much better able to give it them when he had his soldiers inside, than when he had them outside the town. Nevertheless, in Florence they never ceased to blame and abuse M. Imbalt, until at last they came to see that if Beaumont had acted in the same way, they would have got possession Of Pisa as well as of Arezzo.

Applying what has been said to the matter in hand, we find that irresolute republics, unless upon compulsion, never follow wise courses; for wherever there is room for doubt, their weakness will not suffer them to come to any resolve; so that unless their doubts be overcome by some superior force which impels them forward, they remain always in suspense.

CHAPTER XXXIX

That often the same Accidents are seen to befall different Nations.

Any one comparing the present with the past will soon perceive that in all cities and in all nations there prevail the same desires and passions as always have prevailed; for which reason it should be an easy matter for him who carefully examines past events, to foresee those which are about to happen in any republic, and to apply such remedies as the ancients have used in like cases; or finding none which have been used by them, to strike out new ones, such as they might have used in similar circumstances. But these lessons being neglected or not understood by readers, or, if understood by them, being unknown to rulers, it follows that the same disorders are common to all times.

In the year 1494 the Republic of Florence, having lost a portion of its territories, including Pisa and other towns, was forced to make war against those who had taken possession of them, who being powerful, it followed that great sums were spent on these wars to little purpose. This large expenditure had to be met by heavy taxes which gave occasion to numberless complaints on the part of the people; and inasmuch as the war was conducted by a council of ten citizens, who were styled "the Ten of the War," the multitude began to regard these with displeasure, as though they were the cause of the war and of the consequent expenditure; and at last persuaded themselves that if they got rid of this magistracy there would be an end to the war. Wherefore when the magistracy of "the Ten" should have been renewed, the people did not renew it, but, suffering it to lapse, entrusted their affairs to the "Signory." This course was most pernicious, since not only did it fail to put an end to the war, as the people expected it would, but by setting aside men who had conducted it with prudence, led to such mishaps that not Pisa only, but Arezzo also, and many other towns besides were lost to Florence. Whereupon, the people recognizing their mistake, and that the evil was in the disease and not in the physician, reinstated the magistracy of the Ten.

Similar dissatisfaction grew up in Rome against the consular authority. For the people seeing one war follow another, and that they were never allowed to rest, when they should have ascribed this to the ambition of neighbouring nations who desired their overthrow, ascribed it to the ambition of the nobles, who, as they believed, being unable to wreak their hatred against them within the city, where they were protected by the power of the tribunes, sought to lead them outside the city, where they were under the authority of the consuls, that they might crush them where they were without help. In which belief they thought it necessary either to get rid of the consuls altogether, or so to restrict their powers as to leave them no authority over the people, either in the city or out of it.

The first who attempted to pass a law to this effect was the tribune Terentillus, who proposed that a committee of five should be named to consider and regulate the power of the consuls. This roused the anger of the nobles, to whom it seemed that the greatness of their authority was about to set for ever, and that no part would be left them in the administration of the republic. Such, however, was the obstinacy of the tribunes, that they succeeded in abolishing the consular title, nor were satisfied until, after other changes, it was resolved that, in room of consuls, tribunes should be appointed with consular powers; so much greater was their hatred of the name than of the thing. For a long time matters remained on this footing; till eventually, the commons, discovering their mistake, resumed the appointment of consuls in the same way as the Florentines reverted to "the Ten of the War."

CHAPTER XL

Of the creation of the Decemvirate in Rome, and what therein is to be noted. Wherein among other Matters is shown how the same Causes may lead to the Safety or to the Ruin of a Commonwealth.

It being my desire to treat fully of those disorders which arose in Rome on the creation of the decemvirate, I think it not amiss first of all to relate what took place at the time of that creation, and then to discuss those circumstances attending it which seem most to deserve notice. These are numerous, and should be well considered, both by those who would maintain the liberties of a commonwealth and by those who would subvert them. For in the course of our inquiry it will be seen that many mistakes prejudicial to freedom were made by the senate and people, and that many were likewise made by Appius, the chief decemvir, prejudicial to that tyranny which it was his aim to establish in Rome.

After much controversy and wrangling between the commons and the nobles as to the framing of new laws by which the freedom of Rome might be better secured, Spurius Posthumius and two other citizens were, by general consent, despatched to Athens to procure copies of the laws which Solon had drawn up for the Athenians, to the end that these might serve as a groundwork for the laws of Rome. On their return, the next step was to depute certain persons to examine these laws and to draft the new code. For which purpose a commission consisting of ten members, among whom was Appius Claudius, a crafty and ambitious citizen, was appointed for a year; and that the commissioners in framing their laws might act without fear or favour, all the other magistracies, and in particular the consulate and tribuneship, were suspended, and the appeal to the people discontinued; so that the decemvirs came to be absolute in Rome. Very soon the whole authority of the commissioners came to be centred in Appius, owing to the favour in which he was held by the commons. For although before he had been regarded as the cruel persecutor of the people, he now showed himself so conciliatory in his bearing that men wondered at the sudden change in his character and disposition.

This set of commissioners, then, behaved discreetly, being attended by no more than twelve lictors, walking in front of that decemvir whom the rest put forward as their chief; and though vested with absolute authority, yet when a Roman citizen had to be tried for murder, they cited him before the people and caused him to be judged by them. Their laws they wrote upon ten tables, but before signing them they exposed them publicly, that every one might read and consider them, and if any defect were discovered in them, it might be corrected before they were finally passed. At this juncture Appius caused it to be notified throughout the city that were two other tables added to these ten, the laws would be complete; hoping that under this belief the people would consent to continue the decemvirate for another year. This consent the people willingly gave, partly to prevent the consuls being reinstated, and partly because they thought they could hold their ground without the aid of the tribunes, who, as has already been said, were the judges in criminal cases.

On it being resolved to reappoint the decemvirate, all the nobles set to canvass for the office, Appius among the foremost; and such cordiality did he display towards the commons while seeking their votes, that the other candidates, *"unable to persuade themselves that so much affability on the part of so proud a man was wholly disinterested,"* began to suspect him; but fearing to oppose him openly, sought to circumvent him, by putting him forward, though the youngest of them all, to declare to the people the names of the proposed decemvirs; thinking that he would not venture to name himself, that being an unusual course in Rome, and held discreditable. "*But what they meant as a hindrance, he turned to account,*" by proposing, to the surprise and displeasure of the whole nobility, his own name first, and then nominating nine others on whose support he thought he could depend.

The new appointments, which were to last for a year, having been made, Appius soon let both commons and nobles know the mistake they had committed, for throwing off the mask, he allowed his innate arrogance to appear, and speedily infected his colleagues with the same spirit; who, to overawe the people and the senate, instead of twelve lictors, appointed one hundred and twenty. For a time their measures were directed against high and low alike; but presently they began to intrigue with the senate, and to attack the commons; and if any of the latter, on being harshly used by one decemvir, ventured to appeal to another, he was worse handled on the appeal than in the first instance. The commons, on discovering their error, began in their despair to turn their eyes towards the nobles, "*and to look for a breeze of freedom from that very quarter whence fearing slavery they had brought the republic to its present straits.*" To the nobles the sufferings of the commons were not displeasing, from the hope "*that disgusted with the existing state of affairs, they too might come to desire the restoration of the consuls.*"

When the year for which the decemvirs were appointed at last came to an end, the two additional tables of the law were ready, but had not yet been published. This was made a pretext by them for prolonging their magistracy, which they took measures to retain by force, gathering round them for this purpose a retinue of young noblemen, whom they enriched with the goods of those citizens whom they had condemned. "*Corrupted by which gifts, these youths came to prefer selfish licence to public freedom.*"

It happened that at this time the Sabines and Volscians began to stir up a war against Rome, and it was during the alarm thereby occasioned that the decemvirs were first made aware how weak was their position. For without the senate they could take no warlike measures, while by assembling the senate they seemed to put an end to their own authority. Nevertheless, being driven to it by necessity, they took this latter course. When the senate met, many of the senators, but particularly Valerius and Horatius, inveighed against the insolence of the decemvirs, whose power would forthwith have been cut short, had not the senate through jealousy of the commons declined to exercise their authority. For they thought that were the decemvirs to lay down office of their own free will, tribunes might not be reappointed. Wherefore they decided for war, and sent forth the armies under command of certain of the decemvirs. But Appius remaining behind to govern the city, it so fell out that he became enamoured of Virginia, and that when he sought to lay violent hands upon her, Virginius, her father, to save her from dishonour, slew her. Thereupon followed tumults in Rome, and mutiny among the soldiers, who, making common cause with the rest of the plebeians, betook themselves to the Sacred Hill, and there remained until the decemvirs laid down their office; when tribunes and consuls being once more appointed, Rome was restored to her ancient freedom.

In these events we note, first of all, that the pernicious step of creating this tyranny in Rome was due to the same causes which commonly give rise to tyrannies in cities; namely, the excessive love of the people for liberty, and the passionate eagerness of the nobles to govern. For when they cannot agree to pass some measure favourable to freedom, one faction or the other sets itself to support some one man, and a tyranny at once springs up. Both parties in Rome consented to the creation of the decemvirs, and to their exercising unrestricted powers, from the desire which the one had to put an end to the consular name, and the other to abolish the authority of the tribunes. When, on the appointment of the decemvirate, it seemed to the commons that Appius had become favourable to their cause, and was ready to attack the nobles, they inclined to support him. But when a people is led to commit this error of lending its support to some one man, in order that he may attack those whom it holds in hatred, if he only be prudent he will inevitably become the tyrant of that city. For he will wait until, with the support of the people, he can deal a fatal blow to the nobles, and will never set himself to oppress the people until the nobles have been rooted out. But when that time comes, the people, although they recognize their servitude, will have none to whom they can turn for help.

Had this method, which has been followed by all who have successfully established tyrannies in republics, been followed by Appius, his power would have been more stable and lasting; whereas, taking the directly opposite course, he could not have acted more unwisely than he did. For in his eagerness to grasp the tyranny, he made himself obnoxious to those who were in fact conferring it, and who could have maintained him in it; and he destroyed those who were his friends, while he sought friendship from those from whom he could not have it. For although it be the desire of the nobles to tyrannize, that section of them which finds itself outside the tyranny is always hostile to the tyrant, who can never succeed in gaining over the entire body of the nobles by reason of their greed and ambition; for no tyrant can ever have honours or wealth enough to satisfy them all.

In abandoning the people, therefore, and siding with the nobles, Appius committed a manifest mistake, as well for the reasons above given, as because to hold a thing by force, he who uses force must needs be stronger than he against whom it is used. Whence it happens that those tyrants who have the mass of the people for their friends and the nobles for their enemies, are more secure than those who have the people for their enemies and the nobles for their friends; because in the former case their authority has the stronger support. For with such support a ruler can maintain himself by the internal strength of his State, as did Nabis, tyrant of Sparta, when attacked by the Romans and by the whole of Greece; for making sure work with the nobles, who were few in number, and having the people on his side, he was able with their assistance to defend himself; which he could not have done had they been against him. But in the case of a city, wherein the tyrant has few friends, its internal strength will not avail him for its defence, and he will have to seek aid from without in one of three shapes. For either he must hire foreign guards to defend his person; or he must arm the peasantry, so that they may play the part which ought to be played by the citizens; or he must league with powerful neighbours for his defence. He who follows these methods and observes them well, may contrive to save himself, though he has the people for his enemy. But Appius could not follow the plan of gaining over the peasantry, since in Rome they and the people were one. And what he might have done he knew not how to do, and so was ruined at the very outset.

In creating the decemvirate, therefore, both the senate and the people made grave mistakes. For although, as already explained, when speaking of the dictatorship, it is those magistrates who make themselves, and not those made by the votes of the people, that are hurtful to freedom; nevertheless the people, in creating magistrates ought to take such precautions as will make it difficult for these to become bad. But the Romans when they ought to have set a check on the decemvirs in order to keep them good, dispensed with it, making them the sole magistrates of Rome, and setting aside all others; and this from the excessive desire of the senate to get rid of the tribunes, and of the commons to get rid of the consuls; by which objects both were so blinded as to fall into all the disorders which ensued. For, as King Ferrando was wont to say, men often behave like certain of the smaller birds, which are so intent on the prey to which nature incites them, that they discern not the eagle hovering overhead for their destruction.

In this Discourse then the mistakes made by the Roman people in their efforts to preserve their freedom and the mistakes made by Appius in his endeavour to obtain the tyranny, have, as I proposed at the outset, been plainly shown.

CHAPTER XLI

That it is unwise to pass at a bound from leniency to severity, or to a haughty bearing from a humble.

Among the crafty devices used by Appius to aid him in maintaining his authority, this, of suddenly passing from one character to the other extreme, was of no small prejudice to him. For his fraud in pretending to the commons to be well disposed towards them, was happily contrived; as were also the means he took to bring about the reappointment of the decemvirate. Most skilful, too, was his audacity in nominating himself contrary to the expectation of the nobles, and in proposing colleagues on whom he could depend to carry out his ends. But, as I have said already, it was not happily contrived that, after doing all this, he should suddenly turn round, and from being the friend, reveal himself the enemy of the people; haughty instead of humane; cruel instead of kindly; and make this change so rapidly as to leave himself no shadow of excuse, but compel all to recognize the doubleness of his nature. For he who has once seemed good, should he afterwards choose, for his own ends, to become bad, ought to change by slow degrees, and as opportunity serves; so that before his altered nature strip him of old favour, he may have gained for himself an equal share of new, and thus his influence suffer no diminution. For otherwise, being at once unmasked and friendless, he is undone:

CHAPTER XLII

How easily Men become corrupted.

In this matter of the decemvirate we may likewise note the ease wherewith men become corrupted, and how completely, although born good and well brought up, they change their nature. For we see how favourably disposed the youths whom Appius gathered round him became towards his tyranny, in return for the trifling benefits which they drew from it; and how Quintus Fabius, one of the second decemvirate and a most worthy man, blinded by a little ambition, and misled by the evil counsels of Appius, abandoning his fair fame, betook himself to most unworthy courses, and grew like his master.

Careful consideration of this should make those who frame laws for commonwealths and kingdoms more alive to the necessity of placing restraints on men's evil appetites, and depriving them of all hope of doing wrong with impunity.

CHAPTER XLIII

That Men fighting in their own Cause make good and resolute Soldiers.

From what has been touched upon above, we are also led to remark how wide is the difference between an army which, having no ground for discontent, fights in its own cause, and one which, being discontented, fights to satisfy the ambition of others. For whereas the Romans were always victorious under the consuls, under the decemvirs they were always defeated. This helps us to understand why it is that mercenary troops are worthless; namely, that they have no incitement to keep them true to you beyond the pittance which you pay them, which neither is nor can be a sufficient motive for such fidelity and devotion as would make them willing to die in your behalf. But in those armies in which there exists not such an attachment towards him for whom they fight as makes them devoted to his cause, there never will be valour enough to withstand an enemy if only he be a little brave. And since such attachment and devotion cannot be looked for from any save your own subjects, you must, if you would preserve your dominions, or maintain your commonwealth or kingdom, arm the natives of your country; as we see to have been done by all those who have achieved great things in war.

Under the decemvirs the ancient valour of the Roman soldiers had in no degree abated; yet, because they were no longer animated by the same good will, they did not exert themselves as they were wont. But so soon as the decemvirate came to an end, and the soldiers began once more to fight as free men, the old spirit was reawakened, and, as a consequence, their enterprises, according to former usage, were brought to a successful close.

CHAPTER XLIV

That the Multitude is helpless without a Head: and that we should not with the same breath threaten and ask leave.

When Virginia died by her father's hand, the commons of Rome withdrew under arms to the Sacred Hill. Whereupon the senate sent messengers to demand by what sanction they had deserted their commanders and assembled there in arms. And in such reverence was the authority of the senate held, that the commons, lacking leaders, durst make no reply. "Not," says Titus Livius, "that they were at a loss what to answer, but because they had none to answer for them;" words which clearly show how helpless a thing is the multitude when without a head.

This defect was perceived by Virginius, at whose instance twenty military tribunes were appointed by the commons to be their spokesmen with the senate, and to negotiate terms; who, having asked that Valerius and Horatius might be sent to them, to whom their wishes would be made known, these declined to go until the decemvirs had laid down their office. When this was done, and Valerius and Horatius came to the hill where the commons were assembled, the latter demanded that tribunes of the people should be appointed; that in future there should be an appeal to the people from the magistrates of whatever degree; and that all the decemvirs should be given up to them to be burned alive. Valerius and Horatius approved the first two demands, but rejected the last as inhuman; telling the commons that "they were rushing into that very cruelty which they themselves had condemned in others;" and counselling them to say nothing about the decemvirs, but to be satisfied to regain their own power and authority; since thus the way would be open to them for obtaining every redress.

Here we see plainly how foolish and unwise it is to ask a thing and with the same breath to say, "I desire this that I may inflict an injury." For we should never declare our intention beforehand, but watch for every opportunity to carry it out. So that it is enough to ask another for his weapons, without adding, "With these I purpose to destroy you;" for when once you have secured his weapons, you can use them afterwards as you please.

CHAPTER XLV

That it is of evil example, especially in the Maker of a Law, not to observe the Law when made: and that daily to renew acts of injustice in a City is most hurtful to the Governor.

Terms having been adjusted, and the old order of things restored in Rome, Virginius cited Appius to defend himself before the people; and on his appearing attended by many of the nobles, ordered him to be led to prison. Whereupon Appius began to cry out and appeal to the people. But Virginius told him that he was unworthy to be allowed that appeal which he had himself done away with, or to have that people whom he had wronged for his protectors. Appius rejoined, that the people should not set at nought that right of appeal which they themselves had insisted on with so much zeal. Nevertheless, he was dragged to prison, and before the day of trial slew himself. Now, though the wicked life of Appius merited every punishment, still it was impolitic to violate the laws, more particularly a law which had only just been passed; for nothing, I think, is of worse example in a republic, than to make a law and not to keep it; and most of all, when he who breaks is he that made it.

After the year 1494, the city of Florence reformed its government with the help of the Friar Girolamo Savonarola, whose writings declare his learning, his wisdom, and the excellence of his heart. Among other ordinances for the safety of the citizens, he caused a law to be passed, allowing an appeal to the people from the sentences pronounced by "the Eight" and by the "Signory" in trials for State offences; a law he had long contended for, and carried at last with great difficulty. It so happened that a very short time after it was passed, five citizens were condemned to death by the "Signory" for State offences, and that when they sought to appeal to the people they were not permitted to do so, and the law was violated. This, more than any other mischance, helped to lessen the credit of the Friar; since if his law of appeal was salutary, he should have caused it to be observed; if useless, he ought not to have promoted it. And his inconsistency was the more remarked, because in all the sermons which he preached after the law was broken, he never either blamed or excused the person who had broken it, as though unwilling to condemn, while unable to justify what suited his purposes. This, as betraying the ambitious and partial turn of his mind, took from his reputation and exposed him to much obloquy.

Another thing which greatly hurts a government is to keep alive bitter feelings in men's minds by often renewed attacks on individuals, as was done in Rome after the decemvirate was put an end to. For each of the decemvirs, and other citizens besides, were at different times accused and condemned, so that the greatest alarm was spread through the whole body of the nobles, who came to believe that these prosecutions would never cease until their entire order was exterminated. And this must have led to grave mischief had not Marcus Duilius the tribune provided against it, by an edict which forbade every one, for the period of a year, citing or accusing any Roman citizen, an ordinance which had the effect of reassuring the whole nobility. Here we see how hurtful it is for a prince or commonwealth to keep the minds of their subjects in constant alarm and suspense by continually renewed punishments and violence. And, in truth, no course can be more pernicious. For men who are in fear for their safety will seize on every opportunity for securing themselves against the dangers which surround them, and will grow at once more daring, and less scrupulous in resorting to new courses. For these reasons we should either altogether avoid inflicting injury, or should inflict every injury at a stroke, and then seek to reassure men's minds and suffer them to settle down and rest.

CHAPTER XLVI

That Men climb from one step of Ambition to another, seeking at first to escape Injury and then to injure others.

As the commons of Rome on recovering their freedom were restored to their former position — nay, to one still stronger since many new laws had been passed which confirmed and extended their authority, — it might reasonably have been hoped that Rome would for a time remain at rest. The event, however, showed the contrary, for from day to day there arose in that city new tumults and fresh dissensions. And since the causes which brought this about have been most judiciously set forth by Titus Livius, it seems to me much to the purpose to cite his own words when he says, that "whenever either the commons or the nobles were humble, the others grew haughty; so that if the commons kept within due bounds, the young nobles began to inflict injuries upon them, against which the tribunes, who were themselves made the objects of outrage, were little able to give redress; while the nobles on their part, although they could not close their eyes to the ill behaviour of their young men, were yet well pleased that if excesses were to be committed, they should be committed by their own faction, and not by the commons. Thus the desire to secure its own liberty prompted each faction to make itself strong enough to oppress the other. For this is the common course of things, that in seeking to escape cause for fear, men come to give others cause to be afraid by inflicting on them those wrongs from which they strive to relieve themselves; as though the choice lay between injuring and being injured."

Herein, among other things, we perceive in what ways commonwealths are overthrown, and how men climb from one ambition to another; and recognize the truth of those words which Sallust puts in the mouth of Caesar, that *"all ill actions have their origin in fair beginnings."* For, as I have said already, the ambitious citizen in a commonwealth seeks at the outset to secure himself against injury, not only at the hands of private persons, but also of the magistrates; to effect which he endeavours to gain himself friends. These he obtains by means honourable in appearance, either by supplying them with money or protecting them against the powerful. And because such conduct seems praiseworthy, every one is readily deceived by it, and consequently no remedy is applied. Pursuing these methods without hindrance, this man presently comes to be so powerful that private citizens begin to fear him, and the magistrates to treat him with respect. But when he has advanced thus far on the road to power without encountering opposition, he has reached a point at which it is most dangerous to cope with him; it being dangerous, as I have before explained, to contend with a disorder which has already made progress in a city. Nevertheless, when he has brought things to this pass, you must either endeavour to crush him, at the risk of immediate ruin, or else, unless death or some like accident interpose, you incur inevitable slavery by letting him alone. For when, as I have said, it has come to this that the citizens and even the magistrates fear to offend him and his friends, little further effort will afterwards be needed to enable him to proscribe and ruin whom he pleases.

A republic ought, therefore, to provide by its ordinances that none of its citizens shall, under colour of doing good, have it in their power to do evil, but shall be suffered to acquire such influence only as may aid and not injure freedom. How this may be done, shall presently be explained.

CHAPTER XLVII

That though Men deceive themselves in Generalities, in Particulars they judge truly.

The commons of Rome having, as I have said, grown disgusted with the consular name, and desiring either that men of plebeian birth should be admitted to the office or its authority be restricted, the nobles, to prevent its degradation in either of these two ways, proposed a middle course, whereby four tribunes, who might either be plebeians or nobles, were to be created with consular authority. This compromise satisfied the commons, who thought they would thus get rid of the consulship, and secure the highest offices of the State for their own order. But here a circumstance happened worth noting. When the four tribunes came to be chosen, the people, who had it in their power to choose all from the commons, chose all from the nobles. With respect to which election Titus Livius observes, that *"the result showed that the people when declaring their honest judgment after controversy was over, were governed by a different spirit from that which had inspired them while contending for their liberties and for a share in public honours."* The reason for this I believe to be, that men deceive themselves more readily in generals than in particulars. To the commons of Rome it seemed, in the abstract, that they had every right to be admitted to the consulship, since their party in the city was the more numerous, since they bore the greater share of danger in their wars, and since it was they who by their valour kept Rome free and made her powerful. And because it appeared to them, as I have said, that their desire was a reasonable one, they were resolved to satisfy it at all hazards. But when they had to form a particular judgment on the men of their own party, they recognized their defects, and decided that individually no one of them was deserving of what, collectively, they seemed entitled to; and being ashamed of them, turned to bestow their honours on those who deserved them. Of which decision Titus Livius, speaking with due admiration, says, "*Where shall we now find in any one man, that modesty, moderation, and magnanimity which were then common to the entire people?*"

As confirming what I have said, I shall cite another noteworthy incident, which occurred in Capua after the rout of the Romans by Hannibal at Cannae. For all Italy being convulsed by that defeat, Capua too was threatened with civil tumult, through the hatred which prevailed between her people and senate. But Pacuvius Calavius, who at this time filled the office of chief magistrate, perceiving the danger, took upon himself to reconcile the contending factions. With this object he assembled the Senate and pointed out to them the hatred in which they were held by the people, and the risk they ran of being put to death by them, and of the city, now that the Romans were in distress, being given up to Hannibal. But he added that, were they to consent to leave the matter with him, he thought he could contrive to reconcile them; in the meanwhile, however, he must shut them up in the palace, that, by putting it in the power of the people to punish them, he might secure their safety.

The senate consenting to this proposal, he shut them up in the palace, and summoning the people to a public meeting, told them the time had at last come for them to trample on the insolence of the nobles, and requite the wrongs suffered at their hands; for he had them all safe under bolt and bar; but, as he supposed they did not wish the city to remain without rulers, it was fit, before putting the old senators to death, they should appoint others in their room. Wherefore he had thrown the names of all the old senators into a bag, and would now proceed to draw them out one by one, and as they were drawn would cause them to be put to death, so soon as a successor was found for each. When the first name he drew was declared, there arose a great uproar among the people, all crying out against the cruelty, pride, and arrogance of that senator whose name it was. But on Pacuvius desiring them to propose a substitute, the meeting was quieted, and after a brief pause one of the commons was nominated. No sooner, however, was his name mentioned than one began to whistle, another to laugh, some jeering at him in one way and some in another. And the same thing happening in every case, each and all of those nominated were judged unworthy of senatorial rank. Whereupon Pacuvius, profiting by the opportunity, said, "Since you are agreed that the city would be badly off without a senate, but are not agreed whom to appoint in the room of the old senators, it will, perhaps, be well for you to be reconciled to them; for the fear into which they have been thrown must have so subdued them, that you are sure to find in them that affability which hitherto you have looked for in vain." This proposal being agreed to, a reconciliation followed between the two orders; the commons having seen their error so soon as they were obliged to come to particulars.

A people therefore is apt to err in judging of things and their accidents in the abstract, but on becoming acquainted with particulars, speedily discovers its mistakes. In the year 1494, when her greatest citizens were banished from Florence, and no regular government any longer existed there, but a spirit of licence prevailed, and matters went continually from bad to worse, many Florentines perceiving the decay of their city, and discerning no other cause for it, blamed the ambition of this or the other powerful citizen, who, they thought, was fomenting these disorders with a view to establish a government to his own liking, and to rob them of their liberties. Those who thought thus, would hang about the arcades and public squares, maligning many citizens, and giving it to be understood that if ever they found themselves in the Signory, they would expose the designs of these citizens and have them punished. From time to time it happened that one or another of those who used this language rose to be of the chief magistracy, and so soon as he obtained this advancement, and saw things nearer, became aware whence the disorders I have spoken of really came, the dangers attending them, and the difficulty in dealing with them; and recognizing that they were the growth of the times, and not occasioned by particular men, suddenly altered his views and conduct; a nearer knowledge of facts freeing him from the false impressions he had been led into on a general view of affairs. But those who had heard him speak as a private citizen, when they saw him remain inactive after he was made a magistrate, believed that this arose not from his having obtained any better knowledge of things, but from his having been cajoled or corrupted by the great. And this happening with many men and often, it came to be a proverb among the people, that *"men had one mind in the market-place, another in the palace."*

Reflecting on what has been said, we see how quickly men's eyes may be opened, if knowing that they deceive themselves in generalities, we can find a way to make them pass to particulars; as Pacuvius did in the case of the Capuans, and the senate in the case of Rome. Nor do I believe that any prudent man need shrink from the judgment of the people in questions relating to particulars, as, for instance, in the distribution of honours and dignities. For in such matters only, the people are either never mistaken, or at any rate far seldomer than a small number of persons would be, were the distribution entrusted to them.

It seems to me, however, not out of place to notice in the following Chapter, a method employed by the Roman senate to enlighten the people in making this distribution.

CHAPTER XLVIII

He who would not have an Office bestowed on some worthless or wicked Person, should contrive that it be solicited by one who is utterly worthless and wicked, or else by one who is in the highest degree noble and good.

Whenever the senate saw a likelihood of the tribunes with consular powers being chosen exclusively from the commons, it took one or other of two ways, — either by causing the office to be solicited by the most distinguished among the citizens; or else, to confess the truth, by bribing some base and ignoble fellow to fasten himself on to those other plebeians of better quality who were seeking the office, and become a candidate conjointly with them. The latter device made the people ashamed to give, the former ashamed to refuse.

This confirms what I said in my last Chapter, as to the people deceiving themselves in generalities but not in particulars.

CHAPTER XLIX

That if Cities which, like Rome, had their beginning in Freedom, have had difficulty in framing such Laws as would preserve their Freedom, Cities which at the first have been in Subjection will find this almost impossible.

How hard it is in founding a commonwealth to provide it with all the laws needed to maintain its freedom, is well seen from the history of the Roman Republic. For although ordinances were given it first by Romulus, then by Numa, afterwards by Tullus Hostilius and Servius, and lastly by the Ten created for the express purpose, nevertheless, in the actual government of Rome new needs were continually developed, to meet which, new ordinances had constantly to be devised; as in the creation of the censors, who were one of the chief means by which Rome was kept free during the whole period of her constitutional government. For as the censors became the arbiters of morals in Rome, it was very much owing to them that the progress of the Romans towards corruption was retarded. And though, at the first creation of the office, a mistake was doubtless made in fixing its term at five years, this was corrected not long after by the wisdom of the dictator Mamercus, who passed a law reducing it to eighteen months; a change which the censors then in office took in such ill part, that they deprived Mamercus of his rank as a senator. This step was much blamed both by the commons and the Fathers; still, as our History does not record that Mamercus obtained any redress, we must infer either that the Historian has omitted something, or that on this head the laws of Rome were defective; since it is never well that the laws of a commonwealth should suffer a citizen to incur irremediable wrong because he promotes a measure favourable to freedom.

But returning to the matter under consideration, we have, in connection with the creation of this new office, to note, that if those cities which, as was the case with Rome, have had their beginning in freedom, and have by themselves maintained that freedom, have experienced great difficulty in framing good laws for the preservation of their liberties, it is little to be wondered at that cities which at the first were dependent, should find it not difficult merely but impossible so to shape their ordinances as to enable them to live free and undisturbed. This difficulty we see to have arisen in the case of Florence, which, being subject at first to the power of Rome and subsequently to that of other rulers, remained long in servitude, taking no thought for herself; and even afterwards, when she could breathe more freely and began to frame her own laws, these, since they were blended with ancient ordinances which were bad, could not themselves be good; and thus for the two hundred years of which we have trustworthy record, our city has gone on patching her institutions, without ever possessing a government in respect of which she could truly be termed a commonwealth.

The difficulties which have been felt in Florence are the same as have been felt in all cities which have had a like origin; and although, repeatedly, by the free and public votes of her citizens, ample authority has been given to a few of their number to reform her constitution, no alteration of general utility has ever been introduced, but only such as forwarded the interests of the party to which those commissioned to make changes belonged. This, instead of order, has occasioned the greatest disorder in our city.

But to come to particulars, I say, that among other matters which have to be considered by the founder of a commonwealth, is the question into whose hands should be committed the power of life and death over its citizens' This was well seen to in Rome, where, as a rule, there was a right of appeal to the people, but where, on any urgent case arising in which it might have been dangerous to delay the execution of a judicial sentence, recourse could be had to a dictator with powers to execute justice at once; a remedy, however, never resorted to save in cases of extremity. But Florence, and other cities having a like origin, committed this power into the hands of a foreigner, whom they styled Captain, and as he was open to be corrupted by powerful citizens this was a pernicious course. Altering this arrangement afterwards in consequence of changes in their government, they appointed eight citizens to discharge the office of Captain. But this, for a reason already mentioned, namely that a few will always be governed by the will of a few and these the most powerful, was a change from bad to worse.

The city of Venice has guarded herself against a like danger. For in Venice ten citizens are appointed with power to punish any man without appeal; and because, although possessing the requisite authority, this number might not be sufficient to insure the punishment of the powerful, in addition to their council of Ten, they have also constituted a council of Forty, and have further provided that the council of the "*Pregai*," which is their supreme council, shall have authority to chastise powerful offenders. So that, unless an accuser be wanting, a tribunal is never wanting in Venice to keep powerful citizens in check.

But when we see how in Rome, with ordinances of her own imposing, and with so many and so wise legislators, fresh occasion arose from day to day for framing new laws favourable to freedom, it is not to be wondered at that, in other cities less happy in their beginnings, difficulties should have sprung up which no ordinances could remedy.

CHAPTER L

That neither any Council nor any Magistrate should have power to bring the Government of a City to a stay.

T.Q. CINCINNATUS and Cn. Julius Mento being consuls of Rome, and being at variance with one another, brought the whole business of the city to a stay; which the senate perceiving, were moved to create a dictator to do what, by reason of their differences, the consuls would not. But though opposed to one another in everything else, the consuls were of one mind in resisting the appointment of a dictator; so that the senate had no remedy left them but to seek the help of the tribunes, who, supported by their authority, forced the consuls to yield.

Here we have to note, first, the usefulness of the tribunes' authority in checking the ambitious designs, not only of the nobles against the commons, but also of one section of the nobles against another; and next, that in no city ought things ever to be so ordered that it rests with a few to decide on matters, which, if the ordinary business of the State is to proceed at all, must be carried out. Wherefore, if you grant authority to a council to distribute honours and offices, or to a magistrate to administer any branch of public business, you must either impose an obligation that the duty confided shall be performed, or ordain that, on failure to perform, another may and shall do what has to be done. Otherwise such an arrangement will be found defective and dangerous; as would have been the case in Rome, had it not been possible to oppose the authority of the tribunes to the obstinacy of the consuls.

In the Venetian Republic, the great council distributes honours and offices. But more than once it has happened that the council, whether from ill-humour or from being badly advised, has declined to appoint successors either to the magistrates of the city or to those administering the government abroad. This gave rise to the greatest confusion and disorder; for, on a sudden, both the city itself and the subject provinces found themselves deprived of their lawful governors; nor could any redress be had until the majority of the council were pacified or undeceived. And this disorder must have brought the city to a bad end, had not provision been made against its recurrence by certain of the wiser citizens, who, finding a fit opportunity, passed a law that no magistracy, whether within or without the city, should ever be deemed to have been vacated until it was filled up by the appointment of a successor. In this way the council was deprived of its facilities for stopping public business to the danger of the State.

CHAPTER LI

What a Prince or Republic does of Necessity, should seem to be done by Choice.

In all their actions, even in those which are matters of necessity rather than choice, prudent men will endeavour so to conduct themselves as to conciliate good-will. This species of prudence was well exercised by the Roman senate when they resolved to grant pay from the public purse to soldiers on active service, who, before, had served at their own charges. For perceiving that under the old system they could maintain no war of any duration, and, consequently, could not undertake a siege or lead an army to any distance from home, and finding it necessary to be able to do both, they decided on granting the pay I have spoken of. But this, which they could not help doing, they did in such a way as to earn the thanks of the people, by whom the concession was so well received that all Rome was intoxicated with delight. For it seemed to them a boon beyond any they could have ventured to hope for, or have dreamed of demanding. And although the tribunes sought to make light of the benefit, by showing the people that their burthens would be increased rather than diminished by it, since taxes would have to be imposed out of which the soldier's stipend might be paid, they could not persuade them to regard the measure otherwise than with gratitude; which was further increased by the manner in which the senate distributed the taxes, imposing on the nobles all the heavier and greater, and those which had to be paid first.

CHAPTER LII

That to check the arrogance of a Citizen who is growing too powerful in a State, there is no safer Method, or less open to objection, than to forestall him in those Ways whereby he seeks to advance himself.

It has been seen in the preceding chapter how much credit the nobles gained with the commons by a show of goodwill towards them, not only in providing for their military pay, but also in adjusting taxation. Had the senate constantly adhered to methods like these, they would have put an end to all disturbances in Rome, and have deprived the tribunes of the credit they had with the people, and of the influence thence arising. For in truth, in a commonwealth, and especially in one which has become corrupted, there is no better, or easier, or less objectionable way of opposing the ambition of any citizen, than to anticipate him in those paths by which he is seen to be advancing to the ends he has in view. This plan, had it been followed by the enemies of Cosimo de' Medici, would have proved a far more useful course for them than to banish him from Florence; since if those citizens who opposed him had adopted his methods for gaining over the people, they would have succeeded, without violence or tumult, in taking his most effective weapon from his hands.

The influence acquired in Florence by Piero Soderini was entirely due to his skill in securing the affections of the people, since in this way he obtained among them a name for loving the liberties of the commonwealth. And truly, for those citizens who envied his greatness it would have been both easier and more honourable, and at the same time far less dangerous and hurtful to the State, to forestall him in those measures by which he was growing powerful, than to oppose him in such a manner that his overthrow must bring with it the ruin of the entire republic. For had they, as they might easily have done, deprived him of the weapons which made him formidable, they could then have withstood him in all the councils, and in all public deliberations, without either being suspected or feared. And should any rejoin that, if the citizens who hated Piero Soderini committed an error in not being beforehand with him in those ways whereby he came to have influence with the people, Piero himself erred in like manner, in not anticipating his enemies in those methods whereby they grew formidable to him; I answer that Piero is to be excused, both because it would have been difficult for him to have so acted, and because for him such a course would not have been honourable. For the paths wherein his danger lay were those which favoured the Medici, and it was by these that his enemies attacked him, and in the end overthrew him. But these paths Piero could not pursue without dishonour, since he could not, if he was to preserve his fair fame, have joined in destroying that liberty which he had been put forward to defend. Moreover, since favours to the Medicean party could not have been rendered secretly and once for all, they would have been most dangerous for Piero, who, had he shown himself friendly to the Medici, must have become suspected and hated by the people; in which case his enemies would have had still better opportunities than before for his destruction.

Men ought therefore to look to the risks and dangers of any course which lies before them, nor engage in it when it is plain that the dangers outweigh the advantages, even though they be advised by others that it is the most expedient way to take. Should they act otherwise, it will fare with them as with Tullius, who, in seeking to diminish the power of Marcus Antonius, added to it. For Antonius, who had been declared an enemy by the senate, having got together a strong force, mostly made up of veterans who had shared the fortunes of Caesar, Tullius counselled the senate to invest Octavianus with full authority, and to send him against Antonius with the consuls and the army; affirming, that so soon as those veterans who had served with Caesar saw the face of him who was Caesar's nephew and had assumed his name, they would rally to his side and desert Antonius, who might easily be crushed when thus left bare of support.

But the reverse of all this happened. For Antonius persuaded Octavianus to take part with him, and to throw over Tullius and the senate. And this brought about the ruin of the senate, a result which might easily have been foreseen. For remembering the influence of that great captain, who, after overthrowing all opponents, had seized on sovereign power in Rome, the senate should have turned a deaf ear to the persuasions of Tullius, nor ever have believed it possible that from Caesar's heir, or from soldiers who had followed Caesar, they could look for anything that consisted with the name of Freedom.

CHAPTER LIII

That the People, deceived by a false show of Advantage, often desire what would be their Ruin; and that large Hopes and brave Promises easily move them.

When Veii fell, the commons of Rome took up the notion that it would be to the advantage of their city were half their number to go and dwell there. For they argued that as Veii lay in a fertile country and was a well-built city, a moiety of the Roman people might in this way be enriched; while, by reason of its vicinity to Rome, the management of civil affairs would in no degree be affected. To the senate, however, and the wiser among the citizens, the scheme appeared so rash and mischievous that they publicly declared they would die sooner than consent to it. The controversy continuing, the commons grew so inflamed against the senate that violence and bloodshed must have ensued; had not the senate for their protection put forward certain old and esteemed citizens, respect for whom restrained the populace and put a stop to their violence.

Two points are here to be noted. First, that a people deceived by a false show of advantage will often labour for its own destruction; and, unless convinced by some one whom it trusts, that the course on which it is bent is pernicious, and that some other is to be preferred, will bring infinite danger and injury upon the State. And should it so happen, as sometimes is the case, that from having been deceived before, either by men or by events, there is none in whom the people trust, their ruin is inevitable. As to which Dante, in his treatise "De Monarchia," observes that the people will often raise the cry, *"Flourish our death and perish our life."* From which distrust it arises that often in republics the right course is not followed; as when Venice, as has been related, on being attacked by many enemies, could not, until her ruin was complete, resolve to make friends with any one of them by restoring those territories she had taken from them, on account of which war had been declared and a league of princes formed against her.

In considering what courses it is easy, and what it is difficult to persuade a people to follow, this distinction may be drawn: Either what you would persuade them to, presents on the face of it a semblance of gain or loss, or it seems a spirited course or a base one. When any proposal submitted to the people holds out promise of advantage, or seems to them a spirited course to take, though loss lie hid behind, nay, though the ruin of their country be involved in it, they will always be easily led to adopt it; whereas it will always be difficult to persuade the adoption of such courses as wear the appearance of disgrace or loss, even though safety and advantage be bound up with them. The truth of what I say is confirmed by numberless examples both Roman and foreign, modern and ancient. Hence grew the ill opinion entertained in Rome of Fabius Maximus, who could never persuade the people that it behoved them to proceed warily in their conflict with Hannibal, and withstand his onset without fighting. For this the people thought a base course, not discerning the advantage resulting from it, which Fabius could by no argument make plain to them. And so blinded are men in favour of what seems a spirited course, that although the Romans had already committed the blunder of permitting Varro, master of the knights to Fabius, to join battle contrary to the latter's desire, whereby the army must have been destroyed had not Fabius by his prudence saved it, this lesson was not enough; for afterwards they appointed this Varro to be consul, for no other reason than that he gave out, in the streets and market-places, that he would make an end of Hannibal as soon as leave was given him to do so. Whence came the battle and defeat of Cannae, and well-nigh the destruction of Rome.

Another example taken from Roman history may be cited to the same effect. After Hannibal had maintained himself for eight or ten years in Italy, during which time the whole country had been deluged with Roman blood, a certain Marcus Centenius Penula, a man of mean origin, but who had held some post in the army, came forward and proposed to the senate that were leave given him to raise a force of volunteers in any part of Italy he pleased, he would speedily deliver Hannibal into their hands, alive or dead. To the senate this man's offer seemed a rash one; but reflecting that were they to refuse it, and were the people afterwards to hear that it had been made, tumults, ill will, and resentment against them would result, they granted the permission asked; choosing rather to risk the lives of all who might follow Penula, than to excite fresh discontent on the part of the people, to whom they knew that such a proposal would be welcome, and that it would be very hard to dissuade them from it. And so this adventurer, marching forth with an undisciplined and disorderly rabble to meet Hannibal, was, with all his followers, defeated and slain in the very first encounter.

In Greece, likewise, and in the city of Athens, that most grave and prudent statesman, Nicias, could not convince the people that the proposal to go and attack Sicily was disadvantageous; and the expedition being resolved on, contrary to his advice and to the wishes of the wiser among the citizens, resulted in the overthrow of the Athenian power. Scipio, on being appointed consul, asked that the province of Africa might be awarded to him, promising that he would utterly efface Carthage; and when the senate, on the advice of Fabius, refused his request, he threatened to submit the matter to the people as very well knowing that to the people such proposals are always acceptable.

I might cite other instances to the same effect from the history of our own city, as when Messer Ercole Bentivoglio and Antonio Giacomini, being in joint command of the Florentine armies, after defeating Bartolommeo d'Alviano at San Vincenzo, proceeded to invest Pisa. For this enterprise was resolved on by the people in consequence of the brave promises of Messer

Ercole; and though many wise citizens disapproved of it, they could do nothing to prevent it, being carried away by the popular will, which took its rise in the assurances of their captain.

I say, then, that there is no readier way to bring about the ruin of a republic, when the power is in the hands of the people, than to suggest daring courses for their adoption. For wherever the people have a voice, such proposals will always be well received, nor will those persons who are opposed to them be able to apply any remedy. And as this occasions the ruin of States, it likewise, and even more frequently, occasions the private ruin of those to whom the execution of these proposals is committed; because the people anticipating victory, do not when there comes defeat ascribe it to the short means or ill fortune of the commander, but to his cowardice and incapacity; and commonly either put him to death, or imprison or banish him; as was done in the case of numberless Carthaginian generals and of many Athenian, no successes they might previously have obtained availing them anything; for all past services are cancelled by a present loss. And so it happened with our Antonio Giacomini, who not succeeding as the people had expected, and as he had promised, in taking Pisa, fell into such discredit with the people, that notwithstanding his countless past services, his life was spared rather by the compassion of those in authority than through any movement of the citizens in his behalf.

CHAPTER LIV

Of the boundless Authority which a great Man may use to restrain an excited Multitude.

The next noteworthy point in the passage referred to in the foregoing Chapter is, that nothing tends so much to restrain an excited multitude as the reverence felt for some grave person, clothed with authority, who stands forward to oppose them. For not without reason has Virgil said —
"If then, by chance, some reverend chief appear, Known for his deeds and for his virtues dear, Silent they wait his words and bend a listening ear."
He therefore who commands an army or governs a city wherein tumult shall have broken out, ought to assume the noblest and bravest bearing he can, and clothe himself with all the ensigns of his station, that he may make himself more revered. It is not many years since Florence was divided into two factions, the *Frateschi* and *Arrabbiati*, as they were named, and these coming to open violence, the *Frateschi*, among whom was Pagolo Antonio Soderini, a citizen of great reputation in these days, were worsted. In the course of these disturbances the people coming with arms in their hands to plunder the house of Soderini, his brother Messer Francesco, then bishop of Volterra and now cardinal, who happened to be dwelling there, so soon as he heard the uproar and saw the crowd, putting on his best apparel and over it his episcopal robes, went forth to meet the armed multitude, and by his words and mien brought them to a stay; and for many days his behaviour was commended by the whole city. The inference from all which is, that there is no surer or more necessary restraint on the violence of an unruly multitude, than

the presence of some one whose character and bearing command respect.

But to return once more to the passage we are considering, we see how stubbornly the people clung to this scheme of transplanting themselves to Veii, thinking it for their advantage, and not discerning the mischief really involved in it; so that in addition to the many dissensions which it occasioned, actual violence must have followed, had not the senate with the aid of certain grave and reverend citizens repressed the popular fury.

CHAPTER LV

That Government is easily carried on in a City wherein the body of the People is not corrupted: and that a Princedom is impossible where Equality prevails, and a Republic where it does not.

Though what we have to fear or hope from cities that have grown corrupted has already been discussed, still I think it not out of place to notice a resolution passed by the senate touching the vow which Camillus made to Apollo of a tenth of the spoil taken from the Veientines. For this spoil having fallen into the hands of the people, the senate, being unable by other means to get any account of it, passed an edict that every man should publicly offer one tenth part of what he had taken. And although this edict was not carried out, from the senate having afterwards followed a different course, whereby, to the content of the people, the claim of Apollo was otherwise satisfied, we nevertheless see from their having entertained such a proposal, how completely the senate trusted to the honesty of the people, when they assumed that no one would withhold any part of what the edict commanded him to give; on the other hand, we see that it never occurred to the people that they might evade the law by giving less than was due, their only thought being to free themselves from the law by openly manifesting their displeasure. This example, together with many others already noticed, shows how much virtue and how profound a feeling of religion prevailed among the Roman people, and how much good was to be expected from them. And, in truth, in the country where virtue like this does not exist, no good can be looked for, as we should look for it in vain in provinces which at the present day are seen to be corrupted; as Italy is beyond all others, though, in some degree, France and Spain are similarly tainted. In which last two countries, if we see not so many disorders spring up as we see daily springing up in Italy, this is not so much due to the superior virtue of their inhabitants (who, to say truth, fall far short of our countrymen), as to their being governed by a king who keeps them united, not merely by his personal qualities, but also by the laws and ordinances of the realm which are still maintained with vigour. In Germany, however, we do see signal excellence and a devout religious spirit prevail among the people, giving rise to the many free States which there maintain themselves, with such strict observance of their laws that none, either within or without their walls, dare encroach on them.

That among this last-named people a great share of the ancient excellence does in truth still flourish, I shall show by an example similar to that which I have above related of the senate and people of Rome. It is customary with the German Free States when they have to expend any large sum of money on the public account, for their magistrates or councils having authority given them in that behalf, to impose a rate of one or two in the hundred on every man's estate; which rate being fixed, every man, in conformity with the laws of the city, presents himself before the collectors of the impost, and having first made oath to pay the amount justly due, throws into a chest provided for the purpose what he conscientiously believes it fair for him to pay, of which payment none is witness save himself. From this fact it may be gathered what honesty and religion still prevail among this people. For we must assume that each pays his just share, since otherwise the impost would not yield the sum which, with reference to former imposts, it was estimated to yield; whereby the fraud would be detected, and thereupon some other method for raising money have to be resorted to.

At the present time this virtue is the more to be admired, because it seems to have survived in this province only. That it has survived there may be ascribed to two circumstances: *first*, that the natives have little communication with their neighbours, neither visiting them in their countries nor being visited by them; being content to use such commodities, and subsist on such food, and to wear garments of such materials as their own land supplies; so that all occasion for intercourse, and every cause of corruption is removed. For living after this fashion, they have not learned the manners of the French, the Italians, or the Spaniards, which three nations together are the corruption of the world. The *second* cause is, that these republics in which a free and pure government is maintained will not suffer any of their citizens either to be, or to live as gentlemen; but on the contrary, while preserving a strict equality among themselves, are bitterly hostile to all those gentlemen and lords who dwell in their neighbourhood; so that if by chance any of these fall into their hands, they put them to death, as the chief promoters of corruption and the origin of all disorders.

But to make plain what I mean when I speak of *gentlemen*, I say that those are so to be styled who live in opulence and idleness on the revenues of their estates, without concerning themselves with the cultivation of these estates, or incurring any other fatigue for their support. Such persons are very mischievous in every republic or country. But even more mischievous are they who, besides the estates I have spoken of, are lords of strongholds and castles, and have vassals and retainers who render them obedience. Of these two classes of men the kingdom of Naples, the country round Rome, Romagna, and Lombardy are full; and hence it happens that in these provinces no commonwealth or free form of government has ever existed; because men of this sort are the sworn foes to all free institutions.

And since to plant a commonwealth in provinces which are in this condition were impossible, if these are to be reformed at all, it can only be by some one man who is able there to establish a kingdom; the reason being that when the body of the people is grown so corrupted that the laws are powerless to control it, there must in addition to the laws be introduced a stronger force, to wit, the regal, which by its absolute and unrestricted authority may curb the excessive ambition and corruption of the great. This opinion may be supported by the example of Tuscany, in which within a narrow compass of territory there have long existed the three republics of Florence, Lucca, and Siena, while the other cities of that province, although to a certain extent dependent, still show by their spirit and by their institutions that they preserve, or at any rate desire to preserve, their freedom: and this because there are in Tuscany no lords possessed of strongholds, and few or no gentlemen, but so complete an equality prevails, that a prudent statesman, well acquainted with the history of the free States of antiquity, might easily introduce free institutions. Such, however, has been the unhappiness of this our country, that, up to the present hour, it has never produced any man with the power and knowledge which would have enabled him to act in this way.

From what has been said, it follows, that he who would found a commonwealth in a country wherein there are many gentlemen, cannot do so unless he first gets rid of them; and that he who would found a monarchy or princedom in a country wherein great equality prevails, will never succeed, unless he raise above the level of that equality many persons of a restless and ambitious temperament, whom he must make gentlemen not in name merely but in reality, by conferring on them castles and lands, supplying them with riches, and providing them with retainers; that with these gentlemen around him, and with their help, he may maintain his power, while they through him may gratify their ambition; all others being constrained to endure a yoke, which force and force alone imposes on them. For when in this way there comes to be a proportion between him who uses force and him against whom it is used, each stands fixed in his own station.

But to found a commonwealth in a country suited for a kingdom, or a kingdom in a country suited to be a commonwealth, requires so rare a combination of intelligence and power, that though many engage in the attempt, few are found to succeed. For the greatness of the undertaking quickly daunts them, and so obstructs their advance they break down at the very outset. The case of the Venetian Republic, wherein none save gentlemen are permitted to hold any public office, does, doubtless, seem opposed to this opinion of mine that where there are gentlemen it is impossible to found a commonwealth. But it may be answered that the case of Venice is not in truth an instance to the contrary; since the gentlemen of Venice are gentlemen rather in name than in reality, inasmuch as they draw no great revenues from lands, their wealth consisting chiefly in merchandise and chattels, and not one of them possessing a castle or enjoying any feudal authority. For in Venice this name of gentleman is a title of honour and dignity, and does not depend on any of those circumstances in respect of which the name is given in other States. But as in other States the different ranks and classes are divided under different names, so in Venice we have the division into gentlemen (*gentiluomini*) and plebeians (*popolani*), it being understood that the former hold, or have the right to hold all situations of honour, from which the latter are entirely excluded. And in Venice this occasions no disturbance, for reasons which I have already explained.

Let a commonwealth, then, be constituted in the country where a great equality is found or has been made; and, conversely, let a princedom be constituted where great inequality prevails. Otherwise what is constituted will be discordant in itself, and without stability.

CHAPTER LVI

That when great Calamities are about to befall a City or Country, Signs are seen to presage, and Seers arise who foretell them.

Whence it happens I know not, but it is seen from examples both ancient and recent, that no grave calamity has ever befallen any city or country which has not been foretold by vision, by augury, by portent, or by some other Heaven-sent sign. And not to travel too far afield for evidence of this, every one knows that long before the invasion of Italy by Charles VIII. of France, his coming was foretold by the friar Girolamo Savonarola; and how, throughout the whole of Tuscany, the rumour ran that over Arezzo horsemen had been seen fighting in the air. And who is there who has not heard that before the death of the elder Lorenzo de' Medici, the highest pinnacle of the cathedral was rent by a thunderbolt, to the great injury of the building? Or who, again, but knows that shortly before Piero Soderini, whom the people of Florence had made gonfalonier for life, was deprived of his office and banished, the palace itself was struck by lightning? Other instances might be cited, which, not to be tedious, I shall omit, and mention only a circumstance which Titus Livius tells us preceded the invasion of the Gauls. For he relates how a certain plebeian named Marcus Ceditius reported to the senate that as he passed by night along the Via Nova, he heard a voice louder than mortal, bidding him warn the magistrates that the Gauls were on their way to Rome.

The causes of such manifestations ought, I think, to be inquired into and explained by some one who has a knowledge, which I have not, of causes natural and supernatural. It may, however, be, as certain wise men say, that the air is filled with intelligent beings, to whom it is given to forecast future events; who, taking pity upon men, warn them beforehand by these signs to prepare for what awaits them. Be this as it may, certain it is that such warnings are given, and that always after them new and strange disasters befall nations.

CHAPTER LVII

That the People are strong collectively, but individually weak.

After the ruin brought on their country by the invasion of the Gauls, many of the Romans went to dwell in Veii, in opposition to the edicts and commands of the senate, who, to correct this mischief, publicly ordained that within a time fixed, and under penalties stated, all should return to live in Rome. The persons against whom these proclamations were directed at first derided them; but, when the time came for them to be obeyed, all obeyed them. And Titus Livius observes that, *"although bold enough collectively, each separately, fearing to be punished, made his submission."* And indeed the temper of the multitude in such cases, cannot be better described than in this passage. For often a people will be open-mouthed in condemning the decrees of their prince, but afterwards, when they have to look punishment in the face, putting no trust in one another, they hasten to comply. Wherefore, if you be in a position to keep the people well-disposed towards you when they already are so, or to prevent them injuring you in case they be ill-disposed, it is clearly of little moment whether the feelings with which they profess to regard you, be favourable or no. This applies to all unfriendliness on the part of a people, whencesoever it proceed, excepting only the resentment felt by them on being deprived either of liberty, or of a prince whom they love and who still survives. For the hostile temper produced by these two causes is more to be feared than any beside, and demands measures of extreme severity to correct it. The other untoward humours of the multitude, should there be no powerful chief to foster them, are easily dealt with; because, while on the one hand there is nothing more terrible than an uncontrolled and headless mob, on the other, there is nothing feebler. For though it be furnished with arms it is easily subdued, if you have some place of strength wherein to shelter from its first onset. For when its first fury has somewhat abated, and each man sees that he has to return to his own house, all begin to lose heart and to take thought how to insure their personal safety, whether by flight or by submission. For which reason a multitude stirred in this way, if it would avoid dangers such as I speak of, must at once appoint a head from among its own numbers, who may control it, keep it united, and provide for its defence; as did the commons of Rome when, after the death of Virginia, they quitted the city, and for their protection created twenty tribunes from among themselves. Unless this be done, what Titus Livius has observed in the passage cited, will always prove true, namely, that a multitude is strong while it holds together, but so soon as each of those who compose it begins to think of his own private danger, it becomes weak and contemptible.

CHAPTER LVIII

That a People is wiser and more constant than a Prince

That *"nothing is more fickle and inconstant than the multitude"* is affirmed not by Titus Livius only, but by all other historians, in whose chronicles of human actions we often find the multitude condemning some citizen to death, and afterwards lamenting him and grieving greatly for his loss, as the Romans grieved and lamented for Manlius Capitolinus, whom they had themselves condemned to die. In relating which circumstance our author observes *"In a short time the people, having no longer cause to fear him, began to deplore his death."* And elsewhere, when speaking of what took place in Syracuse after the murder of Hieronymus, grandson of Hiero, he says, *"It is the nature of the multitude to be an abject slave, or a domineering master."*

It may be that in attempting to defend a cause, which, as I have said, all writers are agreed to condemn, I take upon me a task so hard and difficult that I shall either have to relinquish it with shame or pursue it with opprobrium. Be that as it may, I neither do, nor ever shall judge it a fault, to support opinion by arguments, where it is not sought to impose them by violence or authority I maintain, then, that this infirmity with which historians tax the multitude, may with equal reason be charged against every individual man, but most of all against princes, since all who are not controlled by the laws, will commit the very same faults as are committed by an uncontrolled multitude. Proof whereof were easy, since of all the many princes existing, or who have existed, few indeed are or have been either wise or good.

I speak of such princes as have had it in their power to break the reins by which they are controlled, among whom I do not reckon those kings who reigned in Egypt in the most remote antiquity when that country was governed in conformity with its laws; nor do I include those kings who reigned in Sparta, nor those who in our own times reign in France, which kingdom, more than any other whereof we have knowledge at the present day, is under the government of its laws. For kings who live, as these do, subject to constitutional restraint, are not to be counted when we have to consider each man's proper nature, and to see whether he resembles the multitude. For to draw a comparison with such princes as these, we must take the case of a multitude controlled as they are, and regulated by the laws, when we shall find it to possess the same virtues which we see in them, and neither conducting itself as an abject slave nor as a domineering master.

Such was the people of Rome, who, while the commonwealth continued uncorrupted, never either served abjectly nor domineered haughtily; but, on the contrary, by means of their magistrates and their ordinances, maintained their place, and when forced to put forth their strength against some powerful citizen, as in the case of Manlius, the decemvirs, and others who sought to oppress them, did so; but when it was necessary for the public welfare to yield obedience to the dictator or consuls, obeyed. And if the Roman people mourned the loss of the dead Manlius, it is no wonder; for they mourned his virtues, which had been of such a sort that their memory stirred the regret of all, and would have had power to produce the same feelings even in a prince; all writers being agreed that excellence is praised and admired even by its enemies. But if Manlius when he was so greatly mourned, could have risen once more from the dead, the Roman people would have pronounced the same sentence against him which they pronounced when they led him forth from the prison-house, and straightway condemned him to die. And in like manner we see that princes, accounted wise, have put men to death, and afterwards greatly lamented them, as Alexander mourned for Clitus and others of his friends, and Herod for Mariamne.

But what our historian says of the multitude, he says not of a multitude which like the people of Rome is controlled by the laws, but of an uncontrolled multitude like the Syracusans, who were guilty of all these crimes which infuriated and ungoverned men commit, and which were equally committed by Alexander and Herod in the cases mentioned. Wherefore the nature of a multitude is no more to be blamed than the nature of princes, since both equally err when they can do so without regard to consequences. Of which many instances, besides those already given, might be cited from the history of the Roman emperors, and of other princes and tyrants, in whose lives we find such inconstancy and fickleness, as we might look in vain for in a people.

I maintain, therefore, contrary to the common opinion which avers that a people when they have the management of affairs are changeable, fickle, and ungrateful, that these faults exist not in them otherwise than as they exist in individual princes; so that were any to accuse both princes and peoples, the charge might be true, but that to make exception in favour of princes is a mistake; for a people in command, if it be duly restrained, will have the same prudence and the same gratitude as a prince has, or even more, however wise he may be reckoned; and a prince on the other hand, if freed from the control of the laws, will be more ungrateful, fickle, and short-sighted than a people. And further, I say that any difference in their methods of acting results not from any difference in their nature, that being the same in both, or, if there be advantage on either side, the advantage resting with the people, but from their having more or less respect for the laws under which each lives. And whosoever attentively considers the history of the Roman people, may see that for four hundred years they never relaxed in their hatred of the regal name, and were constantly devoted to the glory and welfare of their country, and will find numberless proofs given by them of their consistency in both particulars. And should any allege against me the ingratitude they showed to Scipio, I reply by what has already been said at length on that head, where I proved that peoples are less ungrateful than princes. But as for prudence and stability of purpose, I affirm that a people is more prudent, more stable, and of better judgment than a prince. Nor is it without reason that the voice of the people has been likened to the voice of God; for we see that wide-spread beliefs fulfil themselves, and bring about marvellous results, so as to have the appearance of presaging by some occult quality either weal or woe. Again, as to the justice of their opinions on public affairs, seldom find that after hearing two speakers of equal ability urging them in opposite directions, they do not adopt the sounder view, or are unable to decide on the truth of what they hear. And if, as I have said, a people errs in adopting courses which appear to it bold and advantageous, princes will likewise err when their passions are touched, as is far oftener the case with them than with a people.

We see, too, that in the choice of magistrates a people will choose far more honestly than a prince; so that while you shall never persuade a people that it is advantageous to confer dignities on the infamous and profligate, a prince may readily, and in a thousand ways, be drawn to do so. Again, it may be seen that a people, when once they have come to hold a thing in abhorrence, remain for many ages of the same mind; which we do not find happen with princes. For the truth of both of which assertions the Roman people are my sufficient witness, who, in the course of so many hundred years, and in so many elections of consuls and tribunes, never made four appointments of which they had reason to repent; and, as I have said, so detested the name of king, that no obligation they might be under to any citizen who affected that name, could shield him from the appointed penalty.

Further, we find that those cities wherein the government is in the hands of the people, in a very short space of time, make marvellous progress, far exceeding that made by cities which have been always ruled by princes; as Rome grew after the expulsion of her kings, and Athens after she freed herself from Pisistratus; and this we can ascribe to no other cause than that the rule of a people is better than the rule of a prince.

Nor would I have it thought that anything our historian may have affirmed in the passage cited, or elsewhere, controverts these my opinions. For if all the glories and all the defects both of peoples and of princes be carefully weighed, it will appear that both for goodness and for glory a people is to be preferred. And if princes surpass peoples in the work of legislation, in shaping civil institutions, in moulding statutes, and framing new ordinances, so far do the latter surpass the former in maintaining what has once been established, as to merit no less praise than they.

And to state the sum of the whole matter shortly, I say that popular governments have endured for long periods in the same way as the governments of princes, and that both have need to be regulated by the laws; because the prince who can do what he pleases is a madman, and the people which can do as it pleases is never wise. If, then, we assume the case of a prince bound, and of a people chained down by the laws, greater virtue will appear in the people than in the prince; while if we assume the case of each of them freed from all control, it will be seen that the people commits fewer errors than the prince, and less serious errors, and such as admit of readier cure. For a turbulent and unruly people may be spoken to by a good man, and readily brought back to good ways; but none can speak to a wicked prince, nor any remedy be found against him but by the sword. And from this we may infer which of the two suffers from the worse disease; for if the disease of the people may be healed by words, while that of the prince must be dealt with by the sword, there is none but will judge that evil to be the greater which demands the more violent remedy.

When a people is absolutely uncontrolled, it is not so much the follies which it commits or the evil which it actually does that excites alarm, as the mischief which may thence result, since in such disorders it becomes possible for a tyrant to spring up. But with a wicked prince the contrary is the case; for we dread present ill, and place our hopes in the future, persuading ourselves that the evil life of the prince may bring about our freedom. So that there is this distinction between the two, that with the one we fear what is, with the other what is likely to be. Again, the cruelties of a people are turned against him who it fears will encroach upon the common rights, but the cruelties of the prince against those who he fears may assert those rights.

The prejudice which is entertained against the people arises from this, that any man may speak ill of them openly and fearlessly, even when the government is in their hands; whereas princes are always spoken of with a thousand reserves and a constant eye to consequences.

But since the subject suggests it, it seems to me not out of place to consider what alliances we can most trust, whether those made with commonwealths or those made with princes.

CHAPTER LIX

To what Leagues or Alliances we may most trust; whether those we make with Commonwealths or those we make with Princes.

Since leagues and alliances are every day entered into by one prince with another, or by one commonwealth with another, and as conventions and treaties are concluded in like manner between princes and commonwealths, it seems to me proper to inquire whether the faith of a commonwealth or that of a prince is the more stable and the safer to count on. All things considered, I am disposed to believe that in most cases they are alike, though in some they differ. Of one thing, however, I am convinced, namely, that engagements made under duress will never be observed either by prince or by commonwealth; and that if menaced with the loss of their territories, both the one and the other will break faith with you and treat you with ingratitude. Demetrius, who was named the "City-taker," had conferred numberless benefits upon the Athenians; but when, afterwards, on being defeated by his enemies, he sought shelter in Athens, as being a friendly city and under obligations to him, it was refused him; a circumstance which grieved him far more than the loss of his soldiers and army had done. Pompey, in like manner, when routed by Caesar in Thessaly, fled for refuge to Ptolemy in Egypt, who formerly had been restored by him to his kingdom; by whom he was put to death. In both these instances the same causes were at work, although the inhumanity and the wrong inflicted were less in the case of the commonwealth than of the prince. Still, wherever there is fear, the want of faith will be the same.

And even if there be found a commonwealth or prince who, in order to keep faith, will submit to be ruined, this is seen to result from a like cause. For, as to the prince, it may easily happen that he is friend to a powerful sovereign, whom, though he be at the time without means to defend him, he may presently hope to see restored to his dominions; or it may be that having linked his fortunes with another's, he despairs of finding either faith or friendship from the enemies of his ally, as was the case with those Neapolitan princes who espoused the interests of France. As to commonwealths, an instance similar to that of the princes last named, is that of Saguntum in Spain, which awaited ruin in adhering to the fortunes of Rome. A like course was also followed by Florence when, in the year 1512, she stood steadfastly by the cause of the French. And taking everything into account, I believe that in cases of urgency, we shall find a certain degree of stability sooner in commonwealths than in princes. For though commonwealths be like-minded with princes, and influenced by the same passions, the circumstance that their movements must be slower, makes it harder for them to resolve than it is for a prince, for which reason they will be less ready to break faith.

And since leagues and alliances are broken for the sake of certain advantages, in this respect also, commonwealths observe their engagements far more faithfully than princes; for abundant examples might be cited of a very slight advantage having caused a prince to break faith, and of a very great advantage having failed to induce a commonwealth to do so. Of this we have an instance in the proposal made to the Athenians by Themistocles, when he told them at a public meeting that he had certain advice to offer which would prove of great advantage to their city, but the nature of which he could not disclose to them, lest it should become generally known, when the opportunity for acting upon it would be lost. Whereupon the Athenians named Aristides to receive his communication, and to act upon it as he thought fit. To him, accordingly, Themistocles showed how the navy of united Greece, for the safety of which the Athenians stood pledged, was so situated that they might either gain it over or destroy it, and thus make themselves absolute masters of the whole country. Aristides reporting to the Athenians that the course proposed by Themistocles was extremely advantageous but extremely dishonourable, the people utterly refused to entertain it. But Philip of Macedon would not have so acted, nor any of those other princes who have sought and found more profit in breaking faith than in any other way.

As to engagements broken off on the pretext that they have not been observed by the other side, I say nothing, since that is a matter of everyday occurrence, and I am speaking here only of those engagements which are broken off on extraordinary grounds; but in this respect, likewise, I believe that commonwealths offend less than princes, and are therefore more to be trusted.

CHAPTER LX

That the Consulship and all the other Magistracies in Rome were given without respect to Age.

It is seen in the course of the Roman history that, after the consulship was thrown open to the commons, the republic conceded this dignity to all its citizens, without distinction either of age or blood; nay, that in this matter respect for age was never made a ground for preference among the Romans, whose constant aim it was to discover excellence whether existing in old or young. To this we have the testimony of Valerius Corvinus, himself made consul in his twenty-fourth year, who, in addressing his soldiers, said of the consulship that it was *"the reward not of birth but of desert."*

Whether the course thus followed by the Romans was well judged or not, is a question on which much might be said. The concession as to blood, however, was made under necessity, and as I have observed on another occasion, the same necessity which obtained in Rome, will be found to obtain in every other city which desires to achieve the results which Rome achieved. For you cannot subject men to hardships unless you hold out rewards, nor can you without danger deprive them of those rewards whereof you have held out hopes. It was consequently necessary to extend, betimes, to the commons the hope of obtaining the consulship, on which hope they fed themselves for a while, without actually realizing it. But afterwards the hope alone was not enough, and it had to be satisfied. For while cities which do not employ men of plebeian birth in any of those undertakings wherein glory is to be gained, as we have seen was the case with Venice, may treat these men as they please, those other cities which desire to do as Rome did, cannot make this distinction. And if there is to be no distinction in respect of blood, nothing can be pleaded for a distinction in respect of age. On the contrary, that distinction must of necessity cease to be observed. For where a young man is appointed to a post which requires the prudence which are is supposed to bring, it must be, since the choice rests with the people, that he is thus advanced in consideration of some noble action which he has performed; but when a young man is of such excellence as to have made a name for himself by some signal achievement, it were much to the detriment of his city were it unable at once to make use of him, but had to wait until he had grown old, and had lost, with youth, that alacrity and vigour by which his country might have profited; as Rome profited by the services of Valerius Corvinus, of Scipio, of Pompey, and of many others who triumphed while yet very young.

BOOK II

PREFACE

Men do always, but not always with reason, commend the past and condemn the present, and are so much the partisans of what has been, as not merely to cry up those times which are known to them only from the records left by historians, but also, when they grow old, to extol the days in which they remember their youth to have been spent. And although this preference of theirs be in most instances a mistaken one, I can see that there are many causes to account for it; chief of which I take to be that in respect of things long gone by we perceive not the whole truth, those circumstances that would detract from the credit of the past being for the most part hidden from us, while all that gives it lustre is magnified and embellished. For the generality of writers render this tribute to the good fortune of conquerors, that to make their achievements seem more splendid, they not merely exaggerate the great things they have done, but also lend such a colour to the actions of their enemies, that any one born afterwards, whether in the conquering or in the conquered country, has cause to marvel at these men and these times, and is constrained to praise and love them beyond all others.

Again, men being moved to hatred either by fear or envy, these two most powerful causes of dislike are cancelled in respect of things which are past, because what is past can neither do us hurt, nor afford occasion for envy. The contrary, however, is the case with the things we see, and in which we take part; for in these, from our complete acquaintance with them, no part of them being hidden from us, we recognize, along with much that is good, much that displeases us, and so are forced to pronounce them far inferior to the old, although in truth they deserve far greater praise and admiration. I speak not, here, of what relates to the arts, which have such distinction inherent in them, that time can give or take from them but little of the glory which they merit of themselves. I speak of the lives and manners of men, touching which the grounds for judging are not so clear.

I repeat, then, that it is true that this habit of blaming and praising obtains, but not always true that it is wrong applied. For sometimes it will happen that this judgment is just; because, as human affairs are in constant movement, it must be that they either rise or fall. Wherefore, we may see a city or province furnished with free institutions by some great and wise founder, flourish for a while through his merits, and advance steadily on the path of improvement. Any one born therein at that time would be in the wrong to praise the past more than the present, and his error would be occasioned by the causes already noticed. But any one born afterwards in that city or province when the time has come for it to fall away from its former felicity, would not be mistaken in praising the past.

When I consider how this happens, I am persuaded that the world, remaining continually the same, has in it a constant quantity of good and evil; but that this good and this evil shift about from one country to another, as we know that in ancient times empire shifted from one nation to another, according as the manners of these nations changed, the world, as a whole, continuing as before, and the only difference being that, whereas at first Assyria was made the seat of its excellence, this was afterwards placed in Media, then in Persia, until at last it was transferred to Italy and Rome. And although after the Roman Empire, none has followed which has endured, or in which the world has centred its whole excellence, we nevertheless find that excellence diffused among many valiant nations, the kingdom of the Franks, for example, that of the Turks, that of the Soldan, and the States of Germany at the present day; and shared at an earlier time by that sect of the Saracens who performed so many great achievements and gained so wide a dominion, after destroying the Roman Empire in the East.

In all these countries, therefore, after the decline of the Roman power, and among all these races, there existed, and in some part of them there yet exists, that excellence which alone is to be desired and justly to be praised. Wherefore, if any man being born in one of these countries should exalt past times over present, he might be mistaken; but any who, living at the present day in Italy or Greece, has not in Italy become an ultramontane or in Greece a Turk, has reason to complain of his own times, and to commend those others, in which there were many things which made them admirable; whereas, now, no regard being had to religion, to laws, or to arms, but all being tarnished with every sort of shame, there is nothing to redeem the age from the last extremity of wretchedness, ignominy, and disgrace. And the vices of our age are the more odious in that they are practised by those who sit on the judgment seat, govern the State, and demand public reverence.

But, returning to the matter in hand, it may be said, that if the judgment of men be at fault in pronouncing whether the present age or the past is the better in respect of things whereof, by reason of their antiquity, they cannot have the same perfect knowledge which they have of their own times, it ought not to be at fault in old men when they compare the days of their youth with those of their maturity, both of which have been alike seen and known by them. This were indeed true, if men at all periods of their lives judged of things in the same way, and were constantly influenced by the same desires; but since they alter, the times, although they alter not, cannot but seem different to those who have other desires, other pleasures, and other ways of viewing things in their old age from those they had in their youth. For since, when they grow old, men lose in bodily strength but gain in wisdom and discernment, it must needs be that those things which in their youth seemed to them tolerable and good, should in their old age appear intolerable and evil. And whereas they should ascribe this to their judgment, they lay the blame upon the times.

But, further, since the desires of men are insatiable, Nature prompting them to desire all things and Fortune permitting them to enjoy but few, there results a constant discontent in their minds, and a loathing of what they possess, prompting them to find fault with the present, praise the past, and long for the future, even though they be not moved thereto by any reasonable cause.

I know not, therefore, whether I may not deserve to be reckoned in the number of those who thus deceive themselves, if, in these Discourses of mine, I render excessive praise to the ancient times of the Romans while I censure our own. And, indeed, were not the excellence which then prevailed and the corruption which prevails now clearer than the sun, I should proceed more guardedly in what I have to say, from fear lest in accusing others I should myself fall into this self-deception. But since the thing is so plain that every one sees it, I shall be bold to speak freely all I think, both of old times and of new, in order that the minds of the young who happen to read these my writings, may be led to shun modern examples, and be prepared to follow those set by antiquity whenever chance affords the opportunity. For it is the duty of every good man to teach others those wholesome lessons which the malice of Time or of Fortune has not permitted him to put in practice; to the end, that out of many who have the knowledge, some one better loved by Heaven may be found able to carry them out.

Having spoken, then, in the foregoing Book of the various methods followed by the Romans in regulating the domestic affairs of their city, in this I shall speak of what was done by them to spread their Empire.

CHAPTER I

Whether the Empire acquired by the Romans was more due to Valour or to Fortune.

Many authors, and among others that most grave historian Plutarch, have thought that in acquiring their empire the Romans were more beholden to their good fortune than to their valour; and besides other reasons which they give for this opinion, they affirm it to be proved by the admission of the Romans themselves, since their having erected more temples to Fortune than to any other deity, shows that it was to her that they ascribed their success. It would seem, too, that Titus Livius was of the same mind, since he very seldom puts a speech into the mouth of any Roman in which he discourses of valour, wherein he does not also make mention of Fortune. This, however, is an opinion with which I can in no way concur, and which, I take it, cannot be made good. For if no commonwealth has ever been found to grow like the Roman, it is because none was ever found so well fitted by its institutions to make that growth. For by the valour of her armies she spread her empire, while by her conduct of affairs, and by other methods peculiar to herself and devised by her first founder, she was able to keep what she acquired, as shall be fully shown in many of the following Discourses.

The writers to whom I have referred assert that it was owing to their good fortune and not to their prudence that the Romans never had two great wars on their hands at once; as, for instance, that they waged no wars with the Latins until they had not merely overcome the Samnites, but undertook in their defence the war on which they then entered; nor ever fought with the Etruscans until they had subjugated the Latins, and had almost worn out the Samnites by frequent defeats; whereas, had any two of these powers, while yet fresh and unexhausted, united together, it may easily be believed that the ruin of the Roman Republic must have followed. But to whatsoever cause we ascribe it, it never so chanced that the Romans engaged in two great wars at the same time. On the contrary, it always seemed as though on the breaking out of one war, another was extinguished; or that on the termination of one, another broke out. And this we may plainly see from the order in which their wars succeeded one another.

For, omitting those waged by them before their city was taken by the Gauls, we find that during their struggle with the Equians and the Volscians, and while these two nations continued strong, no others rose against them. On these being subdued, there broke out the war with the Samnites; and although before the close of that contest the Latin nations had begun to rebel against Rome, nevertheless, when their rebellion came to a head, the Samnites were in league with Rome, and helped her with their army to quell the presumption of the rebels; on whose defeat the war with Samnium was renewed.

When the strength of Samnium had been drained by repeated reverses, there followed the war with the Etruscans; which ended, the Samnites were once more stirred to activity by the coming of Pyrrhus into Italy. When he, too, had been defeated, and sent back to Greece, Rome entered on her first war with the Carthaginians; which was no sooner over than all the Gallic nations on both sides of the Alps combined against the Romans, by whom, in the battle fought between Populonia and Pisa, where now stands the fortress of San Vincenzo, they were at last routed with tremendous slaughter.

This war ended, for twenty years together the Romans were engaged in no contest of importance, their only adversaries being the Ligurians, and the remnant of the Gallic tribes who occupied Lombardy; and on this footing things continued down to the second Carthaginian war, which for sixteen years kept the whole of Italy in a blaze. This too being brought to a most glorious termination, there followed the Macedonian war, at the close of which succeeded the war with Antiochus and Asia. These subdued, there remained not in the whole world, king or people who either singly or together could withstand the power of Rome.

But even before this last victory, any one observing the order of these wars, and the method in which they were conducted, must have recognized not only the good fortune of the Romans, but also their extraordinary valour and prudence. And were any one to search for the causes of this good fortune, he would have little difficulty in finding them, since nothing is more certain than that when a potentate has attained so great a reputation that every neighbouring prince or people is afraid to engage him single-handed, and stands in awe of him, none will ever venture to attack him, unless driven to do so by necessity; so that it will almost rest on his will to make war as he likes on any of his neighbours, while he studiously maintains peace with the rest; who, on their part, whether through fear of his power, or deceived by the methods he takes to dull their vigilance, are easily kept quiet. Distant powers, in the mean time, who have no intercourse with either, treat the matter as too remote to concern them in any way; and abiding in this error until the conflagration approaches their own doors, on its arrival have no resource for its extinction, save in their own strength, which, as their enemy has by that time become exceedingly powerful, no longer suffices.

I forbear to relate how the Samnites stood looking on while the Romans were subjugating the Equians and the Volscians; and, to avoid being prolix, shall content myself with the single instance of the Carthaginians, who, at the time when the Romans were contending with the Samnites and Etruscans, were possessed of great power and held in high repute, being already masters of the whole of Africa together with Sicily and Sardinia, besides occupying territory in various parts of Spain. And because their empire was so great, and at such a distance from the Roman frontier, they were never led to think of attacking the Romans or of lending assistance to the Etruscans or Samnites. On the contrary, they behaved towards the Romans as men behave towards those whom they see prosper, rather taking their part and courting their friendship. Nor did they discover their mistake until the Romans, after subduing all the intervening nations, began to assail their power both in Spain and Sicily. What happened in the case of the Carthaginians, happened also in the case of the Gauls, of Philip of Macedon, and of Antiochus, each of whom, while Rome was engaged with another of them, believed that other would have the advantage, and that there would be time enough to provide for their own safety, whether by making peace or war. It seems to me, therefore, that the same good fortune which, in this respect, attended the Romans, might be shared by all princes acting as they did, and of a valour equal to theirs.

As bearing on this point, it might have been proper for me to show what methods were followed by the Romans in entering the territories of other nations, had I not already spoken of this at length in my *Treatise on Princedoms*, wherein the whole subject is discussed. Here it is enough to say briefly, that in a new province they always sought for some friend who should be to them as a ladder whereby to climb, a door through which to pass, or an instrument wherewith to keep their hold. Thus we see them effect their entrance into Samnium through the Capuans, into Etruria through the Camertines, into Sicily through the Mamertines, into Spain through the Saguntans, into Africa through Massinissa, into Greece through the Etolians, into Asia through Eumenes and other princes, into Gaul through the Massilians and Eduans; and, in like manner, never without similar assistance in their efforts whether to acquire provinces or to keep them.

The nations who carefully attend to this precaution will be seen to stand in less need of Fortune's help than others who neglect it. But that all may clearly understand how much more the Romans were aided by valour than by Fortune in acquiring their empire, I shall in the following Chapter consider the character of those nations with whom they had to contend, and show how stubborn these were in defending their freedom.

CHAPTER II

With what Nations the Romans had to contend, and how stubborn these were in defending their Freedom.

In subduing the countries round about them, and certain of the more distant provinces, nothing gave the Romans so much trouble, as the love which in those days many nations bore to freedom, defending it with such obstinacy as could not have been overcome save by a surpassing valour. For we know by numberless instances, what perils these nations were ready to face in their efforts to maintain or recover their freedom, and what vengeance they took against those who deprived them of it. We know, too, from history, what hurt a people or city suffers from servitude. And though, at the present day, there is but one province which can be said to contain within it free cities, we find that formerly these abounded everywhere. For we learn that in the ancient times of which I speak, from the mountains which divide Tuscany from Lombardy down to the extreme point of Italy, there dwelt numerous free nations, such as the Etruscans, the Romans, and the Samnites, besides many others in other parts of the Peninsula. Nor do we ever read of there being any kings over them, except those who reigned in Rome, and Porsenna, king of Etruria. How the line of this last-named prince came to be extinguished, history does not inform us; but it is clear that at the time when the Romans went to besiege Veii, Etruria was free, and so greatly rejoiced in her freedom, and so detested the regal name, that when the Veientines, who for their defence had created a king in Veii, sought aid from the Etruscans against Rome, these, after much deliberation resolved to lend them no help while they continued to live under a king; judging it useless to defend a country given over to servitude by its inhabitants.

It is easy to understand whence this love of liberty arises among nations, for we know by experience that States have never signally increased, either as to dominion or wealth, except where they have lived under a free government. And truly it is strange to think to what a pitch of greatness Athens came during the hundred years after she had freed herself from the despotism of Pisistratus; and far stranger to contemplate the marvellous growth which Rome made after freeing herself from her kings. The cause, however, is not far to seek, since it is the well-being, not of individuals, but of the community which makes a State great; and, without question, this universal well-being is nowhere secured save in a republic. For a republic will do whatsoever makes for its interest; and though its measures prove hurtful to this man or to that, there are so many whom they benefit, that these are able to carry them out, in spite of the resistance of the few whom they injure.

But the contrary happens in the case of a prince; for, as a rule, what helps him hurts the State, and what helps the State hurts him; so that whenever a tyranny springs up in a city which has lived free, the least evil which can befall that city is to make no further progress, nor ever increase in power or wealth; but in most cases, if not in all, it will be its fate to go back. Or should there chance to arise in it some able tyrant who extends his dominions by his valour and skill in arms, the advantage which results is to himself only, and not to the State; since he can bestow no honours on those of the citizens over whom he tyrannizes who have shown themselves good and valiant, lest afterwards he should have cause to fear them. Nor can he make those cities which he acquires, subject or tributary to the city over which he rules; because to make this city powerful is not for his interest, which lies in keeping it so divided that each town and province may separately recognize him alone as its master. In this way he only, and not his country, is the gainer by his conquests.

And if any one desire to have this view confirmed by numberless other proofs, let him look into Xenophon's treatise *De Tirannide*.

No wonder, then, that the nations of antiquity pursued tyrants with such relentless hatred, and so passionately loved freedom that its very name was dear to them, as was seen when Hieronymus, grandson of Hiero the Syracusan, was put to death in Syracuse. For when word of his death reached the army, which lay encamped not far off, at first it was greatly moved, and eager to take up arms against the murderers. But on hearing the cry of liberty shouted in the streets of Syracuse, quieted at once by the name, it laid aside its resentment against those who had slain the tyrant, and fell to consider how a free government might be provided for the city.

Nor is it to be wondered at that the ancient nations took terrible vengeance on those who deprived them of their freedom; of which, though there be many instances, I mean only to cite one which happened in the city of Corcyra at the time of the Peloponnesian war. For Greece being divided into two factions, one of which sided with the Athenians, the other with the Spartans, it resulted that many of its cities were divided against themselves, some of the citizens seeking the friendship of Sparta and some of Athens. In the aforesaid city of Corcyra, the nobles getting the upper hand, deprived the commons of their freedom; these, however, recovering themselves with the help of the Athenians, laid hold of the entire body of the nobles, and cast them into a prison large enough to contain them all, whence they brought them forth by eight or ten at a time, pretending that they were to be sent to different places into banishment, whereas, in fact, they put them to death with many circumstances of cruelty. Those who were left, learning what was going on, resolved to do their utmost to escape this ignominious death, and arming themselves with what weapons they could find, defended the door of their prison against all who sought to enter; till the people, hearing the tumult and rushing in haste to the prison, dragged down the roof, and smothered the prisoners in the ruins. Many other horrible and atrocious cruelties likewise perpetrated in

Greece, show it to be true that a lost freedom is avenged with more ferocity than a threatened freedom is defended.

When I consider whence it happened that the nations of antiquity were so much more zealous in their love of liberty than those of the present day, I am led to believe that it arose from the same cause which makes the present generation of men less vigorous and daring than those of ancient times, namely the difference of the training of the present day from that of earlier ages; and this, again, arises from the different character of the religions then and now prevailing. For our religion, having revealed to us the truth and the true path, teaches us to make little account of worldly glory; whereas, the Gentiles, greatly esteeming it, and placing therein their highest good, displayed a greater fierceness in their actions.

This we may gather from many of their customs, beginning with their sacrificial rites, which were of much magnificence as compared with the simplicity of our worship, though that be not without a certain dignity of its own, refined rather than splendid, and far removed from any tincture of ferocity or violence. In the religious ceremonies of the ancients neither pomp nor splendour were wanting; but to these was joined the ordinance of sacrifice, giving occasion to much bloodshed and cruelty. For in its celebration many beasts were slaughtered, and this being a cruel spectacle imparted a cruel temper to the worshippers. Moreover, under the old religions none obtained divine honours save those who were loaded with worldly glory, such as captains of armies and rulers of cities; whereas our religion glorifies men of a humble and contemplative, rather than of an active life. Accordingly, while the highest good of the old religions consisted in magnanimity, bodily strength, and all those other qualities which make men brave, our religion places it in humility, lowliness, and contempt for the things of this world; or if it ever calls upon us to be brave, it is that we should be brave to suffer rather than to do.

This manner of life, therefore, seems to have made the world feebler, and to have given it over as a prey to wicked men to deal with as they please; since the mass of mankind, in the hope of being received into Paradise, think more how to bear injuries than how to avenge them. But should it seem that the world has grown effeminate and Heaven laid aside her arms, this assuredly results from the baseness of those who have interpreted our religion to accord with indolence and ease rather than with valour. For were we to remember that religion permits the exaltation and defence of our country, we would see it to be our duty to love and honour it, and would strive to be able and ready to defend it.

This training, therefore, and these most false interpretations are the causes why, in the world of the present day, we find no longer the numerous commonwealths which were found of old; and in consequence, that we see not now among the nations that love of freedom which prevailed then; though, at the same time, I am persuaded that one cause of this change has been, that the Roman Empire by its arms and power put an end to all the free States and free institutions of antiquity. For although the power of Rome fell afterwards into decay, these States could never recover their strength or resume their former mode of government, save in a very few districts of the Empire.

But, be this as it may, certain it is that in every country of the world, even the least considerable, the Romans found a league of well-armed republics, most resolute in the defence of their freedom, whom it is clear they never could have subdued had they not been endowed with the rarest and most astonishing valour. To cite a single instance, I shall take the case of the Samnites who, strange as it may now seem, were on the admission of Titus Livius himself, so powerful and so steadfast in arms, as to be able to withstand the Romans down to the consulship of Papirius Cursor, son to the first Papirius, a period of six and forty years, in spite of numerous defeats, the loss of many of their towns, and the great slaughter which overtook them everywhere throughout their country. And this is the more remarkable when we see that country, which once contained so many noble cities, and supported so great a population, now almost uninhabited; and reflect that it formerly enjoyed a government and possessed resources making its conquest impossible to less than Roman valour.

There is no difficulty, therefore, in determining whence that ancient greatness and this modern decay have arisen, since they can be traced to the free life formerly prevailing and to the servitude which prevails now. For all countries and provinces which enjoy complete freedom, make, as I have said, most rapid progress. Because, from marriage being less restricted in these countries, and more sought after, we find there a greater population; every man being disposed to beget as many children as he thinks he can rear, when he has no anxiety lest they should be deprived of their patrimony, and knows not only that they are born to freedom and not to slavery, but that they may rise by their merit to be the first men of their country. In such States, accordingly, we see wealth multiply, both that which comes from agriculture and that which comes from manufactures. For all love to gather riches and to add to their possessions when their enjoyment of them is not likely to be disturbed. And hence it happens that the citizens of such States vie with one another in whatever tends to promote public or private well-being; in both of which, consequently, there is a wonderful growth.

But the contrary of all this takes place in those countries which live in servitude, and the more oppressive their servitude, the more they fall short of the good which all desire. And the hardest of all hard servitudes is that wherein one commonwealth is subjected to another. First, because it is more lasting, and there is less hope to escape from it; and, second, because every commonwealth seeks to add to its own strength by weakening and enfeebling all beside. A prince who gets the better of you will not treat you after this fashion, unless he be a barbarian like those eastern despots who lay countries waste and destroy the labours of civilization; but if influenced by the ordinary promptings of humanity, will, as a rule, regard all his subject States with equal favour, and suffer them to pursue their usual employments, and retain almost all their ancient institutions, so that if they flourish not as free States might, they do not dwindle as States that are enslaved; by which I mean enslaved by a stranger, for of that other slavery to which they may be reduced by one of their own citizens, I have already spoken.

Whoever, therefore, shall well consider what has been said above, will not be astonished at the power possessed by the Samnites while they were still free, nor at the weakness into which they fell when they were subjugated. Of which change in their fortunes Livius often reminds us, and particularly in connection with the war with Hannibal, where he relates that the Samnites, being ill-treated by a Roman legion quartered at Nola, sent legates to Hannibal to ask his aid; who in laying their case before him told him, that with their own soldiers and captains they had fought single handed against the Romans for a hundred years, and had more than once withstood two consuls and two consular armies; but had now fallen so low, that they were scarce able to defend themselves against one poor legion.

CHAPTER III

That Rome became great by destroying the Cities which lay round about her, and by readily admitting strangers to the rights of Citizenship.

"Crescit interea Roma Albae ruinis" — *Meanwhile Rome grows on the ruins of Alba.* They who would have their city become a great empire, must endeavour by every means to fill it with inhabitants; for without a numerous population no city can ever succeed in growing powerful. This may be effected in two ways, by gentleness or by force. By gentleness, when you offer a safe and open path to all strangers who may wish to come and dwell in your city, so as to encourage them to come there of their own accord; by force, when after destroying neighbouring towns, you transplant their inhabitants to live in yours. Both of these methods were practised by Rome, and with such success, that in the time of her sixth king there dwelt within her walls eighty thousand citizens fit to bear arms. For the Romans loved to follow the methods of the skilful husbandman, who, to insure a plant growing big and yielding and maturing its fruit, cuts off the first shoots it sends out, that the strength remaining in the stem, it may in due season put forth new and more vigorous and more fruitful branches. And that this was a right and a necessary course for Rome to take for establishing and extending her empire, is proved by the example of Sparta and Athens, which, although exceedingly well-armed States, and regulated by excellent laws, never reached the same greatness as the Roman Republic; though the latter, to all appearance, was more turbulent and disorderly than they, and, so far as laws went, not so perfectly governed. For this we can offer no other explanation than that already given. For

by augmenting the numbers of her citizens in both the ways named, Rome was soon able to place two hundred and eighty thousand men under arms; while neither Sparta nor Athens could ever muster more than twenty thousand; and this, not because the situation of these countries was less advantageous than that of Rome, but simply from the difference in the methods they followed.

For Lycurgus, the founder of the Spartan Republic, thinking nothing so likely to relax his laws as an admixture of new citizens, did all he could to prevent intercourse with strangers; with which object, besides refusing these the right to marry, the right of citizenship, and all such other social rights as induce men to become members of a community, he ordained that in this republic of his the only money current should be of leather, so that none might be tempted to repair thither to trade or to carry on any art.

Under such circumstances the number of the inhabitants of that State could never much increase. For as all our actions imitate nature, and it is neither natural nor possible that a puny stem should carry a great branch, so a small republic cannot assume control over cities or countries stronger than herself; or, doing so, will resemble the tree whose boughs being greater than its trunk, are supported with difficulty, and snapped by every gust of wind. As it proved with Sparta. For after she had spread her dominion over all the cities of Greece, no sooner did Thebes rebel than all the others rebelled likewise, and the trunk was left stripped of its boughs. But this could not have happened with Rome, whose stem was mighty enough to bear any branch with ease.

It was, therefore, by adding to her population, and by, adopting certain other methods presently to be noticed, that Rome became so great and powerful. And this is well expressed by Titus Livius, in the words, *"Crescit interea Roma Albae ruinis."*

CHAPTER IV

That Commonwealths have followed three Methods for extending their Power.

Any one who has read ancient history with attention, must have observed that three methods have been used by republics for extending their power. One of these, followed by the old Etruscans, is to form a confederation of many States, wherein none has precedence over the rest in authority or rank, and each allows the others to share its acquisitions; as do the States of the Swiss League in our days, and as the Achaians and Etolians did in Greece in earlier times. And because the Etruscans were opposed to the Romans in many wars, that I may give a clearer notion of this method of theirs, I shall enlarge a little in my account of the Etruscan people.

In Italy, before the Romans became supreme, the Etruscans were very powerful, both by sea and land; and although we have no separate history of their affairs, we have some slight records left us of them, and some indications of their greatness. We know, for instance, that they planted a colony, to which they gave the name of Hadria, on the coast of the upper sea; which colony became so renowned that it lent its name to the sea itself, which to this day by the Latins is called the Hadriatic. We know, too, that their arms were obeyed from the Tiber to the foot of the mountains which enclose the greater part of the Italian peninsula; although, two hundred years before Rome grew to any great strength, they had lost their supremacy in the province now known as Lombardy, of which the French had possessed themselves. For that people, whether driven by necessity, or attracted by the excellence of the fruits, and still more of the wine of Italy, came there under their chief, Bellovesus; and after defeating and expelling the inhabitants of the country, settled themselves therein, and there built many cities; calling the district Gallia, after the name they then bore: and this territory they retained until they were subdued by the Romans.

These Etruscans, therefore, living with one another on a footing of complete equality, when they sought to extend their power, followed that first method of which I have just now spoken. Their State was made up of twelve cities, among which were Chiusi, Veii, Friuli, Arezzo, Volterra, and the like, and their government was conducted in the form of a league. They could not, however, extend their conquests beyond Italy; while even within the limits of Italy, much territory remained unoccupied by them for reasons presently to be noticed.

The second method is to provide yourself with allies or companions, taking heed, however, to retain in your own hands the chief command, the seat of government, and the titular supremacy. This was the method followed by the Romans.

The third method is to hold other States in direct subjection to you, and not merely associated with you as companions; and this was the plan pursued by the Spartans and Athenians.

Of these three methods, the last is wholly useless, as was seen in the case of the two States named, which came to ruin from no other cause than that they had acquired a dominion greater than they could maintain. For to undertake to govern cities by force, especially such cities as have been used to live in freedom, is a difficult and arduous task, in which you never can succeed without an army and that a great one. But to have such an army you must needs have associates who will help to swell the numbers of your own citizens. And because Athens and Sparta neglected this precaution, whatever they did was done in vain; whereas Rome, which offers an instance of the second of the methods we are considering, by attending to this precaution reached a power that had no limit. And as she alone has lived in this way, so she alone has attained to this pitch of power. For joining with herself many States throughout Italy as her companions, who in most respects lived with her on a footing of equality, while, as has been noted, always reserving to herself the seat of empire and the titular command, it came about that these States, without being aware of it, by their own efforts, and with their own blood, wrought out their own enslavement.

For when Rome began to send armies out of Italy, for the purpose of reducing foreign kingdoms to provinces, and of subjugating nations who, being used to live under kings, were not impatient of her yoke, and who, receiving Roman governors, and having been conquered by armies bearing the Roman name, recognized no masters save the Romans, those companions of Rome who dwelt in Italy suddenly found themselves surrounded by Roman subjects, and weighed down by the greatness of the Roman power; and when at last they came to perceive the mistake in which they had been living, it was too late to remedy it, so vast was the authority which Rome had then obtained over foreign countries, and so great the resources which she possessed within herself; having by this time grown to be the mightiest and best-armed of States. So that although these her companions sought to avenge their wrongs by conspiring against her, they were soon defeated in the attempt, and remained in a worse plight than before, since they too became subjects and no longer associates. This method, then, as I have said, was followed by the Romans alone; but no other plan can be pursued by a republic which desires to extend its power; experience having shown none other so safe and certain.

The method which consists in forming leagues, of which I have spoken above as having been adopted by the Etruscans, the Achaians, and the Etolians of old, and in our own days by the Swiss, is the next best after that followed by the Romans, for as in this way there can be no great extension of power, two advantages result: first, that you do not readily involve yourself in war; and, second, that you can easily preserve any little acquisition which you may make. The reason why you cannot greatly extend your power is, that as your league is made up of separate States with distinct seats of government, it is difficult for these to consult and resolve in concert. The same causes make these States careless to enlarge their territories; because acquisitions which have to be shared among many communities are less thought of than those made by a single republic which looks to enjoy them all to itself. Again, since leagues govern through general councils, they must needs be slower in resolving than a nation dwelling within one frontier.

Moreover, we find from experience that this method has certain fixed limits beyond which there is no instance of its ever having passed; by which I mean that some twelve or fourteen communities may league themselves together, but will never seek to pass beyond that limit: for after associating themselves in such numbers as seem to them to secure their safety against all besides, they desire no further extension of their power, partly because no necessity compels them to extend, and partly because, for the reasons already given, they would find no profit in extending. For were they to seek extension they would have to follow one of two courses: either continuing to admit new members to their league, whose number must lead to confusion; or else making subjects, a course which they will avoid since they will see difficulty in making them, and no great good in having them. Wherefore, when their number has so increased that their safety seems secured, they have recourse to two expedients: either receiving other States under their protection and engaging for their defence (in which way they obtain money from various quarters which they can easily distribute among themselves); or else hiring themselves out as soldiers to foreign States, and drawing pay from this or the other prince who employs them to carry out his enterprises; as we see done by the Swiss at the present day, and as we read was done in ancient times by certain of those nations whom we have named above. To which we have a witness in Titus Livius, who relates that when Philip of Macedon came to treat with Titus Quintius Flamininus, and while terms were being discussed in the presence of a certain Etolian captain, this man coming to words with Philip, the latter taunted him with greed and bad faith; telling him that the Etolians were not ashamed to draw pay from one side, and then send their men to serve on the other; so that often the banner of Etolia might be seen displayed in two hostile camps.

We see, therefore, that the method of proceeding by leagues has always been of the same character, and has led always to the same results. We see, likewise, that the method which proceeds by reducing States to direct subjection has constantly proved a weak one, and produced insignificant gains; and that whenever these gains have passed a certain limit, ruin has ensued. And if the latter of these two methods be of little utility among armed States, among those that are unarmed, as is now the case with the republics of Italy, it is worse than useless. We may conclude, therefore, that the true method was that followed by the Romans; which is the more remarkable as we find none who adopted it before they did, and none who have followed it since. As for leagues, I know of no nations who have had recourse to them in recent times except the Swiss and the Suevians.

But to bring my remarks on this head to an end, I affirm that all the various methods followed by the Romans in conducting their affairs, whether foreign or domestic, so far from being imitated in our day, have been held of no account, some pronouncing them to be mere fables, some thinking them impracticable, others out of place and unprofitable; and so, abiding in this ignorance, we rest a prey to all who have chosen to invade our country. But should it seem difficult to tread in the footsteps of the Romans, it ought not to appear so hard, especially for us Tuscans, to imitate the Tuscans of antiquity, who if, from the causes already assigned, they failed to establish an empire like that of Rome, succeeded in acquiring in Italy that degree of power which their method of acting allowed, and which they long preserved in security, with the greatest renown in arms and government, and the highest reputation for manners and religion. This power and this glory of theirs were first impaired by the Gauls, and afterwards extinguished by the Romans, and so utterly extinguished, that of the Etruscan Empire, so splendid two thousand years ago, we have at the present day barely a record. This it is which has led me to inquire whence this oblivion of things arises, a question of which I shall treat in the following Chapter.

CHAPTER V

That changes in Sects and Tongues, and the happening of Floods and Pestilences, obliterate the Memory of the Past.

To those philosophers who will have it that the world has existed from all eternity, it were, I think, a good answer, that if what they say be true we ought to have record of a longer period than five thousand years; did it not appear that the memory of past times is blotted out by a variety of causes, some referable to men, and some to Heaven.

Among the causes which have a human origin are the changes in sects and tongues; because when a new sect, that is to say a new religion, comes up, its first endeavour, in order to give itself reputation, is to efface the old; and should it so happen that the founders of the new religion speak another tongue, this may readily be effected. This we know from observing the methods which Christianity has followed in dealing with the religion of the Gentiles, for we find that it has abolished all the rites and ordinances of that worship, and obliterated every trace of the ancient belief. True, it has not succeeded in utterly blotting out our knowledge of things done by the famous men who held that belief; and this because the propagators of the new faith, retaining the Latin tongue, were constrained to use it in writing the new law; for could they have written this in a new tongue, we may infer, having regard to their other persecutions, that no record whatever would have survived to us of past events. For any one who reads of the methods followed by Saint Gregory and the other heads of the Christian religion, will perceive with what animosity they pursued all ancient memorials; burning the works of poets and historians; breaking images; and destroying whatsoever else afforded any trace of antiquity. So that if to this persecution a new language had been joined, it must soon have been found that everything was forgotten.

We may believe, therefore, that what Christianity has sought to effect against the sect of the Gentiles, was actually effected by that sect against the religion which preceded theirs; and that, from the repeated changes of belief which have taken place in the course of five or six thousand years, the memory of what happened at a remote date has perished, or, if any trace of it remain, has come to be regarded as a fable to which no credit is due; like the Chronicle of Diodorus Siculus, which, professing to give an account of the events of forty or fifty thousand years, is held, and I believe justly, a lying tale.

As for the causes of oblivion which we may refer to Heaven, they are those which make havoc of the human race, and reduce the population of certain parts of the world to a very small number. This happens by plague, famine, or flood, of which three the last is the most hurtful, as well because it is the most universal, as because those saved are generally rude and ignorant mountaineers, who possessing no knowledge of antiquity themselves, can impart none to those who come after them. Or if among the survivors there chance to be one possessed of such knowledge, to give himself consequence and credit, he will conceal and pervert it to suit his private ends, so that to his posterity there will remain only so much as he may have been pleased to communicate, and no more.

That these floods, plagues, and famines do in fact happen, I see no reason to doubt, both because we find all histories full of them, and recognize their effect in this oblivion of the past, and also because it is reasonable that such things should happen. For as when much superfluous matter has gathered in simple bodies, nature makes repeated efforts to remove and purge it away, thereby promoting the health of these bodies, so likewise as regards that composite body the human race, when every province of the world so teems with inhabitants that they can neither subsist where they are nor remove elsewhere, every region being equally crowded and over-peopled, and when human craft and wickedness have reached their highest pitch, it must needs come about that the world will purge herself in one or another of these three ways, to the end that men, becoming few and contrite, may amend their lives and live with more convenience.

Etruria, then, as has been said above, was at one time powerful, abounding in piety and valour, practising her own customs, and speaking her own tongue; but all this was effaced by the power of Rome, so that, as I have observed already, nothing is left of her but the memory of a name.

CHAPTER VI

Of the Methods followed by the Romans in making War.

Having treated of the methods followed by the Romans for increasing their power, we shall now go on to consider those which they used in making war; and in all they did we shall find how wisely they turned aside from the common path in order to render their progress to supreme greatness easy.

Whosoever makes war, whether from policy or ambition, means to acquire and to hold what he acquires, and to carry on the war he has undertaken in such a manner that it shall enrich and not impoverish his native country and State. It is necessary, therefore, whether for acquiring or holding, to consider how cost may be avoided, and everything done most advantageously for the public welfare. But whoever would effect all this, must take the course and follow the methods of the Romans; which consisted, first of all, in making their wars, as the French say, *great and short*. For entering the field with strong armies, they brought to a speedy conclusion whatever wars they had with the Latins, the Samnites, or the Etruscans.

And if we take note of all the wars in which they were engaged, from the foundation of their city down to the siege of Veii, all will be seen to have been quickly ended some in twenty, some in ten, and some in no more than six days. And this was their wont: So soon as war was declared they would go forth with their armies to meet the enemy and at once deliver battle. The enemy, on being routed, to save their country from pillage, very soon came to terms, when the Romans would take from them certain portions of their territory. These they either assigned to particular persons, or made the seat of a colony, which being settled on the confines of the conquered country served as a defence to the Roman frontier, to the advantage both of the colonists who had these lands given them, and of the Roman people whose borders were thus guarded at no expense to themselves. And no other system of defence could have been at once so safe, so strong, and so effectual. For while the enemy were not actually in the field, this guard was sufficient; and when they came out in force to overwhelm the colony, the Romans also went forth in strength and gave them battle; and getting the better of them, imposed harder terms than before, and so returned home. And in this way they came gradually to establish their name abroad, and to add to their power.

These methods they continued to employ until they changed their system of warfare, which they did during the siege of Veii; when to enable them to carry on a prolonged war, they passed a law for the payment of their soldiers, whom, up to that time they had not paid, nor needed to pay, because till then their wars had been of brief duration. Nevertheless, while allowing pay to their soldiers that they might thus wage longer wars, and keep their armies longer in the field when employed on distant enterprises, they never departed from their old plan of bringing their campaigns to as speedy an end as place and circumstances allowed, nor ever ceased to plant colonies.

Their custom of terminating their wars with despatch, besides being natural to the Romans, was strengthened by the ambition of their consuls, who, being appointed for twelve months only, six of which they had to spend in the city, were eager to bring their wars to an end as rapidly as they could, that they might enjoy the honours of a triumph. The usage of planting colonies was recommended by the great advantage and convenience which resulted from it. In dealing with the spoils of warfare their practice, no doubt, in a measure changed, so that in this respect they were not afterwards so liberal as they were at first; partly, because liberality did not seem so necessary when their soldiers were in receipt of pay; and, partly, because the spoils themselves being greater than before, they thought by their help so to enrich the public treasury as to be able to carry on their wars without taxing the city; and, in fact, by pursuing this course the public revenues were soon greatly augmented. The methods thus followed by the Romans in dividing plunder and in planting colonies had, accordingly, this result, that whereas other less prudent princes and republics are impoverished by war, Rome was enriched by it; nay, so far was the system carried, that no consul could hope for a triumph unless he brought back with him for the public treasury much gold and silver and spoils of every kind.

By methods such as these, at one time bringing their wars to a rapid conclusion by invasion and actual defeat, at another wearing out an enemy by protracted hostilities, and again by concluding peace on advantageous terms, the Romans continually grew richer and more powerful.

CHAPTER VII

Of the Quantity of Land assigned by the Romans to each Colonist.

It would, I think, be difficult to fix with certainty how much land the Romans allotted to each colonist, for my belief is that they gave more or less according to the character of the country to which they sent them. We may, however, be sure that in every instance, and to whatever country they were sent, the quantity of land assigned was not very large: first, because, these colonists being sent to guard the newly acquired country, by giving little land it became possible to send more men; and second because, as the Romans lived frugally at home, it is unreasonable to suppose that they should wish their countrymen to be too well off abroad. And Titus Livius tells us that on the capture of Veii, the Romans sent thither a colony, allotting to each colonist three jugera and seven unciae of land, which, according to our measurement would be something under two acres. Besides the above reasons, the Romans may likely enough have thought that it was not so much the quantity of the land allotted as its careful cultivation that would make it suffice. It is very necessary, however, that every colony should have common pasturage where all may send their cattle to graze, as well as woods where they may cut fuel; for without such conveniences no colony can maintain itself.

CHAPTER VIII

Why certain Nations leave their ancestral Seats and overflow the Countries of others.

Having spoken above of the methods followed by the Romans in making war, and related how the Etruscans were attacked by the Gauls, it seems to me not foreign to these topics to explain that of wars there are two kinds. One kind of war has its origin in the ambition of princes or republics who seek to extend their dominions. Such were the wars waged by Alexander the Great, and by the Romans, and such are those which we see every day carried on by one potentate against another. Wars of this sort have their dangers, but do not utterly extirpate the inhabitants of a country; what the conqueror seeks being merely the submission of the conquered people, whom, generally speaking, he suffers to retain their laws, and always their houses and goods.

The other species of war is when an entire people, with all the families of which it is made up, being driven out by famine or defeat, removes from its former seat, and goes in search of a new abode and a new country, not simply with the view to establish dominion over it, but to possess it as its own, and to expel or exterminate the former inhabitants. Of this most terrible and cruel species of warfare Sallust speaks at the end of his history of the war with Jugurtha, where in mentioning that after the defeat of Jugurtha the movement of the Gauls into Italy began to be noticed, he observes that *"in the wars of the Romans with other nations the struggle was for mastery; but that always in their wars with the Gauls the struggle on both sides was for life."* For a prince or commonwealth, when attacking another State, will be content to rid themselves of those only who are at the head of affairs; but an entire people, set in motion in the manner described, must destroy all who oppose them, since their object is to subsist on that whereon those whom they invade have hitherto subsisted.

The Romans had to pass through three of these desperate wars; the first being that in which their city was actually captured by those Gauls who, as already mentioned, had previously taken Lombardy from the Etruscans and made it their seat, and for whose invasion Titus Livius has assigned two causes. First, that they were attracted, as I have said before, by the fruitful soil and by the wine of Italy which they had not in Gaul; second, that their population having multiplied so greatly that they could no longer find wherewithal to live on at home, the princes of their land decided that certain of their number should go forth to seek a new abode; and so deciding, chose as leaders of those who were to go, two Gaulish chiefs, Bellovesus and Siccovesus; the former of whom came into Italy while the latter passed into Spain. From the immigration under Bellovesus resulted the occupation of Lombardy, and, subsequently, the first war of the Gauls with Rome. At a later date, and after the close of the first war with Carthage, came the second Gallic invasion, when more than two hundred thousand Gauls perished in battle between Piombino and Pisa. The third of these wars broke out on the descent into Italy of the Todi and Cimbri, who, after defeating several Roman armies, were themselves defeated by Marius.

In these three most dangerous contests the arms of Rome prevailed; but no ordinary valour was needed for their success. For we see afterwards, when the spirit of the Romans had declined, and their armies had lost their former excellence, their supremacy was overthrown by men of the same race, that is to say by the Goths, the Vandals, and others like them, who spread themselves over the whole of the Western Empire.

Nations such as these, quit, as I have said, their native land, when forced by famine, or by defeat in domestic wars, to seek a new habitation elsewhere. When those thus driven forth are in large numbers, they violently invade the territories of other nations, slaughtering the inhabitants, seizing on their possessions, founding new kingdoms, and giving new names to provinces; as was done by Moses, and by those tribes who overran the Roman Empire. For the new names which we find in Italy and elsewhere, have no other origin than in their having been given by these new occupants; as when the countries formerly known as Gallia Cisalpina and Gallia Transalpina took the names of Lombardy and France, from the Lombards and the Franks who settled themselves there. In the same way Sclavonia was formerly known as Illyria, Hungary as Pannonia, and England as Britain; while many other provinces which it would be tedious to enumerate, have similarly changed their designations; as when the name Judaea was given by Moses to that part of Syria of which he took possession.

And since I have said above that nations such as those I have been describing, are often driven by wars from their ancestral homes, and forced to seek a new country elsewhere, I shall cite the instance of the Maurusians, a people who anciently dwelt in Syria, but hearing of the inroad of the Hebrews, and thinking themselves unable to resist them, chose rather to seek safety in flight than to perish with their country in a vain effort to defend it. For which reason, removing with their families, they went to Africa, where, after driving out the native inhabitants, they took up their abode; and although they could not defend their own country, were able to possess themselves of a country belonging to others. And Procopius, who writes the history of the war which Belisarius conducted against those Vandals who seized on Africa, relates, that on certain pillars standing in places where the Maurusians once dwelt, he had read inscriptions in these words: "*We Maurusians who fled before Joshua, the robber, the son of Nun;*" giving us to know the cause of their quitting Syria. Be this as it may, nations thus driven forth by a supreme necessity, are, if they be in great number, in the highest degree dangerous, and cannot be successfully withstood except by a people who excel in arms.

When those constrained to abandon their homes are not in large numbers, they are not so dangerous as the nations of whom I have been speaking, since they cannot use the same violence, but must trust to their address to procure them a habitation; and, after procuring it, must live with their neighbours as friends and companions, as we find AEneas, Dido, the Massilians, and others like them to have lived; all of whom contrived to maintain themselves in the districts in which they settled, by securing the good will of the neighbouring nations.

Almost all the great emigrations of nations have been and continue to be from the cold and barren region of Scythia, because from the population there being excessive, and the soil ill able to support them, they are forced to quit their home, many causes operating to drive them forth and none to keep them back. And if, for the last five hundred years, it has not happened that any of these nations has actually overrun another country, there are various reasons to account for it. First, the great clearance which that region made of its inhabitants during the decline of the Roman Empire, when more than thirty nations issued from it in succession; and next, the circumstance that the countries of Germany and Hungary, whence also these nations came, are now so much improved that men can live there in comfort, and consequently are not constrained to shift their habitations. Besides which, since these countries are occupied by a very warlike race, they serve as a sort of bulwark to keep back the neighbouring Scythians, who for this reason do not venture to attack them, nor attempt to force a passage. Nevertheless, movements on a great scale have oftentimes been begun by the Tartars, and been at once withstood by the Hungarians and Poles, whose frequent boast it is, that but for them, Italy and the Church would more than once have felt the weight of the Tartar arms.

Of the nations of whom I have been speaking, I shall now say no more.

CHAPTER IX

Of the Causes which commonly give rise to Wars between States.

The occasion which led to war between the Romans and Samnites, who for long had been in league with one another, is of common occurrence in all powerful States, being either brought about by accident, or else purposely contrived by some one who would set war a-foot. As between the Romans and the Samnites, the occasion of war was accidental. For in making war upon the Sidicinians and afterwards on the Campanians, the Samnites had no thought of involving themselves with the Romans. But the Campanians being overpowered, and, contrary to the expectation of Romans and Samnites alike, resorting to Rome for aid, the Romans, on whose protection they threw themselves, were forced to succour them as dependants, and to accept a war which, it seemed to them, they could not with honour decline. For though they might have thought it unreasonable to be called on to defend the Campanians as friends against their own friends the Samnites, it seemed to them shameful not to defend them as subjects, or as a people who had placed themselves under their protection. For they reasoned that to decline their defence would close the gate against all others who at any future time might desire to submit themselves to their power. And, accordingly, since glory and empire, and not peace, were the ends which they always had in view, it became impossible for them to refuse this protectorship.

A similar circumstance gave rise to the first war with the Carthaginians, namely the protectorate assumed by the Romans of the citizens of Messina in Sicily, and this likewise came about by chance. But the second war with Carthage was not the result of chance. For Hannibal the Carthaginian general attacked the

Saguntans, who were the friends of Rome in Spain, not from any desire to injure them, but in order to set the arms of Rome in motion, and so gain an opportunity of engaging the Romans in a war, and passing on into Italy. This method of picking a quarrel is constantly resorted to by powerful States when they are bound by scruples of honour or like considerations. For if I desire to make war on a prince with whom I am under an ancient and binding treaty, I shall find some colour or pretext for attacking the friend of that prince, very well knowing that when I attack his friend, either the prince will resent it, when my scheme for engaging him in war will be realized; or that, should he not resent it, his weakness or baseness in not defending one who is under his protection will be made apparent; either of which alternatives will discredit him, and further my designs.

We are to note, therefore, in connection with this submission of the Campanians, what has just now been said as to provoking another power to war; and also the remedy open to a State which, being unequal to its own defence, is prepared to go all lengths to ruin its assailant, — that remedy being to give itself up unreservedly to some one whom it selects for its defender; as the Campanians gave themselves up to the Romans, and as the Florentines gave themselves up to King Robert of Naples, who, after refusing to defend them as his friends against Castruccio of Lucca by whom they were hard pressed, defended them as his subjects.

CHAPTER X

That contrary to the vulgar opinion, Money is not the Sinews of War.

Since any man may begin a war at his pleasure, but cannot at his pleasure bring it to a close, a prince before he engages in any warlike enterprise ought to measure his strength and govern himself accordingly. But he must be prudent enough not to deceive himself as to his strength, which he will always do, if he measure it by money, by advantage of position, or by the good-will of his subjects, while he is unprovided with an army of his own. These are things which may swell your strength but do not constitute it, being in themselves null and of no avail without an army on which you can depend.

Without such an army no amount of money will meet your wants, the natural strength of your country will not protect you, and the fidelity and attachment of your subjects will not endure, since it is impossible that they should continue true to you when you cannot defend them. Lakes, and mountains, and the most inaccessible strongholds, where valiant defenders are wanting, become no better than the level plain; and money, so far from being a safeguard, is more likely to leave you a prey to your enemy; since nothing can be falser than the vulgar opinion which affirms it to be the sinews of war.

This opinion is put forward by Quintus Curtius, where, in speaking of the war between Antipater the Macedonian and the King of Sparta, he relates that the latter, from want of money, was constrained to give battle and was defeated; whereas, could he have put off fighting for a few days the news of Alexander's death would have reached Greece, and he might have had a victory without a battle. But lacking money, and fearing that on that account his soldiers might desert him, he was forced to hazard an engagement. It was for this reason that Quintus Curtius declared money to be the sinews of war, a maxim every day cited and acted upon by princes less wise than they should be. For building upon this, they think it enough for their defence to have laid up great treasures; not reflecting that were great treasures all that is needed for victory, Darius of old had conquered Alexander, the Greeks the Romans, and in our own times Charles of Burgundy the Swiss; while the pope and the Florentines together would have had little difficulty in defeating Francesco Maria, nephew of Pope Julius II., in the recent war of Urbino; and yet, in every one of these instances, the victory remained with him who held the sinews of war to consist, not in money, but in good soldiers.

Croesus, king of Lydia, after showing Solon the Athenian much besides, at last displayed to him the boundless riches of his treasure-house, and asked him what he thought of his power. Whereupon Solon answered that he thought him no whit more powerful in respect of these treasures, for as war is made with iron and not with gold, another coming with more iron might carry off his gold. After the death of Alexander the Great a tribe of Gauls, passing through Greece on their way into Asia, sent envoys to the King of Macedonia to treat for terms of accord; when the king, to dismay them by a display of his resources, showed them great store of gold and silver. But these barbarians, when they saw all this wealth, in their greed to possess it, though before they had looked on peace as settled, broke off negotiations; and thus the king was ruined by those very treasures he had amassed for his defence. In like manner, not many years ago, the Venetians, with a full treasury, lost their whole dominions without deriving the least advantage from their wealth.

I maintain, therefore, that it is not gold, as is vulgarly supposed, that is the sinews of war, but good soldiers; or while gold by itself will not gain you good soldiers, good soldiers may readily get you gold. Had the Romans chosen to make war with gold rather than with iron all the treasures of the earth would not have sufficed them having regard to the greatness of their enterprises and the difficulties they had to overcome in carrying them out. But making their wars with iron they never felt any want of gold; for those who stood in fear of them brought gold into their camp.

And supposing it true that the Spartan king was forced by lack of money to risk the chances of a battle, it only fared with him in respect of money as it has often fared with others from other causes; since we see that where an army is in such straits for want of victual that it must either fight or perish by famine, it will always fight, as being the more honourable course and that on which fortune may in some way smile. So, too, it has often happened that a captain, seeing his enemy about to be reinforced, has been obliged either to trust to fortune and at once deliver battle, or else, waiting till the reinforcement is complete, to fight then, whether he will or no, and at whatever disadvantage. We find also, as in the case of Hasdrubal when beset, in the March of Ancona, at once by Claudius Nero and by the other Roman consul, that a captain, when he must either fight or fly, will always fight, since it will seem to him that by this course, however hazardous, he has at least a chance of victory, while by the other his ruin is certain.

There are many circumstances, therefore, which may force a captain to give battle contrary to his intention, among which the want of money may sometimes be one. But this is no ground for pronouncing money to be the sinews of war, any more than those other things from the want of which men are reduced to the same necessity. Once more, therefore, I repeat that not gold but good soldiers constitute the sinews of war. Money, indeed, is most necessary in a secondary place; but this necessity good soldiers will always be able to supply, since it is as impossible that good soldiers should lack money, as that money by itself should secure good soldiers. And that what I say is true is shown by countless passages in history. When Pericles persuaded the Athenians to declare war against the whole Peloponnesus, assuring them that their dexterity, aided by their wealth, was sure to bring them off victorious, the Athenians, though for a while they prospered in this war, in the end were overpowered, the prudent counsels and good soldiers of Sparta proving more than a match for the dexterity and wealth of Athens. But, indeed, there can be no better witness to the truth of my contention than Titus Livius himself. For in that passage of his history wherein he discusses whether if Alexander the Great had invaded Italy, he would have succeeded in vanquishing the Romans, three things are noted by him as essential to success in war; to wit, many and good soldiers, prudent captains, and favourable fortune; and after examining whether the Romans or Alexander would have had the advantage in each of these three particulars, he arrives at his conclusion without any mention of money.

The Campanians, therefore, when asked by the Sidicinians to arm in their behalf, must have measured their strength by wealth and not by soldiers; for after declaring in their favour and suffering two defeats, to save themselves they were obliged to become tributary to Rome.

CHAPTER XI

That it were unwise to ally yourself a Prince who has Reputation rather than Strength.

To mark the mistake made by the Sidicinians in trusting to the protection of the Campanians, and by the Campanians in supposing themselves able to protect the Sidicinians, Titus Livius could not have expressed himself in apter words than by saying, that *"the Campanians rather lent their name to the Sidicinians than furnished any substantial aid towards their defence."*

Here we have to note that alliances with princes who from dwelling at a distance have no facility, or who from their own embarrassments, or from other causes, have no ability to render aid, afford rather reputation than protection to those who put their trust in them. As was the case in our own times with the Florentines, when, in the year 1479, they were attacked by the Pope and the King of Naples. For being friends of the French king they drew from that friendship more reputation than help. The same would be the case with that prince who should engage in any enterprise in reliance on the Emperor Maximilian, his being one of those friendships which, in the words of our historian, *nomen magis quam praesidium adferunt.*

On this occasion, therefore, the Campanians were misled by imagining themselves stronger than they really were. For often, from defect of judgment, men take upon them to defend others, when they have neither skill nor ability to defend themselves. Of which we have a further instance in the Tarentines, who, when the Roman and Samnite armies were already drawn up against one another for battle, sent messengers to the Roman consul to acquaint him that they desired peace between the two nations, and would themselves declare war against whichsoever of the two first began hostilities. The consul, laughing at their threats, in the presence of the messengers, ordered the signal for battle to sound, and bade his army advance to meet the enemy; showing the Tarentines by acts rather than words what answer he thought their message deserved.

Having spoken in the present Chapter of unwise courses followed by princes for defending others, I shall speak in the next, of the methods they follow in defending themselves.

CHAPTER XII

Whether when Invasion is imminent it is better to anticipate or to await it.

I have often heard it disputed by men well versed in military affairs, whether, when there are two princes of nearly equal strength, and the bolder of the two proclaims war upon the other, it is better for that other to await attack within his own frontier, or to march into the enemy's country and fight him there; and I have heard reasons given in favour of each of these courses.

They who maintain that an enemy should be attacked in his own country, cite the advice given by Croesus to Cyrus, when the latter had come to the frontiers of the Massagetae to make war on that people. For word being sent by Tomyris their queen that Cyrus might, at his pleasure, either enter her dominions, where she would await him, or else allow her to come and meet him; and the matter being debated, Croesus, contrary to the opinion of other advisers, counselled Cyrus to go forward and meet the queen, urging that were he to defeat her at a distance from her kingdom, he might not be able to take it from her, since she would have time to repair her strength; whereas, were he to defeat her within her own dominions, he could follow her up on her flight, and, without giving her time to recover herself, deprive her of her State. They cite also the advice given by Hannibal to Antiochus, when the latter was meditating a war on the Romans. For Hannibal told him that the Romans could not be vanquished except in Italy, where an invader might turn to account the arms and resources of their friends, whereas any one making war upon them out of Italy, and leaving that country in their hands, would leave them an unfailing source whence to draw whatever reinforcement they might need; and finally, he told him, that the Romans might more easily be deprived of Rome than of their empire, and of Italy more easily than of any of their other provinces. They likewise instance Agathocles, who, being unequal to support a war at home, invaded the Carthaginians, by whom he was being attacked, and reduced them to sue for peace. They also cite Scipio, who to shift the war from Italy, carried it into Africa.

Those who hold a contrary opinion contend that to have your enemy at a disadvantage you must get him away from his home, alleging the case of the Athenians, who while they carried on the war at their convenience in their own territory, retained their superiority; but when they quitted that territory, and went with their armies to Sicily, lost their freedom. They cite also the fable of the poets wherein it is figured that Antaeus, king of Libya, being assailed by the Egyptian Hercules, could not be overcome while he awaited his adversary within the bounds of his own kingdom; but so soon as he was withdrawn from these by the craft of Hercules, lost his kingdom and his life. Whence the fable runs that Antaeus, being son to the goddess Earth, when thrown to the ground drew fresh strength from the Earth, his mother; and that Hercules, perceiving this, held him up away from the Earth.

Recent opinions are likewise cited as favouring this view. Every one knows how Ferrando, king of Naples, was in his day accounted a most wise prince; and how two years before his death there came a rumour that Charles VIII of France was meditating an attack upon him; and how, after making great preparations for his defence, he sickened; and being on the point of death, among other counsels left his son Alfonso this advice, that nothing in the world should tempt him to pass out of his own territory, but to await the enemy within his frontier, and with his forces unimpaired; a warning disregarded by Alfonso, who sent into Romagna an army, which he lost, and with it his whole dominions, without a battle.

Other arguments on both sides of the question in addition to those already noticed, are as follows: He who attacks shows higher courage than he who stands on his defence, and this gives his army greater confidence. Moreover, by attacking your enemy you deprive him of many opportunities for using his resources, since he can receive no aid from subjects who have been stripped of their possessions; and when an enemy is at his gates, a prince must be careful how he levies money and imposes taxes; so that, as Hannibal said, the springs which enable a country to support a war come to be dried up. Again, the soldiers of an invader, finding themselves in a foreign land, are under a stronger necessity to fight, and necessity, as has often been said, is the parent of valour.

On the other hand, it may be argued that there are many advantages to be gained by awaiting the attack of your enemy. For without putting yourself much about, you may harass him by intercepting his supplies, whether of victual or of whatsoever else an army stands in need: from your better knowledge of the country you can impede his movements; and because men muster more willingly to defend their homes than to go on distant expeditions, you can meet him with more numerous forces, if defeated you can more easily repair your strength, because the bulk of your army, finding shelter at hand, will be able to save itself, and your reserves will have no distance to come. In this way you can use your whole strength without risking your entire fortunes; whereas, in leaving your country, you risk your entire fortunes, without putting forth your whole strength. Nay, we find that to weaken an adversary still further, some have suffered him to make a march of several days into their country, and then to capture certain of their towns, that by leaving garrisons in these, he might reduce the numbers of his army, and so be attacked at greater disadvantage.

But now to speak my own mind on the matter, I think we should make this distinction. Either you have your country strongly defended, as the Romans had and the Swiss have theirs, or, like the Carthaginians of old and the King of France and the

Italians at the present day, you have it undefended. In the latter case you must keep the enemy at a distance from your country, for as your strength lies not in men but in money, whenever the supply of money is cut off you are undone, and nothing so soon cuts off this supply as a war of invasion. Of which we have example in the Carthaginians, who, while their country was free from invasion, were able by means of their great revenues to carry on war in Italy against the Romans, but when they were invaded could not defend themselves even against Agathocles. The Florentines, in like manner, could make no head against Castruccio, lord of Lucca, when he attacked them in their own country; and to obtain protection, were compelled to yield themselves up to King Robert of Naples. And yet, after Castruccio's death, these same Florentines were bold enough to attack the Duke of Milan in his own country, and strong enough to strip him of his dominions. Such valour did they display in distant wars, such weakness in those that were near.

But when a country is armed as Rome was and Switzerland now is, the closer you press it, the harder it is to subdue; because such States can assemble a stronger force to resist attack than for attacking others. Nor does the great authority of Hannibal move me in this instance, since resentment and his own advantage might lead him to speak as he spoke to Antiochus. For had the Romans suffered in Gaul, and within the same space of time, those three defeats at the hands of Hannibal which they suffered in Italy, it must have made an end of them; since they could not have turned the remnants of their armies to account as they did in Italy, not having the same opportunity for repairing their strength; nor could they have met their enemy with such numerous armies. For we never find them sending forth a force of more than fifty thousand men for the invasion of any province; whereas, in defending their own country against the inroad of the Gauls at the end of the first Carthaginian war, we hear of them bringing some eighteen hundred thousand men into the field; and their failure to vanquish the Gauls in Lombardy as they had vanquished those in Tuscany arose from their inability to lead a great force so far against a numerous enemy, or to encounter him with the same advantages. In Germany the Cimbrians routed a Roman army who had there no means to repair their disaster; but when they came into Italy, the Romans could collect their whole strength, and destroy them. Out of their native country, whence they can bring no more than thirty or forty thousand men, the Swiss may readily be defeated; but in their own country, where they can assemble a hundred thousand, they are well-nigh invincible.

In conclusion, therefore, I repeat that the prince who has his people armed and trained for war, should always await a great and dangerous war at home, and never go forth to meet it. But that he whose subjects are unarmed, and whose country is not habituated to war, should always carry the war to as great a distance as he can from home. For in this way each will defend himself in the best manner his means admit.

CHAPTER XIII

That Men rise from humble to high Fortunes rather by Fraud than by Force.

I hold it as most certain that men seldom if ever rise to great place from small beginnings without using fraud or force, unless, indeed, they be given, or take by inheritance the place to which some other has already come. Force, however, will never suffice by itself to effect this end, while fraud often will, as any one may plainly see who reads the lives of Philip of Macedon, Agathocles of Sicily, and many others like them, who from the lowest or, at any rate, from very low beginnings, rose either to sovereignty or to the highest command.

This necessity for using deceit is taught by Xenophon in his life of Cyrus; for the very first expedition on which Cyrus is sent, against the King of Armenia, is seen to teem with fraud; and it is by fraud, and not by force, that he is represented as having acquired his kingdom; so that the only inference to be drawn from his conduct, as Xenophon describes it, is, that the prince who would accomplish great things must have learned how to deceive. Xenophon, moreover, represents his hero as deceiving his maternal grandsire Cyaxares, king of the Medians, in a variety of ways; giving it to be understood that without such deceit he could not have reached the greatness to which he came. Nor do I believe that any man born to humble fortunes can be shown to have attained great station, by sheer and open force, whereas this has often been effected by mere fraud, such as that used by Giovanni Galeazzo to deprive his uncle Bernabo of the State and government of Lombardy.

The same arts which princes are constrained to use at the outset of their career, must also be used by commonwealths, until they have grown powerful enough to dispense with them and trust to strength alone. And because Rome at all times, whether from chance or choice, followed all such methods as are necessary to attain greatness, in this also she was not behindhand. And, to begin with, she could have used no greater fraud than was involved in her method above noticed, of making for herself companions; since under this name she made for herself subjects, for such the Latins and the other surrounding nations, in fact, became. For availing herself at first of their arms to subdue neighbouring countries and gain herself reputation as a State, her power was so much increased by these conquests that there was none whom she could not overcome. But the Latins never knew that they were enslaved until they saw the Samnites twice routed and forced to make terms. This success, while it added greatly to the fame of the Romans among princes at a distance, who were thereby made familiar with the Roman name though not with the Roman arms, bred at the same time jealousy and distrust among those who, like the Latins, both saw and felt these arms; and such were the effects of this jealousy and distrust, that not the Latins only but all the Roman colonies in Latium, along with the Campanians whom a little while before the Romans had defended leagued themselves together against the authority of Rome. This war was set on foot by the Latins in the manner in which, as I have already explained, most wars are begun, not by directly attacking the Romans, but by defending the Sidicinians against the Samnites who were making war upon them with the permission of the Romans. And that it was from their having found out the crafty policy of the Romans that the Latins were led to take this step, is plain from the words which Titus Livius puts in the mouth of Annius Setinus the Latin praetor, who, in addressing the Latin council, is made to say, *"For if even now we can put up with slavery under the disguise of an equal alliance, etc"*

We see, therefore, that the Romans, from the time they first began to extend their power, were not unfamiliar with the art of deceiving, an art always necessary for those who would mount to great heights from low beginnings; and which is the less to be condemned when, as in the case of the Romans, it is skilfully concealed.

CHAPTER XIV

That Men often err in thinking they can subdue Pride by Humility.

You shall often find that humility is not merely of no service to you, but is even hurtful, especially when used in dealing with insolent men, who, through envy or other like cause, have conceived hatred against you. Proof whereof is supplied by our historian where he explains the causes of this war between the Romans and the Latins. For on the Samnites complaining to the Romans that the Latins had attacked them, the Romans, desiring not to give the Latins ground of offence, would not forbid them proceeding with the war. But the endeavour to avoid giving offence to the Latins only served to increase their confidence, and led them the sooner to declare their hostility. Of which we have evidence in the language used by the same Latin Praetor, Annius Setinus, at the aforesaid council, when he said: — "You have tried their patience by refusing them, soldiers. Who doubts but that they are offended? Still they have put up with the affront. They have heard that we are assembling an army against their allies the Samnites; and yet they have not stirred from their city. Whence this astonishing forbearance, but from their knowing our strength and their own weakness?" Which words give us clearly to understand how much the patience of the Romans increased the arrogance of the Latins.

A prince, therefore, should never stoop from his dignity, nor should he if he would have credit for any concession make it voluntarily, unless he be able or believe himself able to withhold it. For almost always when matters have come to such a pass that you cannot give way with credit it is better that a thing be taken from you by force than yielded through fear of force. For if you yield through fear and to escape war, the chances are that you do not escape it; since he to whom, out of manifest cowardice you make this concession, will not rest content, but will endeavour to wring further concessions from you, and making less account of you, will only be the more kindled against you. At the same time you will find your friends less zealous on your behalf, since to them you will appear either weak or cowardly. But if, so soon as the designs of your enemy are disclosed, you at once prepare to resist though your strength be inferior to his, he will begin to think more of you, other neighbouring princes will think more; and many will be willing to assist you, on seeing you take up arms, who, had you relinquished hope and abandoned yourself to despair, would never have stirred a finger to save you.

The above is to be understood as applying where you have a single adversary only; but should you have several, it will always be a prudent course, even after war has been declared, to restore to some one of their number something you have of his, so as to regain his friendship and detach him from the others who have leagued themselves against you.

CHAPTER XV

That weak States are always dubious in their Resolves; and that tardy Resolves are always hurtful.

Touching this very matter, and with regard to these earliest beginnings of war between the Latins and the Romans, it may be noted, that in all our deliberations it behoves us to come quickly to a definite resolve, and not to remain always in dubiety and suspense. This is plainly seen in connection with the council convened by the Latins when they thought to separate themselves from the Romans. For the Romans suspecting the hostile humour wherewith the Latins were infected, in order to learn how things really stood, and see whether they could not win back the malcontents without recourse to arms, gave them to know that they must send eight of their citizens to Rome, as they had occasion to consult with them. On receiving which message the Latins, knowing that they had done many things contrary to the wishes of the Romans, called a council to determine who of their number should be sent, and to instruct them what they were to say. But Annius, their praetor, being present in the council when these matters were being discussed, told them *"that he thought it of far greater moment for them to consider what they were to do than what they were to say; for when their resolves were formed, it would be easy to clothe them in fit words."* This, in truth, was sound advice and such as every prince and republic should lay to heart. Because, where there is doubt and uncertainty as to what we may decide on doing, we know not how to suit our words to our conduct; whereas, with our minds made up, and the course we are to follow fixed, it is an easy matter to find words to declare our resolves. I have noticed this point the more readily, because I have often found such uncertainty hinder the public business of our own republic, to its detriment and discredit. And in all matters of difficulty, wherein courage is needed for resolving, this uncertainty will always be met with, whenever those who have to deliberate and decide are weak.

Not less mischievous than doubtful resolves are those which are late and tardy, especially when they have to be made in behalf of a friend. For from their lateness they help none, and hurt ourselves. Tardy resolves are due to want of spirit or want of strength, or to the perversity of those who have to determine, who being moved by a secret desire to overthrow the government, or to carry out some selfish purpose of their own, suffer no decision to be come to, but only thwart and hinder. Whereas, good citizens, even when they see the popular mind to be bent on dangerous courses, will never oppose the adoption of a fixed plan, more particularly in matters which do not brook delay.

After Hieronymus, the Syracusan tyrant, was put to death, there being at that time a great war between the Romans and the Carthaginians, the citizens of Syracuse fell to disputing among themselves with which nation they should take part; and so fierce grew the controversy between the partisans of the two alliances, that no course could be agreed on, and they took part with neither; until Apollonides, one of the foremost of the Syracusan citizens, told them in a speech replete with wisdom, that neither those who inclined to hold by the Romans, nor those who chose rather to side with the Carthaginians, were deserving of blame; but that what was utterly to be condemned was doubt and delay in taking one side or other; for from such uncertainty he clearly foresaw the ruin of their republic; whereas, by taking a decided course, whatever it might be, some good might come. Now Titus Livius could not show more clearly than he does in this passage, the mischief which results from resting in suspense. He shows it, likewise, in the case of the Lavinians, of whom he relates, that being urged by the Latins to aid them against Rome, they were so long in making up their minds, that when the army which they at last sent to succour the Latins was issuing from their gates, word came that the Latins were defeated. Whereupon Millionius, their praetor, said, "*With the Romans this short march will cost us dear.*" But had the Lavinians resolved at once either to grant aid or to refuse it, taking a latter course they would not have given offence to the Romans, taking the former, and rendering timely help, they and the Latins together might have had a victory. But by delay they stood to lose in every way, as the event showed.

This example, had it been remembered by the Florentines, might have saved them from all that loss and vexation which they underwent at the hands of the French, at the time King Louis XII. of France came into Italy against Lodovico, duke of Milan. For when Louis first proposed to pass through Tuscany he met with no objection from the Florentines, whose envoys at his court arranged with him that they should stand neutral, while the king, on his arrival in Italy, was to maintain their government and take them under his protection; a month's time being allowed the republic to ratify these terms. But certain persons, who, in their folly, favoured the cause of Lodovico, delayed this ratification until the king was already on the eve of victory; when the Florentines suddenly becoming eager to ratify, the king would not accept their ratification, perceiving their consent to be given under constraint and not of their own good-will. This cost the city of Florence dear, and went near to lose her freedom, whereof she was afterwards deprived on another like occasion. And the course taken by the Florentines was the more to be blamed in that it was of no sort of service to Duke Lodovico, who, had he been victorious, would have shown the Florentines many more signs of his displeasure than did the king.

Although the hurt which results to republics from weakness of this sort has already been discussed in another Chapter, nevertheless, since an opportunity offered for touching upon it again, I have willingly availed myself of it, because to me it seems a matter of which republics like ours should take special heed.

CHAPTER XVI

That the Soldiers of our days depart widely from the methods of ancient Warfare.

In all their wars with other nations, the most momentous battle ever fought by the Romans, was that which they fought with the Latins when Torquatus and Decius were consuls. For it may well be believed that as by the loss of that battle the Latins became subject to the Romans, so the Romans had they not prevailed must have become subject to the Latins. And Titus Livius is of this opinion, since he represents the armies as exactly equal in every respect, in discipline and in valour, in numbers and in obstinacy, the only difference he draws being, that of the two armies the Romans had the more capable commanders. We find, however, two circumstances occurring in the conduct of this battle, the like of which never happened before, and seldom since, namely, that to give steadiness to the minds of their soldiers, and render them obedient to the word of command and resolute to fight, one of the consuls put himself, and the other his son, to death.

The equality which Titus Livius declares to have prevailed in these two armies, arose from this, that having long served together they used the same language, discipline, and arms; that in disposing their men for battle they followed the same system; and that the divisions and officers of their armies bore the same names. It was necessary, therefore, that as they were of equal strength and valour, something extraordinary should take place to render the courage of the one army more stubborn and unflinching than that of the other, it being on this stubbornness, as I have already said, that victory depends. For while this temper is maintained in the minds of the combatants they will never turn their backs on their foe. And that it might endure longer in the minds of the Romans than of the Latins, partly chance, and partly the valour of the consuls caused it to fall out that Torquatus slew his son, and Decius died by his own hand.

In pointing out this equality of strength, Titus Livius takes occasion to explain the whole system followed by the Romans in the ordering of their armies and in disposing them for battle; and as he has treated the subject at length, I need not go over the same ground, and shall touch only on what I judge in it most to deserve attention, but, being overlooked by all the captains of our times, has led to disorder in many armies and in many battles.

From this passage of Titus Livius, then, we learn that the Roman army had three principal divisions, or battalions as we might now call them, of which they named the first *hastati*, the second *principes*, and the third *triarii*, to each of which cavalry were attached. In arraying an army for battle they set the *hastati* in front. Directly behind them, in the second rank, they placed the *principes*; and in the third rank of the same column, the *triarii*. The cavalry of each of these three divisions they disposed to the right and left of the division to which it belonged; and to these companies of horse, from their form and position, they gave the name wings (*alae*), from their appearing like the two wings of the main body of the army. The first division, the *hastati*, which was in front, they drew up in close order to enable it to withstand and repulse the enemy. The second division, the *principes*, since it was not to be engaged from the beginning, but was meant to succour the first in case that were driven in, was not formed in close order but kept in open file, so that it might receive the other into its ranks whenever it was broken and forced to retire. The third division, that, namely, of the *triarii*, had its ranks still more open than those of the second, so that, if occasion required, it might receive the first two divisions of the *hastati* and *principes*. These divisions, therefore, being drawn up in this order, the engagement began, and if the *hastati* were overpowered and driven back, they retired within the loose ranks of the *principes*, when both these divisions, being thus united into one, renewed the conflict. If these, again, were routed and forced back, they retreated within the open ranks of the *triarii*, and all three divisions, forming into one, once more renewed the fight, in which, if they were overpowered, since they had no further means of recruiting their strength, they lost the battle. And because whenever this last division, of the *triarii*, had to be employed, the army was in jeopardy, there arose the proverb, *"Res redacta est ad triarios,"* equivalent to our expression of *playing a last stake*.

The captains of our day, as they have abandoned all the other customs of antiquity, and pay no heed to any part of the ancient discipline, so also have discarded this method of disposing their men, though it was one of no small utility. For to insure the defeat of a commander who so arranges his forces as to be able thrice during an engagement to renew his strength, Fortune must thrice declare against him, and he must be matched with an adversary able three times over to defeat him; whereas he whose sole chance of success lies in his surviving the first onset, as is the case with all the armies of Christendom at the present day, may easily be vanquished, since any slight mishap, and the least failure in the steadiness of his men, may deprive him of victory.

And what takes from our armies the capacity to renew their strength is, that provision is now no longer made for one division being received into the ranks of another, which happens because at present an army is arranged for battle in one or other of two imperfect methods. For either its divisions are placed side by side, so as to form a line of great width but of no depth or solidity; or if, to strengthen it, it be drawn up in columns after the fashion of the Roman armies, should the front line be broken, no provision having been made for its being received by the second, it is thrown into complete disorder, and both divisions fall to pieces. For if the front line be driven back, it jostles the second, if the second line endeavour to advance, the first stands in its way: and thus, the first driving against the second, and the second against the third, such confusion follows that often the most trifling accident will cause the ruin of an entire army.

At the battle of Ravenna, where M. de Foix, the French commander, was slain, although according to modern notions this was a well-fought field, both the French and the Spanish armies were drawn up in the first of the faulty methods above described; that is to say, each army advanced with the whole of its battalions side by side, so that each presented a single front much wider than deep; this being always the plan followed by modern armies when, as at Ravenna, the ground is open. For knowing the disorder they fall into on retreat, forming themselves in a single line, they endeavour, as I have said, as much as possible to escape confusion by extending their front. But where the ground confines them they fall at once into the disorder spoken of, without an effort to prevent it.

Troops traversing an enemy's country, whether to pillage or carry out any other operation of war, are liable to fall into the same disorder; and at S. Regolo in the Pisan territory, and at other places where the Florentines were beaten by the Pisans during the war which followed on the revolt of Pisa after the coming of Charles of France into Italy, our defeat was due to no other cause than the behaviour of our own cavalry, who being posted in front, and being repulsed by the enemy, fell back on the infantry and threw them into confusion, whereupon the whole army took to flight; and Messer Ciriaco del Borgo, the veteran leader of the Florentine foot, has often declared in my presence that he had never been routed by any cavalry save those who were fighting on his side. For which reason the Swiss, who are the greatest proficients in modern warfare, when serving with the French, make it their first care to place themselves on their flank, so that the cavalry of their friends, if repulsed, may not throw them into disorder.

But although these matters seem easy to understand and not difficult to put in practice, none has yet been found among the commanders of our times, who attempted to imitate the ancients or to correct the moderns. For although these also have a tripartite division of their armies into van-guard, main-body, and rear-guard, the only use they make of it is in giving orders when their men are in quarters; whereas on active service it rarely happens that all divisions are not equally exposed to the same onset.

And because many, to excuse their ignorance, will have it that the destructive fire of artillery forbids our employing at the present day many of the tactics used by the ancients, I will discuss this question in the following Chapter, and examine whether artillery does in fact prevent us from using the valiant methods of antiquity.

CHAPTER XVII

What importance the Armies of the present day should allow to Artillery; and whether the commonly received opinion concerning it be just.

Looking to the number of pitched battles, or what are termed by the French *journees*, and by the Italians *fatti d'arme*, fought by the Romans at divers times, I am led further to examine the generally received opinion, that had artillery been in use in their day, the Romans would not have been allowed, or at least not with the same ease, to subjugate provinces and make other nations their tributaries, and could never have spread their power in the astonishing way they did. For it is said that by reason of these fire-arms men can no longer use or display their personal valour as they could of old; that there is greater difficulty now than there was in former times in joining battle; that the tactics followed then cannot be followed now; and that in time all warfare must resolve itself into a question of artillery.

Judging it not out of place to inquire whether these opinions are sound, and how far artillery has added to or taken from the strength of armies, and whether its use lessens or increases the opportunities for a good captain to behave valiantly, I shall at once address myself to the first of the averments noticed above, namely, that the armies of the ancient Romans could not have made the conquests they did, had artillery then been in use.

To this I answer by saying that, since war is made for purposes either of offence or defence, we have first to see in which of these two kinds of warfare artillery gives the greater advantage or inflicts the greater hurt. Now, though something might be said both ways, I nevertheless believe that artillery is beyond comparison more hurtful to him who stands on the defensive than to him who attacks. For he who defends himself must either do so in a town or in a fortified camp. If within a town, either the town will be a small one, as fortified towns commonly are, or it will be a great one. In the former case, he who is on the defensive is at once undone. For such is the shock of artillery that there is no wall so strong that in a few days it will not batter down, when, unless those within have ample room to withdraw behind covering works and trenches, they must be beaten; it being impossible for them to resist the assault of an enemy who forces an entrance through the breaches in their walls. Nor will any artillery a defender may have be of any service to him; since it is an established axiom that where men are able to advance in numbers and rapidly, artillery is powerless to check them.

For this reason, in storming towns the furious assaults of the northern nations prove irresistible, whereas the attacks of our Italian troops, who do not rush on in force, but advance to the assault in small knots of skirmishers (*scaramouches*, as they are fitly named), may easily be withstood. Those who advance in such loose order, and with so little spirit, against a breach covered by artillery, advance to certain destruction, and as against them artillery is useful. But when the assailants swarm to the breach so massed together that one pushes on another, unless they be brought to a stand by ditches and earthworks, they penetrate everywhere, and no artillery has any effect to keep them back; and though some must fall, yet not so many as to prevent a victory.

The frequent success of the northern nations in storming towns, and more particularly the recovery of Brescia by the French, is proof sufficient of the truth of what I say. For the town of Brescia rising against the French while the citadel still held out, the Venetians, to meet any attack which might be made from the citadel upon the town, ranged guns along the whole line of road which led from the one to the other, planting them in front, and in flank, and wherever else they could be brought to bear. Of all which M. de Foix making no account, dismounted with his men-at-arms from horseback, and, advancing with them on foot through the midst of the batteries, took the town; nor do we learn that he sustained any considerable loss from the enemy's fire. So that, as I have said, he who has to defend himself in a small town, when his walls are battered down and he has no room to retire behind other works, and has only his artillery to trust to, is at once undone.

But even where the town you defend is a great one, so that you have room to fall back behind new works, artillery is still, by a long way, more useful for the assailant than for the defender. For to enable your artillery to do any hurt to those without, you must raise yourself with it above the level of the ground, since, if you remain on the level, the enemy, by erecting any low mound or earth-work, can so secure himself that it will be impossible for you to touch him. But in raising yourself above the level of the ground, whether by extending yourself along the gallery of the walls, or otherwise, you are exposed to two disadvantages; for, first, you cannot there bring into position guns of the same size or range as he who is without can bring to bear against you, since it is impossible to work large guns in a confined space; and, secondly, although you should succeed in getting your guns into position, you cannot construct such strong and solid works for their protection as those can who are outside, and on level ground, and who have all the room and every other advantage which they could desire. It is consequently impossible for him who defends a town to maintain his guns in position at any considerable height, when those who are outside have much and powerful artillery; while, if he place it lower, it becomes, as has been explained, to a great extent useless. So that in the end the defence of the city has to be effected, as in ancient times, by hand to hand fighting, or else by means of the smaller kinds of fire-arms, from which if the defender derive some slight advantage, it is balanced by the injury he sustains from the great artillery of his enemy, whereby the walls of the city are battered down and almost buried in their ditches; so that when it comes once more to an encounter at close quarters, by reason of his walls being demolished and his ditches filled up, the defender is now at a far greater disadvantage than he was formerly. Wherefore I repeat that these arms are infinitely more useful for him who attacks a town than for him who defends it.

As to the remaining method, which consists in your taking up your position in an entrenched camp, where you need not fight unless you please, and unless you have the advantage, I say that this method commonly affords you no greater facility for avoiding an engagement than the ancients had; nay, that sometimes, owing to the use of artillery, you are worse off than they were. For if the enemy fall suddenly upon you, and have some slight advantage (as may readily be the case from his being on higher ground, or from your works on his arrival being still incomplete so that you are not wholly sheltered by them), forthwith, and without your being able to prevent him, he dislodges you, and you are forced to quit your defences and deliver battle: as happened to the Spaniards at the battle of Ravenna. For having posted themselves between the river Ronco and an earthwork, from their not having carried this work high enough, and from the French having a slight advantage of ground, they were forced by the fire of the latter to quit their entrenchments come to an engagement.

But assuming the ground you have chosen for your camp to be, as it always should, higher than that occupied by the enemy, and your works to be complete and sufficient, so that from your position and preparations the enemy dare not attack you, recourse will then be had to the very same methods as were resorted to in ancient times when an army was so posted that it could not be assailed; that is to say, your country will be wasted, cities friendly to you besieged or stormed, and your supplies intercepted; until you are forced, at last, of necessity to quit your camp and to fight a pitched battle, in which, as will presently appear, artillery will be of little service to you.

If we consider, therefore, for what ends the Romans made wars, and that attack and not defence was the object of almost all their campaigns, it will be clear, if what I have said be true, that they would have had still greater advantage, and might have achieved their conquests with even greater ease, had artillery been in use in their times.

And as to the second complaint, that by reason of artillery men can no longer display their valour as they could in ancient days, I admit it to be true that when they have to expose themselves a few at a time, men run more risks now than formerly; as when they have to scale a town or perform some similar exploit, in which they are not massed together but must advance singly and one behind another. It is true, also, that Captains and commanders of armies are subjected to a greater risk of being killed now than of old, since they an be reached everywhere by the enemy's fire; and it is no protection to them to be with those of their men who are furthest from the enemy, or to be surrounded by the bravest of their guards. Still, we do not often find either of these two dangers occasioning extraordinary loss. For towns strongly fortified are not attacked by escalade, nor will the assailing army advance against them in weak numbers; but will endeavour, as in ancient times, to reduce them by regular siege. And even in the case of towns attacked by storm, the dangers are not so very much greater now than they were formerly; for in those old days also, the defenders of towns were not without warlike engines, which if less terrible in their operation, had, so far as killing goes, much the same effect. And as for the deaths of captains and leaders of companies, it may be said that during the last twenty-four years of war in Italy, we have had fewer instances of such deaths than might be found in a period of ten years of ancient warfare. For excepting the Count Lodovico della Mirandola, who fell at Ferrara, when the Venetians a few years ago attacked that city, and the Duke de Nemours, slain at Cirignuola, we have no instance of any commander being killed by artillery. For, at Ravenna, M. de Foix died by steel and not by shot. Wherefore I say that if men no longer perform deeds of individual prowess, it results not so much from the use of artillery, as from the faulty discipline and weakness of our armies, which being collectively without valour cannot display it in particular instances.

As to the third assertion, that armies can no longer be brought to engage one another, and that war will soon come to be carried on wholly with artillery, I maintain that this allegation is utterly untrue, and will always be so held by those who are willing in handling their troops to follow the usages of ancient valour. For whosoever would have a good army must train it, either by real or by mimic warfare, to approach the enemy, to come within sword-thrust, and to grapple with him; and must rely more on foot soldiers than on horse, for reasons presently to be explained. But when you trust to your foot-soldiers, and to the methods already indicated, artillery becomes powerless to harm you. For foot-soldiers, in approaching an enemy, can with more ease escape the fire of his artillery than in ancient times they could have avoided a charge of elephants or of scythed chariots, or any other of those strange contrivances which had to be encountered by the Romans, and against which they always devised some remedy. And, certainly, as against artillery, their remedy would have been easier, by as much as the time during which artillery can do hurt is shorter than the time during which elephants and chariots could. For by these you were thrown into disorder after battle joined, whereas artillery harasses you only before you engage; a danger which infantry can easily escape, either by advancing so as to be covered by the inequalities of the ground, or by lying down while the firing continues; nay, we find from experience that even these precautions may be dispensed with, especially as against great artillery, which can hardly be levelled with such precision that its fire shall not either pass over your head from the range being too high, or fall short from its being too low.

So soon, however, as the engagement is begun, it is perfectly clear that neither small nor great artillery can harm you any longer; since, if the enemy have his artillerymen in front, you take them; if in rear, they will injure him before they injure you; and if in flank, they can never fire so effectively as to prevent your closing, with the result already explained. Nor does this admit of much dispute, since we have proof of it in the case of the Swiss at Novara, in the year 1513, when, with neither guns nor cavalry, they advanced against the French army, who had fortified themselves with artillery behind entrenchments, and routed them without suffering the slightest check from their fire. In further explanation whereof it is to be noted, that to work artillery effectively it should be protected by walls, by ditches, or by earthworks; and that whenever, from being left without such protection it has to be defended by men, as happens in pitched battles and engagements in the open field, it is either taken or otherwise becomes useless. Nor can it be employed on the flank of an army, save in the manner in which the ancients made use of their warlike engines, which they moved out from their columns that they might be worked without inconvenience, but withdrew within them when driven back by cavalry or other troops. He who looks for any further advantage from artillery does not rightly understand its nature, and trusts to what is most likely to deceive him. For although the Turk, using artillery, has gained victories over the Soldan and the Sofi, the only advantage he has had from it has been the terror into which the horses of the enemy, unused to such sounds, are thrown by the roar of the guns.

And now, to bring these remarks to a conclusion, I say briefly that, employed by an army wherein there is some strain of the ancient valour, artillery is useful; but employed otherwise, against a brave adversary, is utterly useless.

CHAPTER XVIII

That the authority of the Romans and the example of ancient Warfare should make us hold Foot Soldiers of more account than Horse.

By many arguments and instances it can be clearly established that in their military enterprises the Romans set far more store on their infantry than on their cavalry, and trusted to the former to carry out all the chief objects which their armies were meant to effect. Among many other examples of this, we may notice the great battle which they fought with the Latins near the lake Regillus, where to steady their wavering ranks they made their horsemen dismount, and renewing the combat on foot obtained a victory. Here we see plainly that the Romans had more confidence in themselves when they fought on foot than when they fought on horseback. The same expedient was resorted to by them in many of their other battles, and always in their sorest need they found it their surest stay.

Nor are we to condemn the practice in deference to the opinion of Hannibal, who, at the battle of Cannae, on seeing the consuls make the horsemen dismount, said scoffingly, *"Better still had they delivered their knights to me in chains."* For though this saying came from the mouth of a most excellent soldier, still, if we are to regard authority, we ought rather to follow the authority of a commonwealth like Rome, and of the many great captains who served her, than that of Hannibal alone. But, apart from authority, there are manifest reasons to bear out what I say. For a man may go on foot into many places where a horse cannot go; men can be taught to keep rank, and if thrown into disorder to recover form; whereas, it is difficult to keep horses in line, and impossible if once they be thrown into disorder to reform them. Moreover we find that with horses as with men, some have little courage and some much; and that often a spirited horse is ridden by a faint-hearted rider, or a dull horse by a courageous rider, and that in whatever way such disparity is caused, confusion and disorder result. Again, infantry, when drawn up in column, can easily break and is not easily broken by cavalry. This is vouched, not only by many ancient and many modern instances, but also by the authority of those who lay down rules for the government of States, who show that at first wars were carried on by mounted soldiers, because the methods for arraying infantry were not yet understood, but that so soon as these were discovered, the superiority of foot over horse was at once recognized. In saying this, I would not have it supposed that horsemen are not of the greatest use in armies, whether for purposes of observation, for harrying and laying waste the enemy's country, for pursuing a retreating foe or helping to repulse his cavalry. But the substance and sinew of an army, and that part of it which ought constantly to be most considered, should always be the infantry. And among sins of the Italian princes who have made their country the slave of foreigners, there is none worse than that they have held these arms in contempt, and turned their whole attention to mounted troops.

  This error is due to the craft of our captains and to the ignorance of our rulers. For the control of the armies of Italy for the last five and twenty years resting in the hands of men, who, as having no lands of their own, may be looked on as mere soldiers of fortune, these fell forthwith on contriving how they might maintain their credit by being supplied with the arms which the princes of the country were without. And as they had no subjects of their own of whom they could make use, and could not obtain constant employment and pay for a large number of foot-soldiers, and as a small number would have given them no importance, they had recourse to horsemen. For a *condottiere* drawing pay for two or three hundred horsemen was maintained by them in the highest credit, and yet the cost was not too great to be met by the princes who employed him. And to effect their object with more ease, and increase their credit still further, these adventurers would allow no merit or favour to be due to foot-soldiers, but claimed all for their horsemen. And to such a length was this bad system carried, that in the very greatest army only the smallest sprinkling of infantry was to be found. This, together with many other ill practices which accompanied it, has so weakened the militia of Italy, that the country has easily been trampled upon by all the nations of the North.

That it is a mistake to make more account of cavalry than of infantry, may be still more clearly seen from another example taken from Roman history. The Romans being engaged on the siege of Sora, a troop of horse a sally from the town to attack their camp; when the Roman master of the knights advancing with his own horsemen to give them battle, it so chanced that, at the very first onset, the leaders on both sides were slain. Both parties being thus left without commanders, and the combat, nevertheless, continuing, the Romans thinking thereby to have the advantage of their adversaries, alighted from horseback, obliging the enemy's cavalry, in order to defend themselves, to do the like. The result was that the Romans had the victory. Now there could be no stronger instance than this to show the superiority of foot over horse. For while in other battles the Roman cavalry were made by their consuls to dismount in order to succour their infantry who were in distress and in need of such aid, on this occasion they dismounted, not to succour their infantry, nor to encounter an enemy contending on foot, but because they saw that though they could not prevail against the enemy fighting as horsemen against horsemen, on foot they readily might. And from this I conclude that foot-soldiers, if rightly handled, can hardly be beaten except by other soldiers fighting on foot.

With very few cavalry, but with a considerable force of infantry, the Roman commanders, Crassus and Marcus Antonius, each for many days together overran the territories of the Parthians, although opposed by the countless horsemen of that nation. Crassus, indeed, with the greater part of his army, was left there dead, and Antonius only saved himself by his valour; but even in the extremities to which the Romans were then brought, see how greatly superior foot-soldiers are to horse. For though fighting in an open country, far from the sea-coast, and cut off from his supplies, Antonius proved himself a valiant soldier in the judgment even of the Parthians themselves, the whole strength of whose cavalry never ventured to attack the columns of his army. And though Crassus perished there, any one who reads attentively the account of his expedition must see that he was rather outwitted than defeated, and that even when his condition was desperate, the Parthians durst not close with him, but effected his destruction by hanging continually on the flanks of his army, and intercepting his supplies, while cajoling him with promises which they never kept.

It might, I grant, be harder to demonstrate this great superiority of foot over horse, had we not very many modern examples affording the clearest proof of it. For instance, at the battle of Novara, of which we have already spoken, nine thousand Swiss foot were seen to attack ten thousand cavalry together with an equal number of infantry, and to defeat them; the cavalry being powerless to injure them, while of the infantry, who were mostly Gascons, and badly disciplined, they made no account. On another occasion we have seen twenty-six thousand Swiss march on Milan to attack Francis I. of France, who had with him twenty thousand men-at-arms, forty thousand foot, and a hundred pieces of artillery; and although they were not victorious as at Novara, they nevertheless fought valiantly for two days together, and, in the end, though beaten, were able to bring off half their number. With foot-soldiers only Marcus Attilius Regulus ventured to oppose himself, not to cavalry merely, but to elephants; and if the attempt failed it does not follow that he was not justified by the valour of his men in believing them equal to surmount this danger.

I repeat, therefore, that to prevail against well-disciplined infantry, you must meet them with infantry disciplined still better, and that otherwise you advance to certain destruction. In the time of Filippo Visconti, Duke of Milan, some sixteen thousand Swiss made a descent on Lombardy, whereupon the Duke, who at that time had Il Carmagnola as his captain, sent him with six thousand men-at-arms and a slender following of foot-soldiers to meet them. Not knowing their manner of fighting, Carmagnola fell upon them with his horsemen, expecting to put them at once to rout; but finding them immovable, after losing many of his men he withdrew. But, being a most wise captain, and skilful in devising new remedies to meet unwonted dangers, after reinforcing his company he again advanced to the attack; and when about to engage made all his men-at-arms dismount, and placing them in front of his foot-soldiers, fell once more upon the Swiss, who could then no longer withstand him. For his men, being on foot and well armed, easily penetrated the Swiss ranks without hurt to themselves; and getting among them, had no difficulty in cutting them down, so that of the entire army of the Swiss those only escaped who were spared by his humanity.

Of this difference in the efficiency of these two kinds of troops, many I believe are aware; but such is the unhappiness and perversity of the times in which we live, that neither ancient nor modern examples, nor even the consciousness of error, can move our present princes to amend their ways, or convince them that to restore credit to the arms of a State or province, it is necessary to revive this branch of their militia also, to keep it near them, to make much of it, and to give it life, that in return, it may give back life and reputation to them. But as they have departed from all those other methods already spoken of, so have they departed from this, and with this result, that to them the acquisition of territory is rather a loss than a gain, as presently shall be shown.

CHAPTER XIX

That Acquisitions made by ill-governed States and such as follow not the valiant methods of the Romans, tend rather to their Ruin than to their Aggrandizement.

To these false opinions, founded on the pernicious example first set by the present corrupt age, we owe it, that no man thinks of departing from the methods which are in use. It had been impossible, for instance, some thirty years ago, to persuade an Italian that ten thousand foot-soldiers could, on plain ground, attack ten thousand cavalry together with an equal number of infantry; and not merely attack, but defeat them; as we saw done by the Swiss at that battle of Novara, to which I have already referred so often. For although history abounds in similar examples, none would have believed them, or, believing them, would have said that nowadays men are so much better armed, that a squadron of cavalry could shatter a rock, to say nothing of a column of infantry. With such false pleas would they have belied their judgment, taking no account that with a very scanty force of foot-soldiers, Lucullus routed a hundred and fifty thousand of the cavalry of Tigranes, among whom were a body of horsemen very nearly resembling our own men-at-arms. Now, however, this error is demonstrated by the example of the northern nations.

And since what history teaches as to the superiority of foot-soldiers is thus proved to be true, men ought likewise to believe that the other methods practised by the ancients are in like manner salutary and useful. And were this once accepted, both princes and commonwealths would make fewer blunders than they do, would be stronger to resist sudden attack, and would no longer place their sole hope of safety in flight; while those who take in hand to provide a State with new institutions would know better what direction to give them, whether in the way of extending or merely of preserving; and would see that to augment the numbers of their citizens, to assume other States as companions rather than reduce them to subjection, to send out colonies for the defence of acquired territories, to hold their spoils at the credit of the common stock, to overcome enemies by inroads and pitched battles rather than by sieges, to enrich the public purse, keep down private wealth, and zealously, to maintain all military exercises, are the true ways to aggrandize a State and to extend its empire. Or if these methods for adding to their power are not to their mind, let them remember that acquisitions made in any other way are the ruin of republics, and so set bounds to their ambition, wisely regulating the internal government of their country by suitable laws and ordinances, forbidding extension, and looking only to defence, and taking heed that their defences are in good order, as do those republics of Germany which live and for long have lived, in freedom.

And yet, as I have said on another occasion, when speaking of the difference between the methods suitable for acquiring and those suitable for maintaining, it is impossible for a republic to remain long in the peaceful enjoyment of freedom within a restricted frontier. For should it forbear from molesting others, others are not likely to refrain from molesting it; whence must grow at once the desire and the necessity to make acquisitions; or should no enemies be found abroad, they will be found at home, for this seems to be incidental to all great States. And if the free States of Germany are, and have long been able to maintain themselves on their present footing, this arises from certain conditions peculiar to that country, and to be found nowhere else, without which these communities could not go on living as they do.

The district of Germany of which I speak was formerly subject to the Roman Empire, in the same way as France and Spain; but on the decline of the Empire, and when its very name came to be limited to this one province, its more powerful cities taking advantage of the weakness and necessities of the Emperors, began to free themselves by buying from them their liberty, subject to the payment of a trifling yearly tribute; until, gradually, all the cities which held directly from the Emperor, and were not subject to any intermediate lord, had, in like manner, purchased their freedom. While this went on, it so happened that certain communities subject to the Duke of Austria, among which were Friburg, the people of Schweitz, and the like, rose in rebellion against him, and meeting at the outset with good success, by degrees acquired such accession of strength that so far from returning under the Austrian yoke, they are become formidable to all their neighbours These are the States which we now name Swiss.

Germany is, consequently, divided between the Swiss, the communities which take the name of Free Towns, the Princes, and the Emperor; and the reason why, amid so many conflicting interests, wars do not break out, or breaking out are of short continuance, is the reverence in which all hold this symbol of the Imperial authority. For although the Emperor be without strength of his own, he has nevertheless such credit with all these others that he alone can keep them united, and, interposing as mediator, can speedily repress by his influence any dissensions among them.

The greatest and most protracted wars which have taken place in this country have been those between the Swiss and the Duke of Austria; and although for many years past the Empire and the dukedom of Austria have been united in the same man, he has always failed to subdue the stubbornness of the Swiss, who are never to be brought to terms save by force. Nor has the rest of Germany lent the Emperor much assistance in his wars with the Swiss, the Free Towns being little disposed to attack others whose desire is to live as they themselves do, in freedom; while the Princes of the Empire either are so poor that they cannot, or from jealousy of the power of the Emperor will not, take part with him against them.

These communities, therefore, abide contented within their narrow confines, because, having regard to the Imperial authority, they have no occasion to desire greater; and are at the same time obliged to live in unity within their walls, because an enemy is always at hand, and ready to take advantage of their divisions to effect an entrance. But were the circumstances of the country other than they are these communities would be forced to make attempts to extend their dominions, and be constrained to relinquish their present peaceful mode of life. And since the same conditions are not found elsewhere, other nations cannot adopt this way of living, but are compelled to extend their power either by means of leagues, or else by the methods used by the Romans; and any one who should act otherwise would find not safety but rather death and destruction. For since in a thousand ways, and from causes innumerable, conquests are surrounded with dangers, it may well happen that in adding to our dominions, we add nothing to our strength; but whosoever increases not his strength while he adds to his dominions, must needs be ruined. He who is impoverished by his wars, even should he come off victorious, can add nothing to his strength, since he spends more than he gains, as the Venetians and Florentines have done. For Venice has been far feebler since she acquired Lombardy, and Florence since she acquired Tuscany, than when the one was content to be mistress of the seas, and the other of the lands lying within six miles from her walls. And this from their eagerness to acquire without knowing what way to take. For which ignorance these States are the more to be blamed in proportion as there is less to excuse them; since they had seen what methods were used by the Romans, and could have followed in their footsteps; whereas the Romans, without any example set them, were able by their own prudence to shape a course for themselves.

But even to well-governed States, their conquests may chance to occasion much harm; as when some city or province is acquired abounding in luxury and delights, by whose manners the conqueror becomes infected; as happened first to the Romans, and afterwards to Hannibal on taking possession of Capua. And had Capua been at such a distance from Rome that a ready remedy could not have been applied to the disorders of the soldiery, or had Rome herself been in any degree tainted with corruption, this acquisition had certainly proved her ruin. To which Titus Livius bears witness when he says, *"Most mischievous at this time to our military discipline was Capua; for ministering to all delights, she turned away the corrupted minds of our soldiers from the remembrance of their country."* And, truly, cities and provinces like this, avenge themselves on their conquerors without blood or blow; since by infecting them with their own evil customs they prepare them for defeat at the hands of any assailant. Nor could the subject have been better handled than by Juvenal, where he says in his Satires, that into the hearts of the Romans, through their conquests in foreign lands, foreign manners found their way; and in place of frugality and other admirable virtues —

"Came luxury more mortal than the sword, And settling down, avenged a vanquished world."

And if their conquests were like to be fatal to the Romans at a time when they were still animated by great virtue and prudence, how must it fare with those who follow methods altogether different from theirs, and who, to crown their other errors of which we have already said enough, resort to auxiliary and mercenary arms, bringing upon themselves those dangers whereof mention shall be made in the Chapter following.

CHAPTER XX

Of the Dangers incurred by Princes or Republics who resort to Auxiliary or Mercenary Arms.

Had I not already, in another treatise, enlarged on the inutility of mercenary and auxiliary, and on the usefulness of national arms, I should dwell on these matters in the present Discourse more at length than it is my design to do. For having given the subject very full consideration elsewhere, here I would be brief. Still when I find Titus Livius supplying a complete example of what we have to look for from auxiliaries, by whom I mean troops sent to our assistance by some other prince or ruler, paid by him and under officers by him appointed, it is not fit that I should pass it by in silence.

It is related, then, by our historian, that the Romans, after defeating on two different occasions armies of the Samnites with forces sent by them to succour the Capuans, whom they thus relieved from the war which the Samnites Were waging against them, being desirious to return to Rome, left behind two legions to defend the Capuans, that the latter might not, from being altogether deprived of their protection, once more become a prey to the Samnites. But these two legions, rotting in idleness began to take such delight therein, that forgetful of their country and the reverence due to the senate, they resolved to seize by violence the city they had been left to guard by their valour. For to them it seemed that the citizens of Capua were unworthy to enjoy advantages which they knew not how to defend. The Romans, however, getting timely notice of this design, at once met and defeated it, in the manner to be more fully noticed when I come to treat of conspiracies.

Once more then, I repeat, that of all the various kinds of troops, auxiliaries are the most pernicious, because the prince or republic resorting to them for aid has no authority over them, the only person who possesses such authority being he who sends them. For, as I have said, auxiliary troops are those sent to your assistance by some other potentate, under his own flag, under his own officers, and in his own pay, as were the legions sent by the Romans to Capua. Such troops, if victorious, will for the most part plunder him by whom, as well as him against whom, they are hired to fight; and this they do, sometimes at the instigation of the potentate who sends them, sometimes for ambitious ends of their own. It was not the purpose of the Romans to violate the league and treaty which they had made with Capua; but to their soldiers it seemed so easy a matter to master the Capuans, that they were readily led into this plot for depriving them of their town and territories. Many other examples might be given to the same effect, but it is enough to mention besides this instance, that of the people of Regium, who were deprived of their city and of their lives by another Roman legion sent for their protection.

Princes and republics, therefore, should resort to any other expedient for the defence of their States sooner than call in hired auxiliaries, when they have to rest their entire hopes of safety on them; since any accord or terms, however hard, which you may make with your enemy, will be carefully studied and current events well considered, it will be seen that for one who has succeeded with such assistance, hundreds have been betrayed. Nor, in truth, can any better opportunity for usurping a city or province present itself to an ambitious prince or commonwealth, than to be asked to send an army for its defence. On the other hand, he who is so greedy of conquest as to summon such help, not for purposes of defence but in order to attack others, seeks to have what he can never hold and is most likely to be taken from him by the very person who helps him to gain it. Yet such is the perversity of men that, to gratify the desire of the moment, they shut their eyes to those ills which must speedily ensue and are no more moved by example in this matter than in all those others of which I have spoken; for were they moved by these examples they would see that the more disposed they are to deal generously with their neighbours, and the more averse they are to usurp authority over them, the readier will these be to throw themselves into their arms; as will at once appear from the case of the Capuans.

CHAPTER XXI

That Capua was the first City to which the Romans sent a Praetor; nor there, until four hundred years after they began to make War.

The great difference between the methods followed by the ancient Romans in adding to their dominions, and those used for that purpose by the States of the present time, has now been sufficiently discussed. It has been seen, too how in dealing with the cities which they did not think fit to destroy, and even with those which had made their submission not as companions but as subjects, it was customary with the Romans to permit them to live on under their own laws, without imposing any outward sign of dependence, merely binding them to certain conditions, or complying with which they were maintained in their former dignity and importance. We know, further, that the same methods continued to be followed by the Romans until they passed beyond the confines of Italy, and began to reduce foreign kingdoms and States to provinces: as plainly appears in the fact that Capua was the first city to which they sent a praetor, and him from no motive of ambition, but at the request of the Capuans themselves who, living at variance with one another, thought it necessary to have a Roman citizen in their town who might restore unity and good order among them. Influenced by this example, and urged by the same need, the people of Antium were the next to ask that they too might have a praetor given them; touching which request and in connection with which new method of governing, Titus Livius observes, *"that not the arms only but also the laws of Rome now began to exert an influence,"* showing how much the course thus followed by the Romans promoted the growth of their authority.

For those cities, more especially, which have been used to freedom or to be governed by their own citizens, rest far better satisfied with a government which they do not see, even though it involve something of oppression, than with one which standing constantly before their eyes, seems every day to reproach them with the disgrace of servitude. And to the prince there is another advantage in this method of government, namely, that as the judges and magistrates who administer the laws civil and criminal within these cities, are not under his control, no decision of theirs can throw responsibility or discredit upon him; so that he thus escapes many occasions of calumny and hatred. Of the truth whereof, besides the ancient instances which might be noted, we have a recent example here in Italy. For Genoa, as every one knows, has many times been occupied by the French king, who always, until lately, sent thither a French governor to rule in his name. Recently, however, not from choice but of necessity, he has permitted the town to be self-governed under a Genoese ruler; and any one who had to decide which of these two methods of governing gives the greater security to the king's authority and the greater content to the people themselves, would assuredly have to pronounce in favour of the latter.

Men, moreover, in proportion as they see you averse to usurp authority over them, grow the readier to surrender themselves into your hands; and fear you less on the score of their freedom, when they find you acting towards them with consideration and kindness. It was the display of these qualities that moved the Capuans to ask the Romans for a praetor; for had the Romans betrayed the least eagerness to send them one, they would at once have conceived jealousy and grown estranged.

But why turn for examples to Capua and Rome, when we have them close at hand in Tuscany and Florence? Who is there but knows what a time it is since the city of Pistoja submitted of her own accord to the Florentine supremacy? Who, again, but knows the animosity which down to the present day exists between Florence and the cities of Pisa, Lucca, and Siena? This difference of feeling does not arise from the citizens of Pistoja valuing their freedom less than the citizens of these other towns or thinking themselves inferior to them, but from the Florentines having always acted towards the former as brothers, towards the latter as foes. This it was that led the Pistojans to come voluntarily under our authority while the others have done and do all in their power to escape it. For there seems no reason to doubt, that if Florence, instead of exasperating these neighbours of hers, had sought to win them over, either by entering into league with them or by lending them assistance, she would at this hour have been mistress of Tuscany. Not that I would be understood to maintain that recourse is never to be had to force and to arms, but that these are only to be used in the last resort, and when all other remedies are unavailing.

CHAPTER XXII

That in matters of moment Men often judge amiss.

How falsely men often judge of things, they who are present at their deliberations have constant occasion to know. For in many matters, unless these deliberations be guided by men of great parts, the conclusions come to are certain to be wrong. And because in corrupt republics, and especially in quiet times, either through jealousy or from other like causes, men of great ability are often obliged to stand aloof, it follows that measures not good in themselves are by a common error judged to be good, or are promoted by those who seek public favour rather than the public advantage. Mistakes of this sort are found out afterwards in seasons of adversity, when recourse must be had to those persons who in peaceful times had been, as it were, forgotten, as shall hereafter in its proper place be more fully explained. Cases, moreover, arise in which those who have little experience of affairs are sure to be misled, from the matters with which they have to deal being attended by many deceptive appearances such as lead men to believe whatsoever they are minded to believe.

These remarks I make with reference to the false hopes which the Latins, after being defeated by the Romans, were led to form on the persuasion of their praetor Numitius, and also with reference to what was believed by many a few years ago, when Francis, king of France, came to recover Milan from the Swiss. For Francis of Angouleme, succeeding on the death of Louis XII. to the throne of France, and desiring to recover for that realm the Duchy of Milan, on which, some years before, the Swiss had seized at the instance of Pope Julius, sought for allies in Italy to second him in his attempt; and besides the Venetians, who had already been gained over by King Louis, endeavoured to secure the aid of the Florentines and Pope Leo X.; thinking that were he to succeed in getting these others to take part with him, his enterprise would be easier. For the forces of the Spanish king were then in Lombardy, and the army of the Emperor at Verona.

Pope Leo, however, did not fall in with the wishes of Francis, being, it is said, persuaded by his advisers that his best course was to stand neutral. For they urged that it was not for the advantage of the Church to have powerful strangers, whether French or Swiss, in Italy; but that to restore the country to its ancient freedom, it must be delivered from the yoke of both. And since to conquer both, whether singly or together, was impossible, it was to be desired that the one should overthrow the other, after which the Church with her friends might fall upon the victor. And it was averred that no better opportunity for carrying out this design could ever be found than then presented itself; for both the French and the Swiss were in the field; while the Pope had his troops in readiness to appear on the Lombard frontier and in the vicinity of the two armies, where, under colour of watching his own interests, he could easily keep them until the opposed hosts came to an engagement; when, as both armies were full of courage, their encounter might be expected to be a bloody one, and likely to leave the victor so weakened that it would be easy for the Pope to attack and defeat him; and so, to his own great glory, remain master of Lombardy and supreme throughout Italy.

How baseless this expectation was, was seen from the event. For the Swiss being routed after a protracted combat, the troops of the Pope and Spain, so far from venturing to attack the conqueror, prepared for flight; nor would flight have saved them, had not the humanity or indifference of the king withheld him from pursuing his victory, and disposed him to make terms with the Church.

The arguments put forward by the Pope's advisers had a certain show of reason in their favour, which looked at from a distance seemed plausible enough; but were in reality wholly contrary to truth; since it rarely happens that the captain who wins a victory loses any great number of his men, his loss being in battle only, and not in flight. For in the heat of battle, while men stand face to face, but few fall, chiefly because such combats do not last long; and even when they do last, and many of the victorious army are slain, so splendid is the reputation which attends a victory, and so great the terror it inspires, as far to outweigh any loss the victor suffers by the slaughter of his soldiers; so that an enemy who, trusting to find him weakened, should then venture to attack him, would soon be taught his mistake, unless strong enough to give him battle at any time, before his victory as well as after. For in that case he might, as fortune and valour should determine, either win or lose; though, even then, the army which had first fought and won would have an advantage. And this we know for a truth from what befell the Latins in consequence of the mistake made by Numitius their praetor, and their blindness in believing him. For when they had already suffered defeat at the hands of the Romans, Numitius caused it to be proclaimed throughout the whole country of Latium, that now was the time to fall upon the enemy, exhausted by a struggle in which they were victorious only in name, while in reality suffering all those ills which attend defeat, and who might easily be crushed by any fresh force brought against them. Whereupon the Latins believed him, and getting together a new army, were forthwith routed with such loss as always awaits those who listen to like counsels.

CHAPTER XXIII

That in chastising their Subjects when circumstances required it the Romans always avoided half-measures.

"Such was now the state of affairs in Latium, that peace and war seemed alike intolerable." No worse calamity can befall a prince or commonwealth than to be reduced to such straits that they can neither accept peace nor support war; as is the case with those whom it would ruin to conclude peace on the terms offered, while war obliges them either to yield themselves a spoil to their allies, or remain a prey to their foes. To this grievous alternative are men led by evil counsels and unwise courses, and, as already said, from not rightly measuring their strength. For the commonwealth or prince who has rightly measured his strength, can hardly be brought so low as were the Latins, who made war with the Romans when they should have made terms, and made terms when they should have made war, and so mismanaged everything that the friendship and the enmity of Rome were alike fatal. Whence it came that, in the first place, they were defeated and broken by Manlius Torquatus, and afterwards utterly subdued by Camillus; who, when he had forced them to surrender at discretion to the Roman arms, and had placed garrisons in all their towns, and taken hostages from all, returned to Rome and reported to the senate that the whole of Latium now lay at their mercy.

And because the sentence then passed by the senate is memorable, and worthy to be studied by princes that it may be imitated by them on like occasion, I shall cite the exact words which Livius puts into the mouth of Camillus, as confirming what I have already said touching the methods used by the

Romans to extend their power, and as showing how in chastising their subjects they always avoided half-measures and took a decided course. For government consists in nothing else than in so controlling your subjects that it shall neither be in their power nor for their interest to harm you. And this is effected either by making such sure work with them as puts it out of their power to do you injury, or else by so loading them with benefits that it would be folly in them to seek to alter their condition. All which is implied first in the measures proposed by Camillus, and next in the resolutions passed on these proposals by the senate. The words of Camillus were as follows: "The immortal gods have made you so entirely masters in the matter you are now considering, that it lies with you to pronounce whether Latium shall or shall not longer exist. So far as the Latins are concerned, you can secure a lasting peace either by clemency or by severity. Would you deal harshly with those whom you have conquered and who have given themselves into your hands, you can blot out the whole Latin nation. Would you, after the fashion of our ancestors, increase the strength of Rome by admitting the vanquished to the rights of citizenship, here you have opportunity to do so, and with the greatest glory to yourselves. That, assuredly, is the strongest government which they rejoice in who obey it. Now, then, is your time, while the minds of all are bent on what is about to happen, to obtain an ascendency over them, either by punishment or by benefits."

Upon this motion the senate resolved, in accordance with the advice given by the consul, to take the case of each city separately, and either destroy utterly or else treat with tenderness all the more important of the Latin towns. To those cities they dealt with leniently, they granted exemptions and privileges, conferring upon them the rights of citizenship, and securing their welfare in every particular. The others they razed to the ground, and planting colonies in their room, either removed the inhabitants to Rome, or so scattered and dispersed them that neither by arms nor by counsels was it ever again in their power to inflict hurt. For, as I have said already, the Romans never, in matters of moment, resorted to half-measures. And the sentence which they then pronounced should be a pattern for all rulers, and ought to have been followed by the Florentines when, in the year 1502, Arezzo and all the Val di Chiana rose in revolt. For had they followed it, they would have established their authority on a surer footing, and added much to the greatness of their city by securing for it those lands which are needed to supply it with the necessaries of life. But pursuing that half-hearted policy which is most mischievous in executing justice, some of the Aretines they outlawed, some they condemned to death, and all they deprived of their dignities and ancient importance in their town, while leaving the town itself untouched. And if in the councils then held any Florentine recommended that Arezzo should be dismantled, they who thought themselves wiser than their fellows objected, that to do so would be little to the honour of our republic, since it would look as though she lacked strength to hold it. Reasons like this are of a sort which seem sound, but are not really so; for, by the same rule, no parricide should be put to death, nor any other malefactor, however atrocious his crimes; because, forsooth, it would be discreditable to the ruler to appear unequal to the control of a single criminal. They who hold such opinions fail to see that when men individually, or entire cities collectively, offend against the State, the prince for his own safety, and as a warning to others, has no alternative but to make an end of them; and that true honour lies in being able and in knowing how to chastise such offenders, and not in incurring endless dangers in the effort to retain them. For the prince who does not chastise offenders in a way that puts it out of their power to offend again, is accounted unwise or worthless.

How necessary it was for the Romans to execute Justice against the Latins, is further seen from the course took with the men of Privernum. And here the text of Livius suggests two points for our attention: first, as already noted, that a subjugated people is either to be caressed or crushed; and second, how much it is for our advantage to maintain a manly bearing, and to speak the truth fearlessly in the presence of the wise. For the senate being met to determine the fate of the citizens of Privernum, who after rebelling had been reduced to submission by the Roman arms, certain of these citizens were sent by their countrymen to plead for pardon. When these had come into the presence of the senate, one of them was asked by a senator, "*What punishment he thought his fellow citizens deserved?*" To which he of Privernum answered, "*Such punishment as they deserve who deem themselves worthy of freedom.*" "But," said the consul, "should we remit your punishment, what sort of peace can we hope to have with you?" To which the other replied, "If granted on fair terms, a firm and lasting peace; if on unfair, a peace of brief duration." Upon this, though many of the senators were displeased, the wiser among them declared "that they had heard the voice of freedom and manhood, and would never believe that the man or people who so spoke ought to remain longer than was needful in a position which gave them cause for shame; since that was a safe peace which was accepted willingly; whereas good faith could not be looked for where it was sought to impose servitude." So saying, they decided that the people of Privernum should be admitted to Roman citizenship, with all the rights and privileges thereto appertaining; declaring that "men whose only thought was for freedom, were indeed worthy to be Romans." So pleasing was this true and high answer to generous minds, while any other must have seemed at once false and shameful. And they who judge otherwise of men, and of those men, especially, who have been used to be free, or so to think themselves, are mistaken; and are led through their mistake to adopt courses unprofitable for themselves and affording no content to others. Whence, the frequent rebellions and the downfall of States.

But, returning to our subject, I conclude, as well from this instance of Privernum, as from the measures followed with the Latins, that when we have to pass sentence upon powerful States accustomed to live in freedom, we must either destroy them utterly, or else treat them with much indulgence; and that any other course we may take with them will be unprofitable. But most carefully should we avoid, as of all courses the most pernicious, such half-measures as were followed by the Samnites when they had the Romans shut up in the Caudine Forks, and would not listen to the counsels of the old man who urged them either to send their captives away with every honourable attention, or else put them all to death; but adopted a middle course, and after disarming them and making them pass under the yoke, suffered them to depart at once disgraced and angered. And no long time after, they found to their sorrow that the old man's warning was true, and that the course they had themselves chosen was calamitous; as shall, hereafter, in its place be shown.

CHAPTER XXIV

That, commonly, Fortresses do much more Harm than Good

To the wise men of our day it may seem an oversight on the part of the Romans, that, when they sought to protect themselves against the men of Latium and Privernum, it never occurred to them to build strongholds in their cities to be a curb upon them, and insure their fidelity, especially when we remember the Florentine saying which these same wise men often quote, to the effect that Pisa and other like cities must be held by fortresses Doubtless, had those old Romans been like-minded with our modern sages, they would not have neglected to build themselves fortresses, but because they far surpassed them in courage, sense, and vigour, they refrained. And while Rome retained her freedom, and adhered to her own wise ordinances and wholesome usages, she never built a single fortress with the view to hold any city or province, though, sometimes, she may have suffered those to stand which she found already built.

Looking, therefore, to the course followed by the Romans in this particular, and to that adopted by our modern rulers, it seems proper to consider whether or not it is advisable to build fortresses, and whether they are more likely to help or to hurt him who builds them In the first place, then, we are to remember that fortresses are built either as a defence against foreign foes or against subjects In the former case, I pronounce them unnecessary, in the latter mischievous. And to state the reasons why in the latter case they are mischievous, I say that when princes or republics are afraid of their subjects and in fear lest they rebel, this must proceed from knowing that their subjects hate them, which hatred in its turn results from their own ill conduct, and that again from their thinking themselves able to rule their subjects by mere force, or from their governing with little prudence. Now one of the causes which lead them to suppose that they can rule by mere force, is this very circumstance of their people having these fortresses on their backs So that the conduct which breeds hatred is itself mainly occasioned by these princes or republics being possessed of fortresses, which, if this be true, are really far more hurtful than useful First, because, as has been said already, they render a ruler bolder and more violent in his bearing towards his subjects, and, next, because they do not in reality afford him that security which he believes them to give For all those methods of violence and coercion which may be used to keep a people under, resolve themselves into two; since either like the Romans you must always have it in your power to bring a strong army into the field, or else you must dissipate, destroy, and disunite the subject people, and so divide and scatter them that they can never again combine to injure you For should you merely strip them of their wealth, *spoliatis arma supersunt,* arms still remain to them, or if you deprive them of their weapons, *furor arma ministrat,* rage will supply them, if you put their chiefs to death and continue to maltreat the rest, heads will renew themselves like those Hydra; while, if you build fortresses, these may serve in time of peace to make you bolder in outraging your subjects, but in time of war they will prove wholly useless, since they will be attacked at once by foes both foreign and domestic, whom together it will be impossible for you to resist. And if ever fortresses were useless they are so at the present day, by reason of the invention of artillery, against the fury of which, as I have shown already, a petty fortress which affords no room for retreat behind fresh works, cannot be defended.

But to go deeper into the matter, I say, either you are a prince seeking by means of these fortresses to hold the people of your city in check; or you are a prince, or it may be a republic, desirous to control some city which you have gained in war. To the prince I would say, that, for the reasons already given, nothing can be more unserviceable than a fortress as a restraint upon your subjects, since it only makes you the readier to oppress them, and less scrupulous how you do so; while it is this very oppression which moves them to destroy you, and so kindles their hatred, that the fortress, which is the cause of all the mischief, is powerless to protect you. A wise and good prince, therefore, that he may continue good, and give no occasion or encouragement to his descendants to become evil, will never build a fortress, to the end that neither he nor they may ever be led to trust to it rather than to the good-will of their subjects. And if Francesco Sforza, who was accounted a wise ruler, on becoming Duke of Milan erected a fortress in that city, I say that herein he was unwise, and that the event has shown the building of this fortress to have been hurtful and not helpful to his heirs. For thinking that by its aid they could behave as badly as they liked to their citizens and subjects, and yet be secure, they refrained from no sort of violence or oppression, until, becoming beyond measure odious, they lost their State as soon as an enemy attacked it. Nor was this fortress, which in peace had occasioned them much hurt, any defence or of any service them in war. For had they being without it, through thoughtlessness, treated their subjects inhumanely, they must soon have discovered and withdrawn from their danger; and might, thereafter, with no other help than that of attached subjects, have withstood the attacks of the French far more successfully than they could with their fortress, but with subjects whom they had estranged.

And, in truth, fortresses are unserviceable in every way, since they may be lost either by the treachery of those to whom you commit their defence, or by the overwhelming strength of an assailant, or else by famine. And where you seek to recover a State which you have lost, and in which only the fortress remains to you, if that fortress is to be of any service or assistance to you, you must have an army wherewith to attack the enemy who has driven you out. But with such an army you might succeed in recovering your State as readily without a fortress as with one; nay, perhaps, even more readily, since your subjects, had you not used them ill, from the overweening confidence your fortress gave you, might then have felt better disposed towards you. And the event shows that in times of adversity this very fortress of Milan has been of no advantage whatever, either to the Sforzas or to the French; but, on the contrary, has brought ruin on both, because, trusting to it, they did not turn their thoughts to nobler methods for preserving that State. Guido Ubaldo, duke of Urbino and son to Duke Federigo, who in his day was a warrior of much renown, but who was driven from his dominions by Cesare Borgia, son to Pope Alexander VI., when afterwards, by a sudden stroke of good fortune, he was restored to the dukedom caused all the fortresses of the country to be dismantled, judging them to be hurtful. For as he was beloved by his subjects, so far as they were concerned he had no need for fortresses; while, as against foreign enemies, he saw he could not defend them, since this would have required an army kept constantly in the field. For which reasons he made them be razed to the ground.

When Pope Julius II. had driven the Bentivogli from Bologna, after erecting a citadel in that town, he caused the people to be cruelly oppressed by his governor; whereupon, the people rebelled, and he forthwith lost the citadel; so that his citadel, and the oppressions to which it led, were of less service to him than different behaviour on his part had been. When Niccolo da Castello, the ancestor of the Vitelli, returned to his country out of exile, he straightway pulled down the two fortresses built there by Pope Sixtus IV., perceiving that it was not by fortresses, but by the good-will of the people, that he could be maintained in his government.

But the most recent, and in all respects most noteworthy instance, and that which best demonstrates the futility of building, and the advantage of destroying fortresses, is what happened only the other day in Genoa. Every one knows how, in 1507, Genoa rose in rebellion against Louis XII. of France, who came in person and with all his forces to recover it; and after recovering it built there a citadel stronger than any before known, being, both from its position and from every other circumstance, most inaccessible to attack. For standing on the extremity of a hill, named by the Genoese Codefa, which juts out into the sea, it commanded the whole harbour and the greater part of the town. But, afterwards, in the year 1512, when the French were driven out of Italy, the Genoese, in spite of this citadel, again rebelled, and Ottaviano Fregoso assuming the government, after the greatest efforts, continued over a period of sixteen months, at last succeeded in reducing the citadel by famine. By all it was believed that he would retain it as a rock of refuge in case of any reverse of fortune, and by some he was advised to do so; but he, being a truly wise ruler, and knowing well that it is by the attachment of their subjects and not by the strength of their fortifications that princes are maintained in their governments, dismantled this citadel; and founding his authority, not upon material defences, but on his own valour and prudence, kept and still keeps it. And whereas, formerly, a force of a thousand foot-soldiers could effect a change in the government of Genoa, the enemies of Ottaviano have assailed him with ten thousand, without being able to harm him.

Here, then, we see that, while to dismantle this fortress occasioned Ottaviano no loss, its construction gave the French king no sort of advantage. For when he could come into Italy with an army, he could recover Genoa, though he had no citadel there; but when he could not come with an army, it was not in his power to hold the city by means of the citadel. Moreover it was costly for the king to build, and shameful for him to lose this fortress; while for Ottaviano it was glorious to take, and advantageous to destroy it.

Let us turn now to those republics which build fortresses not within their own territories, but in towns whereof they have taken possession. And if the above example of France and Genoa suffice not to show the futility of this course, that of Florence and Pisa ought, I think, to be conclusive. For in erecting fortresses to hold Pisa, the Florentines failed to perceive that a city which had always been openly hostile to them, which had lived in freedom, and which could cloak rebellion under the name of liberty, must, if it were to be retained at all, be retained by those methods which were used by the Romans, and either be made a companion or be destroyed. Of how little service these Pisan fortresses were, was seen on the coming of Charles VIII. of France into Italy, to whom, whether through the treachery of their defenders or from fear of worse evils, they were at once delivered up; whereas, had there been no fortresses in Pisa, the Florentines would not have looked to them as the means whereby the town was to be held; the king could not by their assistance have taken the town from the Florentines; and the methods whereby it had previously been preserved might, in all likelihood, have continued sufficient to preserve it; and, at any rate, had served that end no worse than the fortresses.

These, then, are the conclusions to which I come, namely, that fortresses built to hold your own country under are hurtful, and that those built to retain acquired territories are useless; and I am content to rely on the example of the Romans, who in the towns they sought to hold by the strong hand, rather pulled down fortresses than built them. And if any, to controvert these views of mine, were to cite the case of Tarentum in ancient times, or of Brescia in recent, as towns which when they rebelled were recovered by means of their citadels; I answer, that for the recovery of Tarentum, Fabius Maximus was sent at the end of a year with an army strong enough to retake it even had there been no fortress there; and that although he availed himself of the fortress for the recovery of the town, he might, without it, have resorted to other means which would have brought about the same result. Nor do I see of what service a citadel can be said to be, when to recover the city you must employ a consular army under a Fabius Maximus. But that the Romans would, in any case, have recovered Tarentum, is plain from what happened at Capua, where there was no citadel, and which they retook, simply by the valour of their soldiers.

Again, as regards Brescia, I say that the circumstances attending the revolt of that town were such as occur but seldom, namely, that the citadel remaining in your hands after the defection of the city, you should happen to have a great army nigh at hand, as the French had theirs on this occasion. For M. de Foix being in command of the king's forces at Bologna, on hearing of the loss of Brescia, marched thither without an hour's delay, and reaching Brescia in three days, retook the town with the help of the citadel. But here, again, we see that, to be of any service, the citadel of Brescia had to be succoured by a de Foix, and by that French army which in three days' time marched to its relief. So that this instance cannot be considered conclusive as against others of a contrary tendency. For, in the course of recent wars, many fortresses have been taken and retaken, with the same variety of fortune with which open country has been acquired or lost; and this not only in Lombardy, but also in Romagna, in the kingdom of Naples, and in all parts of Italy.

And, further, touching the erection of fortresses as a defence against foreign enemies, I say that such defences are not needed by the prince or people who possess a good army; while for those who do not possess a good army, they are useless. For good armies without fortresses are in themselves a sufficient defence: whereas, fortresses without good armies avail nothing. And this we see in the case of those nations which have been thought to excel both in their government and otherwise, as, for instance, the Romans and the Spartans. For while the Romans would build no fortresses, the Spartans not merely abstained from building them, but would not even suffer their cities to be enclosed with walls; desiring to be protected by their own valour only, and by no other defence. So that when a Spartan was asked by an Athenian what he thought of the walls of Athens, he answered "that they were fine walls if meant to hold women only."

If a prince who has a good army has likewise, on the seafront of his dominions, some fortress strong enough to keep an enemy in check for a few days, until he gets his forces together, this, though not necessary, may sometimes be for his advantage. But for a prince who is without a strong army to have fortresses erected throughout his territories, or upon his frontier, is either useless or hurtful, since they may readily be lost and then turned against him; or, supposing them so strong that the enemy is unable to take them by assault, he may leave them behind, and so render them wholly unprofitable. For a brave army, unless stoutly met, enters an enemy's country without regard to the towns or fortified places it leaves in its rear, as we read of happening in ancient times, and have seen done by Francesco Maria della Rovere, who no long while ago, when he marched against Urbino, made little of leaving ten hostile cities behind him.

The prince, therefore, who can bring together a strong army can do without building fortresses, while he who has not a strong army ought not to build them, but should carefully strengthen the city wherein he dwells, and keep it well stored with supplies, and its inhabitants well affected, so that he may resist attack till an accord be agreed on, or he be relieved by foreign aid. All other expedients are costly in time of peace, and in war useless.

Whoever carefully weighs all that has now been said will perceive, that the Romans, as they were most prudent in all their other methods, so also showed their wisdom in the measures they took with the men of Latium and Privernum, when, without ever thinking of fortresses, they sought security in bolder and more sagacious courses.

CHAPTER XXV

That he who attacks a City divided against itself, must not think to get possession of it through its Divisions.

Violent dissensions breaking out in Rome between the commons and the nobles, it appeared to the Veientines and Etruscans that now was their time to deal a fatal blow to the Roman supremacy. Accordingly, they assembled an army and invaded the territories of Rome. The senate sent Caius Manlius and Marcus Fabius to meet them, whose forces encamping close by the Veientines, the latter ceased not to reproach and vilify the Roman name with every sort of taunt and abuse, and so incensed the Romans by their unmeasured insolence that, from being divided they became reconciled, and giving the enemy battle, broke and defeated them. Here, again, we see, what has already been noted, how prone men are to adopt wrong courses, and how often they miss their object when they think to secure it. The Veientines imagined that they could conquer the Romans by attacking them while they were at feud among themselves; but this very attack reunited the Romans and brought ruin on their assailants. For the causes of division in a commonwealth are, for the most part, ease and tranquillity, while the causes of union are fear and war. Wherefore, had the Veientines been wise, the more divided they saw Rome to be, the more should they have sought to avoid war with her, and endeavoured to gain an advantage over her by peaceful arts. And the best way to effect this in a divided city lies in gaining the confidence of both factions, and in mediating between them as arbiter so long as they do not come to blows; but when they resort to open violence, then to render some tardy aid to the weaker side, so as to plunge them deeper in hostilities, wherein both may exhaust their forces without being led by your putting forth an excess of strength to suspect you of a desire to ruin them and remain their master. Where this is well managed, it will almost always happen that you succeed in effecting the object you propose to yourself.

The city of Pistoja, as I have said already in connection with another matter, was won over to the Florentine republic by no other artifice than this. For the town being split by factions, the Florentines, by now favouring one side and now the other, without incurring the suspicions of either, brought both to such extremities that, wearied out with their harassed life, they threw themselves at last of their own accord into the arms of Florence. The city of Siena, again, has never made any change in her government which has had the support of the Florentines, save when that support has been slight and insignificant; for whenever the interference of Florence has been marked and decided, it has had the effect of uniting all parties in support of things as they stood.

One other instance I shall add to those already given. Oftener than once Filippo Visconti, duke of Milan, relying on their divisions, set wars on foot against the Florentines, and always without success; so that, in lamenting over these failures, he was wont to complain that the mad humours of the Florentines had cost him two millions of gold, without his having anything to show for it. The Veientines and Etruscans, therefore, as I have said already, were misled by false hopes, and in the end were routed by the Romans in a single pitched battle; and any who should look hereafter to prevail on like grounds and by similar means against a divided people, will always find themselves deceived.

CHAPTER XXVI

That Taunts and Abuse breed Hatred against him who uses them, without yielding him any Advantage.

To abstain from threats and injurious language, is, methinks, one of the wisest precautions a man can use. For abuse and menace take nothing from the strength of an adversary; the latter only making him more cautious, while the former inflames his hatred against you, and leads him to consider more diligently how he may cause you hurt.

This is seen from the example of the Veientines, of whom I spoke in the last Chapter, who, to the injury of war against the Romans, added those verbal injuries from which all prudent commanders should compel their soldiers to refrain. For these are injuries which stir and kindle your enemy to vengeance, and yet, as has been said, in no way disable him from doing you hurt; so that, in truth, they are weapons which wound those who use them. Of this we find a notable instance in Asia, in connection with the siege of Amida. For Gabade, the Persian general, after besieging this town for a great while, wearied out at last by its protracted defence, determined on withdrawing his army; and had actually begun to strike his camp, when the whole inhabitants of the place, elated by their success, came out upon the walls to taunt and upbraid their enemies with their cowardice and meanness of spirit, and to load them with every kind of abuse. Stung by these insults, Gabade, changing his resolution, renewed the siege with such fury that in a few days he stormed and sacked the town. And the very same thing befell the Veientines, who, not content, as we have seen, to make war on the Romans with arms, must needs assail them with foul reproaches, advancing to the palisade of their camp to revile them, and molesting them more with their tongues than with their swords, until the Roman soldiers, who at first were most unwilling to fight, forced the consuls to lead them to the attack. Whereupon, the Veientines, like those others of whom mention has just now been made, had to pay the penalty of their insolence.

Wise captains of armies, therefore, and prudent governors of cities, should take all fit precautions to prevent such insults and reproaches from being used by their soldiers and subjects, either amongst themselves or against an enemy. For when directed against an enemy they lead to the mischiefs above noticed, while still worse consequences may follow from our not preventing them among ourselves by such measures as sensible rulers have always taken for that purpose.

The legions who were left behind for the protection of Capua having, as shall in its place be told, conspired against the Capuans, their conspiracy led to a mutiny, which was presently suppressed by Valerius Corvinus; when, as one of the conditions on which the mutineers made their submission, it was declared that whosoever should thereafter upbraid any soldier of these legions with having taken part in this mutiny, should be visited with the severest punishment. So likewise, when Tiberius Gracchus was appointed, during the war with Hannibal, to command a body of slaves, whom the Romans in their straits for soldiers had furnished with arms, one of his first acts was to pass an order making it death for any to reproach his men with their servile origin. So mischievous a thing did the Romans esteem it to use insulting words to others, or to taunt them with their shame. Whether this be done in sport or earnest, nothing vexes men more, or rouses them to fiercer indignation; "for the biting jest which flavours too much of truth, leaves always behind it a rankling memory."

CHAPTER XXVII

That prudent Princes and Republics should be content to have obtained a Victory; for, commonly, when they are not, theft-Victory turns to Defeat.

The use of dishonouring language towards an enemy is mostly caused by an insolent humour, bred by victory or the false hope of it, whereby men are oftentimes led not only to speak, but also to act amiss. For such false hopes, when they gain an entry into men's minds, cause them to overrun their goal, and to miss opportunities for securing a certain good, on the chance of obtaining some thing better, but uncertain. And this, being a matter that deserves attention, because in deceiving themselves men often injure their country, I desire to illustrate it by particular instances, ancient and recent, since mere argument might not place it in so clear a light.

After routing the Romans at Cannae, Hannibal sent messengers to Carthage to announce his victory, and to ask support. A debate arising in the Carthaginian senate as to what was to be done, Hanno, an aged and wise citizen, advised that they should prudently take advantage of their victory to make peace with the Romans, while as conquerors they might have it on favourable terms, and not wait to make it after a defeat; since it should be their object to show the Romans that they were strong enough to fight them, but not to peril the victory they had won in the hope of winning a greater. This advice was not followed by the Carthaginian senate, but its wisdom was well seen later, when the opportunity to act upon it was gone.

When the whole East had been overrun by Alexander of Macedon, the citizens of Tyre (then at the height of its renown, and very strong from being built, like Venice, in the sea), recognizing his greatness, sent ambassadors to him to say that they desired to be his good servants, and to yield him all obedience, yet could not consent to receive either him or his soldiers within their walls. Whereupon, Alexander, displeased that a single city should venture to close its gates against him to whom all the rest of the world had thrown theirs open, repulsed the Tyrians, and rejecting their overtures set to work to besiege their town. But as it stood on the water, and was well stored with victual and all other munitions needed for its defence, after four months had gone, Alexander, perceiving that he was wasting more time in an inglorious attempt to reduce this one city than had sufficed for most of his other conquests, resolved to offer terms to the Tyrians, and to make them those concessions which they themselves had asked. But they, puffed up by their success, not merely refused the terms offered, but put to death the envoy sent to propose them. Enraged by this, Alexander renewed the siege, and with such vigour, that he took and destroyed the city, and either slew or made slaves of its inhabitants.

In the year 1512, a Spanish army entered the Florentine territory, with the object of restoring the Medici to Florence, and of levying a subsidy from the town; having been summoned thither by certain of the citizens, who had promised them that so soon as they appeared within the Florentine confines they would arm in their behalf. But when the Spaniards had come into the plain of the Arno, and none declared in their favour, being in sore need of supplies, they offered to make terms. This offer the people of Florence in their pride rejected, and so gave occasion for the sack of Prato and the overthrow of the Florentine Republic.

A prince, therefore, who is attacked by an enemy much more powerful than himself, can make no greater mistake than to refuse to treat, especially when overtures are made to him; for however poor the terms offered may be, they are sure to contain some conditions advantageous for him who accepts them, and which he may construe as a partial success. For which reason it ought to have been enough for the citizens of Tyre that Alexander was brought to accept terms which he had at first rejected; and they should have esteemed it a sufficient triumph that, by their resistance in arms, they had forced so great a warrior to bow to their will. And, in like manner, it should have been a sufficient victory for the Florentines that the Spaniards had in part yielded to their wishes, and abated something of their own demands, the purport of which was to change the government of Florence, to sever her from her allegiance to France, and, further, to obtain money from her. For if of these three objects the Spaniards had succeeded in securing the last two, while the Florentines maintained the integrity of their government, a fair share of honour and contentment would have fallen to each. And while preserving their political existence, the Florentines should have made small account of the other two conditions; nor ought they, even with the possibility and almost certainty of greater advantages before them, to have left matters in any degree to the arbitration of Fortune, by pushing things to extremes, and incurring risks which no prudent man should incur, unless compelled by necessity.

Hannibal, when recalled by the Carthaginians from Italy, where for sixteen years he had covered himself with glory, to the defence of his native country, found on his arrival that Hasdrubal and Syphax had been defeated, the kingdom of Numidia lost, and Carthage confined within the limits of her walls, and left without other resource save in him and his army. Perceiving, therefore, that this was the last stake his country had to play, and not choosing to hazard it until he had tried every other expedient, he felt no shame to sue for peace, judging that in peace rather than in war lay the best hope of safety for his country. But, when peace was refused him, no fear of defeat deterred him from battle, being resolved either to conquer, if conquer he might, or if he must fall, to fall gloriously. Now, if a commander so valiant as Hannibal, at the head of an unconquered army, was willing to sue for peace rather than appeal to battle when he saw that by defeat his country must be enslaved, what course ought to be followed by another commander, less valiant and with less experience than he? But men labour under this infirmity, that they know not where to set bounds to their hopes, and building on these without otherwise measuring their strength, rush headlong on destruction.

CHAPTER XXVIII

That to neglect the redress of Grievances, whether public or private, is dangerous for a Prince or Commonwealth.

Certain Gauls coming to attack Etruria, and more particularly Clusium its chief city, the citizens of Clusium sought aid from Rome; whereupon the Romans sent the three Fabii, as envoys to these Gauls, to notify to them, in the name of the Roman people, that they must refrain from making war on the Etruscans. From what befell the Romans in connection with this embassy, we see clearly how far men may be carried in resenting an affront. For these envoys arriving at the very moment when the Gauls and Etruscans were about to join battle, being readier at deeds than words, took part with the Etruscans and fought in their foremost ranks. Whence it came that the Gauls recognizing the Roman envoys, turned against the Romans all the hatred which before they had felt for the Etruscans; and grew still more incensed when on making complaint to the Roman senate, through their ambassador, of the wrong done them, and demanding that the Fabii should be given up to them in atonement for their offence, not merely were the offenders not given up or punished in any way, but, on the contrary, when the comitia met were created tribunes with consular powers. But when the Gauls found these men honoured who deserved to be chastised, they concluded that what had happened had been done by way of slight and insult to them, and, burning with fury and resentment, hastened forward to attack Rome, which they took with the exception of the Capitol.

Now this disaster overtook the Romans entirely from their disregard of justice. For their envoys, who had violated the law of nations, and had therefore deserved punishment, they had on the contrary treated with honour. And this should make us reflect, how carefully all princes and commonwealths ought to refrain from committing like wrongs, not only against communities, but also against particular men. For if a man be deeply wronged, either by a private hand or by a public officer, and be not avenged to his satisfaction, if he live in a republic, he will seek to avenge himself, though in doing so he bring ruin on his country; or if he live under a prince, and be of a resolute and haughty spirit, he will never rest until he has wreaked his resentment against the prince, though he knows it may cost him dear. Whereof we have no finer or truer example than in the death of Philip of Macedon, the father of Alexander. For Pausanias, a handsome and high-born youth belonging to Philip's court, having been most foully and cruelly dishonoured by Attalus, one of the foremost men of the royal household, repeatedly complained to Philip of the outrage; who for a while put him off with promises of vengeance, but in the end, so far from avenging him, promoted Attalus to be governor of the province of Greece. Whereupon, Pausanias, seeing his enemy honoured and not punished, turned all his resentment from him who had outraged, against him who had not avenged him, and on the morning of the day fixed for the marriage of Philip's daughter to Alexander of Epirus, while Philip walked between the two Alexanders, his son and his son-in-law, towards the temple to celebrate the nuptials, he slew him.

  This instance nearly resembles that of the Roman envoys; and offers a warning to all rulers never to think so lightly of any man as to suppose, that when wrong upon wrong has been done him, he will not bethink himself of revenge, however great the danger he runs, or the punishment he thereby brings upon himself.

CHAPTER XXIX

That Fortune obscures the minds of Men when she would not have them hinder her Designs.

If we note well the course of human affairs, we shall often find things come about and accidents befall, against which it seems to be the will of Heaven that men should not provide. And if this were the case even in Rome, so renowned for her valour, religion, and wise ordinances, we need not wonder if it be far more common in other cities and provinces wherein these safeguards are wanting.

Having here a notable opportunity to show how Heaven influences men's actions, Titus Livius turns it to account, and treats the subject at large and in pregnant words, where he says, that since it was Heaven's will, for ends of its own, that the Romans should feel its power, it first of all caused these Fabii, who were sent as envoys to the Gauls, to act amiss, and then by their misconduct stirred up the Gauls to make war on Rome; and, lastly, so ordered matters that nothing worthy of their name was done by the Romans to withstand their attack. For it was fore-ordained by Heaven that Camillus, who alone could supply the remedy to so mighty an evil, should be banished to Ardea; and again, that the citizens, who had often created a dictator to meet attacks of the Volscians and other neighbouring hostile nations, should fail to do so when the Gauls were marching upon Rome. Moreover, the army which the Romans got together was but a weak one, since they used no signal effort to make it strong; nay, were so dilatory in arming that they were barely in time to meet the enemy at the river Allia, though no more than ten miles distant from Rome. Here, again, the Roman tribunes pitched their camp without observing any of the usual precautions, attending neither to the choice of ground, nor to surround themselves with trench or Palisade, nor to avail themselves of any other aid, human or Divine. In ordering their army for battle, moreover, disposed it in weak columns, and these far apart: so that neither men nor officers accomplished anything worthy of the Roman discipline. The battle was bloodless for the Romans fled before they were attacked; most of them retreating to Veii, the rest to Rome, where, without turning aside to visit their homes, they made straight for the Capitol.

Meanwhile, the senate, so far from bethinking themselves how they might defend the city, did not even attend to closing the gates; and while some of them made their escape from Rome, others entered the Capitol along with those who sought shelter there. It was only in the defence of the Capitol that any method was observed, measures being taken to prevent it being crowded with useless numbers, and all the victual which could be got, being brought into it to enable it to stand a siege. Of the women, the children, and the men whose years unfitted them for service, the most part fled for refuge to the neighbouring towns, the rest remained in Rome a prey to the invaders; so that no one who had heard of the achievements of the Romans in past years, on being told of what took place on this occasion, could have believed that it was of the same people that things so contrary were related.

Wherefore, Titus Livius, after setting forth all these disorders, concludes with the words, *"So far does Fortune darken men's minds when she would not have her ascendency gainsaid."* Nor could any juster observation be made. And hence it is that those who experience the extremes whether of good or of evil fortune, are, commonly, little deserving either of praise or blame; since it is apparent that it is from Heaven having afforded them, or denied them opportunities for acting worthily, that they have been brought to their greatness or to their undoing. Fortune, doubtless, when she seeks to effect great ends, will often choose as her instrument a man of such sense and worth that he can recognize the opportunities which she holds out to him; and, in like manner, when she desires to bring about great calamities, will put forward such men as will of themselves contribute to that result. And all who stand in her way, she either removes by death, or deprives of the means of effecting good. And it is well seen in the passage we are considering, how Fortune, to aggrandize Rome, and raise her to the height she reached, judged it necessary, as shall be more fully shown in the following Book, to humble her; yet would not have her utterly undone. For which reason we find her causing Camillus to be banished, but not put to death; suffering Rome to be taken, but not the Capitol; and bringing it to pass that, while the Romans took no wise precaution for the defence of their city, they neglected none in defending their citadel. That Rome might be taken, Fortune caused the mass of the army, after the rout at the Allia, to direct its flight to Veii, thus withdrawing the means wherewith the city might have been defended; but while thus disposing matters, she at the same time prepared all the needful steps for its recovery, in bringing an almost entire Roman array to Veii, and Camillus to Ardea, so that a great force might be assembled for the rescue of their country, under a captain in no way compromised by previous reverses, but, on the contrary, in the enjoyment of an untarnished renown. I might cite many modern instances to confirm these opinions, but since enough has been said to convince any fair mind, I pass them over. But once more I repeat what, from all history, may be seen to be most true, that men may aid Fortune, but not withstand her; may interweave their threads with her web, but cannot break it But, for all that, they must never lose heart, since not knowing what their end is to be, and moving towards it by cross-roads and untravelled paths, they have always room for hope, and ought never to abandon it, whatsoever befalls, and into whatsoever straits they come.

CHAPTER XXX

That really powerful Princes and, Commonwealths do not buy Friendships with Money, but with their Valour and the Fame of their Prowess.

When besieged in the Capitol, the Romans although expecting succour from Veii and from Camillus, nevertheless, being straitened by famine, entered into an agreement to buy off the Gauls with gold But at the very moment when, in pursuance of this agreement, the gold was being weighed out, Camillus came up with his army. This, says our historian, was contrived by Fortune, *"that the Romans might not live thereafter as men ransomed for a price,"* and the matter is noteworthy, not only with reference to this particular occasion, but also as it bears on the methods generally followed by this republic. For we never find Rome seeking to acquire towns, or to purchase peace with money, but always confiding in her own warlike valour, which could not, I believe, be said of any other republic.

Now, one of the tests whereby to gauge the strength of any State, is to observe on what terms it lives with its neighbours: for when it so carries itself that, to secure its friendship, its neighbours pay it tribute, this is a sure sign of its strength, but when its neighbours, though of less reputation, receive payments from it, this is a clear proof of its weakness In the course of the Roman history we read how the Massilians, the Eduans, the Rhodians, Hiero of Syracuse, the Kings Eumenes and Massinissa, all of them neighbours to the Roman frontiers, in order to secure the friendship of Rome, submitted to imposts and tribute whenever Rome had need of them, asking no return save her protection. But with a weak State we find the reverse of all this happening And, to begin with our own republic of Florence, we know that in times past, when she was at the height of her renown, there was never a lordling of Romagna who had not a subsidy from her, to say nothing of what she paid to the Perugians, to the Castellans, and to all her other neighbours But had our city been armed and strong, the direct contrary would have been the case, for, to obtain her protection, all would have poured money into her lap, not seeking to sell their friendship but to purchase hers.

Nor are the Florentines the only people who have lived on this dishonourable footing The Venetians have done the same, nay, the King of France himself, for all his great dominions, lives tributary to the Swiss and to the King of England; and this because the French king and the others named, with a view to escape dangers rather imaginary than real, have disarmed their subjects; seeking to reap a present gain by wringing money from them, rather than follow a course which would secure their own safety and the lasting welfare of their country. Which ill-practices of theirs, though they quiet things for a time, must in the end exhaust their resources, and give rise in seasons of danger to incurable mischief and disorder. It would be tedious to count up how often in the course of their wars, the Florentines, the Venetians, and the kingdom of France have had to ransom themselves from their enemies, and to submit to an ignominy to which, once only, the Romans were very near being subjected. It would be tedious, too, to recite how many towns have been bought by the Florentines and by the Venetians, which, afterwards, have only been a trouble to them, from their not knowing how to defend with iron what they had won with gold. While the Romans continued free they adhered to this more generous and noble method, but when they came under the emperors, and these, again, began to deteriorate, and to love the shade rather than the sunshine, they also took to purchasing peace, now from the Parthians, now from the Germans, and at other times from other neighbouring nations. And this was the beginning of the decline of their great empire.

Such are the evils that befall when you withhold arms from your subjects; and this course is attended by the still greater disadvantage, that the closer an enemy presses you the weaker he finds you. For any one who follows the evil methods of which I speak, must, in order to support troops whom he thinks can be trusted to keep off his enemies, be very exacting in his dealings with those of his subjects who dwell in the heart of his dominions; since, to widen the interval between himself and his enemies, he must subsidize those princes and peoples who adjoin his frontiers. States maintained on this footing may make a little resistance on their confines; but when these are passed by the enemy no further defence remains. Those who pursue such methods as these seem not to perceive that they are opposed to reason and common sense. For the heart and vital parts of the body, not the extremities, are those which we should keep guarded, since we may live on without the latter, but must die if the former be hurt. But the States of which I speak, leaving the heart undefended, defend only the hands and feet. The mischief which has thus been, and is at this day wrought in Florence is plain enough to see. For so soon as an enemy penetrates within her frontiers, and approaches her heart, all is over with her. And the same was witnessed a few years ago in the case of the Venetians, whose city, had it not been girdled by the sea, must then have found its end. In France, indeed, a like result has not been seen so often, she being so great a kingdom as to have few enemies mightier than herself. Nevertheless, when the English invaded France in the year 1513, the whole kingdom tottered; and the King himself, as well as every one else, had to own that a single defeat might have cost him his dominions.

But with the Romans the reverse of all this took place. For the nearer an enemy approached Rome, the more completely he found her armed for resistance; and accordingly we see that on the occasion of Hannibal's invasion of Italy, the Romans, after three defeats, and after the slaughter of so many of their captains and soldiers, were still able, not merely to withstand the invader, but even, in the end, to come off victorious. This we may ascribe to the heart being well guarded, while the extremities were but little heeded. For the strength of Rome rested on the Roman people themselves, on the Latin league, on the confederate towns of Italy, and on her colonies, from all of which sources she drew so numerous an army, as enabled her to subdue the whole world and to keep it in subjection.

The truth of what I say may be further seen from the question put by Hanno the Carthaginian to the messengers sent to Carthage by Hannibal after his victory at Cannae. For when these were vaunting the achievements of Hannibal, they were asked by Hanno whether any one had come forward on behalf of the Romans to propose terms of peace, and whether any town of the Latin league or of the colonized districts had revolted from the Romans. And when to both inquiries the envoys answered, "No," Hanno observed that the war was no nearer an end than on the day it was begun.

We can understand, therefore, as well from what has now been said, as from what I have often said before, how great a difference there is between the methods followed by the republics of the present times, and those followed by the republics of antiquity; and why it is that we see every day astounding losses alternate with extraordinary gains. For where men are weak, Fortune shows herself strong; and because she changes, States and Governments change with her; and will continue to change, until some one arise, who, following reverently the example of the ancients, shall so control her, that she shall not have opportunity with every revolution of the sun to display anew the greatness of her power.

CHAPTER XXXI

Of the Danger of trusting banished Men.

The danger of trusting those who are in exile from their own country, being one to which the rulers of States are often exposed, may, I think, be fitly considered in these Discourses; and I notice it the more willingly, because I am able to illustrate it by a memorable instance which Titus Livius, though with another purpose, relates in his history. When Alexander the Great passed with his army into Asia, his brother-in-law and uncle, Alexander of Epirus, came with another army into Italy, being invited thither by the banished Lucanians, who gave him to believe that, with their aid, he might get possession of the whole of that country. But when, confiding in the promises of these exiles, and fed by the hopes they held out to him, he came into Italy, they put him to death, their fellow-citizens having offered to restore them to their country upon this condition. It behoves us, therefore, to remember how empty are the promises, and how doubtful the faith, of men in banishment from their native land. For as to their faith, it may be assumed that whenever they can effect their return by other means than yours, notwithstanding any covenants they may have made with you, they will throw you over, and take part with their countrymen. And as for the empty promises and delusive hopes which they set before you, so extreme is their desire to return home that they naturally believe many things which are untrue, and designedly misrepresent many others; so that between their beliefs and what they say they believe, they fill you with false impressions, on which if you build, your labour is in vain, and you are led to engage in enterprises from which nothing but ruin can result.

To this instance of Alexander I shall add only one other, that, namely, of Themistocles the Athenian, who, being proclaimed a traitor, fled into Asia to Darius, to whom he made such lavish promises if he would only attack Greece, that he induced him to undertake the enterprise. But afterwards, when he could not fulfil what he had promised, either from shame, or through fear of punishment, he poisoned himself. But, if such a mistake as this was made by a man like Themistocles, we may reckon that mistakes still greater will be made by those who, being of a feebler nature, suffer themselves to be more completely swayed by their feelings and wishes Wherefore, let a prince be careful how he embarks in any enterprise on the representations of an exile; for otherwise, he is likely either to be put to shame, or to incur the gravest calamities.

Because towns are sometimes, though seldom, taken by craft, through secret practices had with their inhabitants, I think it not out of place to discuss the matter in the following Chapter, wherein I shall likewise show in how many ways the Romans were wont to make such acquisitions.

CHAPTER XXXII

In how many Ways the Romans gained Possession of Towns.

Turning their thoughts wholly to arms, the Romans always conducted their military enterprises in the most advantageous way, both as to cost and every other circumstance of war. For which reason they avoided attempting towns by siege, judging the expense and inconvenience of this method of carrying on war greatly to outweigh any advantage to be gained by it. Accordingly, they thought it better and more for their interest to reduce towns in any other way than this; and in all those years during which they were constantly engaged in wars we find very few instances of their proceeding by siege.

For the capture of towns, therefore, they trusted either to assault or to surrender. Assaults were effected either by open force, or by force and stratagem combined. When a town was assailed by open force, the walls were stormed without being breached, and the assailants were said *"aggredi urbem corona,"* because they encircled the city with their entire strength and kept up an attack on all sides. In this way they often succeeded in carrying towns, and even great towns, at a first onset, as when Scipio took new Carthage in Spain. But when they failed to carry a town by storm, they set themselves to breach the walls with battering rams and other warlike engines; or they dug mines so as to obtain an entrance within the walls, this being the method followed in taking Veii; or else, to be on a level with the defenders, they erected towers of timber or threw up mounds of earth against the outside of the walls so as to reach the top.

Of these methods of attack, the first, wherein the city was entirely surrounded, exposed the defenders to more sudden perils and left them more doubtful remedies. For while it was necessary for them to have a sufficient force at all points, it might happen that the forces at their disposal were not numerous enough to be everywhere at once, or to relieve one another. Or if their numbers were sufficient, they might not all be equally resolute in standing their ground, and their failure at any one point involved a general defeat. Consequently, as I have said, this method of attack was often successful. But when it did not succeed at the first, it was rarely renewed, being a method dangerous to the attacking army, which having to secure itself along an extended line, was left everywhere too weak to resist a sally made from the town; nay, of itself, was apt to fall into confusion and disorder. This method of attack, therefore, could be attempted once only and by way of surprise.

Against breaches in the walls the defence was, as at the present day, to throw up new works; while mines were met by counter-mines, in which the enemy were either withstood at the point of the sword, or baffled by some other warlike contrivance; as by filling casks with feathers, which, being set on fire and placed in the mine, choked out the assailants by their smoke and stench. Where towers were employed for the attack, the defenders sought to destroy them with fire; and where mounds of earth were thrown up against the walls, they would dig holes at the base of the wall against which the mound rested, and carry off the earth which the enemy were heaping up; which, being removed from within as fast as it was thrown up from without, the mound made no progress.

None of these methods of attack can long be persisted in and the assailant, if unsuccessful, must either strike his camp and seek victory in some other direction, as Scipio did when he invaded Africa and, after failing in the attempt to storm Utica, withdrew from his attack on that town and turned his strength against the Carthaginian army in the field; or else recourse must be had to regular siege, as by the Romans at Veii, Capua, Carthage, Jerusalem, and divers other cities which they reduced in this way.

The capture of towns by stratagem combined with force is effected, as by the Romans at Palaeopolis, through a secret understanding with some within the walls. Many attempts of this sort have been made, both by the Romans and by others, but few successfully, because the least hindrance disarranges the plan of action, and because such hindrances are very likely to occur. For either the plot is discovered before it can be carried out, as it readily may, whether from treachery on the part of those to whom it has been communicated, or from the difficulties which attend its inception, the preliminary arrangements having to be made with the enemy and with persons with whom it is not permitted, save under some pretext or other, to hold intercourse; or if it be not discovered while it is being contrived, a thousand difficulties will still be met with in its execution. For if you arrive either before or after the appointed time, all is ruined. The faintest sound, as of the cackling of the geese in the Capitol, the least departure from some ordinary routine, the most trifling mistake or error, mars the whole enterprise. Add to which, the darkness of night lends further terror to the perils of such undertakings; while the great majority of those engaged in them, having no knowledge of the district or places into which they are brought, are bewildered and disconcerted by the least mishap, and put to flight by every imaginary danger. In secret nocturnal enterprises of this sort, no man was ever more successful than Aratus of Sicyon, although in any encounter by day there never was a more arrant coward. This we must suppose due rather to some special and occult quality inherent in the man, than to success being naturally to be looked for in the like attempts. Such enterprises, accordingly, are often planned, but few are put into execution, and fewer still with success.

When cities are acquired by surrender, the surrender is either voluntary or under compulsion; voluntary, when the citizens appeal to you for protection against some threatened danger from without, as Capua submitted to the Romans; or where they are moved by a desire to be better governed, and are attracted by the good government which he to whom they surrender is seen exercising over others who have placed themselves in his hands; as was the case with the Rhodians, the Massilians, and others who for like causes gave themselves up to the Roman people. Compulsory surrenders take place, either as the result of a protracted siege, like those we have spoken of above; or from the country being continually wasted by incursions, forays, and similar severities, to escape which a city makes its submission.

Of the methods which have been noticed, the Romans, in preference to all others, used this last; and for four hundred and fifty years made it their aim to wear out their neighbours by invasion and by defeat in the open field, while endeavouring, as I have elsewhere said, to establish their influence over them by treaties and conventions. It was to this method of warfare therefore that they always mainly trusted, because, after trying all others, they found none so free from inconvenience and disadvantage — the procedure by siege involving expense and delay, that by assault, difficulty and danger, and that by secret practice, uncertainty and doubt. They found, likewise, that while in subduing one obstinate city by siege many years might be wasted, a kingdom might be gained in a single day by the defeat of a hostile army in the field.

CHAPTER XXXIII

That the Romans intrusted the Captains of their Armies with the fullest Powers.

In reading this History of Titus Livius with a view to profit by it, I think that all the methods of conduct followed by the Roman people and senate merit attention. And among other things fit to be considered, it should be noted, with how ample an authority they sent forth their consuls, their dictators, and the other captains of their armies, all of whom we find clothed with the fullest powers: no other prerogative being reserved to itself by the senate save that of declaring war and making peace, while everything else was left to the discretion and determination of the consul. For so soon as the people and senate had resolved on war, for instance on a war against the Latins, they threw all further responsibility upon the consul, who might fight or decline battle as he pleased, and attack this or the other city as he thought fit.

That this was so, is seen in many instances, and especially from what happened during an expedition made against the Etruscans. For the consul Fabius having routed that people near Sutrium, and thinking to pass onward through the Ciminian forest into Etruria, so far from seeking the advice of the senate, gave them no hint whatever of his design, although for its execution the war had to be carried into a new, difficult, and dangerous country. We have further witness to the same effect, in the action taken in respect of this enterprise by the senate, who being informed of the victory obtained by Fabius, and apprehending that he might decide to pass onward through the aforesaid forest, and deeming it inexpedient that he should incur risk by attempting this invasion, sent two messengers to warn him not to enter Etruria. These messengers, however, did not come up with the consul until he had already made his way into that country and gained a second victory; when, instead of opposing his further advance, they returned to Rome to announce his good fortune and the glory which he had won.

Whoever, therefore, shall well consider the character of the authority whereof I speak, will see that it was most wisely accorded; since had it been the wish of the senate that a consul, in conducting a war, should proceed step by step as they might direct him, this must have made him at once less cautious and more dilatory; because the credit of victory would not then have seemed to be wholly his own, but shared by the senate on whose advice he acted. Besides which, the senate must have taken upon itself the task of advising on matters which it could not possibly understand; for although it might contain among its members all who were most versed in military affairs, still, since these men were not on the spot, and were ignorant of many particulars which, if they were to give sound advice, it was necessary for them to know, they must in advising have made numberless mistakes. For these reasons they desired that the consul should act on his own responsibility, and that the honours of success should be wholly his; judging that the love of fame would act on him at once as a spur and as a curb, making him do whatever he had to do well.

This matter I have the rather dwelt upon because I observe that our modern republics, such as the Venetian and the Florentine, view it in a different light; so that when their captains, commissaries, or *provedditori* have a single gun to place in position, the authorities at home must be informed and consulted; a course deserving the same approval as is due to all those other methods of theirs, which, one with another, have brought Italy to her present condition.

BOOK III

CHAPTER I

For a Sect or Commonwealth to last long, it must often be brought back to its Beginnings.

Doubtless, all the things of this world have a limit set to their duration; yet those of them the bodies whereof have not been suffered to grow disordered, but have been so cared for that either no change at all has been wrought in them, or, if any, a change for the better and not for the worse, will run that course which Heaven has in a general way appointed them. And since I am now speaking of mixed bodies, for States and Sects are so to be regarded, I say that for them these are wholesome changes which bring them back to their first beginnings.

Those States consequently stand surest and endure longest which, either by the operation of their institutions can renew themselves, or come to be renewed by accident apart from any design. Nothing, however, can be clearer than that unless thus renewed these bodies do not last. Now the way to renew them is, as I have said, to bring them back to their beginnings, since all beginnings of sects, commonwealths, or kingdoms must needs have in them a certain excellence, by virtue of which they gain their first reputation and make their first growth. But because in progress of time this excellence becomes corrupted, unless something be done to restore it to what it was at first, these bodies necessarily decay; for as the physicians tell us in speaking of the human body, *"Something or other is daily added which sooner or later will require treatment."*

As regards commonwealths, this return to the point of departure is brought about either by extrinsic accident or by intrinsic foresight. As to the first, we have seen how it was necessary that Rome should be taken by the Gauls, that being thus in a manner reborn, she might recover life and vigour, and resume the observances of religion and justice which she had suffered to grow rusted by neglect. This is well seen from those passages of Livius wherein he tells us that when the Roman army was 'sent forth against the Gauls, and again when tribunes were created with consular authority, no religious rites whatever were celebrated, and wherein he further relates how the Romans not only failed to punish the three Fabii, who contrary to the law of nations had fought against the Gauls, but even clothed them with honour. For, from these instances, we may well infer that the rest of the wise ordinances instituted by Romulus, and the other prudent kings, had begun to be held of less account than they deserved, and less than was essential for the maintenance of good government.

And therefore it was that Rome was visited by this calamity from without, to the end that all her ordinances might be reformed, and the people taught that it behoved them not only to maintain religion and justice, but also to esteem their worthy citizens, and to prize their virtues beyond any advantages of which they themselves might seem to have been deprived at their instance. And this, we find, was just the effect produced. For no sooner was the city retaken, than all the ordinances of the old religion were at once restored; the Fabii, who had fought in violation of the law of nations, were punished; and the worth and excellence of Camillus so fully recognized, that the senate and the whole people, laying all jealousies aside, once more committed to him the entire charge of public affairs.

It is necessary then, as I have said already, that where men dwell together in a regulated society, they be often reminded of those ordinances in conformity with which they ought to live, either by something inherent in these, or else by some external accident. A reminder is given in the former of these two ways, either by the passing of some law whereby the members of the society are brought to an account; or else by some man of rare worth arising among them, whose virtuous life and example have the same effect as a law. In a Commonwealth, accordingly, this end is served either by the virtues of some one of its citizens, or by the operation of its institutions.

The institutions whereby the Roman Commonwealth was led back to its starting point, were the tribuneship of the people and the censorship, together with all those laws which were passed to check the insolence and ambition of its citizens. Such institutions, however, require fresh life to be infused into them by the worth of some one man who fearlessly devotes himself to give them effect in opposition to the power of those who set them at defiance.

Of the laws being thus reinforced in Rome, before its capture by the Gauls, we have notable examples in the deaths of the sons of Brutus, of the Decemvirs, and of Manlius Frumentarius; and after its capture, in the deaths of Manlius Capitolinus, and of the son of Manlius Torquatus in the prosecution of his master of the knights by Papirius Cursor, and in the impeachment of the Scipios. Such examples as these, being signal and extraordinary, had the effect, whenever they took place, of bringing men back to the true standard of right; but when they came to be of rarer occurrence, they left men more leisure to grow corrupted, and were attended by greater danger and disturbance. Wherefore, between one and another of these vindications of the laws, no more than ten years, at most, ought to intervene; because after that time men begin to change their manners and to disregard the laws; and if nothing occur to recall the idea of punishment, and unless fear resume its hold on their minds, so many offenders suddenly spring up together that it is impossible to punish them without danger. And to this purport it used to be said by those who ruled Florence from the year 1434 to 1494, that their government could hardly be maintained unless it was renewed every five years; by which they meant that it was necessary for them to arouse the same terror and alarm in men's minds, as they inspired when they first assumed the government, and when all who offended against their authority were signally chastised. For when the recollection of such chastisement has died out, men are emboldened to engage in new designs, and to speak ill of their rulers; for which the only remedy is to restore things to what they were at first.

A republic may, likewise, be brought back to its original form, without recourse to ordinances for enforcing justice, by the mere virtues of a single citizen, by reason that these virtues are of such influence and authority that good men love to imitate them, and bad men are ashamed to depart from them. Those to whom Rome owed most for services of this sort, were Horatius Cocles, Mutius Scaevola, the two Decii, Atilius Regulus, and divers others, whose rare excellence and generous example wrought for their city almost the same results as might have been effected by ordinances and laws. And if to these instances of individual worth had been added, every ten years, some signal enforcement of justice, it would have been impossible for Rome ever to have grown corrupted. But when both of these incitements to virtuous behavior began to recur less frequently, corruption spread, and after the time of Atilius Regulus, no like example was again witnessed. For though the two Catos came later, so great an interval had elapsed before the elder Cato appeared, and again, so long a period intervened between him and the younger, and these two, moreover, stood so much alone, that it was impossible for them, by their influence, to work any important change; more especially for the younger, who found Rome so much corrupted that he could do nothing to improve his fellow-citizens.

This is enough to say concerning commonwealths, but as regards sects, we see from the instance of our own religion that here too a like renewal is needed. For had not this religion of ours been brought back to its original condition by Saint Francis and Saint Dominick, it must soon have been utterly extinguished. They, however, by their voluntary poverty, and by their imitation of the life of Christ, rekindled in the minds of men the dying flame of faith; and by the efficacious rules which they established averted from our Church that ruin which the ill lives of its prelates and heads must otherwise have brought upon it. For living in poverty, and gaining great authority with the people by confessing them and preaching to them, they got them to believe that it is evil to speak ill even of what is evil; and that it is good to be obedient to rulers, who, if they do amiss, may be left to the judgment of God. By which teaching these rulers are encouraged to behave as badly as they can, having no fear of punishments which they neither see nor credit. Nevertheless, it is this renewal which has maintained, and still maintains, our religion.

Kingdoms also stand in need of a like renewal, and to have their laws restored to their former force; and we see how, by attending to this, the kingdom of France has profited. For that kingdom, more than any other, lies under the control of its laws and ordinances, which are maintained by its parliaments, and more especially by the parliament of Paris, from which last they derive fresh vigour whenever they have to be enforced against any prince of the realm; for this assembly pronounces sentence even against the king himself. Heretofore this parliament has maintained its name as the fearless champion of the laws against the nobles of the land; but should it ever at any future time suffer wrongs to pass unpunished, and should offences multiply, either these will have to be corrected with great disturbance to the State, or the kingdom itself must fall to pieces.

This, then, is our conclusion — that nothing is so necessary in any society, be it a religious sect, a kingdom, or a commonwealth, as to restore to it that reputation which it had at first, and to see that it is provided either with wholesome laws, or with good men whose actions may effect the same ends, without need to resort to external force. For although this last may sometimes, as in the case of Rome, afford an efficacious remedy, it is too hazardous a remedy to make us ever wish to employ it.

And that all may understand how much the actions of particular citizens helped to make Rome great, and how many admirable results they wrought in that city, I shall now proceed to set them forth and examine them; with which survey this Third

Book of mine, and last division of the First Decade of Titus Livius, shall be brought to a close. But, although great and notable actions were done by the Roman kings, nevertheless, since history has treated of these at much length, here I shall pass them over, and say no more about these princes, save as regards certain things done by them with an eye to their private interest. I shall begin, therefore, with Brutus, the father of Roman freedom.

CHAPTER II

That on occasion it is wise to feign Folly.

Never did any man by the most splendid achievements gain for himself so great a name for wisdom and prudence as is justly due to Junius Brutus for feigning to be a fool. And although Titus Livius mentions one cause only as having led him to assume this part, namely, that he might live more securely and look after his patrimony; yet on considering his behavior we may believe that in counterfeiting folly it was also his object to escape notice, and so find better convenience to overthrow the kings, and to free his country whenever an occasion offered. That this was in his mind is seen first of all from the interpretation he gave to the oracle of Apollo, when, to render the gods favourable to his designs, he pretended to stumble, and secretly kissed his mother earth; and, again, from this, that on the death of Lucretia, though her father, her husband, and others of her kinsmen were present, he was the first to draw the dagger from her wound, and bind the bystanders by oath never more to suffer king to reign in Rome.

From his example all who are discontented with their prince are taught, first of all, to measure, and to weigh their strength, and if they find themselves strong enough to disclose their hostility and proclaim open war, then to take that course as at once the nobler and less dangerous; but, if too weak to make open war, then sedulously to court the favour of the prince, using to that end all such methods as they may judge needful, adapting themselves to his pleasures, and showing delight in whatever they see him delight in. Such an intimacy, in the first place, enables you to live securely, and permits you, without incurring any risk, to share the happy fortunes of the prince, while it affords you every facility for carrying out your plans. Some, no doubt, will tell you that you should not stand so near the prince as to be involved in his downfall; nor yet at such a distance that when he falls you shall be too far off to use the occasion for rising on his ruin. But although this mean course, could we only follow it, were certainly the best, yet, since I believe it to be impracticable, we must resort to the methods above indicated, and either keep altogether aloof, or else cleave closely to the prince. Whosoever does otherwise, if he be of great station, lives in constant peril; nor will it avail him to say, "I concern myself with nothing; I covet neither honours nor preferment; my sole wish is to live a quiet and peaceful life." For such excuses, though they be listened to, are not accepted; nor can any man of great position, however much and sincerely he desire it, elect to live this life of tranquillity since his professions will not be believed; so that although he might be contented to be let alone, others will not suffer him to be so. Wherefore, like Brutus, men must feign folly; and to play the part effectively, and so as to please their prince, must say, do, see, and praise things contrary to their inclinations.

But now, having spoken of the prudence shown by Brutus when he sought to recover the freedom of Rome, let us next speak of the severity which he used to maintain it.

CHAPTER III

That to preserve a newly acquired Freedom we must slay the Sons of Brutus.

The severity used by Brutus in preserving for Rome the freedom he had won for her, was not less necessary than useful. The spectacle of a father sitting on the judgment, and not merely sentencing his own sons to death, but being himself present at their execution, affords an example rare in history. But those who study the records of ancient times will understand, that after a change in the form of a government, whether it be from a commonwealth to a tyranny or from a tyranny to a commonwealth, those who are hostile to the new order of things must always be visited with signal punishment. So that he who sets up as a tyrant and slays not Brutus, and he who creates a free government and slays not the sons of Brutus, can never maintain himself long. But since I have elsewhere treated of this matter at large, I shall merely refer to what has there been said concerning it, and shall cite here one instance only, happening in our own days, and memorable in the history of our country.

I speak of Piero Soderini, who thought by his patience and goodness to overcome the very same temper which prompted the sons of Brutus to revert to the old government, and who failed in the endeavour. For although his sagacity should have taught him the necessity, while chance and the ambition of those who attacked him furnished him with the opportunity of making an end of them, he never could resolve to strike the blow; and not merely believed himself able to subdue disaffection by patience and kindness, and to mitigate the enmity of particular men by the rewards he held out to them, but also persuaded himself, and often declared in the presence of his friends, that he could not confront opposition openly, nor crush his adversaries, without assuming extraordinary powers and passing laws destructive of civil equality; which measures, although not afterward used by him for tyrannical ends, would so alarm the community, that after his death they would never again consent to appoint a Gonfalonier for life, an office which he judged it essential both to maintain and strengthen. Now although these scruples of his were wise and good, we ought never out of regard for what is good, to suffer an evil to run its course, since it may well happen that the evil will prevail over the good. And Piero should have believed that as his acts and intentions were to be judged by results, he might, if he lived and if fortune befriended him, have made it clear to all, that what he did was done to preserve his country, and not from personal ambition; and he might have so contrived matters that no successor of his could ever turn to bad ends the means which he had used for good ends. But he was misled by a preconceived opinion, and failed to understand that ill-will is not to be vanquished by time nor propitiated by favours. And, so, from not knowing how to resemble Brutus, he lost power, and fame, and was driven an exile from his country.

That it is as hard a matter to preserve a princedom as it is to preserve a commonwealth, will be shown in the Chapter following.

CHAPTER IV

That an Usurper is never safe in his Princedom while those live whom he has deprived of it.

From what befell the elder Tarquin at the hands of the sons of Ancus, and Servius Tullius at the hands of Tarquin the Proud, we see what an arduous and perilous course it is to strip a king of his kingdom and yet suffer him to live on, hoping to conciliate him by benefits. We see, too, how the elder Tarquin was ruined by his belief that he held the kingdom by a just title, since it had been given him by the people and confirmed to him by the senate, never suspecting that the sons of Ancus would be so stirred by resentment that it would be impossible to content them with what contented all the rest of Rome. Servius Tullius again, was ruined through believing that he could conciliate the sons of Ancus by loading them with favours.

By the fate of the first of these kings every prince may be warned that he can never live securely in his princedom so long as those from whom he has taken it survive; while the fate of the second should remind all rulers that old injuries are not to be healed by subsequent benefits, and least of all when the new benefit is less in degree than the injury suffered. And, truly, Servius was wanting in wisdom when he imagined that the sons of Tarquin would contentedly resign themselves to be the sons-in-law of one whom they thought should be their subject. For the desire to reign is so prevailing a passion, that it penetrates the minds not only of those who are rightful heirs, but also of those who are not; as happened with the wife of the younger Tarquin, who was daughter to Servius, but who, possessed by this madness, and setting at naught all filial duty, incited her husband to take her father's kingdom, and with it his life; so much nobler did she esteem it to be a queen than the daughter of a king. But while the elder Tarquin and Servius Tullius lost the kingdom from not knowing how to secure themselves against those whom they had deprived of it, the younger Tarquin lost it from not observing the ordinances of the old kings, as shall be shown in the following Chapter.

CHAPTER V

How an Hereditary King may come to lose his Kingdom.

Tarquin the Proud, when he had put Servius Tullius to death, inasmuch as the latter left no heirs, took secure possession of the kingdom, having nothing to fear from any of those dangers which had stood in the way of his predecessors. And although the means whereby he made himself king were hateful and monstrous, nevertheless, had he adhered to the ancient ordinances of the earlier kings, he might have been endured, nor would he have aroused both senate and people to combine against him and deprive him of his government. It was not, therefore, because his son Sextus violated Lucretia that Tarquin was driven out, but because he himself had violated the laws of the kingdom, and governed as a tyrant, stripping the senate of all authority, and bringing everything under his own control. For all business which formerly had been transacted in public, and with the sanction of the senate, he caused to be transacted in his palace, on his own responsibility, and to the displeasure of every one else, and so very soon deprived Rome of whatever freedom she had enjoyed under her other kings.

Nor was it enough for him to have the Fathers his enemies, but he must needs also kindle the commons against him, wearing them out with mere mechanic labours, very different from the enterprises in which they had been employed by his predecessors; so that when Rome overflowed with instances of his cruelty and pride, he had already disposed the minds of all the citizens to rebel whenever they found the opportunity. Wherefore, had not occasion offered in the violence done to Lucretia, some other had soon been found to bring about the same result. But had Tarquin lived like the other kings, when Sextus his son committed that outrage, Brutus and Collatinus would have had recourse to him to punish the offender, and not to the commons of Rome. And hence let princes learn that from the hour they first violate those laws, customs, and usages under which men have lived for a great while, they begin to weaken the foundations of their authority. And should they, after they have been stripped of that authority, ever grow wise enough to see how easily princedoms are preserved by those who are content to follow prudent counsels, the sense of their loss will grieve them far more, and condemn them to a worse punishment than any they suffer at the hands of others. For it is far easier to be loved by good men than by bad, and to obey the laws than to seek to control them.

And to learn what means they must use to retain their authority, they have only to take example by the conduct of good princes, such as Timoleon of Corinth, Aratus of Sicyone, and the like, in whose lives they will find such security and content, both on the side of the ruler and the ruled, as ought to stir them with the desire to imitate them, which, for the reasons already given, it is easy for them to do. For men, when they are well governed, ask no more, nor look for further freedom; as was the case with the peoples governed by the two whom I have named, whom they constrained to continue their rulers while they lived, though both of them sought repeatedly to return to private life.

But because, in this and the two preceding Chapters, I have noticed the ill-will which arose against the kings, the plots contrived by the sons of Brutus against their country, and those directed against the elder Tarquin and Servius Tullius, it seems to me not out of place to discourse of these matters more at length in the following Chapter, as deserving the attention both of princes and private citizens.

CHAPTER VI

Of Conspiracies.

It were an omission not to say something on the subject of conspiracies, these being a source of much danger both to princes and to private men. For we see that many more princes have lost their lives and states through these than in open warfare; power to wage open war upon a prince being conceded to few, whereas power to conspire against him is denied to none. On the other hand, since conspiracies are attended at every stage by difficulties and dangers, no more hazardous or desperate undertakings can be engaged in by any private citizen; whence it comes that while many conspiracies are planned, few effect their object. Wherefore, to put princes on their guard against these dangers, and to make subjects more cautious how they take part in them, and rather learn to live content under whatever government fortune has assigned them, I shall treat of them at length, without omitting any noteworthy circumstance which may serve for the instruction of either. Though, indeed, this is a golden sentence Of Cornelius Tacitus, wherein he says that *"the past should have our reverence, the present our obedience, and that we should wish for good princes, but put up with any."* For assuredly whosoever does otherwise is likely to bring ruin both on himself and on his country.

But, to go deeper into the matter, we have first of all to examine against whom conspiracies are directed; and we shall find that men conspire either against their country or their prince; and it is of these two kinds of conspiracy that at present I desire to speak. For of conspiracies which have for their object the surrender of cities to enemies who are besieging them, and of all others contrived for like ends, I have already said enough.

First, then, I shall treat of those conspiracies which are directed against a prince, and begin by inquiring into their causes, which are manifold, but of which one is more momentous than all the rest; I mean, the being hated by the whole community. For it may reasonably be assumed, that when a prince has drawn upon himself this universal hatred, he must also have given special offence to particular men, which they will be eager to avenge. And this eagerness will be augmented by the feeling of general ill-will which the prince is seen to have incurred. A prince ought, therefore, to avoid this load of public hatred. How he is to do so I need not stop here to explain, having discussed the matter already in another place; but if he can guard against this, offence given to particular men will expose him to but few attacks. One reason being, that there are few men who think so much of an injury done them as to run great risks to revenge it; another, that assuming them to have both the disposition and the courage to avenge themselves, they are restrained by the universal favour which they see entertained towards the prince.

Injuries are either to a man's life, to his property, or to his honour. As regards the first, they who threaten injuries to life incur more danger than they who actually inflict them; or rather, while great danger is incurred in threatening, none at all is incurred from inflicting such injuries. For the dead are past thinking of revenge; and those who survive, for the most part leave such thoughts to the dead. But he whose life is threatened, finding himself forced by necessity either to do or suffer, becomes a man most dangerous to the prince, as shall be fully explained hereafter.

After menaces to life, injuries to property and honour stir men more than any others, and of these a Prince has most to beware. For he can never strip a man so bare of his possessions as not to leave him some weapon wherewith to redress his wrongs, nor ever so far dishonour him as to quell the stubborn spirit which prompts revenge. Of all dishonours those done to the women of a household are the worst; after which come such personal indignities as nerved the arm of Pausanias against Philip of Macedon, and of many another against other princes; and, in our own days, it was no other reason that moved Giulio Belanti to conspire against Pandolfo, lord of Siena, than that Pandolfo, who had given him his daughter to wife, afterwards took her from him, as presently shall be told. Chief among the causes which led the Pazzi to conspire against the Medici, was the law passed by the latter depriving them of the inheritance of Giovanni Bonromei.

Another most powerful motive to conspire against a prince is the desire men feel to free their country from a usurper. This it was which impelled Brutus and Cassius to conspire against Caesar, and countless others against such tyrants as Phalaris, Dionysius, and the like. Against this humour no tyrant can guard, except by laying down his tyranny; which as none will do, few escape an unhappy end. Whence the verses of Juvenal: —

"Few tyrants die a peaceful death, and few The kings who visit Proserpine's dread lord, Unscathed by wounds and blood."

Great, as I have said already, are the dangers which men run in conspiring; for at all times they are in peril, whether in contriving, in executing, or after execution. And since in conspiracies either many are engaged, or one only (for although it cannot properly be said of *one* man that he *conspires*, there may exist in him the fixed resolve to put the prince to death), it is only the solitary plotter who escapes the first of these three stages of danger. For he runs no risk before executing his design, since as he imparts it to none, there is none to bring it to the ear of the prince. A deliberate resolve like this may be conceived by a person in any rank of life, high or low, base or noble, and whether or no he be the familiar of his prince. For every one must, at some time or other, have leave to speak to the prince, and whoever has this leave has opportunity to accomplish his design. Pausanias, of whom we have made mention so often, slew Philip of Macedon as he walked between his son and his son-in-law to the temple, surrounded by a thousand armed guards. Pausanias indeed was noble, and known to the prince, but Ferdinand of Spain was stabbed in the neck by a poor and miserable Spaniard; and though the wound was not mortal, it sufficed to show that neither courage nor opportunity were wanting to the would-be-assassin. A Dervish, or Turkish priest, drew his scimitar on Bajazet, father of the Sultan now reigning, and if he did not wound him, it was from no lack either of daring or of opportunity. And I believe that there are many who in their minds desire the deed, no punishment or danger attending the mere wish, though there be but few who dare do it. For since few or none who venture, escape death, few are willing to go forward to certain destruction.

But to pass from these solitary attempts to those in which several are engaged, I affirm it to be shown by history that all such plots have been contrived by men of great station, or by those who have been on terms of close intimacy with the prince, since no others, not being downright madmen, would ever think of conspiring. For men of humble rank, and such as are not the intimates of their prince, are neither fed by the hopes nor possessed of the opportunities essential for such attempts. Because, in the first place, men of low degree will never find any to keep faith with them, none being moved to join in their schemes by those expectations which encourage men to run great risks; wherefore, so soon as their design has been imparted to two or three, they are betrayed and ruined. Or, assuming them fortunate enough to have no traitor of their number, they will be so hampered in the execution of their plot by the want of easy access to the prince, that they are sure to perish in the mere attempt. For if even men of great position, who have ready access to the prince, succumb to the difficulties which I shall presently notice, those difficulties must be infinitely increased in the case of men who are without these advantages. And because when life and property are at stake men are not utterly reckless, on perceiving themselves to be weak they grow cautious, and though cursing the tyrant in their hearts, are content to endure him, and to wait until some one of higher station than they, comes forward to redress their wrongs. So that should we ever find these weaklings attempting anything, we may commend their courage rather than their prudence.

We see, however, that the great majority of conspirators have been persons of position and the familiars of their prince, and that their plots have been as often the consequence of excessive indulgence as of excessive injury; as when Perennius conspired against Commodus, Plautianus against Severus, and Sejanus against Tiberius; all of whom had been raised by their masters to such wealth, honours, and dignities, that nothing seemed wanting to their authority save the imperial name. That they might not lack this also, they fell to conspiring against their prince; but in every instance their conspiracies had the end which their ingratitude deserved.

The only instance in recent times of such attempts succeeding, is the conspiracy of Jacopo IV. d'Appiano against Messer Piero Gambacorti, lord of Pisa. For Jacopo, who had been bred and brought up by Piero, and loaded by him with honours, deprived him of his State. Similar to this, in our own days, was the conspiracy of Coppola against King Ferdinand of Aragon. For Coppola had reached such a pitch of power that he seemed to himself to have everything but sovereignty; in seeking to obtain which he lost his life; though if any plot entered into by a man of great position could be expected to succeed, this certainly might, being contrived, as we may say, by another king, and by one who had the amplest opportunities for its accomplishment. But that lust of power which blinds men to dangers darkened the minds of those to whom the execution of the scheme was committed; who, had they only known how to add prudence to their villainy, could hardly have missed their aim.

The prince, therefore, who would guard himself against plots, ought more to fear those men to whom he has been too indulgent, than those to whom he has done great wrongs. For the latter lack opportunities which the former have in abundance; and the moving cause is equally strong in both, lust of power being at least as strong a passion as lust of revenge. Wherefore, a prince should entrust his friends with so much authority only as leaves a certain interval between his position and theirs; that between the two something be still left them to desire. Otherwise it will be strange if he do not fare like those princes who have been named above.

But to return from this digression, I say, that having shown it to be necessary that conspirators should be men of great station, and such as have ready access to the prince, we have next to consider what have been the results of their plots, and to trace the causes which have made them succeed or fail. Now, as I have said already, we find that conspiracies are attended by danger at three stages: before during, and after their execution; for which reason very few of them have had a happy issue; it being next to impossible to surmount all these different dangers successfully. And to begin with those which are incurred beforehand, and which are graver than all the rest, I say that he must be both very prudent and very fortunate who, when contriving a conspiracy, does not suffer his secret to be discovered.

Conspiracies are discovered either by disclosures made, or by conjecture. Disclosures are made through the treachery or folly of those to whom you communicate your design. Treachery is to be looked for, because you can impart your plans only to such persons as you believe ready to face death on your behalf, or to those who are discontented with the prince. Of men whom you can trust thus implicitly, one or two may be found; but when you have to open your designs to many, they cannot all be of this nature; and their goodwill towards you must be extreme if they are not daunted by the danger and by fear of punishment. Moreover men commonly deceive themselves in respect of the love which they imagine others bear them, nor can ever be sure of it until they have put it to the proof. But to make proof of it in a matter like this is very perilous; and even if you have proved it already, and found it true in some other dangerous trial, you cannot assume that there will be the same fidelity here, since this far transcends every other kind of danger. Again, if you gauge a man's fidelity by his discontent with the prince, you may easily deceive yourself; for so soon as you have taken this discontented man into your confidence, you have supplied him with the means whereby he may become contented; so that either his hatred of the prince must be great indeed, or your influence over him extraordinary, if it keep him faithful. Hence it comes that so many conspiracies have been discovered and crushed in their earliest stage, and that when the secret is preserved among many accomplices for any length of time, it is looked on as a miracle; as in the case of the conspiracy of Piso against Nero, and, in our own days, in that of the Pazzi against Lorenzo and Giuliano de' Medici; which last, though more than fifty persons were privy to it, was not discovered until it came to be carried out.

Conspiracies are disclosed through the imprudence of a conspirator when he talks so indiscreetly that some servant, or other person not in the plot, overhears him; as happened with the sons of Brutus, who, when treating with the envoys of Tarquin, were overheard by a slave, who became their accuser; or else through your own weakness in imparting your secret to some woman or boy whom you love, or to some other such light person; as when Dymnus, who was one of those who conspired with Philotas against Alexander the Great, revealed the plot to Nicomachus, a youth whom he loved, who at once told Cebalinus, and Cebalinus the king.

Of discoveries by conjecture we have an instance in the conspiracy of Piso against Nero; for Scaevinus, one of the conspirators, the day before he was to kill Nero, made his will, liberated all his slaves and gave them money, and bade Milichus, his freedman, sharpen his old rusty dagger, and have bandages ready for binding up wounds. From all which preparations Milichus conjecturing what work was in hand, accused Scaevinus before Nero; whereupon Scaevinus was arrested, and with him Natalis, another of the conspirators, who the day before had been seen to speak with him for a long time in private; and when the two differed in their account of what then passed between them, they were put to the torture and forced to confess the truth. In this way the conspiracy was brought to light, to the ruin of all concerned.

Against these causes of the discovery of conspiracies it is impossible so to guard as that either through treachery, want of caution, or levity, the secret shall not be found out, whenever more than three or four persons are privy to it. And whenever more than one conspirator is arrested, the plot is certain to be detected, because no two persons can perfectly agree in a false account of what has passed between them. If only one be taken, should he be a man of resolute courage, he may refuse to implicate his comrades; but they on their part must have no less courage, to stay quiet where they are, and not betray themselves by flight; for if courage be absent anywhere, whether in him who is taken or in those still at large, the conspiracy is revealed. And what is related by Titus Livius as having happened in the conspiracy against Hieronymus, tyrant of Syracuse, is most extraordinary, namely, that on the capture of one of the conspirators, named Theodorus, he, with great fortitude, withheld the names of all his accomplices, and accused friends of the tyrant; while his companions, on their part, trusted so completely in his courage, that not one of them quitted Syracuse or showed any sign of fear.

All these dangers, therefore, which attend the contrivance of a plot, must be passed through before you come to its execution; or if you would escape them, you must observe the following precautions: Your first and surest, nay, to say truth, your only safeguard, is to leave your accomplices no time to accuse you; for which reason you must impart the affair to them, only at the moment when you mean it to be carried out, and not before. Those who have followed this course have wholly escaped the preliminary dangers of conspiracies, and, generally speaking, the others also; indeed, I may say that they have all succeeded, and that it is open to every prudent man to act as they did. It will be enough to give two instances of plots effected in this way. Nelematus, unable to endure the tyranny of Aristotimus, despot of Epirus, assembling many of his friends and kinsmen in his house, exhorted them to free their country; and when some of them asked for time to consider and mature their plans, he bade his slaves close the doors, and told those assembled that unless they swore to go at once and do as he directed he would make them over to Aristotimus as prisoners. Alarmed by his threats, they bound themselves by a solemn oath, and going forth at once and without delay, successfully carried out his bidding. A certain Magus having fraudulently usurped the throne of Persia; Ortanes, a grandee of that realm, discovering the fraud, disclosed it to six others of the chief nobility, telling them that it behoved them to free the kingdom from the tyranny of this impostor. And when some among them asked for time, Darius, who was one of the six summoned by Ortanes, stood up and said, "Either we go at once to do this deed, or I go to the Magus to accuse you all." Whereupon, all rising together, without time given to any to change his mind, they went forth and succeeded in effecting their end. Not unlike these instances was the plan taken by the Etolians to rid themselves of Nabis, the Spartan tyrant, to whom, under pretence of succouring him, they sent Alasamenes, their fellow-citizen, with two hundred foot soldiers and thirty horsemen. For they imparted their real design to Alasamenes only, charging the rest, under pain of exile, to obey him in whatever he commanded. Alasamenes repaired to Sparta, and never divulged his commission till the time came for executing it; and so succeeded in putting Nabis to death.

It was, therefore, by the precautions they observed, that the persons of whom I have just now spoken escaped all those perils that attend the contrivance of conspiracies; and any following their example may expect the like good fortune. And that all may learn to do as they did I shall notice the case of Piso, of which mention has before been made. By reason of his rank, his reputation, and the intimate terms on which he lived with Nero, who trusted him without reserve, and would often come to his garden to sup with him, Piso was able to gain the friendship of many persons of spirit and courage, and well fitted in every way to take part in his plot against the emperor, which, under these circumstances, might easily have been carried out. For when Nero came to his garden, Piso could readily have communicated his design to those friends of his, and with suitable words have encouraged them to do what, in fact, they would not have had time to withdraw from, and was certain to succeed. And were we to examine all similar attempts, it would be seen that there are few which might not have been effected in the manner shown. But since most men are very ignorant of practical affairs, they commit the gravest blunders, especially in matters which lie, as this does, a little way out of the beaten track.

Wherefore, the contriver of a plot ought never, if he can help it, to communicate his design until the moment when it is to be executed; or if he must communicate it, then to some one man only, with whom he has long been intimate, and whom he knows to be moved by the same feelings as himself. To find one such person is far easier than to find several, and, at the same time, involves less risk; for though this one man play you false, you are not left altogether without resource, as you are when your accomplices are numerous. For I have heard it shrewdly said that to one man you may impart anything, since, unless you have been led to commit yourself by writing, your denial will go as far as his assertion. Shun writing, therefore, as you would a rock, for there is nothing so damning as a letter under your own hand.

Plautianus, desiring to procure the deaths of the Emperor Severus and his son Caracalla, intrusted the business to the tribune Saturninus, who, being more disposed to betray than obey Plautianus, but at the same time afraid that, if it came to laying a charge, Plautianus might be believed sooner than he, asked him for a written authority, that his commission might be credited. Blinded by ambition, Plautianus complied, and forthwith was accused by Saturninus and found guilty; whereas, but for that written warrant, together with other corroborating proofs, he must have escaped by his bold denial of the charge. Against the testimony of a single witness, you have thus some defence, unless convicted by your own handwriting, or by other circumstantial proof against which you must guard. A woman, named Epicharis, who had formerly been a mistress of Nero, was privy to Piso's conspiracy, and thinking it might be useful to have the help of a certain captain of triremes whom Nero had among his bodyguards, she acquainted him with the plot, but not with the names of the plotters. This fellow, turning traitor, and accusing Epicharis to Nero, so stoutly did she deny the charge, that Nero, confounded by her effrontery, let her go.

In imparting a plot to a single person there are, therefore, two risks: one, that he may come forward of his own accord to accuse you; the other, that if arrested on suspicion, or on some proof of his guilt, he may, on being convicted, in the hope to escape punishment, betray you. But in neither of these dangers are you left without a defence; since you may meet the one by ascribing the charge to the malice of your accuser, and the other by alleging that the witness his been forced by torture to say what is untrue. The wisest course, however, is to impart your design to none, but to act like those who have been mentioned above; or if you impart it, then to one only: for although even in this course there be a certain degree of danger, it is far less than when many are admitted to your confidence.

A case nearly resembling that just now noticed, is where an emergency, so urgent as to leave you no time to provide otherwise for your safety, constrains you to do to a prince what you see him minded to do to you. A necessity of this sort leads almost always to the end desired, as two instances may suffice to show. Among the closest friends and intimates of the Emperor Commodus, were two captains of the pretorian guards, Letus and Electus, while among the most favoured of his distresses was a certain Martia. But because these three often reproved him for his manner of living, as disgraceful to himself and to his station, he resolved to rid himself of them; and so wrote their names, along with those of certain others whom he meant should be put to death the next night, in a list which he placed under the pillow of his bed. But on his going to bathe, a boy, who was a favourite of his, while playing about his room and on his bed, found the list, and coming out of the chamber with it in his hand, was met by Martia, who took it from him, and on reading it and finding what it contained, sent for Letus and Electus. And all three recognizing the danger in which they stood, resolved to be beforehand with the tyrant, and losing no time, murdered him that very night.

The Emperor Caracalla, being with his armies in Mesopotamia, had with him Macrinus, who was more of a statesman than a soldier, as his prefect. But because princes who are not themselves good are always afraid lest others treat them as they deserve, Caracalla wrote to his friend Maternianus in Rome to learn from the astrologers whether any man had ambitious designs upon the empire, and to send him word. Maternianus, accordingly, wrote back that such designs were entertained by Macrinus. But this letter, ere it reached the emperor, fell into the hands of Macrinus, who, seeing when he read it that he must either put Caracalla to death before further letters arrived from Rome, or else die himself, committed the business to a centurion, named Martialis, whom he trusted, and whose brother had been slain by Caracalla a few days before, who succeeded in killing the emperor.

We see, therefore, that an urgency which leaves no room for delay has almost the same results as the method already noticed as followed by Nelematus of Epirus. We see, too, what I remarked almost at the outset of this Discourse, that the threats of princes expose them to greater danger than the wrongs they actually inflict, and lead to more active conspiracies: and, therefore, that a prince should be careful not to threaten; since men are either to be treated kindly or else got rid of, but never brought to such a pass that they have to choose between slaying and being slain.

As to the dangers attending the execution of plots, these result either from some change made in the plan, or from a failure in courage on the part of him who is to carry it out; or else from some mistake he falls into through want of foresight, or from his not giving the affair its finishing stroke, as when some are left alive whom it was meant to put to death. Now, nothing causes so much disturbance and hindrance in human affairs, as to be forced, at a moment's notice and without time allowed for reflection, to vary your plan of action and adopt a different one from that fixed on at the first. And if such changes cause confusion anywhere, it is in matters appertaining to war, and in enterprises of the kind we are now speaking of; for in such affairs as these, there is nothing so essential as that men be prepared to do the exact thing intrusted to them. But when men have for many days together turned their whole thoughts to doing a thing in a certain way and in a certain order, and the way and order are suddenly altered, it is impossible but that they should be disconcerted and the whole scheme ruined. For which reason, it is far better to do everything in accordance with the preconcerted plan, though it be seen to be attended with some disadvantages, than, in order to escape these, to involve yourself in an infinity of dangers. And this will happen when you depart from your original design without time given to form a new one. For when time is given you may manage as you please.

The conspiracy of the Pazzi against Lorenzo and Giuliano de' Medici is well known. The scheme agreed on was to give a banquet to the Cardinal S. Giorgio, at which the brothers should be put to death. To each of the conspirators a part was assigned: to one the murder, to another the seizure of the palace, while a third was to ride through the streets and call on the people to free themselves. But it so chanced that at a time when the Pazzi, the Medici, and the Cardinal were all assembled in the cathedral church of Florence to hear High Mass, it became known that Giuliano would not be present at the banquet; whereupon the conspirators, laying their heads together, resolved to do in church what they were to have done elsewhere. This, however, deranged the whole scheme. For Giovambattista of Montesecco, would have no hand in the murder if it was to be done in a church; and the whole distribution of parts had in consequence to be changed; when, as those to whom the new parts were assigned had no time allowed them to nerve their minds to their new tasks, they managed matters so badly that they were overpowered in their attempt.

Courage fails a conspirator either from his own poorness of spirit, or from his being overcome by some feeling of reverence. For such majesty and awe attend the person of a prince, that it may well happen that he softens or dismays his executioners. When Caius Marius was taken by the people of Minturnum, the slave sent in to slay him, overawed by the bearing of the man, and by the memories which his name called up, became unnerved, and powerless to perform his office. And if this influence was exercised by one who was a prisoner, and in chains, and overwhelmed by adverse fortune, how much more must reverence be inspired by a prince who is free and uncontrolled, surrounded by his retinue and by all the pomp and splendour of his station; whose dignity confounds, and whose graciousness conciliates.

Certain persons conspiring against Sitalces, king of Thrace, fixed a day for his murder, and assembled at the place appointed, whither the king had already come. Yet none of them raised a hand to harm him, and all departed without attempting anything against him or knowing why they refrained; each blaming the others. And more than once the same folly was repeated, until the plot getting wind, they were taken and punished for what they might have done, yet durst not do.

Two brothers of Alfonso, Duke of Ferrara, conspired against him, employing as their tool a certain priest named Giennes, a singing-man in the service of the Duke. He, at their request, repeatedly brought the Duke into their company, so that they had full opportunity to make away with him. Yet neither of them ever ventured to strike the blow; till at last, their scheme being discovered, they paid the penalty of their combined cowardice and temerity. Such irresolution can only have arisen from their being overawed by the majesty of the prince, or touched by his graciousness.

In the execution of conspiracies, therefore, errors and mishaps arise from a failure of prudence or courage to which all are subject, when, losing self-control, they are led in their bewilderment to do and say what they ought not. That men are thus confounded, and thrown off their balance, could not be better shown than in the words of Titus Livius, where he describes the behaviour of Alasamenes the Etolian, at the time when he resolved on the death of Nabis the Spartan, of whom I have spoken before. For when the time to act came, and he had disclosed to his followers what they had to do, Livius represents him as "collecting his thoughts which had grown confused by dwelling on so desperate an enterprise." For it is impossible for any one, though of the most steadfast temper and used to the sight of death and to handle deadly weapons, not to be perturbed at such a moment. For which reason we should on such occasions choose for our tools those who have had experience in similar affairs, and trust no others though reputed of the truest courage. For in these grave undertakings, no one who is without such experience, however bold and resolute, is to be trusted.

The confusion of which I speak may either cause you to drop your weapon from your hand, or to use words which will have the same results. Quintianus being commanded by Lucilla, sister of Commodus, to slay him, lay in wait for him at the entrance of the amphitheatre, and rushing upon him with a drawn dagger, cried out, "The senate sends you this;" which words caused him to be seized before his blow descended. In like manner Messer Antonio of Volterra, who as we have elsewhere seen was told off to kill Lorenzo de' Medici, exclaimed as he approached him, "Ah traitor!" and this exclamation proved the salvation of Lorenzo and the ruin of that conspiracy.

For the reasons now given, a conspiracy against a single ruler may readily break down in its execution; but a conspiracy against two rulers is not only difficult, but so hazardous that its success is almost hopeless. For to effect like actions, at the same time, in different places, is well-nigh impossible; nor can they be effected at different times, if you would not have one counteract another. So that if conspiracy against a single ruler be imprudent and dangerous, to conspire against two, is in the last degree foolhardy and desperate. And were it not for the respect in which I hold the historian, I could not credit as possible what Herodian relates of Plautianus, namely, that he committed to the centurion Saturninus the task of slaying single-handed both Severus and

Caracalla, they dwelling in different places; for the thing is so opposed to reason that on no other authority could I be induced to accept it as true.

Certain young Athenians conspired against Diocles and Hippias, tyrants of Athens. Diocles they slew; but Hippias, making his escape, avenged him. Chion and Leonidas of Heraclea, disciples of Plato, conspired against the despots Clearchus and Satirus. Clearchus fell, but Satirus survived and avenged him. The Pazzi, of whom we have spoken so often, succeeded in murdering Giuliano only. From such conspiracies, therefore, as are directed against more heads than one, all should abstain; for no good is to be got from them, whether for ourselves, for our country, or for any one else. On the contrary, when those conspired against escape, they become harsher and more unsufferable than before, as, in the examples given, Florence, Athens, and Heraclea had cause to know. True it is that the conspiracy contrived by Pelopidas for the liberation of his country, had to encounter every conceivable hindrance, and yet had the happiest end. For Pelopidas had to deal, not with two tyrants only, but with ten; and so far from having their confidence, could not, being an outlaw, even approach them. And yet he succeeded in coming to Thebes, in putting the tyrants to death, and in freeing his country. But whatever he did was done with the aid of one of the counsellors of the tyrants, a certain Charon, through whom he had all facilities for executing his design. Let none, however, take this case as a pattern; for that it was in truth a desperate attempt, and its success a marvel, was and is the opinion of all historians, who speak of it as a thing altogether extraordinary and unexampled.

The execution of a plot may be frustrated by some groundless alarm or unforeseen mischance occurring at the very moment when the scheme is to be carried out. On the morning on which Brutus and his confederates were to slay Caesar, it so happened that Caesar talked for a great while with Cneus Pompilius Lenas, one of the conspirators; which some of the others observing, were in terror that Pompilius was divulging the conspiracy to Caesar; whose life they would therefore have attempted then and there, without waiting his arrival in the senate house, had they not been reassured by seeing that when the conference ended he showed no sign of unusual emotion. False alarms of this sort are to be taken into account and allowed for, all the more that they are easily raised. For he who has not a clear conscience is apt to assume that others are speaking of him. A word used with a wholly different purpose, may throw his mind off its balance and lead him to fancy that reference is intended to the matter he is engaged on, and cause him either to betray the conspiracy by flight, or to derange its execution by anticipating the time fixed. And the more there are privy to the conspiracy, the likelier is this to happen.

As to the mischances which may befall, since these are unforeseen, they can only be instanced by examples which may make men more cautious. Giulio Belanti of Siena, of whom I have spoken before, from the hate he bore Pandolfo Petrucci, who had given him his daughter to wife and afterwards taken her from him, resolved to murder him, and thus chose his time. Almost every day Pandolfo went to visit a sick kinsman, passing the house of Giulio on the way, who, remarking this, took measures to have his accomplices ready in his house to kill Pandolfo as he passed. Wherefore, placing the rest armed within the doorway, one he stationed at a window to give the signal of Pandolfo's approach. It so happened however, that as he came nigh the house, and after the look-out had given the signal, Pandolfo fell in with a friend who stopped him to converse; when some of those with him, going on in advance, saw and heard the gleam and clash of weapons, and so discovered the ambuscade; whereby Pandolfo was saved, while Giulio with his companions had to fly from Siena. This plot accordingly was marred, and Giulio's schemes baulked, in consequence of a chance meeting. Against such accidents, since they are out of the common course of things, no provision can be made. Still it is very necessary to take into account all that may happen, and devise what remedies you can.

It now only remains for us to consider those dangers which follow after the execution of a plot. These in fact resolve themselves into one, namely, that some should survive who will avenge the death of the murdered prince. The part of avenger is likely to be assumed by a son, a brother, or other kinsman of the deceased, who in the ordinary course of events might have looked to succeed to the princedom. And such persons are suffered to live, either from inadvertence, or from some of the causes noted already, as when Giovann' Andrea of Lampognano, with the help of his companions, put to death the Duke of Milan. For the son and two brothers of the Duke, who survived him, were able to avenge his death. In cases like this, indeed, the conspirators may be held excused, since there is nothing they can do to help themselves. But when from carelessness and want of due caution some one is allowed to live whose death ought to have been secured, there is no excuse. Certain conspirators, after murdering the lord, Count Girolamo of Forli, made prisoners of his wife and of his children who were still very young. By thinking they could not be safe unless they got possession of the citadel, which the governor refused to surrender, they obtained a promise from Madonna Caterina, for so the Countess was named, that on their permitting her to enter the citadel she would cause it to be given up to them, her children in the mean time remaining with them as hostages. On which undertaking they suffered her to enter the citadel. But no sooner had she got inside than she fell to upbraid them from the walls with the murder of her husband, and to threaten them with every kind of vengeance; and to show them how little store she set upon her children, told them scoffingly that she knew how others could be got. In the end, the rebels having no leader to advise them, and perceiving too late the error into which they had been betrayed, had to pay the penalty of their rashness by perpetual banishment.

But of all the dangers which may follow on the execution of a plot, none is so much or so justly to be feared as that the people should be well affected to the prince whom you have put to death. For against this danger conspirators have no resource which can ensure their safety. Of this we have example in the case of Caesar, who as he had the love of the Roman people was by them avenged; for they it was who, by driving out the conspirators from Rome, were the cause that all of them, at different times and in different places, came to violent ends.

Conspiracies against their country are less danger for those who take part in them than conspiracies against princes; since there is less risk beforehand, and though there be the same danger in their execution, there is none afterwards. Beforehand, the risks are few, because a citizen may use means for obtaining power without betraying his wishes or designs to any; and unless his course be arrested, his designs are likely enough to succeed; nay, though laws be passed to restrain him, he may strike out a new path. This is to be understood of a commonwealth which has to some degree become corrupted; for in one wherein there is no taint of corruption, there being no soil in which evil seed can grow, such designs will never suggest themselves to any citizen.

In a commonwealth, therefore, a citizen may by many means and in many ways aspire to the princedom without risking destruction, both because republics are slower than princes are to take alarm, are less suspicious and consequently less cautious, and because they look with greater reverence upon their great citizens, who are in this way rendered bolder and more reckless in attacking them. Any one who has read Sallust's account of the conspiracy of Catiline, must remember how, when that conspiracy was discovered, Catiline not only remained in Rome, but even made his appearance in the senatehouse, where he was suffered to address the senate in the most insulting terms, — so scrupulous was that city in protecting the liberty of all its citizens. Nay, even after he had left Rome and placed himself at the head of his army, Lentulus and his other accomplices would not have been imprisoned, had not letters been found upon them clearly establishing their guilt. Hanno, the foremost citizen of Carthage, aspiring to absolute power, on the occasion of the marriage of a daughter contrived a plot for administering poison to the whole senate and so making himself prince. The scheme being discovered, the senate took no steps against him beyond passing a law to limit the expense of banquets and marriage ceremonies. So great was the respect they paid to his quality.

True, the *execution* of a plot against your country is attended with greater difficulty and danger, since it seldom happens that, in conspiring against so many, your own resources are sufficient by themselves; for it is not every one who, like Caesar, Agathocles, or Cleomenes, is at the head of an army, so as to be able at a stroke, and by open force to make himself master of his country. To such as these, doubtless, the path is safe and easy enough; but others who have not such an assembled force ready at their command, must effect their ends either by stratagem and fraud, or with the help of foreign troops. Of such stratagems and frauds we have an instance in the case of Pisistratus the Athenian, who after defeating the Megarians and thereby gaining the favour of his fellow-citizens, showed himself to them one morning covered with wounds and blood, declaring that he had been thus outraged through the jealousy of the nobles, and asking that he might have an armed guard assigned for his protection. With the authority which this lent him, he easily rose to such a pitch of power as to become tyrant of Athens. In like manner Pandolfo Petrucci, on his return with the other exiles to Siena, was appointed the command of the public guard, as a mere office of routine which others had declined. Very soon, however, this armed force gave him so much importance that he became the supreme ruler of the State. And many others have followed other plans and methods, and in the course of time, and without incurring danger, have achieved their aim.

Conspirators against their country, whether trusting to their own forces or to foreign aid, have had more or less success in proportion as they have been favoured by Fortune. Catiline, of whom we spoke just now, was overthrown. Hanno, who has also been mentioned, failing to accomplish his object by poison, armed his partisans to the number of many thousands; but both he and they came to an ill end. On the other hand, certain citizens of Thebes conspiring to become its tyrants, summoned a Spartan army to their assistance, and usurped the absolute control of the city. In short, if we examine all the conspiracies which men have engaged in against their country, we shall find that few or none have been quelled in their inception, but that all have either succeeded, or have broken down in their execution. Once executed, they entail no further risks beyond those implied in the nature of a princedom. For the man who becomes a tyrant incurs all the natural and ordinary dangers in which a tyranny involves him, and has no remedies against them save those of which I have already spoken.

This is all that occurs to me to say on the subject of conspiracies. If I have noticed those which have been carried out with the sword rather than those wherein poison has been the instrument, it is because, generally speaking, the method of proceeding is the same in both. It is true, nevertheless, that conspiracies which are to be carried out by poison are, by reason of their uncertainty, attended by greater danger. For since fewer opportunities offer for their execution, you must have an understanding with persons who can command opportunities. But it is dangerous to have to depend on others. Again, many causes may hinder a poisoned draught from proving mortal; as when the murderers of Commodus, on his vomiting the poison given him, had to strangle him.

Princes, then, have no worse enemy than conspiracy, for when a conspiracy is formed against them, it either carries them off, or discredits them: since, if it succeeds, they die; while, if it be discovered, and the conspirators be put to death themselves, it will always be believed that the whole affair has been trumped up by the prince that he might glut his greed and cruelty with the goods and blood of those whom he has made away with. Let me not, however, forget to warn the prince or commonwealth against whom a conspiracy is directed, that on getting word of it, and before taking any steps to punish it, they endeavour, as far as they can, to ascertain its character, and after carefully weighing the strength of the conspirators with their own, on finding it preponderate, never suffer their knowledge of the plot to appear until they are ready with a force sufficient to crush it. For otherwise, to disclose their knowledge will only give the signal for their destruction. They must strive therefore to seem unconscious of what is going on; for conspirators who see themselves detected are driven forward by necessity and will stick at nothing. Of this precaution we have an example in Roman history, when the officers of the two legions, who, as has already been mentioned, were left behind to defend the Capuans from the Samnites, conspired together against the Capuans. For on rumours of this conspiracy reaching Rome, Rutilius the new consul was charged to see to it; who, not to excite the suspicions of the conspirators, publicly gave out that by order of the senate the Capuan legions were continued in their station. The conspirators believing this, and thinking they would have ample time to execute their plans, made no effort to hasten matters, but remained at their ease, until they found that the consul was moving one of the two legions to a distance from the other. This arousing their suspicion, led them to disclose their designs and endeavour to carry them out.

  Now, we could have no more instructive example than this in whatever way we look at it. For it shows how slow men are to move in those matters wherein time seems of little importance, and how active they become when necessity urges them. Nor can a prince or commonwealth desiring for their own ends to retard the execution of a conspiracy, use any more effectual means to do so, than by artfully holding out to the conspirators some special opportunity as likely soon to present itself; awaiting which, and believing they have time and to spare for what they have to do, they will afford that prince or commonwealth all the leisure needed to prepare for their punishment. Whosoever neglects these precautions hastens his own destruction, as happened with the Duke of Athens, and with Guglielmo de' Pazzi. For the Duke, who had made himself tyrant of Florence, on learning that he was being conspired against, without further inquiry into the matter, caused one of the conspirators to be seized; whereupon the rest at once armed themselves and deprived him of his government. Guglielmo, again, being commissary in the Val di Chiana in the year 1501, and learning that a conspiracy was being hatched in Arezzo to take the town from the Florentines and give it over to the Vitelli, repaired thither with all haste; and without providing himself with the necessary forces or giving a thought to the strength of the conspirators, on the advice of the bishop, his son, had one of them arrested. Which becoming known to the others, they forthwith rushed to arms, and taking the town from the Florentines, made Guglielmo their prisoner. Where, however, conspiracies are weak, they may and should be put down without scruple or hesitation.

Two methods, somewhat opposed to one another, which have occasionally been followed in dealing with conspiracies, are in no way to be commended. One of these was that adopted by the Duke of Athens, of whom I have just now spoken, who to have it thought that he confided in the goodwill of the Florentines, caused a certain man who gave information of a plot against him, to be put to death. The other was that followed by Dion the Syracusan, who, to sound the intentions of one whom he suspected, arranged with Calippus, whom he trusted, to pretend to get up a conspiracy against him. Neither of these tyrants reaped any advantage from the course he followed. For the one discouraged informers and gave heart to those who were disposed to conspire, the other prepared an easy road to his own death, or rather was prime mover in a conspiracy against himself. As the event showed. For Calippus having free leave to plot against Dion, plotted to such effect, that he deprived him at once of his State and life.

CHAPTER VII

Why it is that changes from Freedom to Servitude, and from Servitude to Freedom, are sometimes made without Bloodshed, but at other times reek with Blood.

Since we find from history that in the countless changes which have been made from freedom to servitude and from servitude to freedom, sometimes an infinite multitude have perished, while at others not a soul has suffered (as when Rome made her change from kings to consuls, on which occasion none was banished save Tarquin, and no harm was done to any other), it may perhaps be asked, how it happens that of these revolutions, some have been attended by bloodshed and others not.

The answer I take to be this. The government which suffers change either has or has not had its beginning in violence. And since the government which has its beginning in violence must start by inflicting injuries on many, it must needs happen that on its downfall those who were injured will desire to avenge themselves; from which desire for vengeance the slaughter and death of many will result. But when a government originates with, and derives its authority from the whole community, there is no reason why the community, if it withdraw that authority, should seek to injure any except the prince from whom it withdraws it. Now the government of Rome was of this nature, and the expulsion of the Tarquins took place in this way. Of a like character was the government of the Medici in Florence, and, accordingly, upon their overthrow in the year 1494, no injury was done to any save themselves.

In such cases, therefore, the changes I speak of do not occasion any very great danger. But the changes wrought by men who have wrongs to revenge, are always of a most dangerous kind, and such, to say the least, as may well cause dismay in the minds of those who read of them. But since history abounds with instances of such changes I need say no more about them.

CHAPTER VIII

That he who would effect Changes in a Commonwealth, must give heed to its Character and Condition

I have said before that a bad citizen cannot work grave mischief in a commonwealth which has not become corrupted. This opinion is not only supported by the arguments already advanced, but is further confirmed by the examples of Spurius Cassius and Manlius Capitolinus. For Spurius, being ambitious, and desiring to obtain extraordinary authority in Rome, and to win over the people by loading them with benefits (as, for instance, by selling them those lands which the Romans had taken from the Hernici,) his designs were seen through by the senate, and laid him under such suspicion, that when in haranguing the people he offered them the money realized by the sale of the grain brought from Sicily at the public expense, they would have none of it, believing that he offered it as the price of their freedom. Now, had the people been corrupted, they would not have refused this bribe, but would have opened rather than closed the way to the tyranny.

The example of Manlius is still more striking. For in his case we see what excellent gifts both of mind and body, and what splendid services to his country were afterwards cancelled by that shameful eagerness to reign which we find bred in him by his jealousy of the honours paid Camillus. For so darkened did his mind become, that without reflecting what were the institutions to which Rome was accustomed, or testing the material he had to work on, when he would have seen that it was still unfit to be moulded to evil ends, he set himself to stir up tumults against the senate and against the laws of his country.

And herein we recognize the excellence of this city of Rome, and of the materials whereof it was composed. For although the nobles were wont to stand up stoutly for one another, not one of them stirred to succour Manlius, and not one of his kinsfolk made any effort on his behalf, so that although it was customary, in the case of other accused persons, for their friends to put on black and sordid raiment, with all the other outward signs of grief, in order to excite pity for the accused, none was seen to do any of these things for Manlius. Even the tribunes of the people, though constantly ready to promote whatever courses seemed to favour the popular cause, and the more vehemently the more they seemed to make against the nobles, in this instance sided with the nobles to put down the common enemy. Nay the very people themselves, keenly alive to their own interests, and well disposed towards any attempt to damage the nobles, though they showed Manlius many proofs of their regard, nevertheless, when he was cited by the tribunes to appear before them and submit his cause for their decision, assumed the part of judges and not of defenders, and without scruple or hesitation sentenced him to die. Wherefore, I think, that there is no example in the whole Roman history which serves so well as this to demonstrate the virtues of all ranks in that republic. For not a man in the whole city bestirred himself to shield a citizen endowed with every great quality, and who, both publicly and privately, had done so much that deserved praise. But in all, the love of country outweighed every other thought, and all looked less to his past deserts than to the dangers which his present conduct threatened; from which to relieve themselves they put him to death. "Such," says Livius, "was the fate of a man worthy our admiration had he not been born in a free State."

And here two points should be noted. The first, that glory is to be sought by different methods in a corrupt city, and in one which still preserves its freedom. The second, which hardly differs from the first, that in their actions, and especially in matters of moment, men must have regard to times and circumstances and adapt themselves thereto. For those persons who from an unwise choice, or from natural inclination, run counter to the times will for the most part live unhappily, and find all they undertake issue in failure; whereas those who accommodate themselves to the times are fortunate and successful. And from the passage cited we may plainly infer, that had Manlius lived in the days of Marius and Sylla, when the body of the State had become corrupted, so that he could have impressed it with the stamp of his ambition, he might have had the same success as they had, and as those others had who after them aspired to absolute power; and, conversely, that if Sylla and Marius had lived in the days of Manlius, they must have broken down at the very beginning of their attempts.

For one man, by mischievous arts and measures, may easily prepare the ground for the universal corruption of a city; but no one man in his lifetime can carry that corruption so far, as himself to reap the harvest; or granting that one man's life might be long enough for this purpose, it would be impossible for him, having regard to the ordinary habits of men, who grow impatient and cannot long forego the gratification of their desires, to wait until the corruption was complete. Moreover, men deceive themselves in respect of their own affairs, and most of all in respect of those on which they are most bent; so that either from impatience or from self-deception, they rush upon undertakings for which the time is not ripe, and so come to an ill end. Wherefore to obtain absolute authority in a commonwealth and to destroy its liberties, you must find the body of the State already corrupted, and corrupted by a gradual wasting continued from generation to generation; which, indeed, takes place necessarily, unless, as has been already explained, the State be often reinforced by good examples, or brought back to its first beginnings by wise laws.

Manlius, therefore, would have been a rare and renowned man had he been born in a corrupt city; and from his example we see that citizens seeking to introduce changes in the form of their government, whether in favour of liberty or despotism, ought to consider what materials they have to deal with, and then judge of the difficulty of their task. For it is no less arduous and dangerous to attempt to free a people disposed to live in servitude, than to enslave a people who desire to live free.

And because it has been said above, that in their actions men must take into account the character of the times in which they live, and guide themselves accordingly, I shall treat this point more fully in the following Chapter.

CHAPTER IX

That to enjoy constant good Fortune we must change with the Times.

I have repeatedly noted that the good or bad fortune of men depends on whether their methods of acting accord with the character of the times. For we see that in what they do some men act impulsively, others warily and with caution. And because, from inability to preserve the just mean, they in both of these ways overstep the true limit, they commit mistakes in one direction or the other. He, however, will make fewest mistakes, and may expect to prosper most, who, while following the course to which nature inclines him, finds, as I have said, his method of acting in accordance with the times in which he lives.

All know that in his command of the Roman armies, Fabius Maximus displayed a prudence and caution very different from the audacity and hardihood natural to his countrymen; and it was his good fortune that his methods suited with the times. For Hannibal coming into Italy in all the flush of youth and recent success, having already by two defeats stripped Rome of her best soldiers and filled her with dismay, nothing could have been more fortunate for that republic than to find a general able, by his deliberateness and caution, to keep the enemy at bay. Nor, on the other hand, could Fabius have fallen upon times better suited to the methods which he used, and by which he crowned himself with glory. That he acted in accordance with his natural bent, and not from a reasoned choice, we may gather from this, that when Scipio, to bring the war to an end, proposed to pass with his army into Africa, Fabius, unable to depart from his characteristic methods and habits, strenuously opposed him; so that had it rested with him, Hannibal might never have left Italy. For he perceived not that the times had changed, and that with them it was necessary to change the methods of prosecuting the war. Had Fabius, therefore, been King of Rome, he might well have caused the war to end unhappily, not knowing how to accommodate his methods to the change in the times. As it was, he lived in a commonwealth in which there were many citizens, and many different dispositions; and which as it produced a Fabius, excellent at a time when it was necessary to protract hostilities, so also, afterwards gave birth to a Scipio, at a time suited to bring them to a successful close.

And hence it comes that a commonwealth endures longer, and has a more sustained good fortune than a princedom, because from the diversity in the characters of its citizens, it can adapt itself better than a prince can to the diversity of times. For, as I have said before, a man accustomed to follow one method, will never alter it; whence it must needs happen that when times change so as no longer to accord with his method, he will be ruined. Piero Soderini, of whom I have already spoken, was guided in all his actions by patience and gentleness, and he and his country prospered while the times were in harmony with these methods. But, afterwards, when a time came when it behoved him to have done with patience and gentleness, he knew not how to drop them, and was ruined together with his country. Pope Julius II., throughout the whole of his pontificate, was governed by impulse and passion, and because the times were in perfect accord, all his undertakings prospered. But had other times come requiring other qualities, he could not have escaped destruction, since he could not have changed his methods nor his habitual line of conduct.

As to why such changes are impossible, two reasons may be given. One is that we cannot act in opposition to the bent of our nature. The other, that when a man has been very successful while following a particular method, he can never be convinced that it is for his advantage to try some other. And hence it results that a man's fortunes vary, because times change and he does not change with them. So, too, with commonwealths, which, as we have already shown at length, are ruined from not altering their institutions to suit the times. And commonwealths are slower to change than princes are, changes costing them more effort; because occasions must be waited for which shall stir the whole community, and it is not enough that a single citizen alters his method of acting.

But since I have made mention of Fabius Maximus who wore out Hannibal by keeping him at bay, I think it opportune to consider in the following Chapter whether a general who desires to engage his enemy at all risks, can be prevented by that enemy from doing so.

CHAPTER X

That a Captain cannot escape Battle when his Enemy forces it on him at all risks.

>*"Cneius Sulpitius when appointed dictator against the Gauls, being unwilling to tempt Fortune by attacking an enemy whom delay and a disadvantageous position would every day render weaker, protracted the war."*

When a mistake is made of a sort that all or most men are likely to fall into, I think it not amiss to mark it again and again with disapproval. Wherefore, although I have already shown repeatedly how in affairs of moment the actions of the moderns conform not to those of antiquity, still it seems to me not superfluous, in this place, to say the same thing once more. For if in any particular the moderns have deviated from the methods of the ancients, it is especially in their methods of warfare, wherein not one of those rules formerly so much esteemed is now attended to. And this because both princes and commonwealths have devolved the charge of such matters upon others, and, to escape danger, have kept aloof from all military service; so that although one or another of the princes of our times may occasionally be seen present in person with his army, we are not therefore to expect from him any further praiseworthy behaviour. For even where such personages take part in any warlike enterprise, they do so out of ostentation and from no nobler motive; though doubtless from sometimes seeing their soldiers face to face, and from retaining to themselves the title of command, they are likely to make fewer blunders than we find made by republics, and most of all by the republics of Italy, which though altogether dependent upon others, and themselves utterly ignorant of everything relating to warfare, do yet, that they may figure as the commanders of their armies, take upon them to direct their movements, and in doing so commit countless mistakes; some of which have been considered elsewhere but one is of such importance as to deserve notice here.

When these sluggard princes or effeminate republics send forth any of their Captains, it seems to them that the wisest instruction they can give him is to charge him on no account to give battle, but, on the contrary, to do what he can to avoid fighting. Wherein they imagine themselves to imitate the prudence of Fabius Maximus, who by protracting the war with Hannibal, saved the Roman commonwealth; not perceiving that in most instances such advice to a captain is either useless or hurtful. For the truth of the matter is, that a captain who would keep the field, cannot decline battle when his adversary forces it on him at all hazards. So that the instruction to avoid battle is but tantamount to saying, "You shall engage when it pleases your enemy, and not when it suits yourself." For if you would keep the field and yet avoid battle, the only safe course is to interpose a distance of at least fifty miles between you and your enemy, and afterwards to maintain so vigilant a look-out, that should he advance you will have time to make your retreat. Another method is to shut yourself up in some town. But both of these methods are extremely disadvantageous. For by following the former, you leave your country a prey to the enemy, and a valiant prince would far sooner risk the chances of battle than prolong a war in a manner so disastrous to his subjects; while by adopting the latter method, and shutting yourself up in a town with your army, there is manifest danger of your being besieged, and presently reduced by famine and forced to surrender. Wherefore it is most mischievous to seek to avoid battle in either of these two ways.

To intrench yourself in a strong position, as Fabius was wont to do, is a good method when your army is so formidable that the enemy dare not advance to attack you in your intrenchments; yet it cannot truly be said that Fabius avoided battle, but rather that he sought to give battle where he could do so with advantage. For had Hannibal desired to fight, Fabius would have waited for him and fought him. But Hannibal never dared to engage him on his own ground. So that an engagement was avoided as much by Hannibal as by Fabius, since if either had been minded to fight at all hazards the other would have been constrained to take one of three courses, that is to say, one or other of the two just now mentioned, or else to retreat. The truth of this is confirmed by numberless examples, and more particularly by what happened in the war waged by the Romans against Philip of Macedon, the father of Perseus. For Philip being invaded by the Romans, resolved not to give them battle; and to avoid battle, sought at first to do as Fabius had done in Italy, posting himself on the summit of a hill, where he intrenched himself strongly, thinking that the Romans would not venture to attack him there. But they advancing and attacking him in his intrenchments, drove him from his position; when, unable to make further resistance, he fled with the greater part of his army, and was only saved from utter destruction by the difficulty of the ground, which made it impossible for the Romans to pursue him.

Philip, therefore, who had no mind to fight, encamping too near the Romans, was forced to fly; and learning from this experience that to escape fighting it was not enough for him to intrench himself on a hill, yet not choosing to shut himself up in a walled town, he was constrained to take the other alternative of keeping at a distance of many miles from the Roman legions. Accordingly, when the Romans entered one province, he betook himself to another, and when they left a province he entered it. But perceiving that by protracting the war in this way, his condition grew constantly worse, while his subjects suffered grievously, now from his own troops, at another time from those of the enemy, he at last resolved to hazard battle, and so came to a regular engagement with the Romans.

It is for your interest, therefore, not to fight, when you possess the same advantages as Fabius, or as Cneius Sulpitius had; in other words, when your army is so formidable in itself that the enemy dare not attack you in your intrenchments, and although he has got within your territory has yet gained no footing there, and suffers in consequence from the want of necessary supplies. In such circumstances delay is useful, for the reasons assigned by Titus Livius when speaking of Sulpitius. In no other circumstances, however, can an engagement be avoided without dishonour or danger. For to retire as Philip did, is nothing else than defeat; and the disgrace is greater in proportion as your valour has been less put to the proof. And if Philip was lucky enough to escape, another, not similarly favoured by the nature of the ground, might not have the same good fortune.

That Hannibal was not a master in the arts of warfare there is none will venture to maintain. Wherefore, when he had to encounter Scipio in Africa, it may be assumed that had he seen any advantage in prolonging the war he would have done so; and, possibly, being a skilful captain and in command of a valiant army, he might have been able to do what Fabius did in Italy. But since he took not that course, we may infer that he was moved by sufficient reasons. For the captain who has got an army together, and perceives that from want of money or friends he cannot maintain it long, must be a mere madman if he do not at once, and before his army melts away, try the fortunes of battle; since he is certain to lose by delay, while by fighting he may chance to succeed. And there is this also to be kept in view, that we must strive, even if we be defeated, to gain glory; and that more glory is to be won in being beaten by force, than in a defeat from any other cause. And this we may suppose to have weighed with Hannibal. On the other hand, supposing Hannibal to have declined battle, Scipio, even if he had lacked courage to follow him up and attack him in his intrenched camp, would not have suffered thereby; for as he had defeated Syphax, and got possession of many of the African towns, he could have rested where he was in the same security and with the same convenience as if he had been in Italy. But this was not the case with Hannibal when he had to encounter Fabius, nor with the Gauls when they were opposed to Sulpitius.

Least of all can he decline battle who invades with his army the country of another; for seeking to enter his enemy's country, he must fight whenever the enemy comes forward to meet him; and is under still greater necessity to fight, if he undertake the siege of any town. As happened in our own day with Duke Charles of Burgundy, who, when beleaguering Morat, a town of the Swiss, was by them attacked and routed; or as happened with the French army encamped against Novara, which was in like manner defeated by the Swiss.

CHAPTER XI

That one who has to contend with many, though he be weaker than they, will prevail if he can withstand their first onset.

The power exercised in Rome by the tribunes of the people was great, and, as I have repeatedly explained, was necessary, since otherwise there would have been no check on the ambition of the nobles, and the commonwealth must have grown corrupted far sooner than it did. But because, as I have said elsewhere, there is in everything a latent evil peculiar to it, giving rise to new mischances, it becomes necessary to provide against these by new ordinances. The authority of the tribunes, therefore, being insolently asserted so as to become formidable to the nobility and to the entire city, disorders dangerous to the liberty of the State must thence have resulted, had not a method been devised by Appius Claudius for controlling the ambition of the tribunes. This was, to secure that there should always be one of their number timid, or venal, or else a lover of the general good, who could be influenced to oppose the rest whenever these sought to pass any measure contrary to the wishes of the senate. This remedy was a great restraint on the excessive authority of the tribunes, and on many occasions proved serviceable to Rome.

I am led by this circumstance to remark, that when many powerful persons are united against one, who, although no match for the others collectively, is also powerful, the chances are more in favour of this single and less I powerful person, than of the many who together are much stronger. For setting aside an infinity of accidents which can be turned to better account by one than by many, it will always happen that, by exercising a little dexterity, the one will be able to divide the many, and weaken the force which was strong while it was united. In proof whereof, I shall not refer to ancient examples, though many such might be cited, but content myself with certain modern instances taken from the events of our own times.

In the year 1484, all Italy combined against the Venetians, who finding their position desperate, and being unable to keep their army any longer in the field, bribed Signer Lodovico, who then governed Milan, and so succeeded in effecting a settlement, whereby they not only recovered the towns they had lost, but also obtained for themselves a part of the territories of Ferrara; so that those were by peace the gainers, who in war had been the losers. Not many years ago the whole world was banded together against France; but before the war came to a close, Spain breaking with the confederates and entering into a separate treaty with France, the other members of the league also, were presently forced to make terms.

Wherefore we may always assume when we see a war set on foot by many against one, that this one, if he have strength to withstand the first shock, and can temporize and wait his opportunity, is certain to prevail. But unless he can do this he runs a thousand dangers: as did the Venetians in the year 1508, who, could they have temporized with the French, and so got time to conciliate some of those who had combined against them, might have escaped the ruin which then overtook them. But not possessing such a strong army as would have enabled them to temporize with their enemies, and consequently not having the time needed for gaining any to their side, they were undone. Yet we know that the Pope, as soon as he had obtained what he wanted, made friends with them, and that Spain did the like; and that both the one and the other of these powers would gladly have saved the Lombard territory for themselves, nor would, if they could have helped it, have left it to France, so as to augment her influence in Italy.

The Venetians, therefore, should have given up a part to save the rest; and had they done so at a time when the surrender would not have seemed to be made under compulsion, and before any step had been taken in the direction of war, it would have been a most prudent course; although discreditable and probably of little avail after war had been begun. But until the war broke out, few of the Venetian citizens recognized the danger, fewer still the remedy, and none ventured to prescribe it.

But to return to the point whence we started, I say that the same safeguard for their country which the Roman senate found against the ambition of the tribunes in their number, is within the reach of the prince who is attacked by many adversaries, if he only know to use prudently those methods which promote division.

CHAPTER XII

A prudent Captain will do what he can to make it necessary for his own Soldiers to fight, and to relieve his Enemy from that necessity.

Elsewhere I have noted how greatly men are governed in what they do by Necessity, and how much of their renown is due to her guidance, so that it has even been said by some philosophers, that the hands and tongues of men, the two noblest instruments of their fame, would never have worked to perfection, nor have brought their labours to that pitch of excellence we see them to have reached, had they not been impelled by this cause. The captains of antiquity, therefore, knowing the virtues of this necessity, and seeing the steadfast courage which it gave their soldiers in battle, spared no effort to bring their armies under its influence, while using all their address to loosen its hold upon their enemies. For which reason, they would often leave open to an adversary some way which they might have closed, and close against their own men some way they might have left open.

Whosoever, therefore, would have a city defend itself stubbornly, or an army fight resolutely in the field, must before all things endeavour to impress the minds of those whom he commands with the belief that no other course is open to them. In like manner a prudent captain who undertakes the attack of a city, will measure the ease or difficulty of his enterprise, by knowing and considering the nature of the necessity which compels the inhabitants to defend it; and where he finds that necessity to be strong, he may infer that his task will be difficult, but if otherwise, that it will be easy.

And hence it happens that cities are harder to be recovered after a revolt than to be taken for the first time. Because on a first attack, having no occasion to fear punishment, since they have given no ground of offence, they readily surrender; but when they have revolted, they know that they have given ground of offence, and, fearing punishment, are not so easily brought under. A like stubbornness grows from the natural hostility with which princes or republics who are neighbours regard one another; which again is caused by the desire to dominate over those who live near, or from jealousy of their power. This is more particularly the case with republics, as in Tuscany for example; for contention and rivalry have always made, and always will make it extremely hard for one republic to bring another into subjection. And for this reason any one who considers attentively who are the neighbours of Florence, and who of Venice, will not marvel so much as some have done, that Florence should have spent more than Venice on her wars and gained less; since this results entirely from the Venetians finding their neighbouring towns less obstinate in their resistance than the Florentines theirs. For all the towns in the neighbourhood of Venice have been used to live under princes and not in freedom; and those who are used to servitude commonly think little of changing masters, nay are often eager for the change. In this way Venice, though she has had more powerful neighbours than Florence, has been able, from finding their towns less stubborn, to subdue them more easily than the latter, surrounded exclusively by free cities, has had it in her power to do.

But, to return to the matter in hand, the captain who attacks a town should use what care he can, not to drive the defenders to extremities, lest he render them stubborn; but when they fear punishment should promise them pardon, and when they fear for their freedom should assure them that he has no designs against the common welfare, but only against a few ambitious men in their city; for such assurances have often smoothed the way to the surrender of towns. And although pretexts of this sort are easily seen through, especially by the wise, the mass of the people are often beguiled by them, because desiring present tranquillity, they shut their eyes to the snares hidden behind these specious promises. By means such as these, therefore, cities innumerable have been brought into subjection, as recently was the case with Florence. The ruin of Crassus and his army was similarly caused: for although he himself saw through the empty promises of the Parthians, as meant only to blind the Roman soldiers to the necessity of defending themselves, yet he could not keep his men steadfast, they, as we clearly gather in reading the life of this captain, being deceived by the offers of peace held out to them by their enemies.

On the other hand, when the Samnites, who, at the instance of a few ambitious men, and in violation of the terms of the truce made with them, had overrun and pillaged lands belonging to the allies of Rome, afterwards sent envoys to Rome to implore peace, offering to restore whatever they had taken, and to surrender the authors of these injuries and outrages as prisoners, and these offers were rejected by the Romans, and the envoys returned to Samnium bringing with them no hope of an adjustment, Claudius Pontius, who then commanded the army of the Samnites, showed them in a remarkable speech, that the Romans desired war at all hazards, and declared that, although for the sake of his country he wished for peace, necessity constrained him to prepare for war; telling them *"that was a just war which could not be escaped, and those arms sacred in which lay their only hopes."* And building on this necessity, he raised in the minds of his soldiers a confident expectation of success. That I may not have to revert to this matter again, it will be convenient to notice here those examples from Roman history which most merit attention. When Caius Manilius was in command of the legions encamped against Veii, a division of the Veientine army having got within the Roman intrenchments, Manilius ran forward with a company of his men to defend them, and, to prevent the escape of the Veientines, guarded all the approaches to the camp. The Veientines finding themselves thus shut in, began to fight with such fury that they slew Manilius, and would have destroyed all the rest of the Roman army, had not the prudence of one of the tribunes opened a way for the Veientines to retreat. Here we see that so long as necessity compelled, the Veientines fought most fiercely, but on finding a path opened for escape, preferred flight to combat. On another occasion when the Volscians and Equians passed with their armies across the Roman frontier, the consuls were sent out to oppose them, and an engagement ensued. It so happened that when the combat was at its height, the army of the Volscians, commanded by Vectius Mescius, suddenly found themselves shut in between their own camp, which a division of the Romans had occupied, and the body of the Roman army; when seeing that they must either perish or cut a way for themselves with their swords, Vectius said to them, "Come on, my men, here is no wall or rampart to be scaled: we fight man with man; in valour we are their equals, and necessity, that last and mightiest weapon, gives us the advantage." Here, then, necessity is spoken of by Titus Livius as *the last and mightiest weapon.*

Camillus, the wisest and most prudent of all the Roman commanders, when he had got within the town of Veii with his army, to make its surrender easier and not to drive its inhabitants to desperation, called out to his men, so that the Veientines might hear, to spare all whom they found unarmed. Whereupon the defenders throwing away their weapons, the town was taken almost without bloodshed. And this device was afterwards followed by many other captains.

CHAPTER XIII

Whether we may trust more to a valiant Captain with a weak Army, or to a valiant Army with a weak Captain.

Coriolanus being banished from Rome betook himself to the Volscians, and when he had got together an army wherewith to avenge himself on his countrymen, came back to Rome; yet, again withdrew, not constrained to retire by the might of the Roman arms, but out of reverence for his mother. From this incident, says Titus Livius, we may learn that the spread of the Roman power was due more to the valour of her captains than of her soldiers. For before this the Volscians had always been routed, and only grew successful when Coriolanus became their captain.

But though Livius be of this opinion, there are many passages in his history to show that the Roman soldiers, even when left without leaders, often performed astonishing feats of valour, nay, sometimes maintained better discipline and fought with greater spirit after their consuls were slain than they had before. For example, the army under the Scipios in Spain, after its two leaders had fallen, was able by its valour not merely to secure its own safety, but to overcome the enemy and preserve the province for the Roman Republic. So that to state the case fairly, we find many instances in which the valour of the soldiers alone gained the day, as well as many in which success was wholly due to the excellence of the captain. From which it may be inferred that the one stands in need of the other.

And here the question suggests itself: which is the more formidable, a good army badly led, or a good captain commanding an indifferent army; though, were we to adopt the opinion of Caesar on this head, we ought lightly to esteem both. For when Caesar went to Spain against Afranius and Petreius, who were there in command of a strong army, he made little account of them, saying, "that he went to fight an army without a captain," indicating thereby the weakness of these generals. And, conversely, when he went to encounter Pompeius in Thessaly, he said, "I go against a captain without an army."

A further question may also be raised, whether it is easier for a good captain to make a good army, or for a good army to make a good captain. As to this it might be thought there was barely room for doubt, since it ought to be far easier for many who are good to find one who is good or teach him to become so, than for one who is good to find or make many good. Lucullus when sent against Mithridates was wholly without experience in war: but his brave army, which was provided with many excellent officers, speedily taught him to be a good captain. On the other hand, when the Romans, being badly off for soldiers, armed a number of slaves and gave them over to be drilled by Sempronius Gracchus, he in a short time made them into a serviceable army. So too, as I have already mentioned, Pelopidas and Epaminondas after rescuing Thebes, their native city, from Spartan thraldom, in a short time made such valiant soldiers of the Theban peasantry, as to be able with their aid not only to withstand, but even to defeat the Spartan armies. So that the question may seem to be equally balanced, excellence on one side generally finding excellence on the other.

A good army, however, when left without a good leader, as the Macedonian army was on the death of Alexander, or as those veterans were who had fought in the civil wars, is apt to grow restless and turbulent. Wherefore I am convinced that it is better to trust to the captain who has time allowed him to discipline his men, and means wherewith to equip them, than to a tumultuary host with a chance leader of its own choosing. But twofold is the merit and twofold the glory of those captains who not only have had to subdue their enemies, but also before encountering them to organize and discipline their forces. This, however, is a task requiring qualities so seldom combined, that were many of those captains who now enjoy a great name with the world, called on to perform it, they would be much less thought of than they are.

CHAPTER XIV

Of the effect produced in Battle by strange and unexpected Sights or Sounds.

That the disorder occasioned by strange and unexpected sights or sounds may have momentous consequences in combat, might be shown by many instances, but by none better than by what befell in the battle fought between the Romans and the Volscians, when Quintius, the Roman general, seeing one wing of his army begin to waver, shouted aloud to his men to stand firm, for the other wing was already victorious. Which words of his giving confidence to his own troops and striking the enemy with dismay won him the battle. But if a cry like this, produce great effect on a well disciplined army, far greater must be its effect on one which is ill disciplined and disorderly. For by such a wind the whole mass will be moved, as I shall show by a well-known instance happening in our own times.

A few years ago the city of Perugia was split into the two factions of the Baglioni and the Oddi, the former holding the government, the latter being in exile. The Oddeschi, however, with the help of friends, having got together an armed force which they lodged in villages of their own near Perugia, obtained, by the favour of some of their party, an entrance into the city by night, and moving forward without discovery, came as far as the public square. And as all the streets of Perugia are barred with chains drawn across them at their corners, the Oddeschi had in front of them a man who carried an iron hammer wherewith to break the fastenings of the chains so that horsemen might pass. When the only chain remaining unbroken was that which closed the public square, the alarm having now been given, the hammerman was so impeded by the crowd pressing behind him that he could not raise his arm to strike freely. Whereupon, to get more room for his work, he called aloud to the others to stand back; and the word back passing from rank to rank those furthest off began to run, and, presently, the others also, with such precipitancy, that they fell into utter disorder. In this way, and from this trifling circumstance, the attempt of the Oddeschi came to nothing.

Here we may note that discipline is needed in an army, not so much to enable it to fight according to a settled order, as that it may not be thrown into confusion by every insignificant accident. For a tumultuary host is useless in war, simply because every word, or cry, or sound, may throw it into a panic and cause it to fly. Wherefore it behoves a good captain to provide that certain fixed persons shall receive his orders and pass them on to the rest, and to accustom his soldiers to look to these persons, and to them only, to be informed what his orders are. For whenever this precaution is neglected the gravest mishaps are constantly seen to ensue.

As regards strange and unexpected sights, every captain should endeavour while his army is actually engaged with the enemy, to effect some such feint or diversion as will encourage his own men and dismay his adversary since this of all things that can happen is the likeliest to ensure victory. In evidence whereof we may cite the example of Cneius Sulpitius, the Roman dictator, who, when about to give battle to the Gauls, after arming his sutlers and camp followers, mounted them on mules and other beasts of burden, furnished them with spears and banners to look like cavalry, and placing them behind a hill, ordered them on a given signal, when the fight was at the hottest, to appear and show themselves to the enemy. All which being carried out as he had arranged, threw the Gauls into such alarm, that they lost the battle.

A good captain, therefore, has two things to see to: first, to contrive how by some sudden surprise he may throw his enemy into confusion; and next, to be prepared should the enemy use a like stratagem against him to discover and defeat it; as the stratagem of Semiramis was defeated by the King of India. For Semiramis seeing that this king had elephants in great numbers, to dismay him by showing that she, too, was well supplied, caused the skins of many oxen and buffaloes to be sewn together in the shape of elephants and placed upon camels and sent to the front. But the trick being detected by the king, turned out not only useless but hurtful to its contriver. In a battle which the Dictator Mamercus fought against the people of Fidenae, the latter, to strike terror into the minds of the Romans, contrived that while the combat raged a number of soldiers should issue from Fidenae bearing lances tipped with fire, thinking that the Romans, disturbed by so strange a sight, would be thrown into confusion.

We are to note, however, with regard to such contrivances, that if they are to serve any useful end, they should *be* formidable as well as *seem* so; for when they menace a real danger, their weak points are not so soon discerned. When they have more of pretence than reality, it will be well either to dispense with them altogether, or resorting to them, to keep them, like the muleteers of Sulpitius, in the background, so that they be not too readily found out. For any weakness inherent in them is soon discovered if they be brought near, when, as happened with the elephants of Semiramis and the fiery spears of the men of Fidenae, they do harm rather than good. For although by this last-mentioned device the Romans at the first were somewhat disconcerted, so soon as the dictator came up and began to chide them, asking if they were not ashamed to fly like bees from smoke, and calling on them to turn on their enemy, and "*with her own flames efface that Fidenae whom their benefits could not conciliate,*" they took courage; so that the device proved of no service to its contrivers, who were vanquished in the battle.

CHAPTER XV

That one and not many should head an Army: and why it is harmful to have more Leaders than one.

The men of Fidenae rising against the colonists whom the Romans had settled among them, and putting them to the sword, the Romans to avenge the insult appointed four tribunes with consular powers: one of whom they retained to see to the defence of Rome, while the other three were sent against the Fidenati and the Veientines. But these three falling out among themselves, and being divided in their counsels, returned from their mission with discredit though not with loss. Of which discredit they were themselves the cause. That they sustained no loss was due to the valour of their soldiers But the senate perceiving the source of the mischief, to the end that one man might put to rights what three had thrown into confusion, resorted to the appointment of a dictator.

Here we see the disadvantage of having several leaders in one army or in a town which has to defend itself. And the case could not be put in clearer words than by Titus Livius, where he says, "The three tribunes with consular authority gave proof how hurtful it is in war to have many leaders; for each forming a different opinion, and each abiding by his own, they threw opportunities in the way of their enemies." And though this example suffice by itself to show the disadvantage in war of divided commands, to make the matter still plainer I shall cite two further instances, one ancient and one modern.

In the year 1500, Louis XII. of France, after recovering Milan, sent troops to restore Pisa to the Florentines, Giovambattista Ridolfi and Luca d'Antonio Albizzi going with them as commissaries. Now, because Giovambattista had a great name, and was older than Luca, the latter left the whole management of everything to him; and although he did not show his jealousy of him by opposing him, he betrayed it by his silence, and by being so careless and indifferent about everything, that he gave no help in the business of the siege either by word or deed, just as though he had been a person of no account. But when, in consequence of an accident, Giovambattista had to return to Florence, all this was changed; for Luca, remaining in sole charge, behaved with the greatest courage, prudence, and zeal, all which qualities had been hidden while he held a joint command. Further to bear me out I shall again borrow the words of Titus Livius, who, in relating how when Quintius and Agrippa his colleague were sent by the Romans against the Equians, Agrippa contrived that the conduct of the war should rest with Quintius, observes, "Most wholesome is it that in affairs of great moment, supreme authority be vested in one man." Very different, however, is the course followed by the republics and princes of our own days, who, thinking to be better served, are used to appoint several captains or commissioners to fill one command; a practice giving rise to so much confusion, that were we seeking for the causes of the overthrow of the French and Italian armies in recent times, we should find this to be the most active of any.

Rightly, therefore, may we conclude that in sending forth an army upon service, it is wiser to entrust it to one man of ordinary prudence, than to two of great parts but with a divided command.

CHAPTER XVI

That in Times of Difficulty true Worth is sought after; whereas in quiet Times it is not the most deserving, but those who are recommended by Wealth or Connection who are most in favour.

It always has happened and always will, that the great and admirable men of a republic are neglected in peaceful times; because at such seasons many citizens are found, who, envying the reputation these men have justly earned, seek to be regarded not merely as their equals but as their superiors. Touching this there is a notable passage in Thucydides, the Greek historian, where he tells how the republic of Athens coming victorious out of the Peloponessian war, wherein she had bridled the pride of Sparta, and brought almost the whole of Greece under her authority, was encouraged by the greatness of her renown to propose to herself the conquest of Sicily. In Athens this scheme was much debated, Alcibiades and certain others who had the public welfare very little in their thoughts, but who hoped that the enterprise, were they placed in command, might minister to their fame, recommending that it should be undertaken. Nicias, on the other hand, one of the best esteemed of the Athenian citizens, was against it, and in addressing the people, gave it as the strongest reason for trusting his advice, that in advising them not to engage in this war, he urged what was not for his own advantage; for he knew that while Athens remained at peace numberless citizens were ready to take precedence of him: whereas, were war declared, he was certain that none would rank before him or even be looked upon as his equal.

Here we see that in tranquil times republics are subject to the infirmity of lightly esteeming their worthiest citizens. And this offends these persons for two reasons: first, because they are not given the place they deserve; and second, because they see unworthy men and of abilities inferior to their own, as much or more considered than they. Injustice such as this has caused the ruin of many republics. For citizens who find themselves undeservedly slighted, and perceive the cause to be that the times are tranquil and not troubled, will strive to change the times by stirring up wars hurtful to the public welfare. When I look for remedies for this state of things, I find two: first, to keep the citizens poor, so that wealth without worth shall corrupt neither them nor others; second, to be so prepared for war as always to be ready to make war; for then there will always be a need for worthy citizens, as was the case in Rome in early times. For as Rome constantly kept her armies in the field, there was constant opportunity for men to display their valour, nor was it possible to deprive a deserving man of his post and give it to another who was not deserving. Or if ever this were done by inadvertency, or by way of experiment, there forthwith resulted such disorder and danger, that the city at once retraced its steps and reverted to the true path. But other republics which are not regulated on the same plan, and make war only when driven to it by necessity, cannot help committing this injustice, nay, will constantly run into it, when, if the great citizen who finds himself slighted be vindictive, and have some credit and following in the city, disorder will always ensue. And though Rome escaped this danger for a time, she too, as has elsewhere been said, having no longer, after she had conquered Carthage and Antiochus, any fear of war, came to think she might commit her armies to whom she would, making less account of the valour of her captains than of those other qualities which gain favour with the people. Accordingly we find Paulus Emilius rejected oftener than once when he sought the consulship; nor, in fact, obtaining it until the Macedonian war broke out, which, being judged a formidable business, was by the voice of the whole city committed to his management. After the year 1494 our city of Florence was involved in a series of wars, in conducting which none of our citizens had any success until chance threw the command into the hands of one who showed us how an army should be led. This was Antonio Giacomini, and so long as there were dangerous wars on foot, all rivalry on the part of other citizens was suspended; and whenever a captain or commissary had to be appointed he was unopposed. But when a war came to be undertaken, as to the issue of which no misgivings were felt, and which promised both honour and preferment, so numerous were the competitors for command, that three commissaries having to be chosen to conduct the siege of Pisa, Antonio was left out; and though it cannot with certainty be shown that any harm resulted to our republic from his not having been sent on this enterprise, we may reasonably conjecture that such was indeed the case. For as the people of Pisa were then without means either for subsistence or defence, it may be believed that had Antonio been there he would have reduced them to such extremities as would have forced them to surrender at discretion to the Florentines. But Pisa being besieged by captains who knew neither how to blockade nor how to storm it, held out so long, that the Florentines, who should have reduced it by force, were obliged to buy its submission. Neglect like this might well move Antonio to resentment; and he must needs have been both very patient and very forgiving if he felt no desire to revenge himself when he could, by the ruin of the city or by injuries to individual citizens. But a republic should beware not to rouse such feelings, as I shall show in the following Chapter.

CHAPTER XVII

That we are not to offend a Man, and then send him to fill an important Office or Command.

A republic should think twice before appointing to an important command a citizen who has sustained notable wrong at the hands of his fellow-citizens. Claudius Nero, quitting the army with which he was opposing Hannibal, went with a part of his forces into the March of Ancona, designing to join the other consul there, and after joining him to attack Hasdrubal before he came up with his brother. Now Claudius had previously commanded against Hasdrubal in Spain, and after driving him with his army into such a position that it seemed he must either fight at a disadvantage or perish by famine, had been outwitted by his adversary, who, while diverting his attention with proposals of terms, contrived to slip through his hands and rob him of the opportunity for effecting his destruction. This becoming known in Rome brought Claudius into so much discredit both with the senate and people, that to his great mortification and displeasure, he was slightingly spoken of by the whole city. But being afterwards made consul and sent to oppose Hannibal, he took the course mentioned above, which was in itself so hazardous that all Rome was filled with doubt and anxiety until tidings came of Hasdrubal's defeat. When subsequently asked why he had played so dangerous a game, wherein without urgent necessity he had staked the very existence of Rome, Claudius answered, he had done so because he knew that were he to succeed he would recover whatever credit he had lost in Spain; while if he failed, and his attempt had an untoward issue, he would be revenged on that city and on those citizens who had so ungratefully and indiscreetly wronged him.

But if resentment for an offence like this so deeply moved a Roman citizen at a time when Rome was still uncorrupted, we should consider how it may act on the citizen of a State not constituted as Rome then was. And because there is no certain remedy we can apply to such disorders when they arise in republics, it follows that it is impossible to establish a republic which shall endure always; since in a thousand unforeseen ways ruin may overtake it.

CHAPTER XVIII

That it is the highest Quality of a Captain to be able to forestall the designs of his Adversary.

It was a saying of Epaminondas the Theban that nothing was so useful and necessary for a commander as to be able to see through the intentions and designs of his adversary. And because it is hard to come at this knowledge directly, the more credit is due to him who reaches it by conjecture. Yet sometimes it is easier to fathom an enemy's designs than to construe his actions; and not so much those actions which are done at a distance from us, as those done in our presence and under our very eyes. For instance, it has often happened that when a battle has lasted till nightfall, the winner has believed himself the loser, and the loser has believed himself the winner and that this mistake has led him who made it to follow a course hurtful to himself. It was from a mistake of this sort, that Brutus and Cassius lost the battle of Philippi. For though Brutus was victorious with his wing of the army Cassius, whose wing was beaten, believed the entire army to be defeated, and under this belief gave way to despair and slew himself. So too, in our own days, in the battle fought by Francis, king of France, with the Swiss at Santa Cecilia in Lombardy, when night fell, those of the Swiss who remained unbroken, not knowing that the rest had been routed and slain, thought they had the victory; and so believing would not retreat, but, remaining on the field, renewed the combat the following morning to their great disadvantage. Nor were they the only sufferers from their mistake, since the armies of the Pope and of Spain were also misled by it, and well-nigh brought to destruction. For on the false report of a victory they crossed the Po, and had they only advanced a little further must have been made prisoners by the victorious French.

An instance is recorded of a like mistake having been made in the camps both of the Romans and of the Equians. For the Consul Sempronius being in command against the Equians, and giving the enemy battle, the engagement lasted with varying success till nightfall, when as both armies had suffered what was almost a defeat, neither returned to their camp, but each drew off to the neighboring hills where they thought they would be safer. The Romans separated into two divisions, one of which with the consul, the other with the centurion Tempanius by whose valour the army had that day been saved from utter rout. At daybreak the consul, without waiting for further tidings of the enemy, made straight for Rome; and the Equians, in like manner, withdrew to their own country. For as each supposed the other to be victorious, neither thought much of leaving their camp to be plundered by the enemy. It so chanced, however, that Tempanius, who was himself retreating with the second division of the Roman army, fell in with certain wounded Equians, from whom he learned that their commanders had fled, abandoning their camp; on hearing which, he at once returned to the Roman camp and secured it, and then, after sacking the camp of the Equians, went back victorious to Rome. His success, as we see, turned entirely on his being the first to be informed of the enemy's condition. And here we are to note that it may often happen that both the one and the other of two opposed armies shall fall into the same disorder, and be reduced to the same straits; in which case, that which soonest detects the other's distress is sure to come off best.

I shall give an instance of this which occurred recently in our own country. In the year 1498, when the Florentines had a great army in the territory of Pisa and had closely invested the town, the Venetians, who had undertaken its protection, seeing no other way to save it, resolved to make a diversion in its favour by attacking the territories of the Florentines in another quarter. Wherefore, having assembled a strong force, they entered

Tuscany by the Val di Lamona, and seizing on the village of Marradi, besieged the stronghold of Castiglione which stands on the height above it. Getting word of this, the Florentines sought to relieve Marradi, without weakening the army which lay round Pisa. They accordingly raised a new levy of foot-soldiers, and equipped a fresh squadron of horse, which they despatched to Marradi under the joint command of Jacopo IV. d'Appiano, lord of Piombino, and Count Rinuccio of Marciano. These troops taking up their position on the hill above Marradi, the Venetians withdrew from the investment of Castiglione and lodged themselves in the village. But when the two armies had confronted one another for several days, both began to suffer sorely from want of victuals and other necessaries, and neither of them daring to attack the other, or knowing to what extremities the other was reduced, both simultaneously resolved to strike their camps the following morning, and to retreat, the Venetians towards Berzighella and Faenza, the Florentines towards Casaglia and the Mugello. But at daybreak, when both armies had begun to remove their baggage, it so happened that an old woman, whose years and poverty permitted her to pass unnoticed, leaving the village of Marradi, came to the Florentine camp, where were certain of her kinsfolk whom she desired to visit. Learning from her that the Venetians were in retreat, the Florentine commanders took courage, and changing their plan, went in pursuit of the enemy as though they had dislodged them, sending word to Florence that they had repulsed the Venetians and gained a victory. But in truth this victory was wholly due to their having notice of the enemy's movements before the latter had notice of theirs. For had that notice been given to the Venetians first, it would have wrought against us the same results as it actually wrought for us.

CHAPTER XIX

Whether Indulgence or Severity be more necessary for controlling a Multitude.

The Roman Republic was distracted by the feuds of the nobles and commons. Nevertheless, on war breaking out, Quintius and Appius Claudius were sent forth in command of Roman armies. From his harshness and severity to his soldiers, Appius was so ill obeyed by them, that after sustaining what almost amounted to a defeat, he had to resign his command. Quintius, on the contrary, by kindly and humane treatment, kept his men obedient and returned victorious to Rome. From this it might seem that to govern a large body of men, it is better to be humane than haughty, and kindly rather than severe.

And yet Cornelius Tacitus, with whom many other authors are agreed, pronounces a contrary opinion where he says, *"In governing a multitude it avails more to punish than to be compliant."* If it be asked how these opposite views can be reconciled, I answer that you exercise authority either over men used to regard you as their equal, or over men who have always been subject to you. When those over whom you exercise authority are your equals, you cannot trust wholly to punishment or to that severity of which Tacitus speaks. And since in Rome itself the commons had equal weight with the nobles, none appointed their captain for a time only, could control them by using harshness and severity. Accordingly we find that those Roman captains who gained the love of their soldiers and were considerate of them, often achieved greater results than those who made themselves feared by them in an unusual degree, unless, like Manlius Torquatus, these last were endowed with consummate valour. But he who has to govern subjects such as those of whom Tacitus speaks, to prevent their growing insolent and trampling upon him by reason of his too great easiness, must resort to punishment rather than to compliance. Still, to escape hatred, punishment should be moderate in degree, for to make himself hated is never for the interest of any prince. And to escape hatred, a prince has chiefly to guard against tampering with the property of any of his subjects; for where nothing is to be gained by it, no prince will desire to shed blood, unless, as seldom happens, constrained to do so by necessity. But where advantage is to be gained thereby, blood will always flow, and neither the desire to shed it, nor causes for shedding it will ever be wanting, as I have fully shown when discussing this subject in another treatise.

Quintius therefore was more deserving of praise than Appius. Nevertheless the opinion of Tacitus, duly restricted and not understood as applying to a case like that of Appius, merits approval. But since I have spoken of punishment and indulgence, it seems not out of place to show how a single act of humanity availed more than arms with the citizens of Falerii.

CHAPTER XX

How one humane act availed more with the men of Falerii, than all the might of the Roman Arms.

When the besieging army of the Romans lay round Falerii, the master of a school wherein the best-born youths of the city were taught, thinking to curry favour with Camillus and the Romans, came forth from the town with these boys, on pretence of giving them exercise, and bringing them into the camp where Camillus was, presented them to him, saying, "*To ransom these that city would yield itself into your hands.*" Camillus, however, not only rejected this offer, but causing the schoolmaster to be stripped and his hands tied behind him, gave each of the boys a scourge, and bade them lead the fellow back to the town scourging him as they went. When the citizens of Falerii heard of this, so much were they pleased with the humanity and integrity of Camillus, that they resolved to surrender their town to him without further defence.

This authentic instance may lead us to believe that a humane and kindly action may sometimes touch men's minds more nearly than a harsh and cruel one; and that those cities and provinces into which the instruments and engines of war, with every other violence to which men resort, have failed to force a way, may be thrown open to a single act of tenderness, mercy, chastity, or generosity. Whereof history supplies us with many examples besides the one which I have just now noticed. For we find that when the arms of Rome were powerless to drive Pyrrhus out of Italy, he was moved to depart by the generosity of Fabritius in disclosing to him the proposal which his slave had made the Romans to poison him. Again, we read how Scipio gained less reputation in Spain by the capture of New Carthage, than by his virtue in restoring a young and beautiful wife unviolated to her husband; the fame of which action won him the love of the whole province. We see, too, how much this generous temper is esteemed by a people in its great men; and how much it is praised by historians and by those who write the lives of princes, as well as by those who lay down rules of human conduct. Among whom Xenophon has taken great pains to show what honours, and victories, and how fair a fame accrued to Cyrus from his being kindly and gracious, without taint of pride, or cruelty, or luxury, or any other of those vices which cast a stain upon men's lives.

And yet when we note that Hannibal, by methods wholly opposite to these, achieved splendid victories and a great renown, I think I am bound to say something in my next Chapter as to how this happened.

CHAPTER XXI

How it happened that Hannibal pursuing a course contrary to that taken by Scipio, wrought the same results in Italy which the other achieved in Spain.

Some, I suspect, may marvel to find a captain, taking a contrary course, nevertheless arrive at the same ends as those who have pursued the methods above spoken of; since it must seem as though success did not depend on the causes I have named; nay, that if glory and fame are to be won in other ways, these causes neither add to our strength nor advance our fortunes. Wherefore, to make my meaning plain, and not to part company with the men of whom I have been speaking, I say, that as, on the one hand, we see Scipio enter Spain, and by his humane and generous conduct at once secure the good-will of the province, and the admiration and reverence of its inhabitants, so on the other hand, we see Hannibal enter Italy, and by methods wholly opposite, to wit, by violence and rapine, by cruelty and treachery of every kind, effect in that country the very same results. For all the States of Italy revolted in his favour, and all the Italian nations ranged themselves on his side.

When we seek to know why this was, several reasons present themselves, the first being that men so passionately love change, that, commonly speaking, those who are well off are as eager for it as those who are badly off: for as already has been said with truth, men are pampered by prosperity, soured by adversity. This love of change, therefore, makes them open the door to any one who puts himself at the head of new movements in their country, and if he be a foreigner they adopt his cause, if a fellow-countryman they gather round him and become his partisans and supporters; so that whatever methods he may there use, he will succeed in making great progress. Moreover, men being moved by two chief passions, love and fear, he who makes himself feared commands with no less authority than he who makes himself loved; nay, as a rule, is followed and obeyed more implicitly than the other. It matters little, however, which of these two ways a captain chooses to follow, provided he be of transcendent valour, and has thereby won for himself a great name For when, like Hannibal or Scipio, a man is very valiant, this quality will cloak any error he may commit in seeking either to be too much loved or too much feared. Yet from each of these two tendencies, grave mischiefs, and such as lead to the ruin of a prince, may arise. For he who would be greatly loved, if he swerve ever so little from the right road, becomes contemptible; while he who would be greatly feared, if he go a jot too far, incurs hatred. And since it is impossible, our nature not allowing it, to adhere to the exact mean, it is essential that any excess should be balanced by an exceeding valour, as it was in Hannibal and Scipio. And yet we find that even they, while they were exalted by the methods they followed, were also injured by them. How they were exalted has been shown. The injury which Scipio suffered was, that in Spain his soldiers, in concert with certain of his allies, rose against him, for no other reason than that they stood in no fear of him. For men are so restless, that if ever so small a door be opened to their ambition, they forthwith forget all the love they have borne their prince in return for his graciousness and goodness, as did these soldiers and allies of Scipio; when, to correct the mischief, he was forced to use something of a cruelty foreign to his nature.

As to Hannibal, we cannot point to any particular instance wherein his cruelty or want of faith are seen to have been directly hurtful to him; but we may well believe that Naples and other towns which remained loyal to the Roman people, did so by reason of the dread which his character inspired. This, however, is abundantly clear, that his inhumanity made him more detested by the Romans than any other enemy they ever had; so that while to Pyrrhus, in Italy with his army, they gave up the traitor who offered to poison him, Hannibal, even when disarmed and a fugitive, they never forgave, until they had compassed his death.

To Hannibal, therefore, from his being accounted impious, perfidious, and cruel, these disadvantages resulted; but, on the other hand, there accrued to him one great gain, noticed with admiration by all historians, namely, that in his army, although made up of men of every race and country, no dissensions ever broke out among the soldiers themselves, nor any mutiny against their leader. This we can only ascribe to the awe which his character inspired, which together with the great name his valour had won for him, had the effect of keeping his soldiers quiet and united. I repeat, therefore, that it is of little moment which method a captain may follow if he be endowed with such valour as will bear him out in the course which he adopts. For, as I have said, there are disadvantages incident to both methods unless corrected by extraordinary valour.

And now, since I have spoken of Scipio and Hannibal, the former of whom by praiseworthy, the latter by odious qualities, effected the same results, I must not, I think, omit to notice the characters of two Roman citizens, who by different, yet both by honourable methods, obtained a like glory.

Chapter XXII

That the severity of Manlius Torquatus and the gentleness of Valerius Corvinus won for both the same Glory.

There lived in Rome, at the same time, two excellent captains, Manlius Torquatus and Valerius Corvinus, equal in their triumphs and in their renown, and in the valour which in obtaining these they had displayed against the enemy; but who in the conduct of their armies and treatment of their soldiers, followed very different methods. For Manlius, in his command, resorted to every kind of severity, never sparing his men fatigue, nor remitting punishment; while Valerius, on the contrary, treated them with all kindness and consideration, and was easy and familiar in his intercourse with them. So that while the one, to secure the obedience of his soldiers, put his own son to death, the other never dealt harshly with any man. Yet, for all this diversity in their modes of acting, each had the same success against the enemy, and each obtained the same advantages both for the republic and for himself. For no soldier of theirs ever flinched in battle, or rose in mutiny against them, or in any particular opposed their will; though the commands of Manlius were of such severity that any order of excessive rigour came to be spoken of as a *Manlian order*.

Here, then, we have to consider first of all why Manlius was obliged to use such severity; next, why Valerius could behave so humanely; thirdly, how it was that these opposite methods had the same results; and lastly, which of the two methods it is better and more useful for us to follow. Now, if we well examine the character of Manlius from the moment when Titus Livius first begins to make mention of him, we shall find him to have been endowed with a rare vigour both of mind and body, dutiful in his behaviour to his father and to his country, and most reverent to his superiors. All which we see in his slaying the Gaul, in his defence of his father against the tribune, and in the words in which, before going forth to fight the Gaul, he addressed the consul, when he said, "Although assured of victory, never will I without thy bidding engage an enemy." But when such a man as this attains to command, he looks to find all others like himself; his dauntless spirit prompts him to engage in daring enterprises, and to insist on their being carried out. And this is certain, that where things hard to execute are ordered to be done, the order must be enforced with sternness, since, otherwise, it will be disobeyed.

And here be it noted that if you would be obeyed you must know how to command, and that they alone have this knowledge who have measured their power to enforce, with the willingness of others to yield obedience; and who issue their orders when they find these conditions combining, but, otherwise, abstain. Wherefore, a wise man was wont to say that to hold a republic by force, there must be a proportion between him who uses the force and him against whom it is used; and that while this proportion obtains the force will operate; but that when he who suffers is stronger than he who uses the force, we may expect to see it brought to an end at any moment.

But returning to the matter in hand, I say that to command things hard of execution, requires hardness in him who gives the command, and that a man of this temper and who issues such commands, cannot look to enforce them by gentleness. He who is not of such a temper must be careful not to impose tasks of extraordinary difficulty, but may use his natural gentleness in imposing such as are ordinary. For common punishments are not imputed to the prince, but to the laws and ordinances which he has to administer.

We must believe, therefore, that Manlius was constrained to act with severity by the unusual character of the commands which his natural disposition prompted him to issue. Such commands are useful in a republic, as restoring its ordinances to their original efficacy and excellence. And were a republic, as I have before observed, fortunate enough to come frequently under the influence of men who, by their example, reinforce its laws, and not only retard its progress towards corruption, but bring it back to its first perfection, it might endure for ever.

Manlius, therefore, was of those who by the severity of their commands maintained the military discipline of Rome; urged thereto, in the first place, by his natural temper, and next by the desire that whatever he was minded to command should be done. Valerius, on the other hand, could afford to act humanely, because for him it was enough if all were done which in a Roman army it was customary to do. And, since the customs of that army were good customs, they sufficed to gain him honour, while at the same time their maintenance cost him no effort, nor threw on him the burthen of punishing transgressors; as well because there were none who trangressed, as because had there been any, they would, as I have said, have imputed their punishment to the ordinary rules of discipline, and not to the severity of their commander. In this way Valerius had room to exercise that humane disposition which enabled him at once to gain influence over his soldiers and to content them. Hence it was that both these captains obtaining the same obedience, could, while following different methods, arrive at the same ends. Those, however, who seek to imitate them may chance to fall into the errors of which I have already spoken, in connection with Hannibal and Scipio, as breeding contempt or hatred, and which are only to be corrected by the presence of extraordinary valour, and not otherwise.

It rests now to determine which of these two methods is the more to be commended. This, I take it, is matter of dispute, since both methods have their advocates. Those writers, however, who have laid down rules for the conduct of princes, describe a character approaching more nearly to that of Valerius than to that of Manlius; and Xenophon, whom I have already cited, while giving many instances of the humanity of Cyrus, conforms closely to what Livius tells us of Valerius. For Valerius being made consul against the Samnites, on the eve of battle spoke to his men with the same kindliness with which he always treated them; and Livius, after telling us what he said, remarks of him: "Never was there a leader more familiar with his men; cheerfully sharing with the meanest among them every hardship and fatigue. Even in the military games, wherein those of the same rank were wont to make trial of their strength or swiftness, he would good-naturedly take a part, nor disdain any adversary who offered; meeting victory or defeat with an unruffled temper and an unchanged countenance. When called on to act, his bounty and generosity never fell short. When he had to speak, he was as mindful of the feelings of others as of his own dignity. And, what more than anything else secures the popular favour, he maintained when exercising his magistracies the same bearing he had worn in seeking them."

Of Manlius also, Titus Livius speaks in like honourable terms, pointing out that his severity in putting his son to death brought the Roman army to that pitch of discipline which enabled it to prevail against the Latins, nay, he goes so far in his praises that after describing the whole order of the battle, comparing the strength of both armies, and showing all the dangers the Romans ran, and the difficulties they had to surmount, he winds up by saying, that it was the valour of Manlius which alone gained for them this great victory, and that whichever side had Manlius for its leader must have won the day. So that weighing all that the historians tell us of these two captains, it might be difficult to decide between them.

Nevertheless, not to leave the question entirely open, I say, that for a citizen living under a republic, I think the conduct of Manlius more deserving of praise and less dangerous in its consequences. For methods like his tend only to the public good and in no way subserve private ends. He who shows himself harsh and stern at all times and to all men alike, and is seen to care only for the common welfare, will never gain himself partisans, since this is not the way to win personal friends, to whom, as I said before, the name of partisans is given. For a republic, therefore, no line of conduct could be more useful or more to be desired than this, because in following it the public interest is not neglected, and no room is given to suspect personal ambition.

But the contrary holds as to the methods followed by Valerius. For though the public service they render be the same, misgivings must needs arise that the personal good-will which, in the course of a prolonged command, a captain obtains from his soldiers, may lead to consequences fatal to the public liberty. And if this was not found to happen in the case of Valerius, it was because the minds of the Roman people were not yet corrupted, and because they had never remained for a long time and continuously under his command.

Had we, however, like Xenophon, to consider what is most for the interest of a prince, we should have to give up Manlius and hold by Valerius; for, undoubtedly, a prince should strive to gain the love of his soldiers and subjects, as well as their obedience. The latter he can secure by discipline and by his reputation for valour. But for the former he will be indebted to his affability, kindliness, gentleness, and all those other like qualities which were possessed by Valerius, and which are described by Xenophon as existing in Cyrus. That a prince should be personally loved and have his army wholly devoted to him is consistent with the character of his government; but that this should happen to a person of private station does not consist with his position as a citizen who has to live in conformity with the laws and in subordination to the magistrates. We read in the early annals of the Venetian Republic, that once, on the return of the fleet, a dispute broke out between the sailors and the people, resulting in tumults and armed violence which neither the efforts of the public officers, the respect felt for particular citizens, nor the authority of the magistrates could quell. But on a certain gentleman, who the year before had been in command of these sailors, showing himself among them, straightway, from the love they bore him, they submitted to his authority and withdrew from the fray. Which deference on their part aroused such jealousy and suspicion in the minds of the Venetian senators that very soon after they got rid of this gentleman, either by death or exile.

The sum of the matter, therefore, is, that the methods followed by Valerius are useful in a prince, but pernicious in a private citizen, both for his country and for himself, for his country, because such methods pave the way to a tyranny; for himself, because his fellow-citizens, growing suspicious of his conduct, are constrained to protect themselves to his hurt. And conversely, I maintain, that the methods of Manlius, while hurtful in a prince are useful in a citizen, and in the highest degree for his country; and, moreover, seldom give offence, unless the hatred caused by his severity be augmented by the jealousy which the fame of his other virtues inspires: a matter now to be considered in connection with the banishment of Camillas.

CHAPTER XXIII

Why Camillus was banished from Rome.

It has been shown above how methods like those of Valerius are hurtful to the citizen who employs them and to his country, while methods like those of Manlius are advantageous for a man's country, though sometimes they be hurtful to the man himself. This is well seen in the example of Camillus, whose bearing more nearly resembled that of Manlius than that of Valerius, so that Titus Livius, in speaking of him, says, *"His virtues were at once hated and admired by his soldiers."* What gained him their admiration was his care for their safety, his prudence, his magnanimity, and the good order he maintained in conducting and commanding them. What made him hated was his being more stern to punish than bountiful to reward; and Livius instances the following circumstances as giving rise to this hatred. First, his having applied the money got by the sale of the goods of the Veientines to public purposes, and not divided it along with the rest of the spoils. Second, his having, on the occasion of his triumph, caused his chariot to be drawn by four white horses, seeking in his pride, men said, to make himself the equal of the sun god. And, third, his having vowed to Apollo a tenth of the Veientine plunder, which, if he was to fulfil his vow, he had to recover from his soldiers, into whose hands it had already come.

Herein we may well and readily discern what causes tend to make a prince hateful to his people; the chief whereof is the depriving them of some advantage. And this is a matter of much importance. For when a man is deprived of what is in itself useful, he never forgets it, and every trifling occasion recalls it to his mind; and because such occasions recur daily, he is every day reminded of his loss. Another error which we are here taught to guard against, is the appearing haughty and proud, than which nothing is more distasteful to a people, and most of all to a free people; for although such pride and haughtiness do them no hurt, they nevertheless hold in detestation any who display these qualities. Every show of pride, therefore, a prince should shun as he would a rock, since to invite hatred without resulting advantage were utterly rash and futile.

CHAPTER XXIV

That prolonged Commands brought Rome to Servitude.

If we well examine the course of Roman history, we shall find two causes leading to the break-up of that republic: one, the dissensions which arose in connection with the agrarian laws; the other, the prolongation of commands. For had these matters been rightly understood from the first, and due remedies applied, the freedom of Rome had been far more lasting, and, possibly, less disturbed. And although, as touching the prolongation of commands, we never find any tumult breaking out in Rome on that account, we do in fact discern how much harm was done to the city by the ascendency which certain of its citizens thereby gained. This mischief indeed would not have arisen, if other citizens whose period of office was extended had been as good and wise as Lucius Quintius, whose virtue affords a notable example. For terms of accord having been settled between the senate and commons of Rome, the latter, thinking their tribunes well able to withstand the ambition of the nobles, prolonged their authority for a year. Whereupon, the senate, not to be outdone by the commons, proposed, out of rivalry, to extend the consulship of Quintius. He, however, refused absolutely to lend himself to their designs, and insisted on their appointing new consuls, telling them that they should seek to discredit evil examples, not add to them by setting worse. Had this prudence and virtue of his been shared by all the citizens of Rome, the practice of prolonging the terms of civil offices would not have been suffered to establish itself, nor have led to the kindred practice of extending the term of military commands, which in progress of time effected the ruin of their republic.

The first military commander whose term was extended, was Publius Philo; for when his consulship was about to expire, he being then engaged in the siege of Palaeopolis, the senate, seeing he had the victory in his hands, would not displace him by a successor, but appointed him *Proconsul*, which office he was the first to hold. Now, although in thus acting the senate did what they thought best for the public good, nevertheless it was this act of theirs that in time brought Rome to slavery. For the further the Romans carried their arms, the more necessary it seemed to them to grant similar extensions of command, and the oftener they, in fact, did so. This gave rise to two disadvantages: first that a smaller number of men were trained to command; second, that by the long continuance of his command a captain gained so much influence and ascendency over his soldiers that in time they came to hold the senate of no account, and looked only to him. This it was, that enabled Sylla and Marius to find adherents ready to follow them even to the public detriment, and enabled Caesar to overthrow the liberties of his country; whereas, had the Romans never prolonged the period of authority, whether civil or military, though they might have taken longer to build up their empire, they certainly had been later in incurring servitude.

CHAPTER XXV

Of the poverty of Cincinnatus and of many other Roman Citizens.

Elsewhere I have shown that no ordinance is of such advantage to a commonwealth, as one which enforces poverty on its citizens. And although it does not appear what particular law it was that had this operation in Rome (especially since we know the agrarian law to have been stubbornly resisted), we find, as a fact, that four hundred years after the city was founded, great poverty still prevailed there; and may assume that nothing helped so much to produce this result as the knowledge that the path to honours and preferment was closed to none, and that merit was sought after wheresoever it was to be found; for this manner of conferring honours made riches the less courted. In proof whereof I shall cite one instance only.

When the consul Minutius was beset in his camp by the Equians, the Roman people were filled with such alarm lest their army should be destroyed, that they appointed a dictator, always their last stay in seasons of peril. Their choice fell on Lucius Quintius Cincinnatus, who at the time was living on his small farm of little more than four acres, which he tilled with his own hand. The story is nobly told by Titus Livius where he says: "This is worth listening to by those who contemn all things human as compared with riches, and think that glory and excellence can have no place unless accompanied by lavish wealth." Cincinnatus, then, was ploughing in his little field, when there arrived from Rome the messengers sent by the senate to tell him he had been made dictator, and inform him of the dangers which threatened the Republic. Putting on his gown, he hastened to Rome, and getting together an army, marched to deliver Minutius. But when he had defeated and spoiled the enemy, and released Minutius, he would not suffer the army he had rescued to participate in the spoils, saying, "I will not have you share in the plunder of those to whom you had so nearly fallen a prey." Minutius he deprived of his consulship, and reduced to be a subaltern, in which rank he bade him remain till he had learned how to command. And before this he had made Lucius Tarquininus, although forced by his poverty to serve on foot, his master of the knights.

Here, then, we see what honour was paid in Rome to poverty, and how four acres of land sufficed to support so good and great a man as Cincinnatus. We find the same Poverty still prevailing in the time of Marcus Regulus, who when serving with the army in Africa sought leave of senate to return home that he might look after his farm which his labourers had suffered to run to waste. Here again we learn two things worthy our attention: first, the poverty of these men and their contentment under it, and how their sole study was to gain renown from war, leaving all its advantages to the State. For had they thought of enriching themselves by war, it had given them little concern that their fields were running to waste Further, we have to remark the magnanimity of these citizens, who when placed at the head of armies surpassed all princes in the loftiness of their spirit, who cared neither for king nor for commonwealth, and whom nothing could daunt or dismay; but who, on returning to private life, became once more so humble, so frugal, so careful of their slender means, and so submissive to the magistrates and reverential to their superiors, that it might seem impossible for the human mind to undergo so violent a change.

This poverty prevailed down to the days of Paulus Emilius, almost the last happy days for this republic wherein a citizen, while enriching Rome by his triumphs, himself remained poor. And yet so greatly was poverty still esteemed at this time, that when Paulus, in conferring rewards on those who had behaved well in the war, presented his own son-in-law with a silver cup, it was the first vessel of silver ever seen in his house.

I might run on to a great length pointing out how much better are the fruits of poverty than those of riches, and how poverty has brought cities, provinces, and nations to honour, while riches have wrought their ruin, had not this subject been often treated by others.

CHAPTER XXVI

How Women are a cause of the ruin of States.

A feud broke out in Ardea touching the marriage of an heiress, whose hand was sought at the same time by two suitors, the one of plebeian, the other of noble birth. For her father being dead, her guardian wished her to wed the plebeian, her mother the noble. And so hot grew the dispute that resort was had to arms, the whole nobility siding with their fellow-noble, and all the plebeians with the plebeian. The latter faction being worsted, left the town, and sent to the Volscians for help; whereupon, the nobles sought help from Rome. The Volscians were first in the field, and on their arrival encamped round Ardea. The Romans, coming up later, shut in the Volscians between themselves and the town, and, reducing them by famine, forced them to surrender at discretion. They then entered Ardea, and putting all the ringleaders in this dispute to the sword, composed the disorders of the city.

In connection with this affair there are several points to be noted. And in the first place we see how women have been the occasion of many divisions and calamities in States, and have wrought great harm to rulers; as when, according to our historian, the violence done to Lucretia drove the Tarquins from their kingdom, and that done to Virginia broke the power of the decemvirs. And among the chief causes which Aristotle assigns for the downfall of tyrants are the wrongs done by them to their subjects in respect of their women, whether by adultery, rape, or other like injury to their honour, as has been sufficiently noticed in the Chapter wherein we treated *"of Conspiracies."*

I say, then, that neither absolute princes nor the rulers of free States should underrate the importance of matter, but take heed to the disorders which it may breed and provide against them while remedies can still be used without discredit to themselves or to their governments And this should have been done by the rulers of Ardea who by suffering the rivalry between their citizens to come to a head, promoted their divisions, and when they sought to reunite them had to summon foreign help, than which nothing sooner leads to servitude.

But now let us turn to another subject which merits attention, namely, the means whereby divided cities may be reunited; and of this I propose to speak in the following Chapter.

CHAPTER XXVII

How a divided City may be reunited, and how it is a false opinion that to hold Cities in subjection they must be kept divided.

From the example of the Roman consuls who reconciled the citizens of Ardea, we are taught the method whereby the feuds of a divided city may be composed, namely, by putting the ringleaders of the disturbances to death; and that no other remedy should be used. Three courses, indeed, are open to you, since you may either put to death, as these consuls did, or banish, or bind the citizens to live at peace with one another, taking security for their good behaviour. Of which three ways the last is the most hurtful, the most uncertain, and the least effectual; because when much blood has been shed, or other like outrage done, it cannot be that a peace imposed on compulsion should endure between men who are every day brought face to face with one another; for since fresh cause of contention may at any moment result from their meeting, it will be impossible for them to refrain from mutual injury. Of this we could have no better instance than in the city of Pistoja.

Fifteen years ago this city was divided between the Panciatichi and Cancellieri, as indeed it still continues, the only difference being that then they were in arms, whereas, now, they have laid them aside. After much controversy and wrangling, these factions would presently proceed to bloodshed, to pulling down houses, plundering property, and all the other violent courses usual in divided cities. The Florentines, with whom it lay to compose these feuds, strove for a long time to do so by using the third of the methods mentioned; but when this only led to increased tumult and disorder, losing patience, they decided to try the second method and get rid of the ringleaders of both factions by imprisoning some and banishing others. In this way a sort of settlement was arrived at, which continues in operation up to the present hour. There can be no question, however, that the first of the methods named would have been the surest. But because extreme measures have in them an element of greatness and nobility, a weak republic, so far from knowing how to use this first method, can with difficulty be brought to employ even the second. This, as I said at the beginning, is the kind of blunder made by the princes of our times when they have to decide on matters of moment, from their not considering how those men acted who in ancient days had to determine under like conditions. For the weakness of the present race of men (the result of their enfeebling education and their ignorance of affairs), makes them regard the methods followed by the ancients as partly inhuman and partly impracticable. Accordingly, they have their own newfangled ways of looking at things, wholly at variance with the true, as when the sages of our city, some time since, pronounced that *Pistoja was to be held by feuds and Pisa by fortresses*, not perceiving how useless each of these methods is in itself.

Having spoken of fortresses already at some length, I shall not further refer to them here, but shall consider the futility of trying to hold subject cities by keeping them divided. In the first place, it is impossible for the ruling power, whether prince or republic, to be friends with both factions. For wherever there is division, it is human nature to take a side, and to favour one party more than another. But if one party in a subject city be unfriendly to you, the consequence will be that you will lose that city so soon as you are involved in war, since it is impossible for you to hold a city where you have enemies both within and without. Should the ruling power be a republic, there is nothing so likely to corrupt its citizens and sow dissension among them, as having to control a divided city. For as each faction in that city will seek support and endeavour to make friends in a variety of corrupt ways, two very serious evils will result: first, that the governed city will never be contented with its governors, since there can be no good government where you often change its form, adapting yourself to the humours now of one party and now of another; and next, that the factious spirit of the subject city is certain to infect your own republic. To which Biondo testifies, when, in speaking of the citizens of Florence and Pistoja, he says, "In seeking to unite Pistoja the Florentines themselves fell out." It is easy, therefore, to understand how much mischief attends on such divisions. In the year 1501, when we lost Arezzo, and when all the Val di Tevere and Val di Chiana were occupied by the Vitelli and by Duke Valentino, a certain M. de Lant was sent by the King of France to cause the whole of the lost towns to be restored to the Florentines; who finding in all these towns men who came to him claiming to be of the party of the Marnocco, greatly blamed this distinction, observing, that if in France any of the king's subjects were to say that he was of the king's party, he would be punished; since the expression would imply that there was a party hostile to the king, whereas it was his majesty's desire that all his subjects should be his friends and live united without any distinction of party. But all these mistaken methods and opinions originate in the weakness of rulers, who, seeing that they cannot hold their States by their own strength and valour, have recourse to like devices; which, if now and then in tranquil times they prove of some slight assistance to them, in times of danger are shown to be worthless.

CHAPTER XXVIII

That a Republic must keep an eye on what its Citizens are about; since often the seeds of a Tyranny lie hidden under a semblance of generous deeds.

The granaries of Rome not sufficing to meet a famine with which the city was visited, a certain Spurius Melius, a very wealthy citizen for these days, privately laid in a supply of corn wherewith to feed the people at his own expense; gaining thereby such general favour with the commons, that the senate, apprehending that his bounty might have dangerous consequences, in order to crush him before he grew too powerful, appointed a dictator to deal with him and caused him to be put to death.

Here we have to note that actions which seem good in themselves and unlikely to occasion harm to any one, very often become hurtful, nay, unless corrected in time, most dangerous for a republic. And to treat the matter with greater fulness, I say, that while a republic can never maintain itself long, or manage its affairs to advantage, without citizens of good reputation, on the other hand the credit enjoyed by particular citizens often leads to the establishment of a tyranny. For which reasons, and that things may take a safe course, it should be so arranged that a citizen shall have credit only for such behaviour as benefits, and not for such as injures the State and its liberties. We must therefore examine by what ways credit is acquired. These, briefly, are two, public or secret. Public, when a citizen gains a great name by advising well or by acting still better for the common advantage. To credit of this sort we should open a wide door, holding out rewards both for good counsels and for good actions, so that he who renders such services may be at once honoured and satisfied. Reputation acquired honestly and openly by such means as these can never be dangerous. But credit acquired by secret practices, which is the other method spoken of, is most perilous and prejudicial. Of such secret practices may be instanced, acts of kindness done to this or the other citizen in lending him money, in assisting him to marry his daughters, in defending him against the magistrates, and in conferring such other private favours as gain men devoted adherents, and encourage them after they have obtained such support, to corrupt the institutions of the State and to violate its laws.

A well-governed republic, therefore, ought, as I have said, to throw wide the door to all who seek public favour by open courses, and to close it against any who would ingratiate themselves by underhand means. And this we find was done in Rome. For the Roman republic, as a reward to any citizen who served it well, ordained triumphs and all the other honours which it had to bestow; while against those who sought to aggrandize themselves by secret intrigues, it ordained accusations and impeachment; and when, from the people being blinded by a false show of benevolence, these proved insufficient, it provided for a dictator, who with regal authority might bring to bounds any who had strayed beyond them, as instanced in the case of Spurius Melius. And if conduct like his be ever suffered to pass unchastised, it may well be the ruin of a republic, for men when they have such examples set them are not easily led back into the right path.

CHAPTER XXIX

That the Faults of a People are due to its Prince.

Let no prince complain of the faults committed by a people under his control; since these must be ascribed either to his negligence, or to his being himself blemished by similar defects. And were any one to consider what peoples in our own times have been most given to robbery and other like offences, he would find that they have only copied their rulers, who have themselves been of a like nature. Romagna, before those lords who ruled it were driven out by Pope Alexander VI., was a nursery of all the worst crimes, the slightest occasion giving rise to wholesale rapine and murder. This resulted from the wickedness of these lords, and not, as they asserted, from the evil disposition of their subjects. For these princes being poor, yet choosing to live as though they were rich, were forced to resort to cruelties innumerable and practised in divers ways; and among other shameful devices contrived by them to extort money, they would pass laws prohibiting certain acts, and then be the first to give occasion for breaking them; nor would they chastise offenders until they saw many involved in the same offence; when they fell to punishing, not from any zeal for the laws which they had made, but out of greed to realize the penalty. Whence flowed many mischiefs, and more particularly this, that the people being impoverished, but not corrected, sought to make good their injuries at the expense of others weaker than themselves. And thus there sprang up all those evils spoken of above, whereof the prince is the true cause.

The truth of what I say is confirmed by Titus Livius where he relates how the Roman envoys, who were conveying the spoils of the Veientines as an offering to Apollo, were seized and brought on shore by the corsairs of the Lipari islands in Sicily; when Timasitheus, the prince of these islands, on learning the nature of the offering, its destination, and by whom sent, though himself of Lipari, behaved as a Roman might, showing his people what sacrilege it would be to intercept such a gift, and speaking to such purpose that by general consent the envoys were suffered to proceed upon their voyage, taking all their possessions with them. With reference to which incident the historian observes: "The multitude, who always take their colour from their ruler, were filled by Timasitheus with a religious awe." And to like purport we find it said by Lorenzo de' Medici: —

"A prince's acts his people imitate; For on their lord the eyes of all men wait."

CHAPTER XXX

That a Citizen who seeks by his personal influence to render signal service to his Country, must first stand clear of Envy. How a City should prepare for its defence on the approach of an Enemy.

When the Roman senate learned that all Etruria was assembled in arms to march against Rome, and that the Latins and Hernicians, who before had been the friends of the Romans, had ranged themselves with the Volscians the ancient enemies of the Roman name, they foresaw that a perilous contest awaited them. But because Camillus was at that time tribune with consular authority they thought all might be managed without the appointment of a dictator, provided the other tribunes, his colleagues would agree to his assuming the sole direction of affairs. This they willingly did; "nor," says Titus Livius, "did they account anything as taken from their own dignity which was added to his."

On receiving their promise of obedience, Camillus gave orders that three armies should be enrolled. Of the first, which was to be directed against the Etruscans, he himself assumed command. The command of the second, which he meant to remain near Rome and meet any movement of the Latins and Hernicians, he gave to Quintius Servilius. The third army, which he designed for the protection of the city, and the defence of the gates and Curia, he entrusted to Lucius Quintius. And he further directed, that Horatius, one of his colleagues, should furnish supplies of arms, and corn, and of all else needful in time of war. Finally he put forward his colleague Cornelius to preside in the senate and public council, that from day to day he might advise what should be done. For in those times these tribunes were ready either to command or obey as the welfare of their country might require.

We may gather from this passage how a brave and prudent man should act, how much good he may effect, and how serviceable he may be to his country, when by the force of his character and worth he succeeds in extinguishing envy. For this often disables men from acting to the best advantage, not permitting them to obtain that authority which it is essential they should have in matters of importance. Now, envy may be extinguished in one or other of two ways: first, by the approach of some flagrant danger, whereby seeing themselves like to be overwhelmed, all forego their own private ambition and lend a willing obedience to him who counts on his valour to rescue them. As in the case of Camillas, who from having given many proofs of surpassing ability, and from having been three times dictator and always exercised the office for the public good and not for his private advantage, had brought men to fear nothing from his advancement; while his fame and reputation made it no shame for them to recognize him as their superior. Wisely, therefore, does Titus Livius use concerning him the words which I have cited.

The other way in which envy may be extinguished, is by the death, whether by violence or in the ordinary course of nature, of those who have been your rivals in the pursuit of fame or power, and who seeing you better esteemed than themselves, could never acquiesce in your superiority or put up with it in patience. For when these men have been brought up in a corrupt city, where their training is little likely to improve them, nothing that can happen will induce them to withdraw their pretensions; nay, to have their own way and satisfy their perverse humour, they will be content to look on while their country is ruined. For envy such as this there is no cure save by the death of those of whom it has taken possession. And when fortune so befriends a great man that his rivals are removed from his path by a natural death, his glory is established without scandal or offence, since he is then able to display his great qualities unhindered. But when fortune is not thus propitious to him, he must contrive other means to rid himself of rivals, and must do so successfully before he can accomplish anything. Any one who reads with intelligence the lessons of Holy Writ, will remember how Moses, to give effect to his laws and ordinances, was constrained to put to death an endless number of those who out of mere envy withstood his designs. The necessity of this course was well understood by the Friar Girolamo Savonarola, and by the Gonfalonier Piero Soderini. But the former could not comply with it, because, as a friar, he himself lacked the needful authority; while those of his followers who might have exercised that authority, did not rightly comprehend his teaching. This, however, was no fault of his; for his sermons are full of invectives and attacks against *"the wise of this world,"* that being the name he gave to envious rivals and to all who opposed his reforms. As for Piero Soderini, he was possessed by the belief that in time and with favourable fortune he could allay envy by gentleness-and by benefits conferred on particular men; for as he was still in the prime of life, and in the fresh enjoyment of that good-will which his character and opinions had gained for him, he thought to get the better of all who out of jealousy opposed him, without giving occasion for tumult, violence, or disorder; not knowing how time stays not, worth suffices not, fortune shifts, and malice will not be won over by any benefit Wherefore, because they could not or knew not how to vanquish this envy, the two whom I have named came to their downfall.

Another point to be noted in the passage we are considering, is the careful provision made by Camillus for the safety of Rome both within and without the city. And, truly, not without reason do wise historians, like our author, set forth certain events with much minuteness and detail, to the end that those who come after may learn how to protect themselves in like dangers. Further, we have to note that there is no more hazardous or less useful defence than one conducted without method or system. This is shown in Camillus causing a third army to be enrolled that it might be left in Rome for the protection of the city. Many persons, doubtless, both then and now, would esteem this precaution superfluous, thinking that as the Romans were a warlike people and constantly under arms, there could be no occasion for a special levy, and that it was time enough to arm when the need came. But Camillus, and any other equally prudent captain would be of the same mind, judged otherwise, not permitting the multitude to take up arms unless they were to be bound by the rules and discipline of military service. Let him, therefore, who is called on to defend a city, taking example by Camillus, before all things avoid placing arms in the hands of an undisciplined multitude, but first of all select and enroll those whom he proposes to arm, so that they may be wholly governed by him as to where they shall assemble and whither they shall march; and then let him direct those who are not enrolled, to abide every man in his own house for its defence. Whosoever observes this method in a city which is attacked, will be able to defend it with ease; but whosoever disregards it, and follows not the example of Camillus, shall never succeed.

CHAPTER XXXI

That strong Republics and valiant Men preserve through every change the same Spirit and Bearing.

Among other high sayings which our historian ascribes to Camillus, as showing of what stuff a truly great man should be made, he puts in his mouth the words, "My courage came not with my dictatorship nor went with my exile;" for by these words we are taught that a great man is constantly the same through all vicissitudes of Fortune; so that although she change, now exalting, now depressing, he remains unchanged, and retains always a mind so unmoved, and in such complete accordance with his nature as declares to all that over him Fortune has no dominion.

Very different is the behaviour of those weak-minded mortals who, puffed up and intoxicated with their success, ascribe all their felicity to virtues which they never knew, and thus grow hateful and insupportable to all around them. Whence also the changes in their fortunes. For whenever they have to look adversity in the face, they suddenly pass to the other extreme, becoming abject and base. And thus it happens that feeble-minded princes, when they fall into difficulties, think rather of flight than of defence, because, having made bad use of their prosperity, they are wholly unprepared to defend themselves.

The same merits and defects which I say are found in individual men, are likewise found in republics, whereof we have example in the case of Rome and of Venice. For no reverse of fortune ever broke the spirit of the Roman people, nor did any success ever unduly elate them; as we see plainly after their defeat at Cannae, and after the victory they had over Antiochus. For the defeat at Cannae, although most momentous, being the third they had met with, no whit daunted them; so that they continued to send forth armies, refused to ransom prisoners as contrary to their custom, and despatched no envoy to Hannibal or to Carthage to sue for peace; but without ever looking back on past humiliations, thought always of war, though in such straits for soldiers that they had to arm their old men and slaves. Which facts being made known to Hanno the Carthaginian, he, as I have already related, warned the Carthaginian senate not to lay too much stress upon their victory. Here, therefore, we see that in times of adversity the Romans were neither cast down nor dismayed. On the other hand, no prosperity ever made them arrogant. Before fighting the battle wherein he was finally routed, Antiochus sent messengers to Scipio to treat for an accord; when Scipio offered peace on condition that he withdrew at once into Syria, leaving all his other dominions to be dealt with by the Romans as they thought fit. Antiochus refusing these terms, fought and was defeated, and again sent envoys to Scipio, enjoining them to accept whatever conditions the victor might be pleased to impose. But Scipio proposed no different terms from those he had offered before saying that "the Romans, as they lost not heart on defeat, so waxed not insolent with success."

The contrary of all this is seen in the behaviour of the Venetians, who thinking their good fortune due to valour of which they were devoid, in their pride addressed the French king as "Son of St. Mark;" and making no account of the Church, and no longer restricting their ambition to the limits of Italy, came to dream of founding an empire like the Roman. But afterwards, when their good fortune deserted them, and they met at Vaila a half-defeat at the hands of the French king, they lost their whole dominions, not altogether from revolt, but mainly by a base and abject surrender to the Pope and the King of Spain. Nay, so low did they stoop as to send ambassadors to the Emperor offering to become his tributaries, and to write letters to the Pope, full of submission and servility, in order to move his compassion. To such abasement were they brought in four days' time by what was in reality only a half-defeat. For on their flight after the battle of

Vaila only about a half of their forces were engaged, and one of their two provedditori escaped to Verona with five and twenty thousand men, horse and foot. So that had there been a spark of valour in Venice, or any soundness in her military system, she might easily have renewed her armies, and again confronting fortune have stood prepared either to conquer, or, if she must fall, to fall more gloriously; and at any rate might have obtained for herself more honourable terms. But a pusillanimous spirit, occasioned by the defects of her ordinances in so far as they relate to war, caused her to lose at once her courage and her dominions. And so will it always happen with those who behave like the Venetians. For when men grow insolent in good fortune, and abject inn evil, the fault lies in themselves and in the character of their training, which, when slight and frivolous, assimilates them to itself; but when otherwise, makes them of another temper, and giving them better acquaintance with the world, causes them to be less disheartened by misfortunes and less elated by success.

And while this is true of individual men, it holds good also of a concourse of men living together in one republic, who will arrive at that measure of perfection which the institutions of their State permit. And although I have already said on another occasion that a good militia is the foundation of all States, and where that is wanting there can neither be good laws, nor aught else that is good, it seems to me not superfluous to say the same again; because in reading this history of Titus Livius the necessity of such a foundation is made apparent in every page. It is likewise shown that no army can be good unless it be thoroughly trained and exercised, and that this can only be the case with an army raised from your own subjects. For as a State is not and cannot always be at war, you must have opportunity to train your army in times of peace; but this, having regard to the cost, you can only have in respect of your own subjects.

When Camillus, as already related, went forth to meet the Etruscans, his soldiers on seeing the great army of their enemy, were filled with fear, thinking themselves too to withstand its onset. This untoward disposition being reported to Camillus, he showed himself to his men and by visiting their tents, and conversing with this and the other among them, was able to remove their misgivings; and, finally, without other word of command, he bade them "each do his part as he had learned and been accustomed." Now, any one who well considers the methods followed by Camillus, and the words spoken by him to encourage his soldiers to face their enemy, will perceive that these words and methods could never have been used with an army which had not been trained and disciplined in time of peace as well as of war. For no captain can trust to untrained soldiers or look for good service at their hands; nay, though he were another Hannibal, with such troops his defeat were certain. For, as a captain cannot be present everywhere while a battle is being fought, unless he have taken all measures beforehand to render his men of the same temper as himself, and have made sure that they perfectly understand his orders and arrangements, he will inevitably be destroyed.

When a city therefore is armed and trained as Rome was, and when its citizens have daily opportunity, both singly and together, to make trial of their valour and learn what fortune can effect, it will always happen, that at all times, and whether circumstances be adverse or favourable, they will remain of unaltered courage and preserve the same noble bearing. But when its citizens are unpractised in arms, and trust not to their own valour but wholly to the arbitration of Fortune, they will change their temper as she changes, and offer always the same example of behaviour as was given by the Venetians.

CHAPTER XXXII

Of the methods which some have used to make Peace impossible.

The towns of Caere and Velitrae, two of her own colonies, revolted from Rome in expectation of being protected by the Latins. But the Latins being routed and all hopes of help from that quarter at an end, many of the townsmen recommended that envoys should be sent to Rome to make their peace with the senate. This proposal, however, was defeated by those who had been the prime movers of the revolt, who, fearing that the whole punishment might fall on their heads, to put a stop to any talk of an adjustment, incited the multitude to take up arms and make a foray into the Roman territory.

And, in truth, when it is desired that a prince or people should banish from their minds every thought of reconciliation, there is no surer or more effectual plan than to incite them to inflict grave wrong on him with whom you would not have them be reconciled; for, then, the fear of that punishment which they will seem to themselves to have deserved, will always keep them apart. At the close of the first war waged by the Romans against Carthage, the soldiers who had served under the Carthaginians in Sardinia and Sicily, upon peace being proclaimed, returned to Africa; where, being dissatisfied with their pay, they mutinied against the Carthaginians, and choosing two of their number, Mato and Spendio, to be their leaders, seized and sacked many towns subject to Carthage. The Carthaginians, being loath to use force until they had tried all other methods for bringing them to reason, sent Hasdrubal, their fellow-citizen, to mediate with them, thinking that from formerly having commanded them he might be able to exercise some influence over them. But on his arrival,

Spendio and Mato, to extinguish any hope these mutineers might have had of making peace with Carthage, and so leave them no alternative but war, persuaded them that their best course was to put Hasdrubal, with all the other Carthaginian citizens whom they had taken prisoners, to death. Whereupon, they not only put them to death, but first subjected them to an infinity of tortures; crowning their wickedness by a proclamation to the effect that every Carthaginian who might thereafter fall into their hands should meet a like fate. This advice, therefore, and its consummation had the effect of rendering these mutineers relentless and inveterate in their hostility to the Carthaginians.

CHAPTER XXXIII

That to insure victory in battle you must inspire your Men with confidence in one another and in you.

To insure an army being victorious in battle you must inspire it with the conviction that it is certain to prevail. The causes which give it this confidence are its being well armed and disciplined, and the soldiers knowing one another. These conditions are only to be found united in soldiers born and bred in the same country.

It is likewise essential that the army should think so well of its captain as to trust implicitly to his prudence; which it will always do if it see him careful of its welfare, attentive to discipline, brave in battle, and otherwise supporting well and honourably the dignity of his position. These conditions he fulfils when, while punishing faults, he does not needlessly harass his men, keeps his word with them, shows them that the path to victory is easy, and conceals from them, or makes light of things which seen from a distance might appear to threaten danger. The observance of these precautions will give an army great confidence, and such confidence leads to victory.

This confidence the Romans were wont to inspire in the minds of their soldiers by the aid of religion; and accordingly their consuls were appointed, their armies were enrolled, their soldiers marched forth, and their battles were begun, only when the auguries and auspices were favourable; and without attending to all these observances no prudent captain would ever engage in combat; knowing that unless his soldiers were first assured that the gods were on their side, he might readily suffer defeat. But if any consul or other leader ever joined battle contrary to the auspices, the Romans would punish him, as they did Claudius Pulcher.

The truth of what I affirm is plainly seen from the whole course of the Roman history, but is more particularly established by the words which Livius puts into the mouth of Appius Claudius, who, when complaining to the people of the insolence of the tribunes, and taxing them with having caused the corruption of the auspices and other rites of religion, is made to say, "And now they would strip even religion of its authority. For what matters it, they will tell you, that the fowls refuse to peck, or come slowly from the coop, or that a cock has crowed? These are small matters doubtless; but it was by not contemning such small matters as these, that our forefathers built up this great republic." And, indeed, in these small matters lies a power which keeps men united and of good courage, which is of itself the chief condition of success.

But the observances of religion must be accompanied by valour, for otherwise they can nothing avail. The men of Praneste, leading forth their army against the Romans, took up their position near the river Allia, on the very spot where the Romans had been routed by the Gauls, selecting this ground that it might inspire their own side with confidence, and dishearten their enemies with the unhappy memories which it recalled But although, for the reasons already noted, this was a course which promised success, the result nevertheless showed that true valour is not to be daunted by trifling disadvantages. And this the historian well expresses by the words he puts in the mouth of the dictator as spoken to his master of the knights "See how these fellows, in encamping on the banks of the Allia, have chosen their ground in reliance upon fortune. Do you, therefore, relying on discipline and valour, fall upon then centre." For true valour, tight discipline, and the feeling of security gained by repeated victories, are not to be counteracted by things of no real moment, dismayed by empty terrors, or quelled by a solitary mishap. As was well seen when the two Manlii, being consuls in command against the Volscians, rashly allowed a part of their army to go out foraging, and both those who went out and those who stayed behind found themselves attacked at the same moment For from this danger they were saved by the courage of the soldiers, and not by the foresight of the consuls. With regard to which occurrence Titus Livius observes, "Even without a leader the steadfast valour of the soldiers was maintained."

Here I must not omit to notice the device practised by Fabius to give his army confidence, when he led it for the first time into Etruria. For judging such encouragement to be especially needed by his men, since they were entering an unknown country to encounter a new foe, he addressed them before they joined battle, and, after reciting many reasons for expecting a victory, told them, that "he could have mentioned other favourable circumstances making victory certain, had it not been dangerous to disclose them." And as this device was dexterously used it merits imitation.

CHAPTER XXXIV

By what reports, rumours, or surmises the Citizens of a Republic are led to favour a Fellow-citizen: and-whether the Magistracies are bestowed with better judgment by a People or by a Prince.

I have elsewhere related how Titus Manlius, afterwards named Torquatus, rescued his father from the charge laid against him by Marcus Pomponius, tribune of the people. And though the means he took to effect this were somewhat violent and irregular, so pleasing to everyone were his filial piety and affection, that not only did he escape rebuke, but when military tribunes had to be appointed his name was second on the list of those chosen. To explain his good fortune, it will, I think, be useful to consider what are the methods followed by the citizens of a republic in estimating the character of those on whom they bestow honours, so as to see whether what I have already said on this head be true, namely, that a people is more discriminating in awarding honours than a prince.

I say, then, that in conferring honours and offices, the people, when it has no knowledge of a man from his public career, follows the estimate given of him by the general voice, and by common report; or else is guided by some prepossession or preconceived opinion which it has adopted concerning him. Such impressions are formed either from consideration of a man's descent (it being assumed, until the contrary appears, that where his ancestors have been great and distinguished citizens their descendant will resemble them), or else from regard to his manners and habits; and nothing can be more in his favour than that he frequents the company of the grave and virtuous, and such as are generally reputed wise. For as we can have no better clue to a man's character than the company he keeps, he who frequents worthy company deservedly obtains a good name, since there can hardly fail to be some similarity between himself and his associates. Sometimes, however, the popular estimate of a man is founded on some remarkable and noteworthy action, though not of public moment, in which he has acquitted himself well. And of all the three causes which create a prepossession in a man's favour, none is so effectual as this last. For the presumption that he will resemble his ancestors and kinsmen is so often misleading, that men are slow to trust and quick to discard it, unless confirmed by the personal worth of him of whom they are judging.

The criterion of character afforded by a man's manners and conversation is a safer guide than the presumption of inherited excellence, but is far inferior to that afforded by his actions; for until he has given actual proof of his worth, his credit is built on mere opinion, which may readily change. But this third mode of judging, which originates in and rests upon his actions, at once gives him a name which can only be destroyed by his afterwards doing many actions of a contrary nature. Those therefore who live in a republic should conform to this third criterion, and endeavour, as did many of the Roman youth, to make their start in life with some extraordinary achievement, either by promoting a law conducive to the general well-being, or by accusing some powerful citizen as a transgressor of the laws, or by performing some similar new and notable action which cannot fail to be much spoken of.

Actions like this are necessary not only to lay a foundation for your fame, but also to maintain and extend it. To which end, they must continually be renewed, as we find done by Titus Manlius throughout the whole course of his life. For after winning his earliest renown by his bold and singular defence of his father, when some years had passed he fought his famous duel with the Gaul, from whom, when he had slain him, he took the twisted golden collar which gave him the name of Torquatus. Nor was this the last of his remarkable actions, for at a later period, when he was of ripe years, he caused his own son to be put to death, because he had fought without leave, although successfully. Which three actions gained for him at the time a greater name, and have made him more renowned through after ages than all his triumphs and victories, though of these he had as large a share as fell to the lot of any other Roman. The explanation of which is, that while in his victories Manlius had many who resembled him, in these particular actions he stood almost or entirely alone.

So, too, with the elder Scipio, all whose victories together did not obtain for him so much reputation, as did his rescue, while he was yet young, of his father at the Ticino, and his undaunted bearing after the rout at Cannae, when with his naked sword he constrained a number of the Roman youth to swear never to abandon their country, as some among them had before been minded to do. It was these two actions, therefore, which laid the foundation of his future fame and paved the way for his triumphs in Spain and Africa. And the fair esteem in which men held him, was still further heightened when in Spain he restored a daughter to her father, a wife to her husband.

Nor is it only the citizen who seeks reputation as leading to civil honours, who must act in this way; the prince who would maintain his credit in his princedom must do likewise; since nothing helps so much to make a prince esteemed as to give signal proofs of his worth, whether by words or by deeds which tend to promote the public good, and show him to be so magnanimous, generous, and just, that he may well pass into a proverb among his subjects. But to return to the point whence I digressed, I say that if a people, when they first confer honours on a fellow-citizen, rest their judgment on any one of the three circumstances above-mentioned, they build on a reasonable foundation; but, when many instances of noble conduct have made a man favourably known, that the foundation is still better, since then there is hardly room for mistake. I speak merely of those honours which are bestowed on a man at the outset of his career, before he has come to be known by continued proof, or is found to have passed from one kind of conduct to another and dissimilar kind, and I maintain that in such cases, so far as erroneous judgments or corrupt motives are concerned, a people will always commit fewer mistakes than a prince.

But since a people may happen to be deceived as regards the character, reputation, and actions of a man, thinking them better or greater than in truth they are, an error a prince is less likely to fall into from his being informed and warned by his advisers, in order that the people may not lack similar advice, wise founders of republics have provided, that when the highest dignities of the State, to which it would be dangerous to appoint incapable men, have to be filled up, and it appears that some incapable man is the object of the popular choice, it shall be lawful and accounted honourable for any citizen to declare in the public assemblies the defects of the favoured candidate, that the people, being made acquainted therewith, may be better able to judge of his fitness. That this was the practice in Rome we have proof in the speech made by Fabius Maximus to the people during the second Punic war, when in the appointment of consuls public favour leaned towards Titus Ottacilius. For Fabius judging him unequal to the duties of the consulship at such a crisis, spoke against him and pointed out his insufficiency, and so prevented his appointment, turning the popular favour towards another who deserved it more.

In the choice of its magistrates, therefore, a people judges of those among whom it has to choose, in accordance with the surest indications it can get; and when it can be advised as princes are, makes fewer mistakes than they. But the citizen who would make a beginning by gaining the good-will of the people, must, to obtain it, perform, like Titus Manlius, some noteworthy action.

CHAPTER XXXV

Of the Danger incurred in being the first to recommend new Measures; and that the more unusual the Measures the greater the Danger.

How perilous a thing it is to put one's self at the head of changes whereby many are affected, how difficult to guide and bring them to perfection, and when perfected to maintain them, were too wide and arduous a subject to be treated here. Wherefore I reserve it for a fitter occasion, and shall now speak only of those dangers which are incurred by the citizens of a republic or by the counsellors of a prince in being the first to promote some grave and important measure in such manner that the whole responsibility attending it rests with them. For as men judge of things by their results, any evil which ensues from such measures will be imputed to their author. And although if good ensue he will be applauded, nevertheless in matters of this kind, what a man may gain is as nothing to what he may lose.

Selim, the present sultan, or Grand Turk as he is called, being in readiness, as some who come from his country relate, to set forth on an expedition against Egypt and Syria, was urged by one of his bashaws whom he had stationed on the confines of Persia, to make war upon the Sofi. In compliance with which advice he went on this new enterprise with a vast army. But coming to a great plain, wherein were many deserts and few streams, and encountering the same difficulties as in ancient times had proved the ruin of many Roman armies, he suffered so much from pestilence and famine, that, although victorious in battle, he lost a great part of his men. This so enraged him against the bashaw on whose advice he had acted, that he forthwith put him to death.

In like manner, we read of many citizens who having strenuously promoted various measures were banished when these turned out badly. Certain citizens of Rome, for instance, were very active in forwarding a law allowing the appointment of a plebeian to be consul. This law passing, it so happened that the first plebeian consul who went forth with the armies was routed; and had it not been that the party in whose behalf the law was made was extremely powerful, its promoters would have fared badly. It is plain therefore that the counsellors whether of a republic or of a prince stand in this dilemma, that if they do not conscientiously advise whatsoever they think advantageous for their city or prince, they fail in their duty; if they do advise it, they risk their places and their lives; all men being subject to this infirmity of judging advice by the event.

When I consider in what way this reproach or this danger may best be escaped, I find no other remedy to recommend than that in giving advice you proceed discreetly not identifying yourself in a special manner with the measure you would see carried out, but offering your opinion without heat, and supporting it temperately and modestly, so that if the prince or city follow it, they shall do so of their own good-will, and not seem to be dragged into it by your importunity. When you act thus, neither prince nor people can reasonably bear you a grudge in respect of the advice given by you, since that advice was not adopted contrary to the general opinion. For your danger lies in many having opposed you, who afterwards, should your advice prove hurtful, combine to ruin you. And although in taking this course you fall short of the glory which is earned by him who stands alone against many in urging some measure which succeeds, you have nevertheless two advantages to make up for it: first, that you escape danger; and second, that when you have temperately stated your views, and when, in consequence of opposition, your advice has not been taken, should other counsels prevail and mischief come of them, your credit will be vastly enhanced. And although credit gained at the cost of misfortune to your prince or city cannot be matter of rejoicing, still it is something to be taken into account.

On this head, then, I know of no other advice to offer. For that you should be silent and express no opinion at all, were a course hurtful for your prince or city, and which would not absolve you from danger, since you would soon grow to be suspected, when it might fare with you as with the friend of Perseus the Macedonian king. For Perseus being defeated by Paulus Emilius, and making his escape with a few companions, it happened that one of them, in reviewing the past, began to point out to the king many mistakes which he had made and which had been his ruin. Whereupon Perseus turning upon him said, "Traitor, hast thou waited till now when there is no remedy to tell me these things?" and so saying, slew him with his own hand. Such was the penalty incurred by one who was silent when he should have spoken, and who spoke when he should have been silent; and who found no escape from danger in having refrained from giving advice. Wherefore, I believe, that the course which I have recommended should be observed and followed.

CHAPTER XXXVI

Why it has been and still may be affirmed of the Gauls, that at the beginning of a fray they are more than Men, but afterwards less than Women.

The bravery of the Gaul who on the banks of the Anio challenged any among the Romans to fight with him, and the combat that thereupon ensued between him and Titus Manlius, remind me of what Titus Livius oftener than once observes in his history, that "at the beginning of a fray the Gauls are more than men, but ere it is ended show themselves less than women."

Touching the cause of this, many are content to believe that such is their nature, which, indeed, I take to be true; but we are not, therefore, to assume that the natural temper which makes them brave at the outset, may not be so trained and regulated as to keep them brave to the end. And, to prove this, I say, that armies are of three kinds. In one of these you have discipline with bravery and valour as its consequence. Such was the Roman army, which is shown by all historians to have maintained excellent discipline as the result of constant military training. And because in a well-disciplined army none must do anything save by rule, we find that in the Roman army, from which as it conquered the world all others should take example, none either eat, or slept, or bought, or sold, or did anything else, whether in his military or in his private capacity, without orders from the consul. Those armies which do otherwise are not true armies, and if ever they have any success, it is owing to the fury and impetuosity of their onset and not to trained and steady valour. But of this impetuosity and fury, trained valour, when occasion requires, will make use; nor will any danger daunt it or cause it to lose heart, its courage being kept alive by its discipline, and its confidence fed by the hope of victory which never fails it while that discipline is maintained.

But the contrary happens with armies of the second sort, those, namely, which have impetuosity without discipline, as was the case with the Gauls whose courage in a protracted conflict gradually wore away; so that unless they succeeded in their first attack, the impetuosity to which they trusted, having no support from disciplined valour, soon cooled; when, as they had nothing else to depend on, their efforts ceased. The Romans, on the other hand, being less disquieted in danger by reason of their perfect discipline, and never losing hope, fought steadily and stubbornly to the last, and with the same courage at the end as at the outset; nay, growing heated by the conflict, only became the fiercer the longer it was continued.

In armies of the third sort both natural spirit and trained valour are wanting; and to this class belong the Italian armies of our own times, of which it may be affirmed that they are absolutely worthless, never obtaining a victory, save when, by some accident, the enemy they encounter takes to flight. But since we have daily proofs of this absence of valour, it were needless to set forth particular instances of it.

That all, however, may know on the testimony of Titus Livius what methods a good army should take, and what are taken by a bad army, I shall cite the words he represents Papirius Cursor to have used when urging that Fabius, his master of the knights, should be punished for disobedience, and denouncing the consequences which would ensue were he absolved, saying: — "Let neither God nor man be held in reverence; let the orders of captains and the Divine auspices be alike disregarded; let a vagrant soldiery range without leave through the country of friend or foe; reckless of their military oath, let them disband at their pleasure; let them forsake their deserted standards, and neither rally nor disperse at the word of command; let them fight when they choose, by day or by night, with or without advantage of ground, with or without the bidding of their leader, neither maintaining their ranks nor observing the order of battle; and let our armies, from being a solemn and consecrated company, grow to resemble some dark and fortuitous gathering of cut-throats." With this passage before us, it is easy to pronounce whether the armies of our times be "a dark and fortuitous gathering," or "a solemn and consecrated company;" nay, how far they fall short of anything worthy to be called an army, possessing neither the impetuous but disciplined valour of the Romans, nor even the mere undisciplined impetuosity of the Gauls.

CHAPTER XXXVII

Whether a general engagement should be preceded by skirmishes; and how, avoiding these, we may get knowledge of a new Enemy.

Besides all the other difficulties which hinder men from bringing anything to its utmost perfection, it appears, as I have already observed, that in close vicinity to every good is found also an evil, so apt to grow up along with it that it is hardly possible to have the one without accepting the other. This we see in all human affairs, and the result is, that unless fortune aid us to overcome this natural and common disadvantage, we never arrive at any excellence. I am reminded of this by the combat between Titus Manlius and the Gaul, concerning which Livius writes that it "determined the issue of the entire war; since the Gauls, abandoning their camp, hastily withdrew to the country about Tivoli, whence they presently passed into Campania."

It may be said, therefore, on the one hand, that a prudent captain ought absolutely to refrain from all those operations which, while of trifling moment in themselves, may possibly produce an ill effect on his army. Now, to engage in a combat wherein you risk your whole fortunes without putting forth your entire strength, is, as I observed before, when condemning the defence of a country by guarding its defiles, an utterly foolhardy course. On the other hand, it is to be said that a prudent captain, when he has to meet a new and redoubtable adversary, ought, before coming to a general engagement, to accustom his men by skirmishes and passages of arms, to the quality of their enemy; that they may learn to know him, and how to deal with him, and so free themselves from the feeling of dread which his name and fame inspire.

This for a captain is a matter of the very greatest importance, and one which it might be almost fatal for him to neglect, since to risk a pitched battle without first giving your soldiers such opportunities to know their enemy and shake off their fear of him, is to rush on certain destruction. When Valerius Corvinus was sent by the Romans with their armies against the Samnites, these being new adversaries with whom up to that time they had not measured their strength, Titus Livius tells us that before giving battle he made his men make trial of the enemy in several unimportant skirmishes, "lest they should be dismayed by a new foe and a new method of warfare." Nevertheless, there is very great danger that, if your soldiers get the worst in these encounters, their alarm and self-distrust may be increased, and a result follow contrary to that intended, namely, that you dispirit where you meant to reassure.

This, therefore, is one of those cases in which the evil lies so nigh the good, and both are so mixed up together that you may readily lay hold of the one when you think to grasp the other. And with regard to this I say, that a good captain should do what he can that nothing happen which might discourage his men, nor is there anything so likely to discourage them as to begin with a defeat. For which reason skirmishes are, as a rule, to be avoided, and only to be allowed where you fight to great advantage and with a certainty of victory. In like manner, no attempt should be made to defend the passes leading into your country unless your whole army can co-operate; nor are any towns to be defended save those whose loss necessarily involves your ruin. And as to those towns which you do defend, you must so arrange, both in respect of the garrison within and the army without, that in the event of a siege your whole forces can be employed. All other towns you must leave undefended. For, provided your army be kept together, you do not, in losing what you voluntarily abandon, forfeit your military reputation, or sacrifice your hopes of final success. But when you lose what it was your purpose, and what all know it was your purpose to hold, you suffer a real loss and injury, and, like the Gauls on the defeat of their champion, you are ruined by a mishap of no moment in itself.

Philip of Macedon, the father of Perseus, a great soldier in his day, and of a great name, on being invaded by the Romans, laid waste and relinquished much of his territory which he thought he could not defend; rightly judging it more hurtful to his reputation to lose territory after an attempt to defend it, than to abandon it to the enemy as something he cared little to retain. So, likewise, after the battle of Cannae, when their affairs were at their worst, the Romans refused aid to many subject and protected States, charging them to defend themselves as best they could. And this is a better course than to undertake to defend and then to fail; for by refusing to defend, you lose only your friend; whereas in failing, you not only lose your friend, but weaken yourself.

But to return to the matter in hand, I affirm, that even when a captain is constrained by inexperience of his enemy to make trial of him by means of skirmishes, he ought first to see that he has so much the advantage that he runs no risk of defeat; or else, and this is his better course, he must do as Marius did when sent against the Cimbrians, a very courageous people who were laying Italy waste, and by their fierceness and numbers, and from the fact of their having already routed a Roman army, spreading terror wherever they came. For before fighting a decisive battle, Marius judged it necessary to do something to lessen the dread in which these enemies were held by his army; and being a prudent commander, he, on several occasions, posted his men at points where the Cimbrians must pass, that seeing and growing familiar with their appearance, while themselves in safety and within the shelter of their intrenched camp, and finding them to be a mere disorderly rabble, encumbered with baggage, and either without weapons, or with none that were formidable, they might at last assume courage and grow eager to engage them in battle. The part thus prudently taken by Marius, should be carefully imitated by others who would escape the dangers above spoken of and not have to betake themselves like the Gauls to a disgraceful flight, on sustaining some trifling defeat.

But since in this Discourse I have referred by name to Valerius Corvinus, in my next Chapter I shall cite his words to show what manner of man a captain ought to be.

CHAPTER XXXVIII

Of the Qualities of a Captain in whom his Soldiers can confide.

Valerius Corvinus, as I have said already, was sent in command of an army against the Samnites, who were then new enemies to Rome. Wherefore, to reassure his soldiers and familiarize them with their adversaries, he made them engage with them in various unimportant passages of arms. But not thinking this enough, he resolved before delivering battle to address his men, and by reminding them of their valour and his own, to make it plain how little they should esteem such enemies. And from the words which Titus Livius puts in his mouth we may gather what manner of man the captain ought to be in whom an army will put its trust. For he makes him say: — "Bear ye also this in mind under whose conduct and auspices you are about to fight, and whether he whom you are to obey be great only in exhorting, bold only in words, and all unpractised in arms; or whether he be one who himself knows how to use his spear, to march before the eagles, and play his part in the thickest of the fight. Soldiers! I would have you follow my deeds and not my words, and look to me for example rather than for commands; for with this right hand I have won for myself three consulships, and an unsurpassed renown." Which words rightly understood give every one to know what he must do to merit a captain's rank. And if any man obtain it by other means, he will soon discover that advancement due to chance or intrigue rather takes away than brings reputation, since it is men who give lustre to titles and not titles to men.

From what has been said it will likewise be understood that if great captains when matched against an unfamiliar foe have had to resort to unusual methods for reassuring the minds even of veteran soldiers, much more will it be necessary for them to use all their address when in command of a raw and untried army which has never before looked an enemy in the face. For if an unfamiliar adversary inspire terror even in a veteran army, how much greater must be the terror which any army will inspire in the minds of untrained men. And yet we often find all these difficulties overcome by the supreme prudence of a great captain like the Roman Gracchus or the Theban Epaminondas, of whom I have before spoken, who with untried troops defeated the most practised veterans. And the method they are said to have followed was to train their men for some months in mimic warfare, so as to accustom them to discipline and obedience, after which they employed them with complete confidence on actual service.

No man, therefore, of warlike genius, need despair of creating a good army if only he have the men; for the prince who has many subjects and yet lacks soldiers, has only to thank his own inertness and want of foresight, and must not complain of the cowardice of his people.

CHAPTER XXXIX

That a Captain should have good knowledge of Places.

Among other qualifications essential in a good captain is a knowledge, both general and particular, of places and countries, for without such knowledge it is impossible for him to carry out any enterprise in the best way. And while practice is needed for perfection in every art, in this it is needed in the highest degree. Such practice, or particular knowledge as it may be termed, is sooner acquired in the chase than in any other exercise; and, accordingly, we find it said by ancient historians that those heroes who, in their day, ruled the world, were bred in the woods and trained to the chase; for this exercise not merely gives the knowledge I speak of, but teaches countless other lessons needful in war. And Xenophon in his life of Cyrus tells us, that Cyrus, on his expedition against the King of Armenia, when assigning to each of his followers the part he was to perform, reminded them that the enterprise on which they were engaged, differed little from one of those hunting expeditions on which they had gone so often in his company; likening those who were to lie in ambush in the mountains, to the men sent to spread the toils on the hill-tops; and those who were to overrun the plain, to the beaters whose business it is to start the game from its lair that it may be driven into the toils. Now, this is related to show how, in the opinion of Xenophon, the chase is a mimic representation of war, and therefore to be esteemed by the great as useful and honourable.

Nor can that knowledge of countries which I have spoken of as necessary in a commander, be obtained in any convenient way except by the chase. For he who joins therein gains a special acquaintance with the character of the country in which it is followed; and he who has made himself specially familiar with one district, will afterwards readily understand the character of any strange country into which he comes. For all countries, and the districts of which they are made up, have a certain resemblance to one another, so that from a knowledge of one we can pass easily to the knowledge of another. He therefore who is without such practical acquaintance with some one country, can only with difficulty, and after a long time, obtain a knowledge of another, while he who possesses it can take in at a glance how this plain spreads, how that mountain slopes, whither that valley winds, and all other like particulars in respect of which he has already acquired a certain familiarity.

The truth of what I affirm is shown by Titus Livius in the case of Publius Decius, who, being military tribune in the army which the consul Cornelius led against the Samnites, when the consul advanced into a defile where the Roman army were like to be shut in by the enemy, perceiving the great danger they ran, and noting, as Livius relates, a hill which rose by a steep ascent and overhung the enemy's camp, and which, though hard of access for heavy-armed troops, presented little difficulty to troops lightly armed, turned to the consul and said: — "Seest thou, Aulus Cornelius, yonder height over above the enemy, which they have been blind enough to neglect? There, were we manfully to seize it, might we find the citadel of our hopes and of our safety." Whereupon, he was sent by the consul with three thousand men to secure the height, and so saved the Roman army. And as it was part of his plan to make his own escape and carry off his men safely under shelter of night, Livius represents him as saying to his soldiers: — "Come with me, that, while daylight still serves, we may learn where the enemy have posted their guards, and by what exit we may issue hence." Accordingly, putting on the cloak of a common soldier, lest the enemy should observe that an officer was making his rounds he surveyed their camp in all directions.

Now any one who carefully studies the whole of this passage, must perceive how useful and necessary it is for a captain to know the nature of places, which knowledge had Decius not possessed he could not have decided that it would be for the advantage of the Roman army to occupy this hill; nor could he have judged from a distance whether the hill was accessible or no; and when he reached the summit and desired to return to the consul, since he was surrounded on all sides by the enemy, he never could have distinguished the path it was safe for him to take, from those guarded by the foe. For all which reasons it was absolutely essential that Decius should have that thorough knowledge which enabled him by gaining possession of this hill to save the Roman army, and to discover a path whereby, in the event of his being attacked, he and his followers might escape.

CHAPTER XL

That Fraud is fair in War.

Although in all other affairs it be hateful to use fraud, in the operations of war it is praiseworthy and glorious; so that he who gets the better of his enemy by fraud, is as much extolled as he who prevails by force. This appears in the judgments passed by such as have written of the lives of great warriors, who praise Hannibal and those other captains who have been most noted for acting in this way. But since we may read of many instances of such frauds, I shall not cite them here. This, however, I desire to say, that I would not have it understood that any fraud is glorious which leads you to break your plighted word, or to depart from covenants to which you have agreed; for though to do so may sometimes gain you territory and power, it can never, as I have said elsewhere, gain you glory.

The fraud, then, which I here speak of is that employed against an enemy who places no trust in you, and is wholly directed to military operations, such as the stratagem of Hannibal at the Lake of Thrasymene, when he feigned flight in order to draw the Roman consul and his army into an ambuscade; or when to escape from the hands of Fabius Maximus he fastened lights to the horns of his oxen. Similar to the above was the deceit practised by Pontius the Samnite commander to inveigle the Roman army into the Caudine Forks. For after he had drawn up his forces behind the hills, he sent out a number of his soldiers, disguised as herdsmen, to drive great herds of cattle across the plain; who being captured by the Romans, and interrogated as to where the Samnite army was, all of them, as they had been taught by Pontius, agreed in saying that it had gone to besiege Nocera:

which being believed by the consuls, led them to advance within the Caudine Valley, where no sooner were they come than they were beset by the Samnites. And the victory thus won by a fraud would have been most glorious for Pontius had he but taken the advice of his father Herennius, who urged that the Romans should either be set at liberty unconditionally, or all be put to death; but that a mean course "which neither gains friends nor gets rid of foes" should be avoided. And this was sound advice, for, as has already been shown, in affairs of moment a mean course is always hurtful.

CHAPTER XLI

That our Country is to be defended by Honour or by Dishonour; and in either way is well defended.

The consuls together with the whole Roman army fell, as I have related, into the hands of the Samnites, who imposed on them the most ignominious terms, insisting that they should be stripped of their arms, and pass under the yoke before they were allowed to return to Rome. The consuls being astounded by the harshness of these conditions and the whole army overwhelmed with dismay, Lucius Lentulus, the Roman lieutenant, stood forward and said, that in his opinion they ought to decline no course whereby their country might be saved; and that as the very existence of Rome depended on the preservation of her army, that army must be saved at any sacrifice, for whether the means be honourable or ignominious, all is well done that is done for the defence of our country. And he said that were her army preserved, Rome, in course of time, might wipe out the disgrace; but if her army were destroyed, however gloriously it might perish, Rome and her freedom would perish with it. In the event his counsel was followed.

Now this incident deserves to be noted and pondered over by every citizen who is called on to advise his country; for when the entire safety of our country is at stake, no consideration of what is just or unjust, merciful or cruel, praiseworthy or shameful, must intervene. On the contrary, every other consideration being set aside, that course alone must be taken which preserves the existence of the country and maintains its liberty. And this course we find followed by the people of France, both in their words and in their actions, with the view of supporting the dignity of their king and the integrity of their kingdom; for there is no remark they listen to with more impatience than that this or the other course is disgraceful to the king. For their king, they say, can incur no disgrace by any resolve he may take, whether it turn out well or ill; and whether it succeed or fail, all maintain that he has acted as a king should.

CHAPTER XLII

That Promises made on Compulsion are not to be observed.

When, after being subjected to this disgrace, the consuls returned to Rome with their disarmed legions, Spurius Posthumius, himself one of the consuls, was the first to contend in the senate that the terms made in the Caudine Valley were not to be observed. For he argued that the Roman people were not bound by them, though he himself doubtless was, together with all the others who had promised peace; wherefore, if the people desired to set themselves free from every engagement, he and all the rest who had given this promise must be made over as prisoners into the hands of the Samnites. And so steadfastly did he hold to this opinion, that the senate were content to adopt it, and sending him and the rest as prisoners back to Samnium, protested to the Samnites that the peace was not binding. And so kind was Fortune to Posthumius on this occasion, that the Samnites would not keep him as a prisoner, and that on his return to Rome, notwithstanding his defeat, he was held in higher honour by the Romans than the victorious Pontius by his countrymen.

Here two points are to be noted; first, that glory may be won by any action; for although, commonly, it follow upon victory, it may also follow on defeat, if this defeat be seen to have happened through no fault of yours, or if, directly after, you perform some valiant action which cancels it. The other point to be noted is that there is no disgrace in not observing promises wrung from you by force; for promises thus extorted when they affect the public welfare will always be broken so soon as the pressure under which they were made is withdrawn, and that, too, without shame on the part of him who breaks them; of which we read many instances in history, and find them constantly occurring at the present day. Nay, as between princes, not only are such compulsory promises broken when the force which extorted them is removed, but all other promises as well, are in like manner disregarded when the causes which led to them no longer operate.

Whether this is a thing to be commended or no, and whether such methods ought or ought not to be followed by princes, has already been considered by me in my "*Treatise of the Prince*" wherefore I say no more on that subject here.

CHAPTER XLIII

That Men born in the same Province retain through all Times nearly the same Character.

The wise are wont to say, and not without reason or at random, that he who would forecast what is about to happen should look to what has been; since all human events, whether present or to come, have their exact counterpart in the past. And this, because these events are brought about by men, whose passions and dispositions remaining in all ages the same naturally give rise to the same effects; although, doubtless, the operation of these causes takes a higher form, now in one province, and now in another, according to the character of the training wherein the inhabitants of these provinces acquire their way of life.

Another aid towards judging of the future by the past, is to observe how the same nation long retains the same customs, remaining constantly covetous or deceitful, or similarly stamped by some one vice or virtue. Any one reading the past history of our city of Florence, and noting what has recently befallen it, will find the French and German nations overflowing with avarice, pride, cruelty, and perfidy, all of which four vices have at divers times wrought much harm to our city. As an instance of their perfidy, every one knows how often payments of money were made to Charles VIII. of France, in return for which he engaged to restore the fortresses of Pisa, yet never did restore them, manifesting thereby his bad faith and grasping avarice. Or, to pass from these very recent events, all may have heard of what happened in the war in which the Florentines were involved with the Visconti, dukes of Milan, when Florence, being left without other resource, resolved to invite the emperor into Italy, that she might be assisted by his name and power in her struggle with Lombardy. The emperor promised to come with a strong army to take part against the Visconti and to protect Florence from them, on condition that the Florentines paid him a hundred thousand ducats on his setting out, and another hundred thousand on his arrival in Italy; to which terms the Florentines agreed. But although he then received payment of the first instalment and, afterwards, on reaching Verona, of the second, he turned back from the expedition without effecting anything, alleging as his excuse that he was stopped by certain persons who had failed to fulfil their engagements. But if Florence had not been urged by passion or overcome by necessity, or had she read of and understood the ancient usages of the barbarians, she would neither on this, nor on many other occasions, have been deceived by them, seeing that these nations have always been of the same character, and have always, in all circumstances, and with all men alike, used the same methods. For in ancient times we find them behaving after the same fashion to the Etruscans, who, when overpowered by the Romans, by whom they had been repeatedly routed and put to flight, perceiving that they could not stand without help, entered into a compact with the Gauls dwelling in the parts of Italy south of the Alps, to pay them a certain sum if they would unite with them in a campaign against the Romans. But the Gauls, after taking their money, refused to arm on their behalf, alleging that they had not been paid to make war on the enemies of the Etruscans, but only to refrain from pillaging their lands. And thus the people of Etruria, through the avarice and perfidy of the Gauls, were at once defrauded of their money and disappointed of the help which they had counted on obtaining.

From which two instances of the Etruscans in ancient times and of the Florentines in recent, we may see that barbaric races have constantly followed the same methods, and may easily draw our conclusions as to how far princes should trust them.

CHAPTER XLIV

That where ordinary methods fail, Hardihood and Daring often succeed.

When attacked by the Romans, the Samnites as they could not without help stand against them in the field, resolved to leave garrisons in the towns of Samnium, and to pass with their main army into Etruria, that country being then at truce with Rome, and thus ascertain whether their actual presence in arms might not move the Etruscans to renew hostilities against Rome, which they had refused to renew when invited through envoys. During the negotiations which, on this occasion, passed between the two nations, the Samnites in explaining the chief causes that led them to take up arms, used the memorable words — "they had risen because peace is a heavier burthen for slaves than war for freemen" In the end, partly by their persuasions, and partly by the presence of their army, they induced the Etruscans to join forces with them.

Here we are to note that when a prince would obtain something from another, he ought, if the occasion allow, to leave him no time to deliberate, but should so contrive that the other may see the need of resolving at once; as he will, if he perceive that refusal or delay in complying with what is asked of him, will draw upon him a sudden and dangerous resentment.

This method we have seen employed with good effect in our own times by Pope Julius II. in dealing with France, and by M. de Foix, the general of the French king, in dealing with the Marquis of Mantua. For Pope Julius desiring to expel the Bentivogli from Bologna, and thinking that for this purpose he needed the help of French troops, and to have the Venetians neutral, after sounding both and receiving from both hesitating and ambiguous answers, determined to make both fall in with his views, by giving them no time to oppose him; and so, setting forth from Rome with as strong a force as he could get together, he marched on Bologna, sending word to the Venetians that they must stand aloof, and to the King of France to send him troops. The result was that in the brief time allowed them, neither of the two powers could make up their mind to thwart him; and knowing that refusal or delay would be violently resented by the Pope, they yielded to his demands, the king sending him soldiers and the Venetians maintaining neutrality.

M. de Foix, again, being with the king's army in Bologna when word came that Brescia had risen, could not rest till he had recovered that town. But, to get there he had to choose between two routes, one long and circuitous leading through the territories of the king, the other short and direct. In taking the latter route, however, not only would he have to pass through the dominions of the Marquis of Mantua, but also to make his way into these through the lakes and marshes wherewith that country abounds, by following an embanked road, closed and guarded by the marquis with forts and other defensive works. Resolving, nevertheless, to take the shortest road at all hazards, he waited till his men were already on their march before signifying to the marquis that he desired leave to pass through his country, so that no time might be left him to deliberate. Taken aback by the unexpected demand, the marquis gave the leave sought, which he never would have given had De Foix acted with less impetuosity. For he was in league with the Venetians and with the Pope, and had a son in the hands of the latter; all which circumstances would have afforded him fair pretexts for refusal. But carried away by the suddenness and urgency of the demand, he yielded. And in like manner the Etruscans yielded to the instances of the Samnites, the presence of whose army decided them to renew hostilities which before they had declined to renew.

CHAPTER XLV

Whether in battle it is better to await and repel the Enemy's attack, or to anticipate it by an impetuous onset.

Decius and Fabius, the Roman consuls, were each of them in command of a separate army, one directed against the Samnites, the other against the Etruscans: and as both delivered battle, we have to pronounce, in respect of the two engagements, which commander followed the better method. Decius attacked his enemy at once with the utmost fury and with his whole strength. Fabius was content, at first, merely to maintain his ground; for judging that more was to be gained by a later attack, he reserved his forces for a final effort, when the ardour of the enemy had cooled and his energy spent itself. The event showed Fabius to be more successful in his tactics than Decius, who being exhausted by his first onset, and seeing his ranks begin to waver, to secure by death the glory he could no longer hope from victory, followed the example set him by his father, and sacrificed himself to save the Roman legions. Word whereof being brought to Fabius, he, to gain, while he yet lived, as much honour as the other had earned by his death, pushed forward all the troops he had reserved for his final effort, and so obtained an unexampled victory. Whence we see that of the two methods, that of Fabius was the safer and the more deserving our imitation.

CHAPTER XLVI

How the Characteristics of Families come to be perpetuated.

Manners and institutions differing in different cities, seem here to produce a harder and there a softer race; and a like difference may also be discerned in the character of different families in the same city. And while this holds good of all cities, we have many instances of it in reading the history of Rome. For we find the Manlii always stern and stubborn; the Valerii kindly and courteous; the Claudii haughty and ambitious; and many families besides similarly distinguished from one another by their peculiar qualities.

These qualities we cannot refer wholly to the *blood*, for that must change as a result of repeated intermarriages, but must ascribe rather to the different training and education given in different families. For much turns on whether a child of tender years hears a thing well or ill spoken of, since this must needs make an impression on him whereby his whole conduct in after life will be influenced. Were it otherwise we should not have found the whole family of the Claudii moved by the desires and stirred by the passions which Titus Livius notes in many of them, and more especially in one holding the office of censor, who, when his colleague laid down his magistracy, as the law prescribed, at the end of eighteen months, would not resign, maintaining that he was entitled to hold the office for five years in accordance with the original law by which the censorship was regulated. And although his refusal gave occasion to much controversy, and bred great tumult and disturbance, no means could be found to depose him from his office, which he persisted in retaining in opposition to the will of the entire commons and a majority of the senate. And any who shall read the speech made against him by Publius Sempronius, tribune of the people, will find therein all the Claudian insolence exposed, and will recognize the docility and good temper shown by the body of the citizens in respecting the laws and institutions of their country.

CHAPTER XLVII

That love of his Country should lead a good Citizen to forget private Wrongs.

While commanding as consul against the Samnites, Manlius was wounded in a skirmish. His army being thereby endangered, the senate judged it expedient to send Papirius Cursor as dictator to supply his place. But as it was necessary that the dictator should be nominated by Fabius, the other consul, who was with the army in Etruria, and as a doubt was felt that he might refuse to nominate Papirius, who was his enemy, the senate sent two messengers to entreat him to lay aside private animosity, and make the nomination which the public interest required. Moved by love of his country Fabius did as he was asked, although by his silence, and by many other signs, he gave it to be known that compliance was distasteful. From his conduct at this juncture all who would be thought good citizens should take example.

CHAPTER XLVIII

That on finding an Enemy make what seems a grave blunder, we should suspect some fraud to lurk behind.

The consul having gone to Rome to perform certain ceremonial rites, and Fulvius being left in charge of the Roman army in Etruria, the Etruscans, to see whether they could not circumvent the new commander, planting an ambush not far from the Roman camp, sent forward soldiers disguised as shepherds driving large flocks of sheep so as to pass in sight of the Roman army. These pretended shepherds coming close to the wall of his camp, Fulvius, marvelling at what appeared to him unaccountable audacity, hit upon a device whereby the artifice of the Etruscans was detected and their design defeated.

Here it seems proper to note that the captain of an army ought not to build on what seems a manifest blunder on the part of an enemy; for as men are unlikely to act with conspicuous want of caution, it will commonly be found that this blunder is cover to a fraud. And yet, so blinded are men's minds by their eagerness for victory, that they look only to what appears on the surface.

After defeating the Romans on the Allia, the Gauls, hastening on to Rome, found the gates of the city left open and unguarded. But fearing some stratagem, and being unable to believe that the Romans could be so foolish and cowardly as to abandon their city, they waited during the whole of that day and the following night outside the gates, without daring to enter. In the year 1508, when the Florentines Avere engaged in besieging Pisa, Alfonso del Mutolo, a citizen of that town, happening to be taken prisoner, was released on his promise to procure the surrender to the Florentines of one of the gates of the city.

Afterwards, on pretence of arranging for the execution of this surrender, he came repeatedly to confer with those whom the Florentine commissaries had deputed to treat with him, coming not secretly but openly, and accompanied by other citizens of Pisa, whom he caused to stand aside while he conversed with the Florentines. From all which circumstances his duplicity might have been suspected, since, had he meant to do as he had engaged, it was most unlikely that he should be negotiating so openly. But the desire to recover possession of Pisa so blinded the Florentines that they allowed themselves to be conducted under his guidance to the Lucca Gate, where, through his treachery, but to their own disgrace, they lost a large number of their men and officers.

CHAPTER XLIX

That a Commonwealth to preserve its Freedom has constant need of new Ordinances. Of the services in respect of which Quintius Fabius received the surname of Maximus.

It must happen, as I have already said, in every great city, that disorders needing the care of the physician continually spring up; and the graver these disorders are, the greater will be the skill needed for their treatment. And if ever in any city, most assuredly in Rome, we see these disorders assume strange and unexpected shapes. As when it appeared that all the Roman wives had conspired to murder their husbands, many of them being found to have actually administered poison, and many others to have drugs in readiness for the purpose.

Of like nature was the conspiracy of the Bacchanals, discovered at the time of the Macedonian war, wherein many thousands, both men and women, were implicated, and which, had it not been found out, or had the Romans not been accustomed to deal with large bodies of offenders, must have proved perilous for their city. And, indeed, if the greatness of the Roman Republic were not declared by countless other signs, as well as by the manner in which it caused its laws to be observed, it might be seen in the character of the punishments which it inflicted against wrong-doers. For in vindicating justice, it would not scruple or hesitate to put a whole legion to death, to depopulate an entire city, or send eight or ten thousand men at a time into banishment, subject to the most stringent conditions, which had to be observed, not by one of these exiles only, but by all. As in the case of those soldiers who fought unsuccessfully at

Cannae, who were banished to Sicily, subject to the condition that they should not harbour in towns, and should all eat standing.

But the most formidable of all their punishments was that whereby one man out of every ten in an entire army was chosen by lot to be put to death. For correcting a great body of men no more effectual means could be devised; because, when a multitude have offended and the ringleaders are not known, all cannot be punished, their number being too great; while to punish some only, and leave the rest unpunished, were unjust to those punished and an encouragement to those passed over to offend again. But where you put to death a tenth chosen by lot, where all equally deserve death, he who is punished will blame his unlucky fortune, while he who escapes will be afraid that another time the lot may be his, and for that reason will be careful how he repeats his offence. The poisoners and the Bacchanals, therefore, were punished as their crimes deserved.

Although disorders like these occasion mischievous results in a commonwealth, still they are not fatal, since almost always there is time to correct them. But no time is given in the case of disorders in the State itself, which unless they be treated by some wise citizen, will always bring a city to destruction. From the readiness wherewith the Romans conferred the right of citizenship on foreigners, there came to be so many new citizens in Rome, and possessed of so large a share of the suffrage, that the government itself began to alter, forsaking those courses which it was accustomed to follow, and growing estranged from the men to whom it had before looked for guidance. Which being observed by Quintius Fabius when censor, he caused all those new citizens to be classed in four *Tribes*, that being reduced within this narrow limit they might not have it in their power to corrupt the entire State. And this was a wisely contrived measure, for, without introducing any violent change, it supplied a convenient remedy, and one so acceptable to the republic as to gain for Fabius the well-deserved name of Maximus.

www.ingramcontent.com/pod-product-compliance
Lightning Source LLC
Chambersburg PA
CBHW060309230426
43663CB00009B/1644